Welsh Saints
ON THE
Mormon Trail

To Ron, for opening the trail
and to Carys, for coming with me.

Welsh Saints
ON THE
Mormon Trail

THE STORY OF THE WELSH EMIGRATION TO SALT
LAKE CITY DURING THE NINETEENTH CENTURY

WIL AARON

First impression: 2019

© Copyright Wil Aaron and Y Lolfa Cyf., 2019

Every attempt was made to ascertain and contact the source
of all the photographs in this book.

The publishers wish to acknowledge
the support of the Books Council of Wales.

Cover photograph: Courtesy of Utah State Historical Society
Cover design: Y Lolfa
Maps: Elgan Griffiths

ISBN: 978-1-912631-20-9

Published and printed in Wales
on paper from well-maintained forests by
Y Lolfa Cyf., Talybont, Ceredigion SY24 5HE
website www.ylolfa.com
e-mail ylolfa@ylolfa.com
tel 01970 832 304
fax 832 782

Introduction

THE SUN IS already setting. Far below flows the Missouri and, from my vantage point here on Rainbow Point, I can make out the city of Omaha, ten miles away, the tall buildings at its centre rising like rockets from their launch pads. Beyond the city, for two hundred miles, lie the rich grasslands of the Prairies. Beyond the Prairies, stretching a further thousand miles into the sunset, are the Great Plains and the Rockies. And at the far end of the Rockies, somewhere in the reddening haze, are the Great Salt Lake and the Valley of the Great Salt Lake.

Here on Rainbow Point there is a monument to Lewis and Clark, commemorating their epic journey up the Missouri and across the Rockies to the Pacific in 1804. A year earlier, Napoleon had sold over 828,000 square miles of land west of the Mississippi to the United States at a knock-down price of about three cents an acre, doubling the size of the country overnight. It was Lewis and Clark's heroic expedition that revealed to the American people the immensity and splendour of their new acquisition. But they were not the first white men to pass this way. Nine years earlier, John Evans, of Waunfawr in north Wales, had skirted Rainbow Point, paddling up the Missouri for 1,800 miles in a vain attempt to find the Madogwys, a tribe of Indians believed to be descended from Prince Madog, a mythical prince of Gwynedd in north Wales, who was said to have discovered America in 1170. Evans, like most Welshmen of his day, believed implicitly in their existence. With their red hair and their blue eyes and the Welsh language still easy on their lips, he thought they would be easy to find but, two years later, he returned past Rainbow Point, disappointed in his quest. Nevertheless, he had travelled further up the Missouri than any white man before him and in his pocket was a detailed map of the river which was to prove useful to Lewis and Clark.

The voyage of Lewis and Clark inspired half a century of exploration in the new lands by successive waves of explorers. First came the 'Mountain Men', men like Kit Carson, Jedediah Smith, Thomas Fitzpatrick and Jim Bridger, men who made a living hunting beaver and otter for their skins. After the 'Mountain Men' came the traders, buying pelts and selling coffee, sugar, whisky, bullets and guns to white men and Native Americans alike. Then came the priests and missionaries, men like Father De Smet, who crossed the continent four times, looking for souls to save. And finally, the 'pioneers' – weary men and wiry women in straggling trains of tattered wagons, their oxen hunched in the yoke, their cows and sheep and dogs and children following behind in the dust clouds. Some were fleeing failure or escaping persecution; others searching for a way out of poverty or for a better life for their children. All of them imagined an Eldorado, beyond the frontier, somewhere out west.

In the early years it was Oregon that drew them. From the beginning of the 1840s, a wagon train or two had set out every year from the Mississippi, led by one or other of the Mountain Men. They crossed the Plains, climbed the Rockies and wove their way down the Snake and the Columbia rivers into the fertile valley of the Williamette, near Fort Vancouver. In 1843, over a thousand people followed this route to Oregon. By 1845, the numbers had increased fivefold. The floodgates were opening. Thus the memorial at Rainbow Point marks the beginning of this romantic period in the history of the West.

A few miles further down the ridge stands another memorial, looking out this time over Council Bluffs, Omaha's sister city, separated from her only by the Missouri River. This granite pillar was set up by the Daughters of the American Revolution, that busy society responsible for so many of the historical markers of the United States. 'This monument,' it says, 'is to commemorate the visit of Abraham Lincoln to Council Bluffs, August 19, 1859. From this point he viewed the extensive panorama of the valley of the Missouri River and in compliance with the law of Congress on Nov 17, 1863, he selected this city as the eastern terminus of the Union Pacific Railway.' Building a railway across America had been one of Lincoln's dreams, not realised until four years after his assassination. On May 10th, 1869, the Union Pacific Railway finally met the Central Pacific at Promontory Summit in Utah. The cumbersome wagon trains that had cluttered the western trails for over a quarter of a century made way for the great steam locomotives that accomplished in a few effortless days what had previously taken many wearisome months. And with the coming of the locomotives, the Age of the Pioneers came to an end.

These two memorial stones above Omaha, therefore, bracket the days of the American West, a heroic era that forged many of the values of the nation. This was the age of the West in its pristine glory and the pioneers were part of it. They walked with the '49ers' on their way to the goldfields of California. They were passed by the Pony Express and by the first transcontinental stagecoaches. They saw the first telegraph wires strung across the land and the first transcontinental railroad tracks being laid. Behind them, they left a land riven by civil war. Before them flared the first skirmishes of the Plains Indian Wars. Buffalo Bill and Wild Bill Hickok rode the same trails and Crazy Horse watched them pass.

From 1847 to the coming of the railway, over 400,000 people travelled these trails to the west. About 250,000 went to California, another 80,000 to Oregon. A part was also played in the drama by 80,000 Mormons, fleeing their persecutors in the east, intent on establishing a holy city, their Zion, somewhere beyond the Rocky Mountains. And amongst these 80,000 Mormons were a few thousand from Wales.

It is not known exactly how many Welsh emigrated to Salt Lake City during those pioneer years. F.D. Richards, one of the organisers of the emigration, claimed that between 8,000 and 10,000 sailed from Liverpool between the start of the emigration and 1867, but that figure seems improbably high. And of course, not all who left Liverpool arrived in the Salt Lake Valley. The Atlantic crossing was only the beginning of their trials. Many abandoned their dream and elected to remain in the eastern states. Many more died out on the Plains.

Another estimate can be found in the magnificent collection of ships' manifests that is to be read on Brigham Young University's **http://mormonmigration.lib.byu.edu** website. In these lists of Mormon passengers on the Atlantic, their nationality is indicated alongside their names. Between 1851 and 1868, the sum of the emigrants marked with a 'W' for 'Welsh' appears to be a little over 3,000, but this figure is improbably low. Not all the early manifests have survived and many of them fail to indicate the nationality of the passengers. Many emigrants are from the parts of Monmouthshire and Brecknockshire and Radnorshire that the Mormons administered from Hereford and are therefore recorded as English. Passengers are moved from ship to ship; there are last-minute changes; there are failures to show, and the notes of the clerks are often difficult to interpret and baffling.

Another method might be to count the names in the Welsh Mormon website, **http://welshmormon.byu.edu/**, the rich treasury of Welsh Mormon emigrant history created by Professor Ron Dennis and administered now by Brigham Young University. Nearly 5,000 names are listed at the latest count but Professor Dennis believes this could be an underestimate. The figure is based on a trawl made twenty years ago through the names of people listed as born in Wales in the forerunner of Family Search, the genealogical research site administered by the Church of Latter Day Saints. Since then, Professor Dennis has added many new names to the list, based on information sent in by descendants and on his own researches, but there are very many more, he says, who could well be Welsh, but which, because of the lack of detailed information, he cannot include.

However, his overall impression is that somewhere between

5,000 and 6,000 Welsh Mormons reached the Valley of the Salt Lake before the coming of the railway, not a large number compared to the 55,000 Welsh who migrated to other parts of the U.S.A. in the same period, mainly to the iron and coal districts of Pennsylvania and Ohio, but more than three times the number that emigrated to Patagonia, that most famous of Welsh settlements in the Americas.

At various points along the trail west, the Welsh Mormons have left their mark. I can look down on two of them from my vantage point here alongside the Lincoln Memorial. Two miles to the south-west, there is the site of a meeting hall built by Welsh Mormons in 1849 and intended as a place of recuperation, where their fellow countrymen might rest awhile before setting out on the last, most testing stage of their long journey. The community that built it has long since gone and the meeting hall itself was washed away by Missouri floods. A mile to the west, on the main street of Council Bluffs, there used to be, for a short period in the 1850s, a primitive fast-food eatery, run by a Mormon from Marloes in south Pembrokeshire, serving squirrel pies and prairie chicken pasties to hungry pioneers. And there are countless other sites along the trail, telling similar tales of the Welsh Mormon migration. Yet, in Wales today, we know so very little about them despite there being a wealth of material available to the historian.

In the U.S.A., the probable reason for this dearth of early Welsh Mormon history lies in the fact that so few of the documents of the period were written in English. It is only recently that translations of the relevant periodicals and other publications have been made available to researchers by the lifetime industry of Professor Dennis. He has also put together a vast collection of Welsh Mormon memoirs and journals and letters and photographs and made them available to all on his 'welshmormon' website.

The lack of interest here in Wales, on the other hand, has probably more to do with the bitter feuding that characterized Welsh religious life in the mid-1800s. The Baptist, Methodist and Congregational chapels, which dominated Welsh religious life then, were fiercely hostile to these strange Yankee evangelists. They had arrived from America at the beginning of the 1840s, preaching what the Non-conformists considered to be a heretical gospel. Rumours about their ungodly behaviour and un-Christian practices were rife. 'They baptize at night, and those receiving baptism must undress for them and go naked into the water.' They 'rewrite the Gospels and have added another book to the Bible'. They peddle 'the most shameful superstition that has ever been proclaimed in a Christian country'. When the Mormon missionaries returned to Utah, taking their converts with them, the Welsh Non-conformists heaved a sigh of relief. Out of sight, they were soon out of mind and their story forgotten. But it remains a remarkable tale, deserving an honourable place in the history of the Welsh people.

1847

JOHN BENNION AND his family, from Hawarden in Flintshire, were the first Welsh to reach the Great Salt Lake. John Bennion's father was a tenant farmer, renting a cottage and twelve acres of land from the estate of Sir Stephen Glynne of Hawarden Castle. Nothing remains of his cottage today, but its location is known. It stood on a low hill overlooking the broad valley of the Dee, facing out towards the English border. At night, the glow of Birkenhead and Liverpool lit up the eastern sky.

At the beginning of the nineteenth century, when John was growing up, this small corner of Flintshire burst into vigorous industrial life. In the field where the cottage once stood, there are traces of a small tramway that ran from a coal pit at Mancott down to the Dee. The river had been newly straightened and widened to allow for the increased traffic generated by the burgeoning activity along its banks. John's father took note of the bustle around him and understood what it foretold. He realised that the world was changing, that a revolution was in the making, and that the steam engine would emerge as king. So John was given a good education in a local school until he was fourteen and then apprenticed to a company that manufactured steam boilers.

In his journal, John describes the family's religious life. 'My father had been a member of the Methodist Society for many years and had taught his children strict morals and religion; but as I grew up, I became associated with boys who were under less religious influence. Going to Sunday school and to hear preaching became burdensome to me. I chose rather to spend the Sunday with my comrades in some fun.

One Sunday, I, with two others, were rambling through the fields with a dog, when the dog caught a rabbit. A watcher came upon us and declared we were poaching. Next day we were summoned to appear before a justice for trial, but I was determined not to submit to such proceedings. I therefore took my departure another way and came to Liverpool.' He joined his elder brother Samuel who had left home six years earlier to work in his uncle's bakery.

In Liverpool, John, now sixteen, was apprenticed to another boiler maker, signing a three-year contract and receiving a weekly wage of ten shillings. He completed his contract honourably but refused to sign another, feeling his master had not given him adequate training. Instead he joined a rival firm. The impression one gets is of an ambitious but conscientious young man, of sound morals and sturdy principles, confident in his capabilities.

From his early days, despite being uncomfortable in his father's Methodism, he appeared to have had a deep need of religion in his life. When he first came to Liverpool, he had attended the meetings of a small sect called 'Mr Aitken's Society' and had remained faithful to them for over five years. Mr Aitken's ideas were a strange mixture of high church ritual and Wesleyan evangelisms. A powerful preacher, he exhorted his congregations to sing and shout and dance. One of his teachings, one which might well have appealed to John, was that the restoration of the Early Church, as ordained by God and described in Holy Scriptures, was at hand. The 'Last Days' were nigh and Christ would soon return to purify his Church and restore it to its perfection.

This belief had much in common with one of the central tenets of Mormonism. The Mormons believed that God, down the ages, had, many times, established and re-established his one true Church on earth, but that each time, men had defiled it, and corrupted it, and strayed from its truths. It was given to Adam and Eve and again to the Old Testament prophets, but each time its truths had been lost and its commandments forgotten. Then God sent Christ into the world to restore his

Church once more but, when the last of the Apostles died, the Mormons maintain that the believers had again fallen away from the standards demanded of them and that the true Church had again been lost. Finally, in 1830, God gave them one last chance. Through his Prophet, Joseph Smith, he resurrected his Church on earth one last time. This, declared Joseph Smith, was the only Church that preserved and nurtured true Christian values. He preached the importance of miracles and faith healing and speaking with tongues as described in the Bible, and he proclaimed that the time was fast approaching when Christ would return to earth to rule for a thousand years, to judge the sinful and to lead the faithful to eternal life. These truths had been revealed to him, he said, by God himself, with whom he was in constant contact.

It was a time when such ideas flourished on both sides of the Atlantic. In Britain, many listened to Joanna Southcott and were convinced by her sensational proclamations. In 1814, even though she was well past sixty, she announced that she would soon give birth to the Son of God and, for a while, she held the country in thrall, awaiting the event. William Owen Pughe, the most respected Welsh scholar of the age, was one of her most faithful followers. From the same background came John Wroe and the Christian Israelites. In 1825, Wroe built an extravagant temple in the centre of Ashton-under-Lyne on the outskirts of Manchester. This, he said, was the place chosen by God to be His holy city. He built four gatehouses into the city, one of which still stands today. The floors of his temple were of polished oak, the galleries of the best mahogany and the walls were adorned with copper and silver. But a sad ending befell him. He took seven virgins with him on a preaching tour and, on their return, one of them was pregnant. As a consequence, his church in Britain hit the buffers, although it continues to steam on in Australia.

The Millerites came from America. Their leader, William Miller, believed that Christ's second coming would occur between March 21st, 1843, and March 21st, 1844. His followers numbered many thousands, but, alas, when March 22nd, 1844, dawned, and proved to be a fine, calm, spring day, the bottom fell out of this faith also. It was not uncommon in those days for charismatic preachers proclaiming apocalyptical beliefs to fire up fervent followers, but to hold on to them was another matter.

In 1837, the Mormons sent their first missionaries from America to Britain. Amongst their early converts were members of Mr Aitken's Society. In 1840, John Bennion went to listen to a sermon preached by the Mormon missionary John Taylor and was moved by what he heard. 'I resolved to investigate for myself, which, the more I did, the more I became convinced that it was not of man but of God. Next day I attended the Saints meeting three times, forenoon, afternoon and evening, hearing preaching and testimony. I was now fully convinced, and resolved to obey. Accordingly, after the meeting was dismissed, I went, in company with some others, to the seashore and was baptized, and went to my lodgings rejoicing in the truth.'

In those days the Mormons believed that, to be saved, a believer had to withdraw from the company of 'gentiles' or 'Babylonians', as they called those who were not of their faith. To be sure of salvation, they had to gather to the Holy City in America, with other 'Saints', as they called each other. John felt a duty to obey. Nine months after his conversion he married Esther Wainwright, who had been his neighbour in Hawarden, and five days later, they sailed together for New Orleans. At that time, their Zion was a city called Nauvoo, built on a bend of the Mississippi, one thousand miles upriver from the delta.

Nauvoo was unlike other cities. Three years earlier, in 1838, it had consisted of a few cabins precariously clinging to a swampy headland. All that flourished there were mosquitoes and malaria. Then the Mormons arrived. Now Nauvoo was the biggest town in Illinois, bigger even than Chicago, and one of the twenty largest towns in all America. The swamps had been drained, over 1,200 houses had been built and hundreds more were being planned. There were wide streets, fertile gardens, timber and flour mills, shops and schools, and over 7,000 inhabitants. On the hill above the river, a huge temple was being built. When completed, this would be the largest building north of St Louis and west of Chicago. But Nauvoo's glory was short-lived. The temple was never completed. Five years later the houses lay in ruins, the gardens were growing wild, the temple had been destroyed and the people had all fled. The man responsible for the extraordinary growth of the city, and for its equally extraordinary collapse, was the founder and leader and Prophet of the Mormon people, Joseph Smith.

Smith is an enigmatic figure. His life story has been the subject of countless biographies, all of which seem to paint a different picture. 'You don't know me,' he once said in a speech to his followers. 'You never knew my heart. No man knows my history.' Adored, respected, feared, detested, he was the sun around which the Mormon faith spun. Only eleven years had passed since he had established his Church. Four years later, when he was assassinated, he had 26,000 followers. Today the Church claims to have over sixteen million.

There was nothing remarkable about Smith's childhood. He grew up in Palmyra in northern New York State, a farmer's boy, high spirited, popular with the girls, fond of sports of all kinds, poorly educated but with a lively imagination. He once claimed he could communicate with spirits by gazing into a crystal ball. He said the spirits whispered to him of fabulous treasures buried beneath the ground. For a fee, he was ready to reveal the whereabouts of these treasures and many were convinced by him. It led to his conviction in a local court on a charge of being 'a disorderly person and an imposter'.

But to the Saints, Joseph Smith was the vessel chosen by God to deliver His message to the world, to re-establish His Church, to warn mankind that a Day of Judgement was at hand and to make it known that Christ would soon reappear on earth, in a city to be built in the western mountains of the United States. The Mormons also believed that God used Joseph to reveal the lost history of the Mormons. Joseph claimed an angel called Moroni had come to him and recounted to him how one of the lost tribes of Israel had left the Middle East in about 600 B.C., crossed the Atlantic and settled somewhere in the Americas, how Christ had come to them after his Crucifixion and how He had preached and taught amongst them before ascending to Heaven. The true Church, said Moroni, was preserved by this people until well into the fifth century A.D. but it was then torn asunder by warring factions. The Prophet of that time, a man called Mormon, who was Moroni's father, realising that the end was nigh, had gathered together the history of his people and had copied it on to plates of gold. Then, in 421, his people, he said, had been conquered and massacred in a battle near a hill called Cumorah, in present-day New York State. The only survivor was Moroni himself. He took his father's golden plates and buried them on Cumorah in a stone box, where they remained hidden for 1,400 years. God had now sent Moroni, in the form of an angel, to reveal the hiding place to Joseph Smith. Cumorah turned out to be only three miles from his home. Exactly as the angel had described, Joseph said he found the golden plates bound together by three huge D-shaped rings and covered with strange hieroglyphics which he said were 'reformed' Egyptian. In the same hiding place, he said he found a pair of crystals, set in bows of silver. The angel showed him how they could be used as spectacles to decipher the hieroglyphics. So Joseph set about translating the plates, and the translation he made was published as the *Book of Mormon* and is today the chief gospel of the Mormon Church. Joseph said that eleven of his followers had been allowed to see the plates before Moroni retrieved them and, in every copy of the *Book of Mormon*, their testimony is published. 'Be it known unto all nations, kindred, tongues and people unto whom this work shall come that Joseph Smith, the translator of this work, hath shown unto us the plates of which hath been spoken, which have the appearance of gold.'

No shard of hard evidence has ever been produced, no vestige of proof of the existence of the golden book, but whatever one makes of it, it remains an incontrovertible fact that Joseph Smith, the unlettered farm boy, succeeded in producing, in 75 days, during April, May and June of 1829, a manuscript of 275,000 words, half the size of the Bible, which has changed the lives of millions. Amongst them was John Bennion of Hawarden. Such was the book's effect upon him that he was wrenched out of the comfortable ruts of his old life and driven on a desperate adventure, 5,000 miles across the Atlantic and a thousand miles up the Mississippi.

John's journal comes to an end as he sets sail for America. What we know of him and of Esther in Nauvoo, from the day they arrived in 1842 to the morning they left for their new home in the Rockies in 1845, is contained in four letters. One was sent to his brother, Samuel, in Liverpool, one to his father and the other two to Esther's parents in Hawarden.

The first letter was written a month after he and Esther arrived in Nauvoo. They were beginning to find their feet in their new home. 'It is not as in England for everyone to keep to his own trade,' John wrote, 'but a man who comes here must turn to any work and get along as well as he can… I have bought one acre of land in the city and have built a house on it without any help and am now living in it. The land is now ploughed. We had a team of 12 oxen breaking it up. I have planted part of it with Indian corn and tomato plants.' In the main, the tone of the letter is optimistic and hopeful, yet, occasionally, there are undertones of anxiety. 'I have heard this people much spoken against in England,' he writes, 'but more so here. In coming up the river, it is a general outcry, "Don't go to Nauvoo, for it is a place of poverty and oppression," and all manner of evil spoken against Jo Smith. But this is false.'

The Saints had long suffered periods of persecution and it was not only because of their religion. Wherever they settled, they managed to draw down the wrath of their neighbours. Three years previously, in their first settlement in Kirtland, Ohio, they had incurred a heavy debt by over-spending on their first temple. They had then exacerbated the situation by attempting to pay their debts with unsecured paper drawn upon their own bank. The bank crashed, causing furious investors to turn on the owners and the Saints to flee for their lives.

Another group of Mormons had travelled halfway across the continent, to what was then the extreme western frontier of the United States. They had settled on the Missouri River, in a settlement called Independence, then hardly more than a village, today swallowed up by Kansas City. At first, they lived at peace with their 'Babylonian' neighbours but, over time, the relationship soured. It was their very successes that proved the Saints' undoing. Their community was better organised and more efficient than that of their neighbours. They worked as one, under the direction of their Church, with a clear, centralised vision and purpose. The Church, with Joseph Smith at its head, controlled all aspects of community life, the economy, from the distribution of land, the implementation of the law, the policing of society, to the welfare of the people, their education, their social activities and their defence. To the 'Babylonians', it seemed that a Mormon community was an autocratic, despotic dictatorship. But Mormons liked to compare the order within their society to the order of a beehive. It was the hive that mattered, not the individual bee. 'All for one and one for all' was the Mormon tenet, so different from the frontier philosophy of 'Every man for himself'. In addition, the Mormons, faithful to the wishes of God as interpreted by Joseph Smith, tended to vote as one and this gave them considerable power in local government. However weak a Mormon community might be when it first settled in a new area, within no time it became a force to be reckoned with and a threat to the way of life of the original settlers.

By 1834, over a thousand Mormons had come to live in Independence, and more were arriving every day. Before long they would outnumber the original inhabitants. The tensions between the two communities flared into violence. Over two hundred Mormon houses were attacked and burnt to the ground. It was then agreed that they should be given land in a neighbouring county, where they would be left to live in peace. There they set about rebuilding their new community with their usual fervour and many of those who had fled from Kirtland after the bank collapse came to join them, including Joseph Smith himself. But soon the same old tensions flared again. In the autumn of 1838, Lilburn W. Boggs, the Governor of Missouri, ordered that all Mormons should be driven out of the state and that those who refused to go should be done away with. A mob of two hundred Missourians fell on the small Mormon village of Haun's Mill and seventeen of the inhabitants were killed. Once again, the Mormons had to flee. They crossed the state of Missouri and found a haven in Nauvoo, Illinois.

When John and Esther arrived in Nauvoo three years later, the inhabitants had put the atrocities of Haun's Mill behind them and were once again furiously building. As the presence of a queen gives purpose and order to a hive, so Joseph Smith's presence in Nauvoo drove and inspired his Saints. 'Yesterday there was a public meeting for the purpose of improving agriculture,' wrote John in his letter. 'Joseph Smith and others were speaking. I expect this will be carried out. If so, this will soon become a noted place.' Smith had a warm and attractive personality. It was what sustained and stimulated the Saints. He believed in living well. He liked dancing and wrestling. His energy and enthusiasm were infectious. He was a young man at ease amongst his people, enjoying their company, delighting in their friendships. For his sake, they were ready to give all they owned to the Church, to work themselves to a standstill and, if necessary, to suffer hardship and adversity. Living alongside Joseph Smith, seeing him often on the streets, working with him, worshipping with him, listening to his advice, this was one of the reasons why John and his family had come to Nauvoo. God often spoke to Joseph and Joseph discussed His commandments with the faithful in the Sunday services and the conferences of the Saints. The commandments were duly recorded and published in another of the Mormon gospels, *The Book of Doctrine and Covenants*.

God's words, as recorded in *The Book of Doctrine and Covenants*, are often remarkably down-to-earth and business-like. In 1841, for example, when John and Esther first arrived in Nauvoo, God had decreed that a hotel should be built in the town. 'Let my servant George and my servant Lyman and my servant John Snider and others build a house unto my name, such a one as my servant Joseph shall show unto them, upon the place he shall show unto them also. And it shall be a house for boarding, a house that strangers may come from afar to lodge therein; therefore let it be a good house, worthy of all acceptation, that the weary traveller may find health and safety while he shall contemplate the word of the Lord.' In his commandments, God takes care not only of the broad outline of the project but of the details also. For example, He deals with how the capital should be raised and what the value of each share should be. 'And they shall form a constitution, whereby they may receive stock for the building of that house. And they shall not receive less than fifty dollars for a share of stock in that house... And if they do appropriate any portion of that stock anywhere else without the consent of the stockholder, and do not repay fourfold for the stock... they shall be accursed and shall be moved out of their place saith the Lord God; for I, the Lord, am God, and cannot be mocked in any of these things.' And then God goes on to name some of the people He hopes would invest in the project. This is a typical example of the practical, plain-speaking, frank dealings that God had with his Saints in Nauvoo.

But the great excitement in Nauvoo that spring was that God had decreed a temple should be built in the city. 'The people here are employed in building a temple for the worship of almighty God where he will be glorified in the midst of the people,' writes John. The citizens had first heard of the plan in a speech given by Joseph in January. 'Come ye with all your gold and your silver and your precious stones... and with iron and copper and with brass and with zinc and with all your precious things of the earth and build a house to my name, for the Most High to dwell therein.' By April, the foundations of the temple had been laid. By the time John and Esther arrived in May, the gleaming white limestone walls, 165 feet high, were rising on a hill above the Mississippi. There was no building like it in the whole of the west, but the cost to the community was great. Every family was expected to pay tithes to the Church. This had been part of Mormonism from its beginnings and is still practised today. And if they couldn't raise the money or pay in kind, then they could labour for one day in ten.

Yet, despite the speed at which their city grew and the lavish spending on the temple, they were not a wealthy community. Many had abandoned their homes in previous settlements to marauding 'Babylonians', not once, not twice, but three or four times. In their diaries they wrote of leaking roofs, poor diets and unhealthy children. When the storms came, the streets were converted into muddy sloughs. 'In wet weather the roads are dirty and here we have had some heavy rain and more thunder and lightning than ever I knew before.' There were few luxuries in Nauvoo. The only favour John asks of his parents-in-law is that they send his wife some much-needed essentials. 'Esther wishes me to state if you can to send her a pair of half boots for common wear and a pair of clogs and a pair of blue linen aprons, she would be glad of them.' It was a hard life of continuous labour, but they could look forward confidently to better things. 'Now we have ground for a good garden. With it we both can live comfortably for a dollar a week... Through the mercy of our heavenly Father we are this day in health... I did not come here to prove whether the teaching of this church was truth. That much I knew before I started, and had I the privilege, I would teach it with greater confidence than I ever did before.'

In the second letter, a year later, their lives continue to flourish. 'I feel thankful unto God who has been so merciful unto us... When we first came here, things appeared new and strange to me in this new country but now I feel myself at home and can get plenty of work and I like the people.' In Hawarden, his father, also, had been converted to Mormonism and was thinking of following his son to Nauvoo. He had written that he intended to bring a mare with him but John suggests that a good dog would be more useful. 'A year or two ago wolves were very common here. Consequently the dogs are a kind of crossbreed with the wolf and are of little use... The hogs and cattle are apt to get in the garden and fields and root up the murphys [potatoes] and if he would bring a good bitch he would get a cow or the worth of one for a pup when reared.' The city was still growing fast and, after a year in Nauvoo, John's list of what his father should bring out with him is considerably more sophisticated than the list of Esther's needs sent to her brother-in-law twelve months previously. 'An English family have brought their clock safely in a case. Esther thinks you might bring yours the same way and plenty of mugs and plenty of blu [laundry bluing].'

The next letter to have survived is to his brother Samuel in February 1844. Their father was now on his way to New Orleans and Samuel intended to follow him. John eagerly encourages him. 'This forenoon,' he writes, 'we have been hearing Joseph Smith preach in the open air to a congregation of several thousands. I rejoice in the truths which I hear from time to time. All the tribulation and disappointment through which the Saints have to pass is forgotten when the glory and greatness of the Eternal worlds are placed before our mind. I am anxious for you and all the rest of our family to be here. It is then of the greatest importance that we keep the commandments of God given to his Saints, that we may escape the judgments which await the inhabitants of the earth. My desire is that you and I with our families and connections may stand on Mount Zion where there shall be peace and safety.' Yet, despite the enthusiasm, a suggestion of unease is also palpable. 'If any are coming here looking for perfection they must not forget to bring plenty with them, for this plant does not grow spontaneously here but we have to cultivate it with care or it will not grow at all. But the soil here is fertile and plenty of room for it to grow.'

Suspicion of the Mormons in Nauvoo, and doubts about their intentions, were, once again, beginning to stir and fester amongst the citizens of the surrounding towns. This time, some of the blame lay with the Mormons themselves. When first they came to Nauvoo, they were given permission by the state legislature to raise a militia. This militia grew to be a body of between 3,000 and 4,000 men, at a time when the army of the United States consisted of little more than 8,000 or 9,000 men.

To the non-Mormon frontiersmen, imbued with the conviction that religion and politics should be kept well separate and that despots were dangerous, there was something repugnant and un-American in the way Joseph assumed the leadership of the Church and the state and the army. He liked to appear on military manoeuvres clad in a colourful uniform with a peacock plume in his helmet. He liked to be addressed as 'General'. In the communities around Nauvoo, the tensions deepened and people grew more suspicious.

In June 1844, a damaging scandal surfaced in the city. It arose from a quarrel between Joseph and one of his most faithful followers. Before coming to Illinois to join the Mormons, William Law had been a successful businessman in Canada. In Nauvoo, he began to build houses and develop small industrial sites, but was hampered by the high price of land. He came to believe that Joseph, in the name of the Church, was operating an unfair monopoly. He began to doubt the business acumen of the Prophet and publicly gave voice to his suspicions. Joseph did what he always did when confronted by a contentious member of his Church. He excommunicated him. But Law refused to go quietly. He purchased a printing press and published a newspaper to disseminate his opinions. The leader column of the first edition of *The Nauvoo Expositor* attacked Joseph furiously, accusing him of personally profiting from selling land to newcomers at inflated prices, of wasting Church money and of indulging too enthusiastically in the pleasures of this world. And Law added one other charge, a charge which remains a painful thorn in the side of the Church to this day. He claimed to have undeniable proof that Joseph sanctioned polygamy.

He said that, although this had not yet been made public, certain members of Joseph's inner circle had been told and that some of them had taken advantage of the doctrine and had already married more than one wife. Nauvoo was shaken and shocked by his accusations. On Joseph's orders, an unit of the Nauvoo Militia was sent to the offices of the *Nauvoo Expositor* to destroy the press. Law and his fellow-conspirators fled to the neighbouring town of Warsaw and the following week, in the *Warsaw Signal*, Joseph himself was accused of having seduced many of the women of Nauvoo. 'War and extermination is inevitable!' proclaimed the headlines. 'Citizens arise, one and all!!! We have no time for comment. Every man will make his own. Let it be made with powder and balls!' Little urging was needed. Groups of armed men began to encircle Nauvoo and the Nauvoo Militia prepared to defend itself. Joseph knew that, were he to be taken, he was unlikely to escape with his life. Yet, at the last minute, in order to avoid what he feared would be a bloody slaughter, he surrendered to the state militia and ordered his men to lay down their weapons. He and his brother Hyrum were taken to Carthage jail. Three days later, armed men broke into the building and shot them both dead. This was on June 27th, 1844.

Without their Prophet, it was assumed that the Mormon Church would collapse. But Joseph had laid a solid foundation and had appointed good men to guard it. To help him govern, he had appointed a committee of a dozen of his most faithful followers, whom he called his Apostles, and when he died, the reins of power fell into the hands of these men and, in particular, into the hands of their President, a man called Brigham Young.

Brigham Young came to the fore at a critical time in the Church's history. The Mormons were fortunate in their early leaders. (They, of course, would argue that fortune had nothing to do with it.) He had much in common with Joseph. They were both about the same age, Joseph being 38 when he died, six years younger than Brigham. Both came from poor farming families, both were born in the backwoods of Vermont. Joseph was the fifth of eleven children, Brigham the ninth of eleven. Brigham's mother died when he was very young and he was raised by a harsh father. 'It used to be a word and a blow with him,' he once said, 'but the blow came first.' Both their families moved to New York State when the boys were still young. Both had very little schooling. Throughout his life, Brigham's grammar was shaky and his spelling erratic. He starts a letter to his wife thus, 'Having a fue mineuts I atempt to wright a fue lines to you.' And he finishes it with, 'Please read this and keep it to yourself not expose my poore righting and speling.' But, like Joseph, he had an innate wisdom and a sharp mind and he learnt very quickly in the stern school of experience.

There the similarities cease. Joseph, as behoves a prophet, was a man of vivid dreams and powerful imagination, charismatic and captivating, but not particularly practical. Brigham, on the other hand was, by trade, a builder, a carpenter, a painter and a glazier and, throughout his life, he remained a builder, although it was towns and communities and colonies that he was to build in the second half of his career. He had his feet planted solidly upon the ground and his eye fixed securely on the things of this world. 'I preach, comparatively, but little about the eternities and Gods and their wonderful works in eternities,' he once said, 'and do not tell who made them nor how they were made, for I know nothing about that. Life is for us, and it is for us to receive it today and not wait for the Millennium… My desire is to teach the people what they should do now and let the Millennium take care of itself.' The ways of the Kingdom of Heaven might have been something of a mystery to him, but he knew every corner of his own kingdom on earth. An unlikely Prophet, but a consummate leader.

Nothing happened in Zion without Brigham's finger being in the pie. He was a fair man and a just man, possessed of an iron will and an unswerving resolve. He had little to say to the privileged and the wealthy. Throughout his life he worked to better the lot of the poor and he worked very hard indeed. Copies of 30,000 of his letters are preserved in the Church archives and over 10,000 of them are replies to people who had asked his advice on such mundane matters as the best way to plant potatoes, whether or not to open a shop, how to collect a debt, how to build a home or how to find a wife. With Brigham's support, things moved forward. Without it, everything came to a stop. In the interests of his people and his God, he was willing to sail very close to the wind and to cut many corners. Above all, he was faithful unto death to Joseph Smith and his new religion.

Everyone had a story about Brigham. He had a turn of phrase that bordered, at times, on the coarse and boorish. This, to two of his enemies: 'When my old servant had been dead a year, if you will wash your faces clean, you may kiss his arse.' He could appear to be brutishly unpolished. 'If any man queries your authority,' he once instructed a newly formed police unit setting out on its first patrol, 'just knock him down with your cane.' But he could also be tender and warm, sensitively attuned to the anxieties of his people. Gwenllian Williams, for example, had buried her husband in Wales before coming to the Valley and it worried her greatly that she would not be buried by his side. She asked Brigham for his advice and he came to see her at her home. Gwenllian was not fluent in English and her nephew offered to interpret but Brigham refused his help, insisting they would understand each other well enough. And so it proved. Brigham explained to her, said Gwenllian later, that distances didn't matter after death. Her son said that she never worried about it afterwards.

Another time, Brigham was attending a Sunday morning meeting in Wellsville, a small village to the north of the Salt Lake Valley, when he saw a wagon of tired, dirty immigrants roll in. Thomas John and his family were newly arrived that very morning, from Mathry in Pembrokeshire. Brigham, noticing them hesitating outside the meeting hall, came to them, inviting them to enter. But Thomas said that they had not had time to wash off the dust of the trail, and that he felt too dirty to enter. 'Nonsense,' said Brigham, putting his arm through his, 'we're all dirty here.' And with that, led him into the meeting house.

'I saw and heard the Prophet, Brigham Young,' wrote D.F. Thomas, in a letter to his family. 'Even though he is the chief man here, he humbled himself to be everybody's servant.' John S. Davis, in a letter to *Udgorn Seion* [*Zion's Trumpet*], the Church magazine in Wales, wrote, 'It was a joy for me to see the Prophet and to have the honour of having private talks with him many times… He has a sharp eye and his judgements are just and in his presence many a man comes to know himself. He is gentle and kind to the humble and honest, but a roaring lion to the fearsome and wicked. The works of a man he sees from afar and is not easily deceived in anything.'

By November 1845, John Bennion's father and his brother, Samuel, had arrived in Nauvoo. The last surviving letter written by John from Nauvoo was to Esther's parents in Wales. 'Dear Parents… It is now a cold winter here, the river has been froze up several weeks… You will no doubt have heard much about the trouble in this part of the country of late… In the month of September when the people were busy gathering in their crops, the reward of their toil, a mob collected and commenced going to the houses of the Mormons, ordering them that in so many minutes they must be out of their houses for they were going to burn them up… Sick and weakly people were exposed to the hot sun and dampening dews of the night till they could get to Nauvoo, where all fled for safety. Some of these poor people died on account of being thus exposed.'

In the letter, he makes no mention of 'plural marriages' nor of the serious charges that had been made against Joseph Smith six months earlier. Published, as they were, by an enemy of the Church, in a hostile newspaper, the majority of the faithful would have assumed that they were false and malicious. But dark clouds continued to hang over Nauvoo. Rumours of strange and un-Christian practices spread through the surrounding 'Babylonian' countryside, exciting further attacks. The Saints, once again, began to harbour thoughts of escaping further into the West. 'Liberty in a solitary place,' writes John, 'is far more preferable than always being harassed and mobbed in these states and that on account of our religion… We now consider it best to leave this wicked nation.' Their enemies hounded them relentlessly. The special rights given to Nauvoo by the Illinois State Legislature were revoked and the militia was ordered to demobilize. In September, more outlying farms and villages were destroyed. Eventually, to save his people from further harassment, Brigham declared that the Mormons would leave

Illinois in the following spring 'as soon as grass grows and water runs'. But how? And to where?

The Apostles considered many possibilities. They looked for somewhere beyond the borders of the United States, somewhere beyond the reach of 'Babylon', somewhere where they might build a community and worship their God in their own way, with no interference. But such places were becoming few and far between. In California it would be difficult to escape the interference of the Mexican government, in Oregon the British would dictate. There was talk of Texas and Hawaii but, from the start, it was the land around the Great Salt Lake that most appealed to them.

Little was known about it. It lay over a thousand miles to the west, over the Rockies and well clear of the jurisdiction of the United States. Legally, all lands west of the Rockies belonged to Mexico but, apart from California, the Mexicans took little interest in them. The prevalent belief was that the centre of the continent was a bone-dry, barren land in which no community could survive. But, very recently, these views had been challenged. John Charles Frémont, known as 'The Pathfinder', had led an exploratory expedition over the Rockies in 1842 and had written a detailed account of what he had seen. In what had been known until then as 'The Great American Desert', he had seen areas of fertile land, where crops might be raised. On his second journey across the continent in 1845, he passed close by the Great Salt Lake and saw there green lands and grass covered hills. 'In the cove of mountains along its eastern shore, the lake is bordered by a plain where the soil is generally good and in greater part fertile, watered by a delta of prettily timbered streams. This would be an excellent locality for stock farms; it is generally covered with good bunch grass and would abundantly produce the ordinary grains.'

By the autumn of 1845, the Apostles had more or less agreed that the Salt Lake Valley was to be the place. John writes, 'We will leave here in April and May. I expect it will be a summer journey about 2,000 miles west ward. We shall pass through many Indian tribes towards the sea, where I expect to find a more healthy country than this.' His geography might have been questionable, his estimation of the distance vague, but the direction is certain and the resolve beyond doubt. 'The Valley' was now their goal and, although they had little idea of what awaited them there, they were eager to leave. 'There are here about 2,500 families preparing to go,' writes John. 'The people are busy making wagons for the journey.'

Crossing the Great Plains and the Rockies would have been a serious undertaking for a single family, but for a whole town to move en bloc was totally unprecedented. Some families, such as the Bennions, planned to take more than one wagon. Three to four thousand wagons would be needed, and 12,000 to 15,000 oxen. And food to last them many months and all the equipment necessary to pioneer a virgin land. All of them would go, from newborn babies to withered old folk, a population fast approaching 17,000 people. With them, they intended to take, not only their day-to-day needs, but also the things that made them an unique and different people – their institutions, their records, their culture and their church.

With their usual order and drive, the Mormons got to work. All their energies were now channelled into this one project – to have the bulk of their people ready to travel and on the road by spring. Every workshop in town was converted into a wagon maker's shop. Even unfinished sections of the temple were put to this use. Loggers felled trees by the hundreds, wheelwrights made wheels, blacksmiths beat out the rims of iron that were to encircle them, every family was building or strengthening the wagon frames that would ride on the axles. They were buying thousands of oxen, breaking them in, introducing them to harness. The women were salting meat, drying fruit, pickling vegetables. In such an enterprise, working as one under the guidance of the Church, the Mormons were at their best.

It was estimated that the journey to the Valley would take nine months or more. In October, the local paper, *The Nauvoo Neighbour*, published a list of what each family should bring: 1,000 lbs of flour, 1 lb of tea, 5 lbs of coffee, 100 lbs of sugar, 1 lb of cayenne pepper, 1 lb of black pepper, ½ lb of mustard,

10 lbs of rice, 1 lb of cinnamon, ½ lb of cloves, 12 nutmegs, 25 lbs of salt, 10 lbs of dried apples, 5 lbs of saleratus (a form of baking soda for making bread), 28 lbs of beans, many pounds of dried pork or dried beef, 5 lbs of dried peaches, 20 lbs of dried pumpkin, a gallon of alcohol, 20 lbs of soap. In addition, each family was expected to carry an adequate supply of cutlery, plates, cooking utensils, bedding and tents. The women and the younger children would usually plan to sleep in the wagons, the men, the older children and the servants underneath or in tents. Brigham also ordered that each family should carry their share of the heavier equipment that would be needed to clear the land, to plant the crops and to build the houses when they arrived in the Valley. Twenty-five pounds of seed corn to each family, fifteen pounds of scrap iron, between twenty-five and a hundred pounds of agricultural tools and machinery, many pounds of nails, fishing lines and hooks, the tools to build timber mills and flour mills – the list was endless.

In his letter, John worries about the land and the house he would be leaving behind. 'As to selling property,' he writes, 'if we can sell, we gladly will, but if not, we leave it unsold. Most people are the same way. Some few are sold.' He finishes his letter to his parents-in-law in good spirits. 'We have another daughter, Ann, born Nov 19. Our children are all healthy and thriving fast… You have been talking of coming to Nauvoo a long time. We will be glad to see you here early in the spring, in time to go with us to a good and more healthy country than this, where this people will commence a government of their own. Yours affectionately J & E Bennion.' And that's John's last letter from Nauvoo.

But as one window on their lives closes, another opens. Samuel, his brother, had arrived in Nauvoo in May 1845 and Samuel kept a diary. In it he describes how he set about improving his land and building his home. He bought 85 acres and fenced it. He bought 32,000 red bricks and spent $1,000 on a two-storey house with six rooms. But now, a year later, he was leaving for the Valley. Everything had to be sold in a falling market and he faced heavy losses. 'May, 1846. Sold my house and farm for $250.' But that was not his most serious concern. 'During the summer my father, myself and wife and two children, John R. and Elizabeth, were sick with the ague and fever. On the 18th day of February 1846, our little daughter Elizabeth died of the same. We buried her in the Nauvoo burying ground and put a large headstone on her grave.' Before leaving Liverpool, a year earlier, two of his three sons had contracted measles and had also died. Elizabeth had been born less than a month later and now she too was dead. They had hardly had a chance to mourn before the order came to leave. 'We left our Nauvoo home to go west somewhere. Myself, wife, son and father, brother John and his wife, Esther Wainwright and two children, Samuel R. and Mary.' He forgot to mention Ann, John and Esther's new child.

Three thousand people had left Nauvoo before the end of February 1846. As winter turned to spring, 12,000 more followed, grandfathers and grandmothers, pregnant women, little children, the sick and the feeble, all eager to leave 'Babylon', all with their sights set on an unidentified Zion somewhere beyond the Rockies. With them came their animals, thousands of cattle, great flocks of sheep and herds of horses, pigs, chickens, geese, bees. Behind them they left the temple to be vandalized and burnt by the mob. They left their fields, carved by their labour out of the virgin lands of the prairie, to revert again to wilderness. And they left their homes. 'My last act in that precious spot,' remembered one young wife, 'was to tidy the rooms, sweep up the floor and set the broom in its accustomed place behind the door. Then, with emotions in my heart which I could not now pen, I gently closed the door and faced an unknown future.'

John and his family set out for the west in five wagons, one driven by himself, another by his brother Samuel, and the other three by their wives, Esther and Mary, and by their father. They had hoped to complete their journey before autumn, but they soon ran into difficulties. The temperature plummeted to twelve degrees of frost and stayed there for the best part of a month. The Mississippi froze solid, which enabled the early starters to drive their wagons across the ice. This was considered to be a miracle and a sign that God was with them, but then the weather turned around. Even the route over the gentle hills of Iowa proved horrendously difficult. The grass had not yet begun to grow and pasture for the animals was not easy to find. In ceaseless rain, they struggled to make headway. Thick mud clung to the wheels of the wagons and sucked them into quagmires of clay. Small streams swelled into turbulent torrents and there was no foothold for the oxen as they struggled up the steep banks. Within weeks the Saint were strung out across Iowa in disorder, with no hope of reaching the Valley before winter and with very little idea of where they were headed.

Brigham had sent ahead a body of capable men to prepare the way for the thousands that were to follow. Their task was to identify the best routes, clear them of hindrances, cut easy access to the streams and prepare respite camps across Iowa, places where the sick and weary might stop awhile and regain their strength. On April 23rd, these men reached the frontier of the settled part of the state. Between them and the Missouri lay 150 miles of empty, uninhabited lands. The following day, at the sound of the morning trumpet, they began building one of the respite camps. A hundred men to cut down trees, fifty to shape them into logs for hut building. One crew ploughing, another sowing. One crew to dig wells, another to build bridges. One crew to fence, another to construct cabins. When they moved on, eighteen days later, they left a completed village behind them, Garden Grove, which still thrives today. Three hundred acres of land had been cleared, much of it ploughed, some of it planted, 10,000 fence posts had been cut and shaped, and wood enough had been prepared to build forty additional houses. One of the families to take advantage of the respite offered by Garden Grove was the Bennions. They decided to winter there and to leave early in the spring to catch up with Brigham Young and the main column, who were 150 miles ahead, hunkered down for the winter on the banks of the Missouri opposite Council Bluffs, in a camp they called

Winter Quarters. In September, John's father died of a disease described as 'bilious fever and dumb ague'. They buried him under a large oak in the Garden Grove graveyard. In January, another child was born to Mary and Samuel and, in April, a little girl was born to Esther and John. Before the end of the month, they all set out again for the Missouri.

During the journey, Esther's wagon slipped off the trail and she was thrown under a wheel and her arm was broken. The Mormons had little faith in doctors and medicine. An elder would probably have prayed for a cure, blessed her and anointed her arm with holy oil. Perhaps one of the company knew how to set the broken bones. Esther suffered from the after-effects of the accident for the rest of her life but she refused to be excused from her duties on the journey. Years later, she would relate with pride to her grandchildren how she had driven a wagon all the way from Nauvoo to Salt Lake City.

After a difficult winter in Winter Quarters, Brigham was preparing to set out once again for the Valley, still over a thousand miles away. It was evident to all that the previous season's confused, chaotic scramble, should not be repeated. There had to be order. It was then that God gave Brigham detailed instructions about the organizing of wagon trains. 'The word and will of the Lord concerning the camp of Israel in their journeying to the west. Let all the people of the Church of Jesus Christ of Latter-day Saints, and those who journey with them, be organised into companies, with a covenant and promise to keep all the commandments and statutes of the Lord God. Let the companies be ordered with Captains of Hundreds, Captain of Fifties and Captain of Tens, with a president and his two councillors at their head, under the direction of the Twelve Apostles… I am he who led the children of Israel out of Egypt, and my arm is stretched out in the last days to save my people Israel.' In other words, they were to be divided into trains of a hundred wagons; those trains were then to be subdivided into groups of fifty and the fifty into groups of ten. The Captains of Ten were responsible for overseeing the upkeep of the wagons in their groups, for ensuring the animals were well treated, for checking that every man and woman did their fair share of the work and for ensuring that the camp rules were obeyed. When faced with problems beyond their ability to resolve, they were to seek the advice of their Captain of Fifty, and he, in turn, could turn to his Captain of a Hundred. At the top of the chain were the Apostles, and then Brigham Young, and then God. This was the beginning of twenty years of orderly, disciplined and very successful migration.

The Lord also demanded that an advance party be sent out, as had been done the previous year. 'Choose out a sufficient number of able-bodied and expert men to take teams, seeds and farming utensils to go as pioneers to prepare for putting in spring crops... for I am the Lord your God, even the God of your fathers, the God of Abraham and of Isaac and of Jacob.' Brigham Young led the advance party and took 144 men with him to represent the twelve tribes of Israel, twelve men to each tribe. He saw himself as a Moses, leading the Chosen People once more through the desert to their Promised Land. But, at the last minute, his plans were sabotaged by one of the wives who refused to allow her husband to leave without her, and then two other wives had to be taken along to keep her company, and then one of them insisted on bringing a child. Moses, no doubt, had similar problems.

They set out for the Valley at the beginning of April. As in the previous year, they prepared the way for the thousands that were to follow by blazoning the trail, cutting down trees, building bridges, straightening paths and raising milestones. To measure the miles from Winter Quarters, they counted the revolutions of a wheel on one of their wagons. This, they had found, had a circumference of exactly fourteen feet and eight inches, therefore 360 of its revolutions constituted a mile. They then devised a system of wooden cogs to automatically count the revolutions, with the result that, a year later, they were able to produce the best and most accurate map yet published of a western trail. All along the route, they left messages for the main party, scribbled in charcoal on the dried skulls of buffalos or elk. Due perhaps to the comparatively trouble-free

34

passage enjoyed by Brigham and his men, these messages were peculiarly dull. 'Pioneers all well,' said one. 'Short grass, rushes plenty, watch for Indians.'

One of the most important aims of the advance party was to reach the Valley in time to sow and harvest a crop that season. They were still not convinced that the Valley could produce a harvest. Would the snows melt in time to water their crops? Were the summers long enough? Was the soil rich enough? Only by planting and harvesting could they be sure. In the meantime, Brigham ordered everyone to bring with them enough food for eighteen months so that, if the harvest failed, they had the means to try again or to move on to more promising locations.

Ahead of them, across the territory that became known as Nebraska, stretched the wide valley of the Platte River. Brigham intended to follow its course for the first six hundred miles. The Platte is a strange river. At times, especially in early June when the thaw waters from the Rockies came rushing down its channels, it was well-nigh impossible to ford. At other times, a child could wade through. It was subject to much abuse by the pioneers. 'Too muddy to drink and too watery to plough.' 'No fish, plenty of snakes.' 'Too much colour for washing up water, too little for paint.' 'Six miles wide in places and six inches deep in others.' But the river proved a good friend. The grass grew green along its banks. On the islands in its stream, protected from the constant prairie fires that swept the valley, the trees that fuelled their camp fires grew in profusion. And the buffalo and antelope came down to drink.

The Platte was the main road to the Rockies. Two hundred and fifty miles from its confluence with the Missouri, it divides into a southern fork which turns towards Colorado and a northern fork which continues straight out west. This led the pioneers directly to South Pass, which was then the only known route by which a laden wagon might pass through the Rockies. In those years, the years of the 'Manifest Destiny', when the United States began to feel it had the right to straddle the continent from sea to sea, South Pass assumed great importance. Were it not for this notch in the Rockies, the task of populating the west and uniting the two seaboards of the continent would have proved infinitely more difficult. All trails of any importance congregated at South Pass – the Oregon Trail, the California Trail, and later, the Mormon Trail and the Pony Express Trail – before parting to go their separate ways on the other side of the Continental Divide. Only the Santa Fe Trail, far to the south, found another wagon route through the mountains.

From the starting point on the Missouri to as far as South Pass, the California Trail and the Oregon Trail followed the same route, along the south bank of the Platte. It was estimated that between 5,000 and 6,000 emigrants used these two trails in 1847. But the Mormons decided they did not wish to share a trail with 'Babylonians' and unbelievers. They followed a lesser-used trail on the northern bank, a trail which gradually came to be known as 'The Mormon Trail'.

'Trail' is a good word, redolent of the romance of the Old West. On trails, cowboys amble and stagecoaches roll, although no cowboys would amble in these parts for another twenty years. A trail is not a path, nor is it a road, more a series of wagon ruts running side by side. On a flat, empty plain the trail might be a mile wide. In narrow defiles in the hills, it might be reduced to one deep channel carved out of the rock by countless wheels. At times, at the start of a season, it might be difficult to follow through the tall grass. At other times, especially in the 1850s and 1860s, it would cut through the landscape like a motorway.

Two and a half months after Brigham and the advance party had left, the rest of the 2,500 emigrants set out to follow in 566 wagons. John and Samuel Bennion and their families arrived in time to leave with the first company of a hundred. John had with him four oxen, two heifers, seven sheep and one blue mare. He lost six of his sheep *en route*. Samuel had six oxen and two milking cows. Two of his oxen strayed and were lost and one of his cows was killed by Indians. Contrary to the impression given in the cinema, very few horses were used to haul the wagons. Oxen were cheaper, tougher, more patient and could survive on poorer pastures. They were also less likely to be stolen by Indians because they couldn't be made to gallop away swiftly.

The early pioneers had a great fear of Indians. They had all heard lurid tales, culled from the dime novels of the day, of the terrible things that happened to white folk when they fell into Indian hands. They imagined every sort of savagery, from being flayed alive to 'a fate worse than death'. 'We were in fear of the Indians,' wrote one woman, 'and had to keep our guard all night. You can judge the feelings of women and children travelling through Indian country, not knowing what moment we might be attacked by wild savages.' Every man and boy above twelve was advised to carry a gun and some four pounds of powder and a pound of shot. Many men carried considerably more. One wrote that the ten men in his group had sixteen guns between them – nine rifles, four muskets and three pistols – each one primed to fire. Another group of 46 men carried between them fifty rifles, seven pistols, 246 pounds of powder and 138 pounds of shot. Three cannon were also hauled across the Plains, ready to fire into massed ranks of Indians should they charge. Yet, despite this, a member of John's wagon train was shot dead by Indians two days after leaving the Missouri. Some days later, to compound their fears, they came across the body of an unknown man, half eaten by wolves and bearing all the signs of having been killed by Indians. And to cap it all, one of their calves, feeding nearby, came back to camp one evening with an arrow stuck in its rump. Whenever it was believed that Indians were in the vicinity, the men were advised to sleep with their guns loaded and ready for use. As a consequence, far more of the early pioneers were shot by the accidental discharge of their own weaponry than were ever killed by Indians.

The Indian threat was at its height in the more populated areas near the Missouri, where they were being pushed out of their hereditary homes by the incoming white settlers. As the wagon trains left these lands, their relationship with the Indians improved. One emigrant described meeting a band of Indians far out on the Plains. 'They presented a hostile appearance as they approached towards us. Leaving their women and children in the background, the warriors advanced carrying a red flag. Our company was soon thrown into a defensive position. They came to a halt and sent their flag forward which was met by one of our men. The token of friendship was extended by shaking hands and extending the pipe. Women and children then came forward and, with the men, were permitted inside our lines.' No one quite knew what to do next. They shuffled around in mutual wariness until the children broke the ice and began to play together. 'Some of the boys proposed I should turn a somersault for their amusement. I was young then and very nimble. The Indians gathered around and I turned a couple of somersaults. They were amazed. They stood on the spot and jumped up and down as if to see if it would spring with them. Finding the ground was solid, they came and felt my legs and talked amongst themselves, much surprised that such a thing was possible.' From then on, the Indians often came into camp to sell moccasins and buffalo skins and beadwork and to buy bread and sugar and coffee and black powder for their guns. And they staged concerts in which they performed what the diarist described as 'war dances' and in return the emigrants danced to the music of the fife and drum. And then, to round off the evening with a good bang, the cannon were fired.

Despite the improved relations, the Indians still pilfered from the camp at every opportunity. Pots and pans and cutlery disappeared, clothing of all kinds, bits of iron, scraps of food, whatever they could find. Brigham Young's policy was to urge his people to forgive and be generous. Feeding them was cheaper than fighting them, he said. A few pilfered goods was a price he was happy to pay.

Eight hundred miles ahead of John's company, Brigham Young and his men were on the last leg of their journey, with only two hundred miles to go. They had passed through South Pass the previous day and were now out of the United States. As they rolled down the western slopes of the Rockies towards the Little Sandy River, they saw three men coming towards them. One of them turned out to be Jim Bridger, the most experienced and best informed of the Mountain Men. For 25 years, Bridger had lived in these mountains, trapping and exploring, returning to the east only twice in that time. In 1835 he had married an Indian wife, and had three children with her. After her death he had married another, the daughter of a Shoshone chief. He was a kindly and loving father to his children, sending them to schools in the east to be educated. He couldn't write his own name but he spoke many languages – Spanish, French and many Indian tongues, including Indian sign languages. He couldn't read a book, but he could read the terrain like a wild animal. No one knew the lands west of the Rockies better.

For twenty years he had been earning a good living hunting beaver and selling the skins to the traders who came out west every year to buy. But of late, his old way of life was under threat and his livelihood was in decline. The beaver was over-hunted and had become difficult to find. More importantly, beaver hats were going out of fashion in Europe, silk hats becoming all the rage. But, as one business collapsed, another took its place. Bridger offered his services as a guide to the emigrants and to the soldiers who were sent out west to police the trails. In the far west of what became Wyoming, he established Fort Bridger, a trading centre and a smithy, and it grew to be an important stopover on the annual migration trail. He knew the area west of the Rockies better than any man. In 1824, when he was only twenty, he had discovered and explored the Great Salt Lake and the Great Salt Lake Valley.

That night in camp, Brigham eagerly interrogated him, anxious to know if crops could be grown in the Valley, but, alas, Bridger was in no fit state to contribute to an intelligent conversation. He had been drinking and his speech was garbled and confused. No one was quite sure what he'd said. Some believed that he'd said he'd give a thousand dollars to anyone who could grow corn in the Valley. The Saints grew fearful that an arid desert might await them.

Meanwhile, far back along the trail, the Bennions and the

main companies were leaving the Prairies and entering the Great Plains, the territory of the buffalo. One night they were woken by the camp guards. A large herd was approaching and the wagon train was in danger. 'Our slumbers had been disturbed by a loud rumbling, not unlike a strong wind in a dense forest. Men and women and children could be seen tumbling out of their wagons in a half dressed condition. It required all the force we could muster, consisting of men, women and children, with ox whips, tin pans and everything that could make a noise, to prevent them running over and demolishing our wagons. They were easily reached with the ox whips. After considerable exertion we succeeded in inducing them to clamber up the bank a short distance below the camp. The ground fairly trembled as they galloped over the plain leaving us unmolested the remainder of the night.'

Another time, they were again awoken by the sound of galloping hooves. This time it was not buffalo, but their own oxen that were stampeding. A stampede could cause havoc in a wagon train. The least thing could start one, a dog barking, a piece of cloth flapping in the wind or thunder overhead. One animal would panic and the contagion would spread like wildfire through the herd. What was most feared was oxen stampeding whilst still in harness, still attached to their wagons, for then the wagons would be dragged behind the maddened animals for miles. They would smash into each other, scattering their contents, injuring and often killing the occupants. The animals could run for ten or fifteen miles before tiring. It meant hours, sometimes days, of searching for them and then long delays repairing the wagons before the train could move on again.

The first stampede of the season was more of a comedy than a catastrophe. It was caused by a woman shaking the dust from a buffalo robe. 'Woken as if by an earthquake,' wrote one of the company. 'The cattle had taken fright and were rushing with tremendous fury to the gaps in the corral, tramping down all before them. Men in their underwear and women in their night clothes mingled together indiscriminately, endeavouring to allay the fury of the cattle. One guard, a boy, seeing some of our men running after the cattle, took them for Indians, drew up his rifle and blazed away.' Fortunately, his aim was as poor as his judgement, and no one was hit. The animals didn't run far and the damage was not as bad as it might have been – only two wheels broken. But stampedes in other companies were more serious. Jedediah Grant's company lost sixty cattle and, despite searching for days, they were never found. The company was left with too few oxen to pull their wagons. Cows and calves were pushed into service. Eventually they had to beg for replacements from other companies. To further compound their troubles, they lost more animals in the Rockies, poisoned by a strange white powder that was often found scattered on the pasture. Alkaline salts were seeping from the rocks, polluting the pools. When, at the height of summer, these pools evaporated, the powder was left to contaminate the pasture. 'Over a great part of the road the ground is partly covered with Saleratus, or Salt Petre, which is very injurious to the oxen as they eat it freely. Owing to this, many fine oxen died. In fact you cannot go far on the road but you see the carcasses or the bones of cattle.' In years to come, this powder proved to be one of the chief menaces of the trail.

In the Bennion's company, as in all the Mormon companies that year, men were in short supply. A census taken of the population of Winter Quarters, the main camp, during the early spring of 1847 showed that there were 2,983 women and children present, but only five hundred men. A hundred and forty-four men had left with Brigham and another 550 men had gone to fight for the United States in their war against Mexico, not for patriotic reasons, but to earn money to buy food for their families. They spent twelve months in the army before returning. One diarist noted that, of the 87 wagons in the Bennion's company, thirty were without men to drive them. So, with typical frontier fortitude, the women set about teaching themselves to drive. 'Our family being numerous and help scarce,' wrote one of them, 'two of we women rather thought we could manage, with the oversight of my husband, to drive our own team, which consisted of a yoke of cattle, for, though just coming from a large city, and not being used to this kind of life – never having seen cattle yoked together – still I thought, well, what any other women can do, I can. So, shouldering my whip, I drove out of Winter Quarters, and soon learned to manage my team first class.' The Bennion wives were also expected to drive. It was clear that Esther's broken arm still troubled her but she was not excused the duty.

Driving an ox wagon was not a matter of sitting comfortably on a wagon seat, occasionally twitching the reins. An ox cannot be restrained and controlled by a bridle and bit. The driver has to walk alongside his or her animals, pulling their horns, whipping their flanks, beating their muzzles and shouting commands. 'One of my calamities was my lock-chain giving out,' wrote one woman. 'In going down a hill I had to hold the nigh ox by the horn and tap the off one over the face and keep saying, "Whoa, back; Whoa, back," and nearly hold my breath till I got down to the bottom, then stop, draw a breath of relief, see that all was right, then on again, for others were right on our heels and we had to get out of the way.' Mary Jane Tanner remembers her mother driving on the trail. 'The roads were very rough and often she had to spring from the wagon to guide the cattle and keep them from getting upset. One of her oxen would never learn to hold back, and when going downhill, she had to hold his horn with one hand and pound his nose with the other.' Esther, with her broken arm, must have had a hard time of it.

It was reckoned that twenty out of every hundred women who crossed the Plains in covered wagons were pregnant. They received no special attention. In addition to driving the wagon, they were expected to cook and wash and look after the children as usual. George Whitaker, one of Samuel and John's closest friends, describes the birth of his son. 'The first night we arrived at Independence Rock, my wife was blessed with a fine boy. We stopped over the next day on account of our cattle being sick and dying. It was lucky for my wife, as she needed a day's rest.' Another woman in the Bennion's company drove a wagon all the way to the Valley and gave birth five days later. Both mother and daughter survived the experience.

In Captain Jedediah Grant's company, which left Winter Quarters two days after John Bennion's, there was a girl called Martha Jane Williams. She was seventeen years old and pregnant. Two months into the journey, one of the company noted in his diary that the baby's birth was imminent. 'About noon,' he writes, 'Martha Jane was taken sick but we were obliged to travel on or stop where there was neither wood, water nor feed. We travelled on over a very rough road till dark and no camping place yet. Just at dark she was delivered of a son. About this time we found ourselves in a bad fix, behind the rest with a heavy load and no matches, consequently no light and she in a very precarious situation. We travelled on as fast as circumstances would permit till, within a mile of the camp, we was met by a midwife with light. We got into camp a little before midnight. The child was dead.' But at least Martha survived. Not so Jedediah's own wife. She and her newborn son died 75 miles from the Valley. That night, Jedediah made a coffin for his wife and child and wrapped them in a fine linen sheet and loaded them into his wagon and left the camp before dawn, making all haste to the Valley with his sad cargo. His wife and child were buried there, the first white woman and the first white child to be buried in Utah.

One of the happiest days on the journey was the day when Brigham Young came riding into camp on his way back to Winter Quarters. It was early September and the company was on the upper reaches of the Sweetwater, a day or two from South Pass. Brigham brought with him the very good news that the Valley appeared to be fertile and that the crops that had been planted appeared to be thriving. The Salt Lake Valley could well prove to be an ideal home for the Saints. He could have brought no better news. They decided to celebrate. A cow was slaughtered.

But in John Bennion's wagon, there were no celebrations. Ann, his little girl, was very ill. During the afternoon there had been a heavy storm and a blanket of snow had fallen, eight inches thick. Some began to worry that winter was upon them and that there would be no escape from the mountains. During the storm, Ann died. The cause of her death is unknown. Only a few words about the loss have survived, in a letter written later by John to his sister-in-law, Hannah. 'I sent you a letter on Sept. 7, giving you some account of our journeying from Garden Grove to the place of our affliction, on account of the loss of our little girl.' Nothing more.

Brigham was questioned closely about conditions in the Valley. They had begun to plough, he said, within two hours of their arrival. Eight days later, 25 acres had been prepared and planted and, before he left, he had seen the green shoots of corn stand three inches high and the potatoes and beans flourish. At last, the Saints could feel that there was an end to their wanderings and that the Zion promised to them by their God was within their reach. They laid out the best tablecloths and brought out their finest dinner services and feasted and made merry. But in the Bennion wagons that night, they were in mourning.

Next morning, the snow had melted and they moved on. 'We carried her body with us the next day 13 miles,' John wrote, 'and buried it on the morning of the 9th near the camp ground called Pacific Springs, on the left hand side of the road. I put down a headboard with this inscription: Ann Bennion, died Sept. 7, 1847, aged 1 year, 9 months and 19 days.' Pacific Springs were the first springs on the western side of the Continental Divide, the first streams to run down the western flanks of the Rockies, the first water to flow to the Pacific. They were now in Mexico, free of the United States. Perhaps they had carried Ann's body to that place so that she could be buried beyond the reach of their old enemies or perhaps so that, from her grave, she might look towards Zion.

At last, a hundred days after leaving Winter Quarters, John and Samuel and their families came to the end of the trail. 'I shall never forget the last day we travelled,' wrote one of the company. 'The reach of our wagon was broken and tied together after a fashion and the way the front wheels wobbled was a sight to behold. I kept expecting every minute to see the poor old concern draw apart and come to grief, but it held together and when my eyes rested on the beautiful, entrancing sight – the Valley, Oh! How my heart swelled within me. I could have laughed and cried, such a commingling of emotions I cannot describe. My soul was filled with a thankfulness to God for bringing us to a place of rest and safety – a home.'

In truth, their new home was no paradise. Most of Utah is high mountain or desert. Around the small pockets of fertile land were desolate expanses of arid emptiness. And apart from a few scattered bands of Native Americans and the occasional hunter, there was no living soul for hundreds of miles in all directions. But this was why the Mormons had come here. This is what motivated them. 'I want hard times,' declared Brigham, 'so that every person who does not wish to stay for the sake of his religion, will leave… God has appointed this place for the gathering of his Saints. We have been kicked out of the frying pan into the fire, out of the fire onto the middle of the floor, and here we are and here we will stay. God will temper the elements for the good of his Saints… Brethren, go to now and plant out your fruit seeds.'

For John and Samuel, the promises were kept. They lived out the rest of their lives with no discrimination and without persecution. John later wrote, 'If peace dwells upon this earth, it is here, and here are the happiest and most prosperous people in the world, enjoying free soil, pure air and liberty to worship God just as we please.' The two families remained close, working, living and worshipping together. The blue mare, the eight oxen, the two heifers and the cow and the sheep that the brothers had brought with them increased to over a hundred horses, 1,500 head of cattle and about 7,000 sheep. Over the next half century, they invested wisely in flour mills and woollen mills and stores and in many other successful businesses in Salt Lake City and became wealthy men.

In Utah, the Bennions have left their names on many institutions and landmarks. In the Sheeprock Mountains, above one of the family ranches, are Bennion Creek and Bennion

Canyon. On the edge of Salt Lake City is Bennion Hill and in the south-west of the city, where they farmed throughout their lives, there was a suburb called Bennion, which has now become part of the larger suburb of Taylorsville-Bennion. But Bennion Park still survives, as do Bennion Boulevard, Bennion Junior High, Bennion Elementary, and the family's contribution to the early history of the city is still remembered in the township's museum, the Bennion Heritage Centre.

In Wales, on the other hand, even in their home village of Hawarden, they are forgotten. In 1872, John returned to Wales, having been called to serve a term as a missionary. He visited his old haunts in Hawarden. Since he had last been there, the squire's family had advanced in the world. Catherine, the squire's sister, had married the Prime Minister, Mr Gladstone, and, when the House of Commons was not sitting, she and her husband spent much of their time in Hawarden Castle. One afternoon, John and his cousin, Susan Catheral, took a walk through the castle park. Who should pass by in her carriage but Mrs Gladstone herself. 'Mrs. Catheral introduced me to her,' wrote John. 'She asked me how I was suited in my American home and readily remembered me as Betty Bennion's son of Moor Lane, whom she used to visit some 45 years ago. She invited us to the castle for tea.' What an honour! To be invited into the castle! The son of one of the tenants invited to take tea with the Prime Minister's wife! But no! It was not tea in the sitting room that awaited John and his cousin, but tea in the kitchen with the servants. A tenant was always a tenant in Hawarden Castle.

1848

ONE OF THE few Welsh Mormons known to have been on the trail in 1848 is Sarah Price of Hanmer in English Maelor, on the eastern border of Flintshire. She might also have been amongst the very first to have heard the Mormon message being preached in Wales. The earliest Mormon missionaries to Britain had based themselves in the industrial towns of north-west England – in Manchester, Preston and Liverpool – but they made occasional forays into the surrounding countryside to preach and distribute their tracts. On one such mission, in the autumn of 1840, two missionaries, Henry Royle and Frederick Cook, came to Cloy, a collection of farmhouses on the edge of Overton, five miles from Sarah's home, and just over the Welsh border. A fortnight later, Brigham Young himself, newly arrived from the U.S.A., also came to Wales, to preach in Hawarden, 25 miles to the north. He mentions his visit in a letter to his wife written in November that year. 'The report went out that we had the same power that the old Apostles had. It was true we did lay hands on one young man who was quite low with a fever. We rebuked his fever and he got well. We laid our hands on a woman that had very bad eyes. She immediately recovered.' The Cloy mission seems to have flourished mightily, gathering, within a month of the arrival of the missionaries, a congregation of 32 members. By the spring of the following year, it had grown to over 150 members. And then, mysteriously, it disappeared. When the next missionaries visited the area in 1845, no mention was made of it. Perhaps it had been absorbed into the Liverpool Conference or perhaps most of its member had answered the call to gather to Zion, as did Sarah Price. On January 3rd, 1843, Sarah married Charles Smith, a Church missionary from Ellesmere in Cheshire. Two days later they boarded the *Swanton* in Liverpool docks and sailed for New Orleans and Nauvoo. She was then twenty years old.

Charles Smith seems to have been a gentle, unassuming man. He kept a diary, written in Pitman's Shorthand, which suggests that he was well educated. But his education, good though it might have been, guaranteed him no easy living in Nauvoo. His life there was a chronicle of hard, unremitting toil, firstly in a brickworks and then in a ropewalk. But Charles doesn't complain. His diary implies that being in the presence of Joseph Smith, listening to his sermons and conversations, compensated for all the hard work. He willingly undertakes extra unpaid responsibilities on behalf of the Church. He delights in being a member of the Nauvoo Brass Band. He quotes a verse from the Psalms, 'Gather my saints together to me, those that have made a covenant with me by sacrifice.'

In 1844 a son was born, but did not survive. In the autumn of 1845, Charles played his part in the defence of Nauvoo, but when the chance came to leave with the majority of the population for the Salt Lake in the spring of 1846, he found he could not afford the oxen and wagon and the food and equipment that the Church demanded an emigrant family should bring with them. In August Sarah gave birth to another son, Edward. Throughout 1846 and 1847 Charles laboured to earn the means to pay for the journey to the Valley. Three times he went to St Louis looking for work. He worked on a steamboat, he worked in a store, he drove a wagon. He tried to sell a plot of land which he'd cleared and upon which he'd built a cabin. It had cost him $47 to develop. He had to sell it for $10. But by 1848 he had saved enough to buy two oxen, a cow, a wagon and all the paraphernalia necessary to cross the Plains. In the spring, he and Sarah and the boy left for the Missouri and there they joined the two companies that were preparing to set out for the Valley that year – the largest, led by Brigham Young himself, consisting of 1,061 people and the other, of 699, led by Heber Kimball. Sarah and Charles were placed in Kimball's company.

Throughout the journey, Charles continued to keep his diary, but he could not, by any stretch of the imagination, be described as an interesting diarist. Occasionally his entries flicker into life, such as his description of the night when he set his own wagon alight. 'August 30th. Went to Sweetwater 7 miles and camped. Whilst here we had liked to have been burnt up. We took some coals into the wagon at night and the wind rose and blew the coals about, which set several things on fire. Nearly burnt my pants all away. The smell of the smoke awoke me. I got up in alarm and put the fire out.' But such passages are few and far between. More often, he records only the distances travelled and the locations of the camps. 'Sunday, 3rd. Left for Pacific Springs. The next day we went to Little Sandy and the next day to Big Sandy, 17 miles. The next day to Green River. The next day down Green River 5 miles.' And so on.

However, there was no shortage of diarists in the company. Keeping a diary or a 'memory-book' was considered by the Saints to be a religious duty. They believed that a record of their trials would help them to later examine their lives and so learn from their experiences. According to the *Book of Mormon*, when Christ appeared in America, after his crucifixion, one of his commandments was that the faithful should 'write the things that ye have seen and heard… for out of the books which shall be written shall the world be judged'. 'Have the servants of the Lord been faithful in this?' demanded *Udgorn Seion*, the Welsh Church magazine. 'Let us not be negligent nor lazy from now on. Let each buy a small notebook and write therein every relevant event that comes to his notice pertaining to the works of God.' In fair weather or foul, once the tent was up, the cattle taken to water, the wagon repaired, the fire lit, the clothes washed and the meal prepared, the first duty of the conscientious Mormon was to reach for a pencil. 'I rise in the night when my babe and all others are asleep, light a candle and write,' writes one mother. 'It is raining and the wind is blowing so hard it shakes the wagon so hard I can't write good,' writes another. Throughout the twenty years of ox wagon migrations to the Valley, hundreds of others did likewise and many of their diaries have survived. Some, like Charles', are perfunctory and uninteresting but others write with charm and humour and with lively, detailed descriptions of day-to-day life on the trail. Together they constitute a palette of many colours which has enabled historians to paint a vivid and detailed picture of the Mormon migration.

Five good diarists travelled with Sarah and Charles in Kimball's company and ten others in Brigham Young's company, which travelled alongside them. In addition, over eighty biographies and autobiographies, written by or about members of these two companies, have been collected by the Church History Library in Salt Lake City. These, of course, are not as dependable as the diaries. They were often written towards the end of the subject's life, sometimes fifty years or more after the events described. And, of course, when stories get told and re-told to children and to grandchildren, the wolves become more ferocious, the snows deepen, and finding camp is always touch and go. But by dipping into the fifteen diaries, and using the memoirs and the biographies to fill the gaps, we can gain a pretty good impression of what Sarah and Charles experienced on their way to the Valley. Today, the diaries and the biographies can be read on the Mormon pioneer overland travel website hosted by the Church History Library – **http://history.lds.org/overlandtravels/home** – and on Professor Dennis' site – **http://welshmormon.byu.edu/**

Every year, those intent on crossing the Plains would be called to a staging camp, where the inexperienced were prepared for the trials ahead. They were shown how to cook on an open fire, how to put up tents, how to load their wagons. They were introduced to their oxen and taught how to handle them. Before his conversion, Alexander Baird had been in the navy. 'I had never seen a yoke of cattle in my life,' he wrote, 'and knew as much about them as they knew about me. In fact, they probably knew more.' The pioneers had to be taught how to sort their own oxen at the start of the day from the

350 others in the company herd and how to coax the reluctant animals into their yokes. Each animal had its own specific place in the team and woe betide the green-horn who got it wrong. The front left ox in the right back yoke was a recipe for disaster. They were taught to cry 'Gee' to make the oxen turn to the right and 'Haw' to the left, followed each time by the animal's name. But in the heat of the moment, as they approached difficult corners, there was a tendency to panic, and instructions became garbled, and the sound of 'geeing' and 'hawing' would rise to incomprehensible crescendos, leaving the poor animals baffled. Long before they reached journey's end, however, the green-horns would be 'geeing' and 'hawing' with the best of them, as proficiently as prairie-born farm boys. They were taught to emphasise their commands with cracks of the bull whip. 'It was quite a while before I could swing my whip and hit what and where I wanted,' said one, 'which was very necessary to do in order to be a good and safe teamster. Many a red mark I had on my face and neck from my own awkwardness... But before we arrived at Salt Lake I could pick a horsefly off the oxen's ear and never make him jump.'

At the end of the day, when the wagons had been run into a tight circle and locked, wheel to wheel, with chains, to form a sturdy corral, the women would prepare supper. For most of them, boiling a pot of coffee on a camp fire was a challenge. Water had to be fetched, fuel collected, fire lit, coffee beans roasted and ground. And if there was a strong wind or a heavy downpour, it could be well-nigh impossible. Cooking was equally difficult. 'Although there is not much to cook, the difficulty and inconvenience in doing it amounts to a great deal. So by the time one has squatted around the fires and cooked bread and bacon and made several dozen trips to and from the wagon, washed the dishes (with no place to drain them) and gotten things ready for an early breakfast, it is time to go to bed.'

Their diet was sparse, with little variety. 'Our daily exertions made hunger a constant companion,' wrote Mary Scott Pugh, a member of Charles and Sarah's company. 'The quantity of food was limited and the meals were usually scant. Pig Weed, found wild on the prairie, could be cooked and eaten like spinach. Thistles and other greens were gathered at times and cooked to add variety. In some places, an abundance of wild red and black berries were gratefully gleaned.' Bread, which was usually flour mixed with water and fried, was a regular item in the staple diet. As was salted pork. Another popular food was 'mush', a sort of weak porridge made from Indian corn or maize flour. Every kind of bean was popular, French, Lima, Black and Pinto, because, once dried, they kept well. 'We cooked in a camp kettle. It was an iron pot with three legs. It had a heavy lid and could be set right on the bed of coals, and biscuits, cornbread or cake could be put in, then a shovel full of coals would be put on top to bake them.'

The Saints were advised to take a cow with them to give daily supplies of fresh milk. When they set out in the mornings they would fasten a can of milk to the back of the wagon and, by their midday break, it would have been churned into butter. If there were hunters in the party, they might eat elk and deer, small antelope and prairie hens. Later, when they had passed Grand Island, 250 miles from the Missouri, there would be buffalo steaks. Their opinion of buffalo meat varied greatly. 'I think there is no beef in the world to equal a fine buffalo cow.' 'The most offensive meat I ever tasted.' 'Such flavours, so rich, so juicy, it makes the mouth water to think of it.' 'Tasted like the *chef d'œuvre* of the Devil's kitchen.' The pioneers soon discovered that the tastiest and most tender joints were the ribs, the tongue and the hump on the shoulder of the beast. They dried the meat, as they had seen the Indians do, cutting it into long strips and tying it in bloody ribbons on to the sides of their wagon. When dried, it would keep for the rest of the journey.

A few days before leaving the staging camp, Charles noted in his diary that he had attended a company meeting. Such meetings were convened by every company before they set out. Their purpose was to agree a set of rules for the journey and to approve the men chosen to lead them. In theory, every man in the company had the right to vote against the names proposed by the Church authorities but only very rarely did they do so. If the Apostles and the Prophet had made the decision on their behalf, who were they to disagree? Heber Kimball was confirmed as the Captain of the Company and, in accordance with the order laid down by Brigham Young the previous year, the names of the Captains of Hundreds, Fifties and Tens were duly submitted and approved. The emigrants were then allotted their places in the train.

A good Captain contributed greatly to the success of his company. He chose the route. He was expected to lead by example, to be at the fore when there was danger, dependable in a crisis. He would be first across fast-flowing rivers. He would ensure his company was aware of the perils of the trail, how to avoid stampedes, how to handle their weapons responsibly. He made sure the children kept clear of the rolling wheels of the wagons. On him fell the responsibility for choosing the camping sites and making sure that there was clean water nearby and good pasture. He would need to know the ways of the Indians, when to disregard their displays and when to take them seriously. He would keep in contact with other companies crossing the Plains behind and before him. He would sort out quarrels and dispense justice. And he had to ensure harmony within his company, often his most difficult task. 'I am certain that a journey through a desert country of a thousand miles, with five hundred souls, will try the patience of any man who is set to be at the head,' wrote one Captain, 'especially so when the company is made up of different nationalities, having different customs and some without any experience of travelling with ox teams.' 'Some may think the children of Israel in the wilderness were a clamoursome set,' wrote another, 'but they were nothing more than what folks are now.'

Eight camp rules were agreed in Sarah and Charles' organizing meeting. (1) Noise and confusion will not be allowed after 8 p.m. (2) The camp will be summoned by trumpet to morning and evening prayers. (3) Everybody will arise at 4.30 a.m. and assemble for prayers at 5.30 a.m. (4) Card playing will not be allowed. (5) Dogs must be tied up at night. (6) Profane language will not be tolerated. (7) Each man will help in driving the cattle. (8) The rate of travel for oxen will be three miles per hour. (9) The wagon corral will not be broken until all of the cattle have been yoked.

On the morning of June 7th, the order was at last given for the wagon train to move out. Slowly the knot unwound, the wagons snaking out across the prairie. At the head of the column was the Captain on horseback. Then, up front to avoid the clouds of dust raised by the thousands of hooves that followed, came some of the women in their wide sun bonnets with their barefooted children. Then the wagons and the patient oxen, their teamsters walking besides them, cracking commands with the bull whips. Some of the younger children travelled in the wagons, but it was not a comfortable ride and many people preferred to walk. At the rear came the herds of beef cattle and heifers and calves, of sheep and pigs and their bedraggled, dusty minders. 'It was a beautiful sight to see, those covered wagons and teams... everyone keeping in their place and everything kept in order... winding their way over hill and dale, across streams and climbing hills on their way to Utah, through the tops of mountains to where God said he would set up his kingdom in the last days, never more to be torn down, or given to another people.'

Good humour bubbled through the camp. The pioneers, both Mormon and non-Mormon, liked to decorate the canvas covers of their wagons with slogans and symbols and pithy sayings that could be read from afar. The 'Babylonians' scrawled phrases like 'Never say Die', 'Patience and Perseverance' or 'The Sacramento Express' in charcoal or black paint. Sketches of eagles or buffalos, lions or giraffes, were popular. Some of the larger companies displayed their number and company name on the canvas: '21 Wolverine Rangers' or '40 Pittsburgh and California Enterprise Co.' The Mormons, on the other hand, liked religious or pious slogans, such as 'Truth Will Prevail', 'Blessings Follow Sacrifices', 'Zion's Express' or 'Merry

Mormons'. They all helped to make the wagons identifiable at a distance.

For a while, both companies, Kimball's and Young's, travelled together, six hundred wagons, stretching for five or six miles across the prairies, each one following within a hundred feet or so of the one in front. In the column, there were 2,012 oxen in harness and 1,317 other cattle, 904 chickens, 645 sheep, 237 pigs, 134 dogs, 131 horses, 54 cats, 44 mules, 11 doves, five ducks, five hives of bees, three goats, one squirrel and 1,882 humans. Brigham Young must have felt more like Noah than Moses.

At midday they would stop to give the animals a chance to feed and to rest. They themselves ate a light meal prepared the previous evening. Every evening, the wagons drew into a tight corral, locked wheel to wheel, to shelter the more valuable animals. On a good day, they might travel fifteen miles. On a bad day, due perhaps to sickness, a broken wheel or lost cattle, they might not move at all.

Everyone was in high spirits. They were on the final leg of their long journey to Zion, a journey which had started for most of them months if not years earlier. 'When I had been three weeks on the journey, there was not a more mirthful woman in the whole company,' remembered one young girl. 'The grandeur of nature filled me with grateful aspirations… Especially did we admire the flowers which grew in some places in great profusion, handfuls of which daily adorned our wagon and delighted our children.' And even Charles Smith added his pennyworth of excitement, noting in his diary that he and Sarah had spent a 'very pleasant day'.

It was a country unlike any the pioneers had walked in before. Across the wide prairies in those early days, the grass grew in endless profusion, so high a man might stand in his saddle and still not be able to see about him. It grew from horizon to horizon. Now and again, it would give way to patches of unknown flowers. 'We found ourselves decidedly in the Garden of the Lord or rather in the Lord's Flower Garden. For several acres around there was nothing but the most beautiful flowers, pink, yellow and snowy white as if the flora had been apprised of our coming and had arrayed herself accordingly.' They gave them names to match their beauty – Prairie Golden Pea, Snow-on-the-Mountain, Babies' Breath. 'To look around and see a vast plain, interspersed with small groups of timber, it is enough to make a person exclaim, "Surely God in Heaven has constructed the earth to make me rejoice".'

And there were new animals and birds to be admired. 'Morning was beautiful. When I was going with the herd, the Prairie Hens could be heard in every direction singing praises to Him who'd made them... We came into a land alive with what is called Prairie Dogs... They lived in holes in the ground and would make the hills sound with their barking all night long. They are about the size of small puppies and as cunning as can be. They would sit by their holes by hundreds and yelp and bark until the boys almost got up to them and then dodge back in their cells and stick their heads out and bark.' Soon they were in buffalo country, amazed by the size of the herds and awed by the magnificence of the animals. Following the buffalo came the wolves, hungry for abandoned calves, on the lookout for sick animals that failed to keep up with the herd. And then the coyotes, the 'cockerels of the Plains', that would wake up the camp each dawn with their doleful chorus.

No one knows how many buffalo roamed the Great Plains in those days. Forty million say some, a hundred million say others. 'Sometimes we would see the Plains black with them for ten miles around and I don't know how far beyond our sight. All in motion, on the gallop, they would pass by us for hours.' There were herds that were fifty miles long and 25 miles wide. Horace Greeley, the editor of the *New York Tribune*, on a fact-finding tour of the West, was held up by one such herd for two days and two nights as it crossed his path. 'I know that a million is a great many,' he wrote, 'but I am sure I saw more than a million buffalo yesterday.'

On the prairie in those early days there was a sparkle that the pioneers found intoxicating. 'The camping grounds were so clean that one could believe no human foot had ever trodden there, so green was the grass, so delightful the wild flowers.' But it was a splendour that was not to last. In that same year, gold was discovered in California and, within a twelvemonth, the rush would be underway. Before another summer came, the beauty of the trail would be trampled underfoot by the boots of 20,000 miners. The emigrants who crossed in 1848 were therefore privileged. They walked the trails of the west whilst they were still fresh and clean and pristine.

The euphoria of the early days, however, soon gave way to the small niggling annoyances of daily life on the Plains. All along the Platte River Valley, maddening swarms of fleas, flies, ticks, lice, gnats and bed bugs accompanied the wagon trains, but by far the most insufferable of all the obnoxious pests that sucked their blood was the mosquito. 'Day and night they swarm around, completely covering the animals. At night they are worse and if you did not almost suffocate yourself with smoke inside the tent, they would eat you up.' The sound of mosquitoes striking the wagon covers was 'like heavy rain in a storm', 'thousands upon thousands of them swarming about us'. 'There is not room on this river for another mosquito, and they bite, Oh! Mercy!' They would bite through shirts and frocks, and their bite was said to be far more painful than that of their more civilised cousins in the east. 'Mosquitoes! Oh! Dreadful night. I wrapped my head and hands tightly in a blanket for as long as I could stand it and then got up and ran as fast as I could.'

Dust was another constant nuisance. It was formed from the countless ox pats and buffalo pats that lay on the trail, dried to a tinder under the sun and then crushed by the passing of endless wheels. 'You in the East know nothing of dust. It often seems that the cattle must die for want of breath and then, in our wagon, such a spectacle! Beds, clothes, victuals and children all covered,' wrote one mother. It worked its way into the seams of clothes, it clogged noses and matted hair and made eyes sore. It seasoned food and formed a scum on every drink. And mixed with sweat, it formed a hard crust over the face, like a mask. 'The least breeze or trampling of the cattle is sufficient to raise it in such clouds as to envelope a whole train to such an extent as to render it difficult to distinguish the wagons at a few yards distance.'

They were also bothered by sudden storms that fell on them from clear skies, winds that overturned wagons, rain that flooded the trail in minutes, hail the size of quails' eggs, 'frightening beyond anything known in the Old Country'. In such a storm one poor man complained that he 'couldn't lie down without being drowned or stand up without being struck by lightning.' And the lightning, said another, 'illuminated the darkness of midnight with a light so pure, it was possible to pick up a pin from the prairie ground, if one were there.' One storm in 1849 left the cattle 'cut through on the hips and back by the hail'. For Sarah and Charles, such storms meant hot meals having to be abandoned and many miles walked in sodden clothes. They were, says Charles, in another of his terse, laconic diary entries, 'very disagreeable'.

But their gravest problem was weariness. 'No one knows, unless they have had the same experience, what a trial it was to drive teams all day and guard at night. The loss of sleep was something fearful.' 'As soon as we had struck our wagon in the corral, we unyoked the cattle and gathered wood. The next thing was to get the cows and milk them, then drive stakes to tie the cattle. About this time the drove would come in and we would then get the cattle and tie them. Sometimes we had to go a mile and a half for water and sometimes had to dig wells. Each ten herded their cattle and every man and able boy took their regular turn on guard, each turn coming round once every five days. The duty of guarding the camp at night also fell to each man in turn. The herding and guarding, together with my daily tasks, kept me beat down and wore out all the time. The women were as well beat down as the men.' They would doze whilst driving their wagons, leaving the animals to fend for themselves and to find their own way. Accidents inevitably happened. A wagon ran over Lucy Groves' leg, breaking it in two places. Brigham Young set the bone himself. Six-year-old Lucretia Cox fell in front of a wagon, two of the wheels running over her, killing her.

This was not an uncommon accident. It was easy to trip or fall whilst getting on or off the wagons. Oxen, unlike horses, could not be brought to a sudden stop. And it was not only children who were killed beneath the wheels. The women's long, impractical skirts often caused terrible accidents, dragging them into the spokes of a wheel or tripping them into the path of a wagon. 'She had the hem of her dress torn and it hung and dragged on the ground and when she went to get on the wagon, she saw there were others in the wagon. So she said she would wait awhile longer and stepped back and stepped on her torn dress and fell and the wagon ran over her body.' In 1852, women started to wear bloomers on the trail, not the voluminous undergarments worn by our great-grandmothers, but a sort of loose trouser, tied at the ankles and worn with a short skirt. In the cities of the east and in Europe, bloomers were a daring new fashion, but on the western trails, they were sensible, practical, life-saving garments. Even the Welsh Church magazine, *Udgorn Seion*, advocated their use. 'The women are beginning to wear trousers and jackets... Many of the fair sex are seen in America in their new apparel. All success to them in getting hold of something better than the old apparel, so they may follow the men through the mud more easily than at present.' But there are no reports of Welsh women on the Plains flirting with the new fashion. Did not Deuteronomy, 22:5 expressly forbid such a practice? 'The woman shall not wear that which pertaineth unto a man... All that do so are abomination unto thy Lord God.'

When accidents or illnesses occurred on the trail, the medicines available were very primitive. Mormon pioneers never put much store by doctors. They trusted to traditional cures. Some of the remedies appear more deadly than the sicknesses they aspired to cure. A young sister was bitten by a rattlesnake, not an uncommon experience, and her cure was a liberal quantity of whisky which, according to the diarist, 'neutralized the poison'. When one of the brothers suffered the same injury, a poultice of tobacco juice mixed with turpentine was placed on the wound and he was dosed with large swigs of alcohol. He complained of a sore stomach and a dry mouth and his vision, he said, became blurred, but he eventually recovered, both from the bite and the remedy. Naturally, not much was written about treatments that failed. 'A serious complaint usually results in death.'

Both the Saints and the 'Babylonians' put great faith in the efficacy of black powder as a cure-all for man and beast, inside the body or out. In cases of snakebite, dollops of black powder were sometimes mixed with animal fat and rubbed onto the wound. And when an ox belonging to a man called John Davis sank to its knees after drinking poisoned water, he mixed a quarter of a pound of salt dissolved in warm milk with a pound and a half of pig's fat mixed with a quarter of a pound of black powder and stuffed it down its gullet. The animal was on its feet in no time and soon back at work.

Black powder, however, didn't work every time. One woman suffered a painful ulcer on the joint of a finger. She tried to scrape out the putrefaction but the pain worsened. She was advised to bind the finger in a poultice of black powder. Some nights later, preparing the evening meal, she came too close to the fire and the black powder exploded, blowing her hand away. The finger was no problem thereafter.

But the remedy that the Saints reverted to most often was the anointing of the patient with holy oil, followed by the laying on of hands and a blessing. They trusted in the advice given by James, 5:14. 'Is any sick among you? Let him call for the elders of the church, and let them pray over him, anointing him with oil in the name of the Lord.' There were remarkable instances recounted by the Welsh back home of miracles wrought by the holy oil and the laying on of hands. Some years earlier, in a mine in Merthyr Tydfil, a brother suffered a broken back in a roof fall. He was anointed with the holy oil, which was instantly effective. 'You could hear the bones snap back in to place,' wrote an observer, 'like the cracking of an old basket.' So, when Richard Ballantyne's son, travelling in Brigham's company, fell ill on the third day of the journey, his father prayed to God, promising that he would raise the child 'in fear of the Lord, to obey all His commandments... if the Lord would preserve his life and return him to health.' He then took a bottle of the holy oil and anointed the child in the name of the Lord. The boy recovered. This remedy worked equally well on cattle. Rachel Fielding, travelling with Sarah and Charles, remembered that her Aunt Smith's ox got sick and seemed as if it would die. 'But my father poured oil on it and administered to it,' she wrote, 'and it lay perfectly still a few minutes and then got up and shook itself and ate a little grass and father hitched it up and it was all right after that.'

What was this remarkable oil? How was it obtained? The answers are to be found in a short sketch published in *Udgorn Seion*. Two old friends, neither of them Mormons, meet on a street corner in some small south Wales village. Morgan is sober and sensible, Dafydd is rash and raucous and distrusts all Mormons.

> Dafydd: Morgan, did you hear about that man killed by the damned Mormons? They should be transported, every man jack of them.

> Morgan: No. How did they kill him?

> Dafydd: They gave him that old oil they've got for killing people. Whatever they're suffering from, they all get given the same smelly stuff by those devils, damn them! I went round to the doctors' last night to tell him about their foul tricks and he decided to demand an inquest so that he could transport up to a dozen of them. But damnation! In the just opinion of our minister that's much too good for them, by God!

> Morgan: Don't swear, Dafydd lad. What's the oil they've got, do you know? And what's it called. A stop needs to be put to this sort of thing. They might have the right to preach their religion but that doesn't give them the right to kill people.

> Dafydd: I don't know what name they give their stinking, devilish old oil, but they killed that man who had cholera. It's shocking to think that those sorts of devils are allowed to live in a Christian country.

Then a Mormon, who goes by the name of Wil the Saint, enters and they approach him to find out more about the oil. As it happens, Wil has a bottle in his pocket.

Wil: Here's a bottle I've just bought in the druggist. Our master's maid was in there at the same time buying two bottles of the same stuff for his dinner. It's called *best olive oil* or *sweet eating oil*. Try a sip yourselves, both of you. All the big men use it with the various vegetables on their tables.

Dafydd: Does the old devil want to kill us too? Damn his soul! Get away from the fool, Morgan.

But Morgan stays and learns how to use the oil.

Wil: All that needs to be done to the oil before giving it to the patient is for the elders to bless it through prayer; after that they anoint the patient, at his request, in the name of the Lord; and if the sickness is internal, they give him a spoonful or two to drink. Then, laying their hands on his head, they pray for a second time, in the name of Jesus Christ, for God to cure the sick man, according to his promise.

It was a treatment regularly used by the Saints and one in which they had the utmost confidence. Only a week into their journey, Thomas Bullock reports that three people had already fallen under wagon wheels and had survived after being treated with the oil. The most serious case was that of nine-year-old Mary Anne Perkins. 'She had a wagon laden with 2,500 lbs run over her, both wheels across her breast. The brethren administered and in about an hour she fell asleep. No bones broken. A miracle.'

A fortnight into the journey and the landscape began to change. They were leaving the tall grass of the prairie and entering the Great Plains, a dryer, hotter region where the grasses were short and the feed more difficult to come by. The rolling downs gave way to a sandier, more arid soil. In that parched land, the wood of the wagons began to twist and warp. The first signs were usually the iron rims of the wheels loosening. Charles writes in his diary that the wagon train was held up for two days, one day to make charcoal for the forge fire and another to repair the wheels and re-shoe some of the cattle. Finding wood now became more difficult. The emigrants struggled to gather enough to keep their camp fires alight. But as one fuel became scarce, so another became plentiful. Around them in vast quantities lay thousands of pats of dried buffalo dung. These pats burnt well, although more quickly than wood. They gave off a good heat but the women and children had to gather heavy loads to cook a meal. They also burnt to a profusion of fine ash which added to the dirt in their food and the dust in their mouths. But without this unlikely fuel, without the hot food it made possible and the fires around which they gathered of an evening, life on the trail would have been well-nigh impossible.

During the day, the sun blazed pitilessly upon them. The wheels sank deep into the sandhills and the number of oxen had to be doubled and redoubled to haul the wagons through. By the start of the second month, their spirits were sinking as deep as the wheels. Even the most long-suffering Saint came close to the end of his tether. 'The day was very warm, accompanied by a strong wind and clouds of sand, rendering it extremely disagreeable to travel or be out of our wagons. The Lord grant that we may have but little of such weather, as it is wearing and fatiguing to the people. We could not kindle our fires for fear the wagons would get burned up. The land here is very barren and sandy and no timber but a few scanty cottonwoods and willow. A truly miserable looking country.' It was the dreariness that weighed upon them now, the tedium of their days, the monotony of their meals, the same old daily routines and the horizon that never seemed to change. 'Every day's travel was about alike and as near monotony as I ever saw,' one of them wrote, 'the roads all near alike, each camping place alike.'

Eventually they approached Chimney Rock, some 450 miles from their starting point, a graceful pinnacle of rock that towers 470 feet above the Platte and is visible from over forty miles away. All the diarists mention it. 'The greatest wonder I ever saw,' 'like the steeple of an elegant cathedral with its topmost pinnacle flashing golden in the sunset,' 'like the neck of an ostrich,' 'like the ruins of some majestic castle.' On July 15th Charles and Sarah camped in its shadow. The next day was a Sabbath and the camp took a break from travelling. 'An opportunity for the oxen to rest and for the women to do a bit of laundry and bake some bread,' wrote one of the men. After the evening meal, they gathered around their camp fires. From afar, the camps looked like mighty cities suddenly sprung from the empty desert. Six hundred wagons, a glimmering candle or lantern light glowing through each canvas cover, fires blazing and silhouetted figures flickering around them. But beyond their tight corrals lay the empty, unfriendly desert, enclosed by the vast skies and the pitiless stars. It was not wise to leave the warmth of the fire, to stray from the company of family and friends. 'There is an incredible something, a feeling unspeakable, an utter desolation which creeps over a man on the Plains,' wrote one old pioneer. 'Our camp which looked like a little dot on the face of the earth, our insignificance and helplessness without Supreme protection, is forced upon the consciousness. The stillness, the vastness, the night with the moon and stars shining above us, was all so overwhelming.'

Feelings that had been raw when they left their homes were still tender and sore. 'I queried myself, is this what I left parents, kindred and friends for, to die alone on these almost trackless plains?' They remembered their childhood and the close communities of their old neighbourhoods and they regretted that they had ever thought of leaving. The warm memories of home 'contrasted desperately with the awful lonesomeness of the unbroken plain, the terrible despair of the howling wolves and the terror of the snakes scurrying around us'. It made one vulnerable. So they gathered closer round the camp fires and sought to keep up their spirits in storytelling and song.

The Saints were encouraged to bring musical instruments with them and the camp at night resounded to the sound of flutes and penny whistles, fiddles and accordions. The hard work and the weariness of the day was forgotten. Some of the youngsters still had the energy to dance and Brigham would sometimes join them. And then a story from one of the camp storytellers, and prayers to wind up the evening. After prayers the camp retired for the night, lulled to sleep by the gentle sounds of the animals settling down around them. 'The lowing of the cattle and bleating of the sheep mingled with the neighing of the horses in the corrals of wagons. The howling of coyotes and wolves on distant hills and prairies mingled with the half-hourly cry of the faithful guards, "All is well, all is well".'

On Monday, July 24th, Charles wrote that they arrived at Fort John on the Laramie River. Fort John was soon to be purchased by the government and renamed Fort Laramie. It was to become the most famous of all Western forts. But when Sarah and Charles passed by, it was a primitive trading post, run by second generation Mountain Men, half Sioux, half French-Canadian, buying skins and pelts from the white man, selling whisky and guns to the Indians. Indian families had made their homes in the vicinity and some of them came over to the Saints' camp, 'galloping about in high glee, as independent as lords and free as the birds that flit over the plains'. They proved to be unexpectedly friendly and the pioneers bought moccasins and buffalo skins and beadwork from them. 'They seemed much pleased to see us,' wrote Caroline Crosby. 'They would give a good pair of moccasins for a slice of bread. They were willing to trade us anything they had, even their squaws. They offered my husband a young one for me, wanted to buy our children. But notwithstanding their proffered friendship, they stole a number of articles from us.'

In these early years of the Western migrations, before the Indians had understood that there was to be no end to the flood of people crossing their lands and before the white men had started putting down roots and building homes on their hunting grounds, there were occasions when the two races got on well together. A group of young Mormon men remembered spending an evening around the camp fire with a band of braves, showing them photographs of their wives and girlfriends back home. Many kind favours were exchanged, especially between the mothers, who had, perhaps, more in common than their husbands. Susan Harris sympathized greatly with an Indian mother who was hard at work whilst her husband lazed nearby. 'We felt it our duty to interfere and remonstrate with the noble red man. Alas! Our words fell on stony ground and were of no avail.' Mary Snow watched an Indian woman build a tepee whilst her husband lounged nearby. 'She took an axe on her shoulders, cut several long poles, sharpened the points, placed them in a circle, brought the tops of all together, and then skilfully covered the whole with a large buffalo robe.' Then, to Mary's disgust, the woman was not allowed to enter the tepee. It was, apparently, for men's use only. 'At this our womanly feelings rebelled and pointing our fingers at them we shouted "No [*illegible*] lazy be".' Exactly what Mary shouted can no longer be deciphered, which is probably just as well. 'A loud laugh was our reward and they seemed to be rather astonished that we dared be so bold. It is very evident that they are quite behind the times in the great question of Woman's Rights.' The emigrant women often visited the Indian camps and took an interest in their domestic arrangements. 'They were principally occupied in drying buffalo meat and tanning the skins. One large tent caught my attention as having several squaws in it. I made signs about the children and their mothers, and they pointed out the children of each mother. At another tent cooking was underway, and it looked pretty good for a wild people. The old squaw called the other women's attention to my having no teeth, evidently a wonderment on their part, the Indians having very handsome large teeth.' But the Sioux continued to pilfer whenever they had the chance and when they were known to be in the vicinity a double guard was put on the animals.

The fort on the Laramie River was halfway to the Valley, but the worst was yet to come. The corridor between the Platte and the Sweetwater was known to the emigrants as 'The Valley of the Shadow of Death'. Here, the alkaline seepages that poisoned water and contaminated the pasture was at its worst. 'August 13th. Being a Sunday we yet thought it best not to stop, this being a poisonous place.' Charles and Sarah tried to steer their animals clear of the danger but one or two evaded their scrutiny. 'They nearly died. Their insides swelled and they could hardly breathe.' Oliver Huntingdon's ox drank some of the tainted water, but he had a cure. 'I gave him pork and sweet milk and he went on his journey.' Other animals were not so lucky. 'July 5th, Sweetwater. The companies ahead of us have lost a great many animals at this place. The stench was awful and the wolves as thick as sheep. It was as though they had gathered from miles around. There wasn't a wink of sleep that night for any of us. They were so bold they would come right into camp and some of them would put their feet on the wagon tongues and sniff in at the end of the wagons.'

On August 15th they arrived at the famous rock which rises from the banks of the Sweetwater River like the capstone of some vast cromlech. This is Independence Rock, possibly so-called because the early migrants to California knew they had to pass it before Independence Day (July 24th), to be sure of reaching the Sierra Nevada before the winter storms set in. They liked to climb to the summit of the rock, where they would light a fire, cook a meal and enjoy a little music and dancing. It was also a tradition for them to carve their names into the granite, and thousands of these names are still to be seen today, a register of the travellers of the trail. But Charles and Sarah did none of these things. 'On this day one of my cattle gave out,' wrote Charles, 'and it was with extreme difficulty that I managed to reach in to camp.' Other families were suffering similar losses. On the 23rd Charles wrote again, 'Started to go 16 miles but due to one of my oxen giving out again we stopped after 12 miles.' Twenty wagons in the train had now come to a halt because of the loss of oxen to alkaline poisoning.

In crises like these, the Mormons were at their best. There was no thought of leaving anyone behind. Healthy animals from Brigham's train were sent back to aid Kimball's. On the 25th, Charles made another entry in his diary. 'We moved on again. In ascending a very steep hill, we were met by Brother Kimball's brethren going back with cattle, as a good many had lost their cattle entirely. My team being very weak, a young man let me have a yoke of cattle to assist me in to camp. This day's journey was only about 5 miles.' Brigham, with his usual foresight, had arranged for more oxen to be sent out from the Valley to meet them. Over 250 arrived on September 3rd and there were more on the way. By the 5th, most of the wagons were moving again, up and over South Pass.

Spirits rose as they left the United States and started rolling down the western flanks of the Rockies. In amongst the cooking pots and sacks of flour in the back of one of the wagons, Eliza Lyman gave birth to a child. 'This is the second son that I have borne in a wagon,' she wrote, 'and I still think it a most uncomfortable place to be sick in. The journey thus far has not been very pleasant to me as I have been more or less helpless all the way. But it is all right. We are going from the land of our oppressors.' The Saints knew the trail would be tough. They believed that it was God's way of testing them. 'My people must be tried in all things,' the Lord had said to Joseph Smith, 'that they may be prepared to receive the glory that I have for them, even the glory of Zion; and he that will not bear chastisement is not worthy of my kingdom.' Travelling the trail together forged them into tighter bonds of interdependency. They left the Missouri a loose patchwork of clashing cultures and arrived in Salt Lake City woven into a hard-wearing tapestry. John Davis, the leader of a group of Welsh who crossed in 1854, in a letter home described the experience thus. 'Suffice to say that the journey was long, the weather quite warm, the oxen stubborn, the men sometimes more stubborn, the kindly deed often repaid with unkindness, the servant sometimes becoming a master, the maid a mistress. But all is well. All these things serve to test and perfect the Saint.'

The only words in Charles' diary on the day they crossed Big Mountain, the last barrier on the trail, were, 'Went over Big Mountain'. From the top of Big Mountain they would have caught their first glimpse of the Great Salt Lake and the Valley shimmering before it in the distance, an experience that excited most diarists to paroxysms of red-hot emotion and prose of the deepest purple. 'Dusty hats and faded sun bonnets waving in the sunset; tears of joy running down many a careworn cheek.' 'The desert awaits the hand of a husbandman to set it blooming with fruits and flowers; peace at last in the safety of our home in the mountains.' But not Charles. Charles doesn't do purple. He doesn't mention the first sighting of the Valley. The following day, he scribbled one laconic note, 'Went into the last canyon.' The leading wagons slowed down to allow Brigham to come to the fore. Everyone washed and tidied themselves and tried to look their best. And then the Prophet led them, triumphantly, into the city, doubling the population overnight. 'Arrived at the Great Salt Lake City,' was Charles' only comment.

The 1847 crossing proved to be one of the least troublesome of all the annual migrations. When news of its success was published in the Welsh press that winter, many began to seriously consider a fresh start in the New World. It was no longer foolish to dream of turning one's back on 'Babylon' and escaping to Zion in the Great American West. It was now a real option, within the grasp of a Merthyr coal miner or a Llanybydder smallholder or an Abergele stonemason. 'Who is ready to start for home?' asked a headline in the Mormon press. 'After biding our time for so long and after frequent enquiry, the much anticipated moment has come for the Welsh to leave behind oppression, aggression, persecution and tyrannical decrees. Who is ready, we ask?' Over three hundred answered the call and prepared to leave Wales the following spring. But for them the trail was to prove cruel and hard and unforgiving.

1849

ALTHOUGH BOTH JOHN Bennion and Sarah Price were born and raised in Wales, it is unlikely that they spoke Welsh. Hawarden and Hanmer are within a few miles of the English border and for centuries the English language had been commonly spoken there. Both John and Sarah had made contact with Mormonism through the English missions in Cheshire and Liverpool, and, until they emigrated, they continued, as far as we know, to receive their instruction and inspiration from England. The background of the next group of Welsh to leave for the Valley, however, was very different. Many could only speak Welsh. Most had never been outside Wales. They were led by a small, excitable man, bubbling over with an infectious and irrepressible enthusiasm for his country, for the Welsh language and for his religion. This was Captain Dan Jones, the most successful missionary not only in the history of the Mormon Church in Wales but, according to some, in the history of the Mormon Church worldwide.

He first distinguished himself in a meeting convened in Manchester in 1845 to discuss the next steps for the British mission. He rose to his feet and delivered an impassioned and memorable speech. What he said was partly recorded by the conference clerk. 'The Devil tried to prevent me from leaving my home this morning by placing a painful sickness upon me. But I am determined to address this meeting.' He wanted to tell them, he said, about 'a nation renowned in history, one of the most ancient nations of the earth, which had never been subdued, and to which he hoped to be instrumental in bearing the tidings of the work of God, in the last days.' The scribe was swept along by his passion and eloquence. 'He enlarged on the characteristics of his people in a manner that told how ardently he loved his native tribe and his fatherland.' And then became so excited that he failed to take any more notes. 'We would here remark that we are utterly incapable of doing anything like justice to the address of Captain Dan Jones, for though delivered while struggling with disease, such was its effect upon ourselves, and we also believe upon others, that we ceased to write, in order to give way to the effect produced upon our feelings.' 'I came here to preach Mormonism,' roared Dan in a letter to Brigham Young, 'and I will be heard while I have strength, though Satan rage, priests howl, earth trembles and Baal marshal all his hosts.'

Captain Dan was certainly a colourful character, a man of unshakeable convictions which he was quick to express and ready to defend, even, when necessary, with his fists. His drive and pugnaciousness were just what the Welsh Mormons needed at the time, to weather the deluge of prejudice and bigotry stirred up by their highly unorthodox beliefs. He was born in 1810 near the hamlet of Caerfallwch, halfway between Halkyn and Northop, in Flintshire, the sixth child of Ruth and Thomas Jones. His father was a lead miner, a religious man, a deacon in the local Methodist Church. Before he left home at the age of seventeen to go to sea, Dan apparently worked with his father in the mine. When he was 26, he returned home to marry Jane Melling of Denbigh and, soon afterwards, the two emigrated to the States. At the beginning of 1841, they were in St Louis, the busy trading hub of the five great rivers of Central America, the Tennessee, the Ohio, the Illinois, the Missouri and the Mississippi. It was the golden age of the steamboat. Over five hundred of them operated out of St Louis, many of them capable of carrying more than four hundred passengers and seven hundred tons of cargo.

Dan built himself a steamboat which was described in a local newspaper as one of the smallest on the river, 38 tons compared to the thousand tons and more of the giants with which she was in competition. He named her *The Ripple*. At the end of the year, only a few months after the launch, the *Warsaw Signal* reported her sad demise. *The Ripple* had hit a rock 65 miles upstream near New Boston, and had sunk. But, a year later, Captain Dan was back in business. He had built himself another steamboat, *The Maid of Iowa*, twice the size of *The Ripple*, but still a minnow compared to the leviathans of the river.

As he passed up and down the Mississippi, Dan would have caught sight of the temple that was beginning to rise above the swamps of Nauvoo. He would have read about the Mormons and their strange beliefs in the local papers and he would have known how strong was the prejudice against them. Nevertheless, he was intrigued by their ideas and found meaning and hope in them. 'My mind was not satisfied then until I got hold of one of the Mormons, and once I had found him, we sat up many nights investigating the difference of opinion that existed between us about the gospel; and to my great surprise, I perceived that I was almost a fully-fledged Mormon already, which, when I realized it, frightened me greatly, for I could foresee my popularity at an end the minute I had this despicable name, and consequently my livelihood and my all.' Despite these fears, he decided to join the Church and was baptized in the icy waters of the Mississippi in January 1843.

Soon afterwards, *The Maid of Iowa* and her captain were hired by the Mormons to transport three hundred newly arrived European converts from New Orleans to Nauvoo. This was the first time that Dan had put ashore at Nauvoo. 'When we landed, a large crowd of respectable looking people came to greet us very hospitably; such handshaking and kissing among the women, and such a hearty welcome on meeting each other rather surprised me: but to my even greater dismay, when my glance scanned the crowd for the prophet I had pictured, I failed to see anyone similar. A large handsome man came up to me in the crowd on the boat, took my hand, squeezed it kindly, saying, "God bless you, brother," several times; but before I could ask his name, he was out of sight; and then he came by again, when I understood that my eyes had beheld for the second time Joseph Smith, the Mormon Prophet! And although I was so busy, I spared some time to gaze at him, and I saw in him everything contrary to my expectation. His fair countenance, and his cheerful and guileless face rather convinced me that he was not the cunning and deceitful man I had heard about; the wonderful love and respect shown to him by everyone, and his humility, forced me to believe that this was not the cruel oppressor who considered everyone his slaves; yes, in a word, I was soon convinced that much of what I had heard about this man was false accusations.' Joseph Smith invited him to his home and introduced him to his mother, his wife and his children. They became good friends and, soon, good business partners. Joseph bought a half share of *The Maid of Iowa* and the steamer was used thereafter only in the service of the Church.

When he had been in the Church for a month, Dan received a call to go to Wales as a missionary. He would have had no voice in the decision. The practice amongst the Saints was for the Prophet to announce, in the weekly meetings, the names of those who had been chosen to be missionaries and where they were to go. They were expected to leave immediately and to pay for their travel and keep out of their own pockets. They were not to expect any financial help from the Church. Dan's original plan was to sell the half share he still owned in *The Maid of Iowa* to the Church and use the money to pay his fare to Wales and, once there, to buy a press to print Mormon publications. But this plan was thwarted by Joseph's assassination.

The night before Joseph died, Dan was with him in his cell in Carthage, not as a prisoner but as a friend, free to come and go. In the early hours, Joseph had turned to Dan and asked him whether he was afraid to die. 'Has that time come, think you?' answered Dan. 'Engaged in such a cause, I do not think death would have many terrors.' 'You will see Wales and fulfil the mission appointed you ere you die,' answered the Prophet. This, Dan believed, was his last prophecy. 'I believed his word,' he said, 'and relied upon it through the trying scenes which followed.' The next morning, Dan left the jail with a message for the State governor. As he left, he was surrounded by an angry mob but succeeded in escaping. 'I took advantage of their disagreement and no sooner in the saddle than both spurs were put to work, and racehorse and rider were enveloped in a cloud of dust with balls whistling around me.' Before Dan returned, the mob had broken into Joseph's cell, and both Joseph and his brother Hyrum had been shot dead. Two months later, Dan and Jane were on their way back to Wales.

He initially worked in the Wrexham area. Within three months he had written and published a 48-page pamphlet presenting the Mormon truths to the Welsh in their own language. He called it *Yn Farw Wedi ei Chyfodi yn Fyw: neu'r Hen Grefydd Newydd* [*The Dead Raised to Life: or the New Old Religion*]. In it he proclaimed that the only true Church had been re-established on earth and that the powers of the saints of old to speak in tongues, to heal by faith and to work miracles, were restored and at the service of all who truly believed. The response was disappointing. After eight months of proselytising, only three converts had joined the Church. But after his dramatic speech in the April conference, the tide turned. He was given greater responsibility. It was decided that 'as Brother Dan Jones was the only person we had in this country who could speak, read, write and publish in the Welsh language, he should preside over the churches in Wales.'

He set up his headquarters in Merthyr Tydfil, the iron capital of the world. He could not have chosen a better place or a better time to look for troubled, restless souls. It was a time when mighty economic forces were squeezing the agricultural workers out of the overcrowded countryside into the booming industrial towns at the head of the south Wales valleys. It was a time of great social upheaval, of poor harvests, of great want, a time of industrialization, a time of revolution, the time of the Rebecca Riots and the Chartist Rising. In 1840, the Dowlais iron works outside Merthyr was the greatest iron works in the world, employing over 5,000 workers. The second greatest was Cyfarthfa, just three miles down the road. The population of

Merthyr had jumped from 7,705 in 1801 to 46,378 in 1851. This was the California of Wales, enticing the sons and daughters of the impoverished smallholders of the Welsh countryside into her streets to search for gold.

But Merthyr was a dirty, brutal and unhealthy town. There were no sewers in her narrow, overpopulated lanes and no clean water in her houses. When diseases struck they scythed their way through the population. Typhus was responsible for one in ten of the deaths. In 1832, cholera came to Britain for the first time and made a beeline for Merthyr. Sudden death was part of life and, as a consequence, people worried about the state of their souls. Throughout the first half of the nineteenth century, one religious revival followed another, tearing through the decaying fabric of the Established Church in Wales, steering the people away from that Church towards an evangelic, Non-conformist alternative. In 1800, ten per cent of the people of Merthyr considered themselves Non-conformists, i.e. Baptists, Methodists, Congregationalists or any of the host of smaller radical faiths. By 1851, out of the sixty per cent who considered themselves to be religious, ninety per cent described themselves as Non-conformist.

It was an electrifying, disorientating time. The constant storms of revival sweeping over the land left many in confusion, uncertain as to which church, which denomination or which sect they belonged. Dan Jones looked for the driftwood and the debris of the revivals, men of inquiring minds and of independent thought, but without strong roots in a church or a denomination, searching for something to hold on to, for solid rock beneath their feet. In their diaries and memoirs many of these pilgrims dramatically describe the zigzag paths that led to their conversion to Mormonism.

Men like Daniel Edward Williams, born in Penally in Pembrokeshire in 1802. As a boy, he was taught to read and write and as a twelve year old he began to attend the church Sunday school. In his autobiography he describes how, even in those early years, he worried about the state of his soul. He listened to the Congregationalists and the Wesleyan

Methodists, but felt they did not conduct the ordinance of baptism as it was described in the New Testament. He turned to the Baptists when he was seventeen and was faithful to them for nearly twenty years. But the squabbling and feuding between the Baptists and the other denominations pained him and the old restlessness returned. He left the Baptists and formed his own small society of like-minded men, but this again proved a disappointment. 'I found,' he wrote, 'that we were able to talk much, but could do little that would benefit ourselves or others and, in a short time, had become a sect of talkers who could easily upset all their creeds, but had nothing better to offer them than our opinions.' In 1838 he left Penally and went to work in the iron works in Ebbw Vale and there, half-heartedly, after some hesitation, rejoined the Baptists. 'I could no longer be bound by their systems but always taught whatever seemed to me to be the truth whether I pleased them or not... I did sincerely believe they were gone astray from the simplicity of the Gospel of Christ, for nowhere on earth could I find anything like that religion which is described in the New Testament.' In 1846 he came into contact with the Mormons and was immediately convinced by their beliefs.

George Adams was another Pembrokeshire man, a farm worker in his youth, but in his twenties an iron maker in Merthyr. He felt that he and his fellow workers were being mistreated by their bosses. He supported Chartism and early trade unionism. He called himself a Deist and refused to be led by church or chapel. But, in 1849, cholera swept through the Heads of the Valleys and George began to feel that his soul was in need of the protection of a religious institution. He therefore joined the Primitive Methodists, a sect that worshipped in large open-air meetings with noisy enthusiasm. But the more George read about the Early Church in the Bible, the less he saw of it in the beliefs of the Primitive Methodists. So he joined the Mormons because they offered, he believed, the Early Church in its purity.

Edward Ashton was born into an English-speaking family in Caersws. 'We were very poor indeed. I was working in a woollen factory when I was 8 years old. We were working from 6 o'clock in the morning until 9 p.m. in the evening for 3 pence a day. I was there until I was 10 years old when I had an accident. My right hand was caught in the engine and the cards nearly tore it off. This crippled me, so that for a long time I could not do much work.' He was then apprenticed to a shoemaker, but his employer proved to be a cruel, sadistic man and Edward was beaten and abused by him. He took his master to court, seeking to be released from his apprenticeship, and had to show his scars and wounds to the magistrate to prove his case. He then went down to Tredegar and found work in a primitive shoemaking factory. There he fell in with a crowd of ne'er-do-wells and was sucked into a life of gambling and drinking. To save himself, he left his job and found work on a farm nine miles away. He stayed there for close on ten years. Whilst there, he frequented Church of England services but also learnt Welsh so that he could take part in Calvinist Methodist services. However, neither church nor chapel satisfied him and in 1849 he joined the Mormons, leaving for the Salt Lake within the year.

'Mormonism is making rapid progress in England,' said *The Atheneum*, a London literary magazine, in 1841, 'particularly in the manufacturing districts, and it is also spreading in Wales. Furthermore, its converts are not made from the lowest ranks; those sought and obtained by the Mormon apostles are mechanics and tradesmen who have saved a little money and who are remarkable for their moral character.' In the Welsh industrial communities, these were the men who knew how to read the coal seams and how to operate the iron furnaces. In the Welsh countryside, they were the shoemakers, the blacksmiths and the carpenters. From Flintshire and Denbighshire came builders and stonemasons. From the banks of the Cothi and the Towy came smallholders and farm tenants; sensible, hard-working, conscientious men who worried about their salvation. Dan Jones threw himself, head and shoulders, into the battle to save their souls.

Despite the seismic changes of recent years, Merthyr was still a Welsh-speaking town. Most of the workforce had come from the Welsh hinterland. Eighty-eight per cent of the population in 1840 had been born in Wales. English might be the language of its industry, but Welsh was the language of its religious and social life. The all-powerful Non-conformist chapels conducted their business in Welsh. Welsh literary societies such as the Cymmrodorion and the Cymreigyddion flourished and Welsh was the language of the numerous concerts and eisteddfodau. Dan's conviction that the Mormon message had to be brought to the people of south Wales in their mother tongue proved the key that opened the way for the mission's success.

His methods of proselytising suited the evangelical tone of the times. He was the Mormons' Howell Harris, the hellfire preacher who could pour the rapture of the redeemed sinner into his sermons and hold his audience in thrall. Dan Jones saw the work of the Devil about him on all sides and joyfully charged out to meet him. He travelled tirelessly throughout Wales. During the four years of his first mission, he published sixteen tracts of his own work, all in Welsh. He published a book of hymns and a book on the history of Mormonism, the first in any language. He also started a monthly magazine, originally called *Prophwyd y Jubilî* [*Prophet of the Jubilee*], but which later changed its name to *Udgorn Seion* [*Zion's Trumpet*]. Dan filled its pages with his fervid zeal and his fiery enthusiasm.

'The Greetings of the Publisher to his Compatriots. Dear Reader, behold the beginning of a new era of our age, yea, the most remarkable which has ever been, the most wondrous in its preparations, the most goodly in its deeds and the most glorious in its effects of every previous age. Once more the golden keys of heaven have been entrusted to men for them to open all treasures, to unlock all mysteries and to clarify all errors amongst men. Let the inhabitants of the earth rejoice, and let every Welshman give a hearkening ear to the good news of great joy that is sounded through this last trumpet.'

But, like Howell Harris, he was an uneasy man, his life full of troubles and turmoil. He made enemies easily and his chief enemy in the early days in Wales was the Reverend W.R.

Davies, the Baptist minister of Caersalem Chapel, Dowlais. Listen to Dan, in a typically colourful diatribe, laying into the Reverend Davies in an article in *Prophwyd y Jubilî*. 'We remember as a boy the harmful red hot overflowing of Etna and Stromboli when they spewed from their craters rivers of fire and brimstone, destroying every flower, every blade of grass and every living thing within reach of their furious fiery surges... Never have we seen a more exact imitation of the above phenomena than the overflowing of the bowels of [the Rev. W.R. Davies] through the press and over the pulpit, against his innocent neighbours, because of their religion... Certainly, the disturbances and overflow from the bowels of the 'Caersalem Volcano' are not dissimilar at times to those [of Etna and Vesuvius]. By now, the people of Dowlais can tell when he is about to burst and spew his filth all over town, from his aches and pangs, as those who live near Etna and Vesuvius know from their grumbling and their thundering.' And so on and on. Lambasting 'the Fiends of Hell and the Knaves of Beelzebub' was clearly a task Dan Jones relished, and he was very good at it.

As might be expected, the chapels detested both him and his followers. They refused to believe that Mormonism was a Christian religion. Not only did they ridicule the plates of gold and the reformed Egyptian hieroglyphics and mock the holy spectacles, but they refused to accept that the Mormon Christ was the same figure as their Christ. Their Christ was the only Son of God, but the Mormon Christ was the elder brother of other spirit children. Their Christ was part of a Trinity but the Mormon Christ was a stand-alone God. They believed that God was a spirit but the Mormons believed that God was once a 'humanlike' being who had a wife and in fact still had a body of 'flesh and bones'. They believed that there was only one supreme God, but the Mormons believed there were other deities presiding over other worlds. The chapels believed in original sin, the forgiveness of which, by dying on the Cross, was Christ's greatest gift to them, a concept rejected by the Mormons. And how could a Christ who went on a trip to

America after his crucifixion be the true Son of God? The Saints 'were regarded, with some contempt, as lunatics,' reported one Merthyr local historian of the time.

They were also regarded with some alarm, because the end result of a conversion to Mormonism was emigration. Not only did they snatch the faithful from their chapels, but they stole them from their families. They compelled them to leave their homes and their country for ever. 'Come up to build the House of the Lord, from the four corners of the earth, oh you Saints!' cried Brigham Young. 'For as the hen gathers her chicks, so the Lord Jesus Christ shall gather you also in these latter days.' 'Who is ready to start for home?' was Dan Jones' cry. 'Come together!' This was not an invitation but a command. 'Come, gather! Gather yourselves, Oh! You children of the Kingdom, to the place where God has promised you salvation... the country chosen by God as a place of safety for his people in these last days, when the scourges of God's wrath shall destroy the nations and shall depopulate the earth because of the swelling disbelief and obscenity of the populace.'

Despite the growing enmity of the chapels, the Mormon mission, during the late 1840s and early 1850s, proved very successful. When Dan Jones began his mission, it was estimated that there were about five hundred Mormons in Wales. Soon, their numbers began to increase. Throughout 1845, in Merthyr Tydfil alone, about twenty new members joined every month. In 1846, the figure doubled and in 1847, trebled and, from the middle of 1847 until the middle of 1849, 140 and more were being baptized every month. Dan boasted that there were so many followers in Dowlais that the Saints' hall had proved too small and a larger hall had to be hired, which was now, in turn, filled to overflowing every Sunday. And the Monmouthshire Conference had to place props under the floor of its hall lest it collapse under the weight of the delegates. In Merthyr Tydfil, on the Sunday of the 1851 Religious Census, 1,190 Saints attended their places of worship, only 647 less than attended the Church of England's evening services in the town. And in the whole of Wales, it was estimated that the Mormons had

5,244 members in December 1851. In Britain, at the beginning of 1851, there were 30,747 members. Wales therefore made up one sixth of the total British membership.

In the Welsh denominational press, ferocious attacks upon the Mormons became commonplace. In publications such as *Y Bedyddiwr* [*The Baptist*], *Seren Gomer* [*The Star of Gomer*] and *Y Dysgedydd* [*The Teacher*], outlandish slanders were heaped in monthly shovelfuls upon the Saints. Professor Ron Dennis has listed well over five hundred anti-Mormon articles published in Wales in the Forties and Fifties. Mormonism, said one commentator, was 'a mixture of paganism, Judaism, Christianity, Mohammedanism, idolatry and atheism.' *Y Diwygiwr*, in February 1850, printed a typically scurrilous piece of anti-Mormon doggerel.

Beth yw Seintiau crefydd Mormon
Onid cwter chwydfa'r byd,
Tomen scybion yr eglwysi,
Gwartheg culion Pharo nghyd,
Melltith teulu, pla cymdogaeth,
Llwyth yn rhegi llwythau Duw,
Gweision enllib, deistiaid diras,
Un gymdeithas pryfed byw?

[What are the Saints of Mormonism
but the gutter of the world's vomit,
a pile of the churches' sweepings,
Pharaoh's lean cattle all together,
the curse of the family,
the plague of a neighbourhood,
a tribe cursing the people of God,
the servants of slander, wicked deists,
one heap of writhing worms?]

e frequent cases of outright physical assault.
reached in Llandeilo'r-Fan,' wrote one of the
ad stones and potatoes and turnips thrown at

me.' Missionaries were attacked in Llandovery and one was badly beaten. The same tale was told in Abergele, where they were beaten and had stones thrown at them. In Pembrokeshire, Arthur Evans was hung above the river by his hair. Hugh Roberts, the cobbler in Eglwysbach in the Conwy Valley, was very nearly lynched by an angry mob and, in Brecon, David Williams was dragged through the mud and whipped. Towards the end of his stay in Wales, Dan Jones feared for his life. 'It is absolutely true,' reported a correspondent in *Udgorn Seion*, in March 1849, 'that the life of our dear brother, Capt. Jones, was in such danger that his house was attacked almost every night for weeks before his leaving Merthyr.'

There was an understandable sense of relief therefore when they heard that Brigham Young had reached the Valley and that the prospects there were promising. Dan Jones triumphantly announced the good news to his Welsh followers in the Church periodical of January 1848. 'Now, you dear Saints throughout Wales, here is the news that you have long waited to hear. Behold the place, yes, the refuge for deliverance, has been found. The one which from now on will be the goal for all the children of Zion, of every nation, tongue and people... Let us prepare ourselves with haste.' The following month, he describes the route. 'The recommended way is through New Orleans, up the Mississippi river and the Missouri to Council Bluffs, and from there overland in a wagon to the end of the journey.' In October, he was collecting names and down payments. 'Every person or family who intend to go and are able to do so, are requested to send to me their names written in full plainness and the ages of every man, woman and child and every infant that is going and also to send one pound in money for each person, both old and young.' They were all to travel as one group. 'We intend to make up a shipload of Welsh to travel together if there are about three hundred ready by January.' He knew that most of his potential customers were fluent in Welsh but ill at ease in English and would therefore much prefer to travel in an all-Welsh group. 'I need not tell you that it will be much mor[e] pleasant and beneficial for [you] to travel together – especia[lly] because of the language.' He could not yet be completely sure of the cost. Crossing the Atlantic, he thought, would cost at least two pounds and five shillings but not more than five pounds. There would be other costs, of course, such as the fare for the steamboats up the Mississippi and the cost of buying the wagons and oxen and supplies needed to cross the Plains. Here again, the Church could be of help by introducing them to the most reliable suppliers and bargaining on their behalf for the best possible prices. In the same issue, Dan notes that an epidemic of cholera was on its way to Wales. It was even now ravaging London, Hull, Birmingham and Glasgow. 'We hope,' wrote Dan, 'that as many of the Saints as are able, will prepare to escape to the place where they know deliverance is to be had.' But those who did so would soon find to their cost that they were jumping from a frying pan into a raging fire.

In the November issue, the instructions were more immediate and detailed. A steamer, *The Troubadour*, had been hired to take them from the dock in Swansea to Liverpool. They were warned to be on the lookout for the 'sharpers' and 'dodgers' who combed the wharfs of Liverpool, intent on fleecing the inexperienced and the unworldly. 'But we sincerely hope,' says Dan, 'that the Welsh flock know the voice of their shepherd too well to mistake it for the howl of a wolf.' He advises them on the clothes they should take with them and the food they would need on the voyage and he tells them, all being well, a ship, for Welsh speakers only, would be awaiting them in Liverpool.

At the appointed time, 326 Welsh Saints turned up in Liverpool Docks, more than Dan Jones had bargained for. At the last minute, he had to charter another ship. Eventually, 249 of them sailed on the *Buena Vista* on February 26th and the rest on the *Hartley* a week later. According to *Udgorn Seion*, the 'hosts of Babylon' continued to harass them right up to the last moment. The Reverend Henry Rees, a pillar of the Welsh Methodist establishment and the most powerful Welsh preacher of the age, came to the dock to attempt to argue the emigrants out of their folly. He and his fellow ministers were invited on board and allowed to talk to the passengers. They warned them that they were on the road to perdition. A rumour was rife that Capt. Jones meant to stop in Cuba to sell the women into slavery. 'They are trying to frighten the Saints about the sea voyage,' wrote one of the passengers. 'Great are their efforts to poison the relationship between us and Capt. Jones... but up to now they have failed to influence so much as one.' On the day they sailed, a crowd of fellow Mormons gathered at the dock to bid them farewell. In her old age, Sarah Peters remembers the occasion as if it were yesterday. 'I remember holding my father's hand and he was waving his handkerchief and shouting "Farewell" and "Blessings on you" to his friends as they left. I looked up at the ship and saw there Edward Parry playing his large harp and John Parry leading the singing.'

Yes, my native land, I love thee,
All thy scenes I love them well,
Can I bid you all farewell?
Can I leave thee, can I leave thee,
Far in distant lands to dwell?

They were leaving friends and family for ever. As they sang, the gangplank was lifted and the ship slipped out into the stream.

Yes, I hasten from you gladly,
From the scenes I love so well!
Far away ye billows bear me,
Lovely native land, farewell!
Pleased I leave thee, pleased I leave thee,
Far in distant lands to dwell.

A week later they were followed by the *Hartley*.

We know little about the majority of the passengers on the decks of the two ships but one or two have left valuable diaries and memoirs. Perhaps the most interesting of these is the diary written by David D. Bowen. He was born in Felinfoel, outside Llanelli. At eight, he'd been sent down the pit. Ten years later, in 1840, he'd gone to sea. In 1844, he came close to losing his life on a voyage around the Horn, carrying coal to Valparaíso and a cargo of guano back home to Wales. On the return voyage, the ship had begun to leak and they had run her aground and abandoned her, somewhere on the Chilean coast. David came home to Swansea on a ship carrying copper ore. On Christmas Day 1845, he married Mary Davis and decided to leave the sea so that he could be at home with his new wife. He returned to the mines to work alongside his brother and found there, to his surprise, that he was earning far better money than he had ever done at sea. 'I was getting three shillings per day or one pound one shilling per week, for we were paid for Sundays. My brother John was getting thirty shillings per week. I was very happy in my mind these times and lived very comfortable, making money and saving about half of my wages.' A son was born and was named Morgan, after his father-in-law. David was enjoying life. 'Comfortable work and a comfortable home.' But then his conscience began to prick him. 'I became somewhat anxious about religion, and in loss to know where to go and which sect to join.' He found the Mormons and was baptized in the river that ran beside the pit on the morning of June 19th, 1847. The following week, Mary was baptized in the same place.

Two months later, when his employers learnt that he had joined the Saints, David was sacked. The only choice for him now was to return to sea. He looked for a ship that would allow him to come home regularly to Mary and the baby, and he chose *The Jane*, a brig that plied regularly between Llanelli and Portsmouth. But when he arrived in Portsmouth on his first voyage he learnt that *The Jane*'s next port of call was to be Archangel in Russia. It was six months before he returned home and by that time his second child had been born. Soon afterwards, he decided that the place for him and his family was Salt Lake City, and he left on the *Hartley* with Mary, the children, and her father and mother.

John Parry, from Trelogan in Flintshire, was also on the *Buena Vista*. He was the first of many stonemasons and master builders from that part of Wales to go to the Valley. This was the man who had led the singing as the ship left her moorings in Liverpool. He was a talented harpist, a skilled performer on the flute, a fine singer and a 'cynganeddwr' (a poet in the old Welsh strict meters). At the start of his career he had been active in the Church of England. He then joined the Scotch Baptists and later became a minister with an American sect called 'The Campbellites' – people who believed, like the Mormons, that the Early Church had to be revived. Then, in 1846, he came into contact with the Mormons. He is remembered today as the man who formed, at Brigham Young's behest, the world renowned Mormon Tabernacle Choir.

Thomas Jeremy was another passenger on the ship, the son of a well-to-do farmer, an educated man, intended for the Baptist ministry. He will figure largely in the story of the Welsh in Utah. One day, early in 1846, Dan Jones had come knocking on the door of his home, Glantrenfawr, near Llanybydder, Carmarthenshire, and had changed the course of his life. He led the cause in Llanybydder and had established four branches in the area before he emigrated. With him on the *Buena Vista* were his wife, his two sons and five daughters. He also paid for three of his neighbours and their families to accompany him.

Elizabeth Lewis was the landlady of the White Lion Inn in Kidwelly, Carmarthenshire, an establishment whose doors are still open today. She is said to have paid the transport costs of forty people from Wales to the Missouri and 32 from the Missouri to Salt Lake City. She first heard about Joseph Smith across the bar of the White Lion. 'After this,' she said, 'my house became a resort for the elders and I was the special subject of persecution by my neighbours.' She joined the Mormon Church against the wishes of her husband and decided to emigrate without him. But she first wanted to recover the money that she had invested in the White Lion and she persuaded her husband to sell the business so that she might receive her fair share of the proceeds. Mr Lewis then insisted that she'd taken more than her fair share and, in one version of the story, he is said to have followed her across the Atlantic, taking his complaint to Brigham Young himself, who had then compelled Mrs Lewis to pay back some of the money. Whatever the truth of it, Mrs Lewis was undoubtedly a feisty, fearless woman.

Then there was John Ormond, from Marloes in Pembrokeshire. Travelling with him were five of his children. His wife, Elizabeth, had not been converted to the new religion and had not wished to emigrate. So, cruelly, John had left home without saying goodbye, taking with him as many of their children as he could. On the morning of his departure, he had gone to work as usual with his eldest son, but then, later in the day, they had secretly returned. Elizabeth had gone to market with her youngest son, leaving the eldest daughter at home, in charge of her two young sisters and the baby. When Elizabeth and the boy returned, everybody, including the baby, had gone. She never saw any of them again.

The oldest passenger aboard the *Buena Vista* was 92-year-old Evan Jones. 'He says that many of the sectarians in Wales,' says Dan Jones, 'tried to dissuade him from coming, prophesying that he would not arrive across the sea and many other things. "But I am," says he, "determined, through the power of God, to prove them all false prophets." He had lost his hair, except for a few strands white as snow, but now he has an abundant new crop, just like the hair of a child. And he says that he feels younger and younger!'

Dan Jones enjoyed the voyage greatly. 'Fair winds and weather so beautiful throughout the week that it was almost like Wales in June. An occasional squall and cloud breaking to supply us with water for washing. Some singing here, some talking or reading there; some walking arm-in-arm while others prepare foods of as many kinds almost as could be obtained in a cookshop. It is beautiful to see the children playing across the deck and entertaining their parents.' After fifty days at sea, they reached New Orleans. There, they hired a steamboat to take them on the next stage of their journey.

Ahead of them was a ten-day voyage up the Mississippi to

St Louis, a dramatic introduction to their new country. From the banks came a confusion of sights and sounds, exotic calls, flashes of brilliant plumage and heady perfumes the like of which they had never experienced before. Thousands of ducks and geese rose noisily before them and then dropped back quietly onto the water in their wake. Now and again, they passed busy wharfs where black men rolled bales of cotton, bundles of hemp and casks of molasses down to the waiting ships. In places, the boat fought the current, black smoke belching from her stack and white foam frothing under her paddles. Elsewhere, the river flowed gently, the boat gliding as if on a lake.

From her deck Dan wrote a letter to William Phillips, his successor in Wales. 'The cholera is very bad in New Orleans, and many are dying on the steamboats along the rivers, especially the immigrants. On one ship that went before us, there were 42 who died from cholera... but they were not Saints.' Dan believed that the Saints were protected by a heavenly hand and that God would look after them, whatever the perils. But they reached St Louis at the worst possible time. Twenty-six of the town's inhabitants had died of cholera the previous week but during the week of their arrival the numbers jumped to five hundred. Here they had to find a smaller boat with a shallower draught to take them up the Missouri on the final leg of their journey to Council Bluffs. Dan hurried to hire a suitable craft so that they could leave the stricken city as quickly as possible. His choice was unfortunate, a steamboat called the *Highland Mary*. Her upper decks may have appeared comfortable and smart, but down below, squeezed between the cargo and the engines, there were darker decks, musty and stale, with polluted water swashing in the bilges and it was here that most of the Saints hunkered down. They drank water from the polluted river, their stuffy, clammy cabins were breeding grounds for cholera, and the sickness fell upon them with unbridled ferocity.

Five died before leaving St Louis. First, Jenkin Williams, a twenty-year-old engineer from Aberdare; then Benjamin Francis, a blacksmith from Llanybydder. Between St Louis and Council Bluffs twenty more were taken, the fit and healthy as well as the old and feeble. All ages, from newborn babies to Evan Jones, the 92 year old, were cut down by the disease. The cruelty of cholera is that it strikes so suddenly and runs its course so swiftly. 'Be it understood that nobody is counted as having died of cholera unless they die within twenty-four hours,' explained *Udgorn Seion* when assessing the number of deaths in Merthyr Tydfil earlier in the year.

Margaret Francis, the widow of Benjamin the blacksmith, lost three children in three days, as did David and Mary Phillips. 'Sometimes we had to stop the boat three times on the same day and bury seven in the same grave,' wrote Samuel Leigh. 'I buried my wife and the baby on the 6th day of May.' Men and women lay in agony on the deck. Sarah Jeremy remembered 'that their tongues and mouths were parched with thirst and they felt as though they were being consumed with fire.' In a small pocket book, her husband, Thomas, kept a daily record of those who died, a heartbreaking document, now in the keeping of the Church Archives in Salt Lake City. On May 6th, he wrote the names of two of his daughters in his book and, on the 7th, he added a third. The three were buried on the banks of the Mississippi, two of them sharing the same small grave. Little ceremony was practised at the gravesides. The crew would open a shallow ditch and lay the bodies in it, side by side. Then they would be hurriedly covered. No marker was left to denote the spot.

At the beginning of that terrible May, the *Hartley* arrived in New Orleans nine days behind the *Buena Vista*, having had a trouble-free crossing of the Atlantic, 'more like a pleasure cruise', according to one of the company. But in New Orleans the pleasure cruise ended. The pestilence fell upon them with equal savagery and before they had arrived in Council Bluffs at least twenty of their company of 77 were dead. William Owens, a farmer from Ffestiniog, was travelling with his wife and seven children. One of his daughters died on Monday, then two other children on Tuesday. Then Ellenor, his wife, on Wednesday. Then William himself on Friday and another son on the following Friday. Nathaniel Eames also came from Ffestiniog. He lost his wife and four children. Nor did John Ormond's family escape. Elliner, the baby, so cruelly snatched from her mother, died, as did Laetitia, another of the children.

Death by cholera was ugly and dirty. Black vomit and ceaseless diarrhoea, dehydration and excruciating pain. No wonder the faith of some of the Saints crumbled before it. After losing his wife and child, Thomas Davis abandoned his plan to go to the Valley, turned his back on the Saints and decided to settle in Missouri. David Jones and his wife Emma also refused to go on, as did Benjamin Jones and his family, although in their cases it was believed that they had taken advantage of the Mormons from the start, in order to reach America cheaply. Many of the Welsh passengers on the *Hartley* travelled no further than St Louis that year. Some of them stayed to care for their sick relatives, others to look for work to finance the remainder of their journey.

David D. Bowen and his young wife, Mary, were one couple who were compelled to change their plans. 'May 12th. We landed in St. Louis with many sick on board. My wife was very sick at the time. On the same morning that we landed in St. Louis my mother-in-law was attacked with the cholera so severely that we were obliged to send her to the hospital. I took her and my wife to the hospital. They would not take my wife into the same hospital as her mother for she had not got the cholera. I left my mother-in-law in the Charity Hospital with her youngest daughter, Rachel... After leaving her there, I took my wife to the City Hospital about three miles further. I left her there with a lot of strangers and went back to the boat where my children were and my father-in-law and his family. There I had to nurse my little babe eight months old all night without her mother. We had a very miserable night of it. The next morning I started for the Charity Hospital to see how my mother-in-law was getting along. When I arrived there, to my astonishment, she was dead and buried before I got there. I did not see her at all. I then went to the other hospital where my wife was. There I found her very weak and feeble. She said that she had nothing to take while she was in there but water and she begged on me to take her out from such a miserable place. I complied with her desire. I took her out. I had to carry her on my back most of the way from the hospital to the boat through the city of St. Louis, for we had not yet moved from the boat. By the time I and my wife reach the boat it was very near dark and there were two of my sisters-in-law attacked by the cholera. Ann & Rachel were very bad. I spend another miserable night with the sick and with my own little children.'

'May 23rd. With day light this morning my wife was very bad and about four o'clock she sat on the box and leaned her head back on the wall. She died in an instant without uttering a word. Thus she departed this life on the twenty-third day of May 1849 at 4 o'clock in the morning, or with the break of day. She was 24 years, 3 months and 23 days old when she died on the Dry Hill. She was buried in the county graveyard near Blue Ridge in the State of Missouri... As soon as my wife died my little daughter was taken sick. She got worse and worse until 20th June when she died in the same house as her mother and was buried in the same grave.'

It was a bruised and battered and much diminished company that finally reached Council Bluffs, four months after having left Liverpool. To add salt to their wounds, the people on the landing refused to help them disembark, so great was their fear of cholera. 'Nobody would come near us,' wrote Isaac Nash. 'We were put out on the banks of the river with our dead and suffering. Apostle George A. Smith, hearing of our arrival and of the sad condition we were in, came down to the river bank. He sent word to the people that if they would not take us in and give us shelter, the Lord would turn a scourge upon them. It was not long before teams and wagons came down and all were taken care of.'

Most of the party decided not to continue to the Valley that season, so weakened were they by their experiences on the Missouri. In November, a letter from William Morgan, the leader of those who had decided to stay in Council Bluffs, was published in *Udgorn Seion*. 'We, the Welsh people, have divided into two groups. One group has gone ahead towards the plains of the Salt Lake, that is 22 wagons under the presidency of Brother Jones; the other group is staying here for the purpose of establishing a Welsh settlement in this place.' Their hope was to build a small village which would be a staging post for the Welsh emigrants of the future, somewhere where they might rest and recuperate after the Atlantic crossing and the voyage up the rivers. 'Counting adults and children, we number 113 in all. We have almost all our land adjoining; and Brother Jones has purchased a land claim which is 150 or more acres near our lands and has entrusted it to my care as a gift to the Welsh... Our wheat harvest is finished, all of it under cover... We intend to build a meeting house as soon as we can.' Those who could not afford to buy farms were employed on the farms of their richer compatriots. During the winter, when there was no work on the farms, many went back down the river to St Louis to look for work in the coal mines there.

'There would be a welcome,' wrote William Morgan 'for a shipload coming across next spring. If they can find as little as seven pounds a head, they could come as far as this, and if they can't go any further, they will have in three years or two perhaps, enough oxen and cattle to go on ahead. I am sure of this, for some of this company who had not a penny when they landed here, have cattle and sheep now. In fact, I know of no family in this country who has not a cow or two.' The language in this small settlement would be Welsh. 'This will be to the advantage of the monolingual Welsh who follow; for there will be people of the same language and of the same country here, and probably many who will know them and have been associated with them many times, to welcome them to this new country; for there are only English here for several hundreds of miles – and we, a small handful of Welsh in their midst.' Over the next few years, the comfortable life in this small Welsh enclave proved a temptation to many of the Welsh Saints. Why travel on when money could be made so easily and life was so good on this quiet bend of the Missouri?

It was only 83 therefore, out of the 325 who had left Liverpool with Dan Jones, who joined him on the final leg of the journey to the Salt Lake. In the twelve months since Sarah and Charles had walked the trail it had changed beyond recognition. In 1848, only a few hundred settlers had crossed the continent, most of them bound for Oregon. In 1849, there were over 20,000 people on the trail, all, apart from the Mormons, hoping to strike it rich in California. At the beginning of 1848, California was a grubby, unimportant corner of Mexico's untidy empire. Less than eight hundred white people lived within its borders. Then, on the morning of the 24th of January, James Marshall, walking along the banks of the Coloma, a small stream that ran into the Sacramento, looked down into the water and, suddenly, 'my eye was caught by the flash of something... I stretched my hand down to gather it, and my heart leaped in my breast because I knew, without doubt, that it was gold. And then I saw another piece.' And in that instant, the history of California sprung into high gear! On February 2nd, nine days later, before the gold-strike had become national news, a treaty was signed between the Mexicans and the Americans that brought an end to two years of fighting. The whole of the far west beyond the Rockies was conceded to the United States, a huge expanse of territory that stretched from Arizona to Oregon, from California to the Great Salt Lake. The authority of the United States now extended over the whole continent, from sea to sea. For the Mormons, it was a setback. No longer would they be escaping from the clutches of the 'Babylonians' as they slipped over the Rockies into the Valley of the Great Salt Lake.

In the hectic months after the news broke, California became famous throughout the world. In November 1848, Dan Jones had informed the readers of *Prophwyd y Jubilî* in Wales of 'an unusual excitement' in the west. 'Three-fourths of the houses in San Francisco have been left empty,' he wrote, 'even the lawyers closed their books and emigrated in haste, with a shovel in one hand and a wooden pan in the other, to get rich by washing out the gold from the gravel of the Sacramento river.' By the start of the next emigrating season, the 'unusual excitement' had turned into an all-out rush, with both the 'California Trail' on one bank of the Platte and the 'Mormon Trail' on the other, crowded with fortune-seekers. 'It was a grand spectacle when we came, for the first time, in view of the vast emigration, slowly winding its westward way over the broad plain,' wrote one of the participants. 'It was a sight I shall never forget. It seemed as though all humanity had set their sights for the West.' Howard Egan, leading a train of goods wagons to Salt Lake City, saw them ahead as he joined the trail just east of Grand Island. 'There was one continual string of wagons as far as the eye can extend, both before and behind us.' Later that night, he looked out into the darkening plain from his camp. 'This evening there are twenty-nine camps in sight, numbering from fifteen to forty wagons in a company.' 'The trains have the appearance of a vast army, moving in two columns through a boundless plain,' wrote another emigrant. 'The country was so level we could see the long trains of white-topped wagons for many miles. It seemed to me that I had never seen so many human beings before in all my life.' Dan Jones described the trail as 'white with wagonfuls of immigrants. They are like doves flying to their windows from the four corners of the earth.'

So great were the numbers straining to get to the goldfields that tempers flared and men frequently came to blows. 'Fighting for precedence was quite common,' wrote one of them. To cross the Missouri, even the early starters had to queue for two or three days. The ferry boats worked day and night but still the lines on the eastern banks lengthened. Frequent quarrels broke out in the queues. 'A day or two since, two teamsters, in one of these disputes, killed each other with pistols.' Halfway to the Valley, they had to cross the Platte. The river was in flood and there was only one small ferry, operated by Mormons. The first wagon train arrived at the ferry on June 3rd. By the 6th, there were sixty wagons waiting to cross; by the 10th, 175, and by the 14th, there was a twenty-mile jam. They tried building their own ferries, and when these frail, makeshift vessels capsized, as they often did, there was little hope for the men on them.

'Not one in a thousand can save his life by swimming. The river rolls, boils and rushes along with tremendous velocity and the water is cold.' One train lost six men. When a boy called Brown was drowned trying to swim his cattle over, the accident, it was said, 'caused no more excitement than if he'd been a dog'.

This vast host of inexperienced travellers prompted the government to establish two forts on the California Trail that year, partly to keep an eye on them and partly to keep an eye on the Indians. One was Fort Kearny near Grand Island on the Platte and the other was the famous Fort Laramie at the foot of the Rockies. In previous years, the emigrants travelled the nine hundred miles from the Missouri to Jim Bridger's trading post at Fort Bridger in what became Wyoming without passing a single white man's settlement. Now there were two new bases along the way where they could stop to shoe their animals, repair their wagons, get medical help, be warned of dangers ahead, seek shelter from marauding Indians and even replenish their supplies if they were lucky. The process of civilizing and taming the western trails had begun. The Mormons, however, took little interest in such 'Babylonian' enterprises. They kept to themselves and passed by on the far side of the river.

There were 1,500 Mormons on the trail in 1849, travelling in four companies. The Welsh contingent was in the last company, led by Dan Jones and Apostle George A. Smith. Smith was a lively, jolly, genial man, the most colourful of all the Apostles. He measured five feet nine inches in his stockinged feet and weighed over eighteen stone. He wore an unconvincing wig with which he would often wipe the sweat from his brow. It was a sight that amazed the Indians, especially as he would also remove his teeth and his spectacles. They called him 'Non-choko-wicher', 'The-man-who-pulls-himself-to-bits'. But he was a brave and resourceful leader and the Welsh were lucky to have him as their Captain.

For a few weeks after the horrors of the Mississippi and the Missouri, Dan was unusually taciturn. 'It is very likely that some of our readers, like ourselves, are surprised that a letter is so long in coming from Capt. Jones,' complained *Udgorn Seion* in Merthyr. But as the time came to set out over the Plains, his spirits lifted. The letter he wrote to *Udgorn Seion* on the last morning in the staging camp is full of the exuberance and excitement so typical of him. He is champing at the bit to be away. 'In haste, and almost before a dog opens his mouth in camp, I take this early morning opportunity to send you a few lines. There is no time to portray the sights around me nor to write an introduction; for the mosquitoes are biting, the sun is almost up, and I am waiting for the call to get underway with fifty wagons to the far west, beyond the furthest borders of every civilized country.'

They left the Missouri on June 14th, a fortnight later than the last of the big trains of previous years. It was dangerously late in the season. The risk, of course, was that they might be trapped in the Rockies by the winter snows. There were also worries that the pasture along the trail was in poor condition. That was no surprise, said Dan, 'when you consider that from six to seven thousand covered wagons, each pulled by three to six yoke of oxen, beside several thousand cattle, sheep, mules, and horses, have passed along this road during this summer.' It wasn't wise to overwork the oxen when their feed was so poor. 'It caused us to slow down and be content if we could travel but ten to twelve miles each day... There is hardly a day that we do not come across skeletons of the oxen of those who went before us on the roadside, a monument to their foolishness in travelling too fast at the beginning of a journey as long as this one.'

But there were advantages to a late start. Firstly, the worst of the rush was over. Because the '49ers', on their way to the Californian goldfields, had so much further to travel than the Mormons, they had started a good deal earlier in the season and, by mid June, few of them remained on the Platte. Fording rivers late in the season was also less of a problem. The flood waters of the spring thaw had passed and they could now walk their oxen through. More importantly, cholera had run its course for the season. It had wreaked havoc upon the plains earlier in the year. Terrible though its ravages of the white men had been, the Indian tribes had suffered more, for with no natural immunity they fell easy prey to the pestilence. By the time the Welsh took to the trail there were no Indians to be seen. 'They have not molested us,' wrote Smith. 'Indeed we have not seen half a dozen Indians since we left Winter Quarters. The cholera it appears has frightened them, and they have deserted the path of the white man.' Over 2,500 died of cholera on the trail that year and the Welsh passed countless graves between the Missouri and Fort Laramie, but not one of their company was lost. The pestilence had shot its bolt and passed them by.

Yet it proved a difficult crossing for the Welsh. They were an edgy, uneasy lot and the squabbling started even before they had left Council Bluffs. In his autobiography, written many years later, Isaac Nash, the company blacksmith from Kidwelly, described a quarrel that had broken out between himself and Dan Jones over Mrs Lewis, the Kidwelly innkeeper's wife. Isaac had been one of the forty people whose passage from Liverpool to Council Bluffs had been paid by Mrs Lewis. For some unspecified reasons, she was now refusing to finance the rest of his journey to Salt Lake City. He had therefore refused to repair her wagon. He claimed that Dan Jones had then threatened him with a drawn sword. No mention is made of this incident in any other diary or memoir, but Isaac Nash's story is not implausible. We know that Dan greatly admired Mrs Lewis. Indeed, he entered into a polygamous marriage with her some months after their arrival in the Valley. His relationship with her might well have caused tensions in the Welsh camp. Dan's wife, Jane, had been left in Wales because she was pregnant and the birth of her child was imminent. According to Isaac Nash, 'when we left, she was about to be confined and could not come. Jones would not wait for her as he was bound to go with Mrs. Lewis.' But Dan's version of events was that he was forced to leave without Jane because of the threats to his life. 'Why all the persecution,' he asked, 'why all the slander, and the false accusations I suffered for years from the press and the pulpits? Why had a watch to be kept on my home for weeks? Why was my life not safe? Why was I not able to bid farewell to my wife and children?' And then he added, in a melodramatic flourish, 'You holy angels, I charge you to look after my wife and child. Forward heroically I go. Be sure to sustain her until I return. She is precious to my soul. May the great Snowdon Mountain jump into the sea before I ever, ever forget her.' This was Dan at his most florid and least convincing.

What happened next surprised everyone. Jane was delivered of her child and within three days she had risen from her bed and had set out to follow her husband to America. 'She came all alone across the sea,' wrote Isaac Nash, 'and up the river to Council Bluffs with her babe, which was but a few days old.' Clearly Jane was as intrepid and determined a lady as Mrs Lewis. According to Isaac Nash, her arrival did not please Dan. 'Brother Jones and Sister Lewis were quite surprised and also disappointed because she had followed them.' Dan, on the other hand, said he was delighted to have his wife with him. 'My darling wife and my baby arrived here in good health some days ago, and in time to accompany us.' 'This,' said Isaac, 'was the beginning of the trouble which lasted all the way across the Plains.'

'Mrs. Lewis had a spring wagon,' he wrote, 'and Jones wanted his wife to ride with Mrs. Lewis, but she would not do it. She said she would rather walk than ride with Mrs. Lewis. One day she commenced to walk. I saw her walking and took her in my wagon to ride with my wife. Sometimes she would ride with me and sometimes with a brother by the name of Ned Williams and his family. Brother Jones forbade us to let Jane ride in our wagons. I told him she could ride as long as she wanted and Ned Williams told him the same. Jones, after this, felt bitter toward Ned and I.'

Apart from the Welsh, 366 other emigrants travelled in George A. Smith's company, most of them English or Scandinavian. According to the official record they were a happy, contented band, mingling together merrily. 'We are composed of Yankees, English, Welsh, Norwegian, &c.,' reported George to his superiors, 'yet we are one, although of different dialects and nations. The English are doing first rate, as also the Welsh. They are well fitted out with team and provisions; are in good spirits, are joyful, and make the camp resound with the songs of Zion in the evening after corralling.' But, reading between the lines, one suspects that the company was far from united. Time after time, the Welsh managed to infuriate William Appleby, the company's official clerk. He described August 23rd as 'The Day of the Welsh Accidents'. 'Weather very hot, roads heavy over the Sandy Bluffs. Cattle much fatigued, some very nearly giving out. A wagon in the Welsh company was upset in a mire hole in crossing a creek. Another came very near being run into the river. A Welsh woman had her foot nearly mashed. Another was bitten by a dog belonging to Brother Simmons. Accidents enough for one day.' But five days later, the Welsh were in trouble again. 'Aug 28. Journeyed thirteen miles, over sandy and dusty roads again… A gun was accidentally discharged this morning in a wagon belonging to the Welsh company. However it did but little damage, the shot grazed the leg of a Welsh brother and several shots passed through the hat of another, just clearing his head.'

A fortnight later, one of the Welsh contingent brought the whole train to a stop. 'Last evening, Hugh Davis (Welsh) wandered off from the Camp. He was about seventy years of age, and quite infirm. Search was made for him until about three o'clock this morning, with lanterns on horseback, fires built upon the mount near the camps, but without success. This morning the greater part of the camp turned out, scoured the hills &c but unsuccessful. About noon word came to us from Capt. Richards' Camp, which had passed on ahead in the morning, that Bro. Davis had been found by them about five miles ahead, safe, having tarried in the hills all night.' One can sense the clerk hissing between bared teeth, 'Bloody Welsh again!'

Nor did Bathsheba, George A. Smith's wife, have a good

opinion of the Welsh. She complains in her journal that they were very noisy about their camp fire. 'Several Welsh families were camped behind our wagon and they laughed and talked so much after night that it made me quite nervous.' She watched a gang of Welsh preparing their animals for the day's drive. 'They did not understand driving oxen. It was very amusing to see them yoke their cattle; two would have an animal by the horns, one by the tail, and one or two others would do their best to put on the yoke, whilst the apparently astonished ox, not at all enlightened by the guttural sounds of the Welsh tongue, seemed perfectly at a loss what to do, or to know what was wanted of him.' There was also a stampede, for which she blamed the Welsh.

In the midst of all these squabbles and slanging matches, Dan Jones sat down to compose a small booklet, with the help of George Smith and another of the company leaders, Ezra Benson. They called it *Directions to the Emigrants to Salt Lake City* and in it they offered useful and practical advice to all emigrants who would follow in their path. It was eventually published in a Welsh-language version only. Dan sent the manuscript to William Morgan in Council Bluffs and Morgan sent it to Merthyr where it was published the following year and sold for a penny. The copy in the Salisbury Library at Cardiff University is the only copy to have survived in Wales. Four other copies exist in various libraries in the United States.

Is there a book in the Welsh language written in a more exotic setting? They were camped in the shadow of Independence Rock, the great rock register where thousands of those who had travelled the trail before them had carved their names. The Sweetwater ran gently nearby. From the surrounding wagons came the sound of quiet chatter and bursts of music. There would have been oxen lowing nearby and, far away on the distant hills, wolves and coyotes howling and, above them, the cold stars rising in a clear sky. By the light of a candle, they began to write.

'Camp of Israel, on the hills of the Sweetwater,
Near to Independence Rock,
649 miles from Winter Quarters
September 21, 1849.

Dear Brethren,

Though we are far from you, we thought it fitting to offer for your consideration some things we have learnt from experience, which will be of use to you. Build your wagons from the best materials, strong and light, and the wheels six inches higher than they normally are. They will be useful crossing rivers, keeping the water from reaching your food. The most comfortable load is fourteen hundred pounds on a light, strong wagon, and two yokes of good oxen. Such a load will cross wet places without sinking, nor will it get stuck as heavier vehicles are like to do. In your choice of oxen, we advise you to choose animals that are used to the yoke and easy to handle, no more than ten years old nor less than five.'

They counsel against over-whipping the animals.

'We believe that the gold miners lost more of their animals because of the whip and other ill-treatment than because of their load, their journey or the poison in the alkali sinks. The bones of their animals are scattered over the road that we travel and we are amazed to think of their losses as we gaze upon them.'

They write that, above all, they should avoid frightening the animals and starting a stampede.

'A multitude of maddened animals is an unnerving and terrible thing to gaze upon. Terrified, running, the earth trembling, chains rattling, yokes crackling, wagons damaged, bystanders trodden under foot, some perhaps being killed, others injured.'

They worry about how the Welsh will handle alcohol, which was so readily available in America.

'They come from a land where hard liquor is difficult for all but the gentry to obtain, and therefore not often used by poor people. When they come to America, where spirits are so cheap, they are not used to their intoxicating influences and they are very likely to over-indulge, resulting in injury and great loss to themselves. Therefore, advise all under your care to totally abstain, except when it is absolutely necessary, when someone is ill.'

Some pages were added to the booklet by William Morgan in Council Bluffs. He lists the goods which the emigrants best bring with them from Wales and those which were cheaper to obtain in America. 'In my opinion it is better for all to buy their milk pans, that is, the tin ones, in Wales. And the ropes of the old country are generally better than those of this country.' He says it would also be wise to bring knives and forks, bellows and brass candlesticks from home, but that American axes were good. And a word of advice to the ladies. 'To protect themselves from the sun, it would be wise for those who can, to buy parasols. Ladies here are not often seen walking without them, even the Welsh ladies.'

Finally, Dan Jones had some words of advice for young people and all lovers. 'It would be better for those in an engagement,' he says, 'to marry or release each other from their vows before leaving Wales.' He has no faith in the steadfastness of Welsh engagements in the New World. 'The sea is free, the country they are coming to is free, and between the freedom of the sea and the freedom of the land, engagements get broken, even amongst those who travel together.' In America, he suggests, long engagements are very unusual. This is a new country, he implies, a country in a hurry. 'We offer these suggestions to you for your benefit, and the benefit of all who emigrate.' Could Dan's own predicament, torn as he was between two women, have been on his mind as he composed these lines?

By the end of August, high in the Rockies, the weather began to turn and the going got harder. The night of the 29th was bitterly cold. An inch of ice formed in the water buckets. On the morning of September 1st, they noticed patches of the poisonous white alkaline powder, which had so troubled earlier companies, staining nearby pasture. Despite their best efforts to keep the oxen clear of them, one of them died. That afternoon, a sheep fell under the wheels of a wagon and had to be put down. And that night, the Welsh and the English started fighting.

Cadwalader Owen and Robert Berrett came to blows as they took their animals down to the river to drink. The diaries say nothing about the cause. Robert Berrett's father then joined the scuffle and that night all three appeared before the camp court. Every wagon train had its own court, presided over by the company Captain. The three were found guilty of brawling and were given extra hours on watch. The next morning, all three were re-baptized. This was common practice amongst the Saints. When a man had offended and was contrite, re-baptism washed the slate clean. But, unexpectedly, on that same morning, five others were re-baptized alongside them, including Mrs Lewis and Jane, Dan's wife. Then, in the afternoon, seventeen more were re-baptized, all of them Welsh. Amongst them were Dan Jones and other leaders of the Welsh contingent – Thomas Jeremy and Daniel Daniels – respectable men, upstanding elders. These had certainly not been involved in a punch-up with the English. Rather, it appears that the Welsh had been quarrelling amongst themselves again. Could it have been Dan Jones' treatment of his wife that caused the friction?

The weather deteriorated and grew colder. At the end of September, when they were over 7,000 feet up in the Rockies, close to South Pass, it began to snow heavily. It fell without ceasing for a day and a night. They crouched in their wagons, listening to the wind roaring through the pass, unable to light a fire or prepare hot food. Twenty-four oxen and many of the pigs and chickens froze to death. The short summer of the Rockies was at an end. Then, unexpectedly, there was a brief thaw and the company managed to scramble through the pass and slide down the western flanks.

As they approached the Valley, the bickering started afresh. A present of fresh fruit and vegetables had been sent from the city to welcome the company, but, for some reason, the Welsh received no share of it. Dan believed they had been cheated of their due. He called an urgent meeting of the Welsh to discuss the matter. It proved to be a long and dramatic affair. The only evidence we have of what took place is again in Isaac Nash's journal. 'Brother Jones called a meeting and preached a long sermon,' he wrote, 'advising us all to stick together as a nation. He told us that the wagons which came to meet us with onions and potatoes had come primarily for Brother Smith and the Americans. He said that if the company was all Welsh, they would not have come to meet us. He advised us to stick together and all go over Jordan River and settle there as an independent nation, with Mrs. Lewis as our queen. Jones called for a vote. All who were willing to go over Jordan and establish a Welsh nation were requested to raise their hands. All hands went up except Ned Williams' and mine. Then he asked the reason for my not voting with the rest. I told him I had had enough of the Welsh and I was going to try Americans for a while. He then said that I should be cut off from the Book of the Nation and never be restored. With that, I left, went to Brother George A. Smith and told him all that was said and done. Brother Smith came over right away. Jones was still speaking when he arrived. Jones asked Brother Smith if he would talk to the Saints a little; which he did as follows, "Brothers and Sisters, the potatoes and onions and other things have come for you as well as for the Americans. You have no need to go over Jordan and become an independent nation, for all is free in the Valleys of the Mountains. There is no compulsion in Zion."' With these words, he managed, according to Isaac Nash, to quieten the fears of the Welsh and to convince them that there was a place for them in Zion. And with that, Dan Jones' rebellion came to an end.

It was a strange affair. Knowing Dan's great love for and loyalty to the Church, it's hard to imagine that he was ready to sacrifice it all for such a petty cause. There must have been more to it than that. Only Isaac Nash refers to it, and he was no friend of Dan's. On the other hand, Dan also had a great love for Wales and for all things Welsh, and the squabble over the fresh fruit and vegetables might have been a final insult in a long list of discriminatory slights that he believed the Welsh had endured on their journey. His recklessness might well have led him, in the heat of the moment, to conceive the crazy plan of establishing a Welsh kingdom on the plains of the Salt Lake Valley, with his wife-to-be as queen. Whatever the truth, he soon came to his senses.

His disobedience however was not overlooked. He was sent ahead, that night, to Salt Lake City and into the presence of Brigham Young. His punishment, if it was a punishment, was to be called within a week on another exhausting mission, a mission this time to find, of all things, the lost tribe of Welsh Indians, the Madogwys, the descendants of Madog, Prince of Gwynedd. It was commonly believed that they still existed somewhere in the vast expanse of the West.

Like most Welsh people of the age, Dan believed wholeheartedly in the existence of the Madogwys. 'The greatest desire of my soul for more than twenty years,' he once wrote, 'has been to bring them into our ken and the light of day.' For years, he had been collecting evidence of their existence. He believed that they lived somewhere to the south of the Salt Lake Valley, possibly along the banks of the Colorado. He kept records of the reports of men who were said to have met them. One, 'who understood a few words of Welsh, testified that these natives spoke Welsh.' Another said that they wore similar clothes to those 'worn by the common man in Wales.' Two men 'of good character' had visited their villages on the Colorado. 'I know not how much trust we should place in these tales,' wrote Dan, 'yet they are not unbelievable to me. Not often is so much smoke seen as hides the Madogwys from the presence of their fellow-countrymen from age to age, without it coming from some sort of fire.'

When he'd been in Wales, a year or two earlier, Dan had written Brigham Young a letter recounting the Madog story and telling him of the strong belief in Wales that these blue-eyed, red-haired people still wandered the plains of the West. If only Brigham could get hold of one or two of them, he wrote, and convince them of the truths of Mormonism and then send them to Wales as missionaries, what a sensation they would create! 'If I could have but some of them to preach the Gospel to these zealous religionists of their fatherland, that would be something new under the sun; and the whole nation would flock to hear them.' Brigham was intrigued by the idea.

On November 22nd, in the middle of a hard winter, Dan joined a wagon train of Saints on their way to the southern borders of present-day Utah. Their primary purpose was to seek out suitable locations for settlement, but Dan was also to look out for blue-eyed, Welsh-speaking Indians. The company pushed into the unknown lands of the south and discovered, near to the present-day towns of Cedar City and Parowan, a fertile region with promising deposits of coal and iron. Before turning for home, they celebrated their success with a convivial dinner. 'Around the table on the grass sat about fifty of the brave sons of Zion, all in unity and love.' The speeches were long and fervent, a canon was fired, and a song, especially composed for the occasion, was heartily sung. One of the verses referred to Dan's quest.

> Perhaps these solitudes contain
> A remnant who in Maddock's reign
> From Wales came o'er the main, so far, far away.
> O come, Capt. Jones! Your kindly heart is yearning
> O'er kindred dear. Let's find them here! O come, come away!
> Six hundred years they've dwelt alone,
> To friends and kith and kin unknown,
> Arise! Your kindred own, and bring them away.

On that day, singing and feasting with his fellows, listening to the Madogwys being celebrated in poetry and convinced that their villages lay close by, over just one more mountain, beyond just one more horizon, Dan must have felt more convinced than ever that, one day, he would find them. 'I was sad that we had been unable to fulfil all the aims of the expedition this time,' wrote Dan, 'but I believe they will be fulfilled before long.'

In 1852, Dan was sent on another mission to Wales. He

is said to have baptized 2,000 during this second term and brought five hundred of them back with him to the Valley four years later. We shall look at their torturous journey across the Rockies in due course. One of the last paragraphs Dan Jones wrote in *Udgorn Seion*, before leaving Wales for the final time, was an appeal to his fellow countrymen to help him find the Madogwys. As soon as he arrived back in the Valley, he said, he intended to go looking for them once again. 'Despite how much others doubt the story, we obtained satisfactory proofs in our searches across the continent for the "Welsh Indians" during the past twenty years, and since we have decided to re-initiate at the end of this month a search with no turning back... we beseech those who may have [*their story*], to assist us in our venture.' The same old bee still buzzed in his bonnet, the same obsession still haunted him. There is no evidence that he ever set out on this last quest to find the Welsh Indians. He died of TB in 1862.

We should not conclude this brief digression into the Mormons' fascination with the Madog legend without referring briefly to Llewellyn Harris. He deserves to be remembered. He was born somewhere near Llandovery. His father died when he was very young and, in 1840, his mother emigrated to the United States and settled in New York. She died soon afterwards and Llewellyn, now about nine years old, was left to his own resources. He went to work for a Welsh farmer who treated him badly. He ran away and began living rough on the streets of New York, selling newspapers to survive. He drifted to Chicago and then Washington DC, still selling papers. At fifteen, he joined the crew of a freighter, plying between New York and Texas and, at nineteen, he joined the army and was sent to one of the frontier forts out on the plains. There, for the first time, he came into contact with Native Americans. He admired their way of life and found himself comfortable in their company and, such was his disgust at the barbaric way in which they were treated by his fellow soldiers, that he fled the army and went to live with them. Then he stumbled upon the Mormon settlements on the shores of the Great Salt Lake and met fellow Welshmen there and joined with them and was soon baptized and received into the Mormon faith.

Brigham Young set him to work as a missionary. For thirty years, he kept the Church in touch with the tribes in the south of the country. It was said that he could speak more than twenty of the tribal languages, although Welsh, he said, remained his favourite language. In 1878, when working amongst the Zuñi Indians of New Mexico, he believed he had found the Madogwys. He listened to their tribal legends of white forefathers who had come across the sea from the east and he heard in their talk a few words which, he said, might well have been Welsh. 'What people want to believe, they will believe,' was the wry comment of one American historian, 'especially if they are Welsh or Mormons.'

1850

ALTHOUGH THE THOUSANDS of men who crossed to the west during the California Gold Rush are referred to as the '49ers', '50ers' would be a more precise description. There were twice as many of them on the trail in the second year of the rush. 'The cry of "Gold! Gold! Gold!" reverberates through the land,' cried one San Francisco newspaper, 'the field is left half planted, the house half built, and everything neglected but the manufacture of shovels and pickaxes.' One '49er' wrote that being on the trail in 1850 was like walking the streets of New York. 'The road, from morning to night, is crowded like Pearl Street or Broadway.' Over a thousand wagons were counted passing Fort Kearny in one day. From all directions came 'the lowing of cattle, the neighing of horses, the braying of mules and barking of dogs, mingled with the clack of human voices. To this is added the sound of the viol, bugle, tambourine and clarionette. To fill up the chorus, rifles and pistols are almost constantly cracking, responsive to the rumbling, grinding music of carriage wheels.' The old comradeship and the mutual support that had been a feature of life on the trail in previous years gave way to selfish squabbling. If one of the wagons got stuck in a mudhole or broke an axle, no one would stop to help. All would try to squeeze past. 'First there would be shouting and swearing and the cracking of whips. Then they would start to fight, two or three would be felled and suddenly there would be twenty guns snatched from the wagons.' It was not the loneliness and the emptiness that preyed on the mind of the emigrants this year, but the stampede at the end of day to the best pasture and the wild scrum for the best camping sites.

Never had so many people gone west. Amongst the 50,000 on the trail that year there were about 5,000 Mormons, yet very few were British. Most were Americans from the eastern states. That spring, in Liverpool, only two ships had been chartered by the Church. According to *Udgorn Seion* the notice for those who wished to travel had been too short, but Dan Jones' explanation is more plausible. He believed it was the fear of cholera that kept the Saints at home. Ninety-six Welsh left Liverpool this year, once again travelling together, yet only a few of them reached the Valley. Abel Evans, one of their leaders, writes, in a letter from the Missouri, that seven of the group had died on the voyage, thirty had stayed to work in St Louis, and 57 were staying with him in the Welsh enclave in Council Bluffs. 'We were welcomed most heartily, far beyond our expectations,' he wrote. 'All who had the means have taken houses and land, and the others will soon have the means to do the same. All who came with me have stayed here, apart from David Evans and his wife, who have carried on.'

It was not only the new arrivals that refused to move on. William Morgan's followers, the 113 who had originally stayed to build the Welsh community, also decided to postpone their departure to Zion for another year. Many of the Welsh were, for the first time in their lives, earning good money. They were loath to abandon all they had achieved and to uproot their families once again, in order to embark on another dangerous adventure with no certainties at the end of it. They knew that when the emigrating season started again, large profits could be made in Council Bluffs. Many of their neighbours had bought animals and feed cheaply in the winter of 1848 and sold them at exorbitant profits to the '49ers' the following spring. The price of corn had risen from 20¢ a bushel to $3. 'It is expected that the gold diggers will come here in the spring in hoards,' wrote William Morgan in December 1849. 'If they come, there will be the chance to make dollars fairly easily; some make

110

about 400 dollars each in a few months by buying things for the gold miners. The Welsh can do the same thing easily.'

By the time William Morgan wrote his next letter to the *Udgorn* in May, the rush was at its height. Over 5,000 wagons passed through Council Bluffs that spring and so great was the jam that some had to wait for weeks for a ferry across the Missouri. 'Our town is like a boiling pot these days, and as full as Merthyr market on a Saturday, so that one cannot drive a wagon without stopping along the streets. They are gold people, and they leave some of their gold behind.' No wonder the Welsh were unwilling to leave their new homes to take their chances on the trail.

One of the very few Welsh emigrants on the trail that year therefore was 29-year-old Ann Roberts of Denbighshire. She had been a very early member of the Saints, joining in 1842. In the same year she had married Joseph Griffiths in Liverpool and, a fortnight after the wedding, they had sailed for New Orleans. It took them 37 days to get up the Mississippi to St Louis, their progress being halted time after time by blocks of ice crashing down the river. For the final part of the journey, from St Louis to Nauvoo, they had travelled with Dan Jones in *The Maid of Iowa*, on his maiden voyage to that city. Perhaps she had reminisced with Dan about the people and places they both knew in north Wales. On the dock in Nauvoo, Joseph Smith had taken her hand and blessed her.

But before she and her husband had a chance to settle, the hard times had come. Joseph Smith was assassinated, anti-Mormon mobs had attacked the city and the decision was taken to leave for the Valley. But Ann and Joseph were too poor to afford the wagon, the yoke of oxen and the other requirements of trail travel. In the spring of 1846, when the Bennion family, and all those who had the means, left for the Valley, Ann and Joseph had to stay in Nauvoo, with the destitute, the sick and the feeble, every day expecting another attack from the mob and every day fearful for their lives.

By now, they had four small children. How they must have longed to leave. 'Nauvoo is a truly lonely and bleak place,' wrote one old lady in a letter to Brigham Young that summer. She was a widow, one of about a thousand Saints left behind in the city, and Brigham was her only hope of rescue. 'My body is tired by the struggle to keep a roof over my head. Tell my friends that I am still alive and that my faith in the scriptures is as indestructible as the eternal hills. If your advice is that I should go from here, tell me how I can come to you. Advise me as if I was your child, or sister, and whatever you tell me, I shall do.'

In late summer, the attacks on the city began again. Fifteen hundred men, all heavily armed and eager for plunder, fell upon Nauvoo. About 150 Saints were fit and willing to confront them, Joseph being one of them. There were five days of fighting, of wild gunfire, of heroic defence, but there could only be one conclusion. Anne's biography records that 'opposition to the growing mobs was useless. On September 17, 1846, the Saints surrendered, and the mob entered Nauvoo.' Ignoring the terms of surrender, they pillaged and burnt the houses and abused the inhabitants. Entering Ann and Joseph's home, they threw their furniture into the street and set fire to the building. Hastily, Ann and Joseph gathered together a few possessions, and fled across the Mississippi River.

For three weeks, 640 people, Ann and Joseph and their children amongst them, squatted on the western bank of the Mississippi, in the pouring rain, hungry and cold. 'Many,' wrote Thomas Bullock, 'had not a wagon or tent to shelter from the pitiless blast. It is not known how many died there, but, inevitably, death was no stranger.' After eking out a miserable existence for the best part of a month, they were eventually rescued by a wagon train sent by Brigham from Winter Quarters. As they prepared to move out, there occurred one of those 'miracles' that are fondly remembered in the Mormon annals as evidence of God's care for them. A flock of quail descended on the camp and proved easy to catch. 'See,' wrote one of the company, 'the sick knock them down with sticks and the little children catch them alive with their hands... The flocks increase in number, continually flying round the camp...

A section of the trail near Muddy Creek, Wyoming.

Deep ruts carved into the rock by the passage of thousands of wagon wheels.

The same horizon every day, the same heat, the same stubborn oxen, the same endless weariness.

Approaching the end of the trail, thirty miles from Salt Lake City.

A Mormon camp on the Plains. Nebraska, 1866.
(Courtesy of Church History Library of The Church of Jesus Christ of Latter-day Saints)

'It was a beautiful sight to see, those covered wagons, everyone keeping in their place and everything kept in order, winding their way over hill and dale.'
(Courtesy of Scotts Bluff National Monument)

A woman
collecting
buffalo pats to
use as fuel.
(Courtesy of
Liberal Memorial
Library, Kansas)

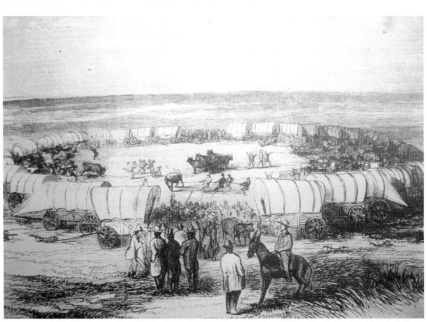

'When I corral, I want to lock wheels with my brothers, just as I would want to lock arms, so we
might be mutually strengthened.' (Brigham Young)

The master mason of the Manti Temple was Edward Lloyd Parry of St George, Denbighshire.

The foundations of the Salt Lake City Temple were laid by Elias Morris of Llanfair Talhaiarn, Denbighshire.

The interior of Brigham City Tabernacle is said to have been influenced by Welsh chapel design.

Catherine Jones Bennett's grave at Muddy Creek.

Mute witnesses of the tragedies of the trail.

A group of American Mormon missionaries in Liverpool, 1855. Capt. Dan Jones is the second from the right in the middle row.

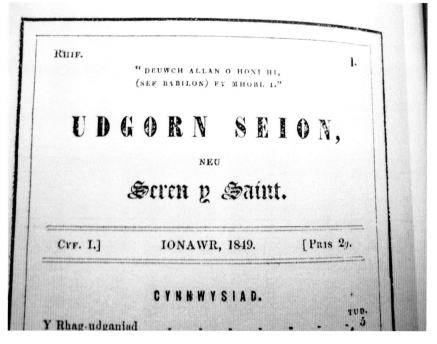

The title-page of the first issue of *Udgorn Seion* [Zion's Trumpet].

The Prophet Joseph Smith. The vessel used by God to deliver his message to the world.

Brigham Young. 'My desire is to teach people what they should do <u>now</u> and let the Millennium take care of itself.'

John Bennion. The first Welshman to enter Salt Lake City.

Mrs Elizabeth Lewis, the 'Welsh Queen', landlady of the White Lion in Kidwelly.

William W. Davies, the keeper of 'The Kingdom of Heaven'.

William's son, Arthur, the 'Walla Walla Jesus'.

Daniel Daniels, a Carmarthen stonemason and gun-runner extraordinaire.

Thomas Jeremy and his wife, Sarah, who lost three little girls on their journey up the Mississippi.

Thomas Giles of Tredegar, the Blind Harpist of Utah.

The harp that he probably carried from Wales.

One of the many statues of handcarters to be found all over Utah.

A handcarters' camp. The men on the left are busily repairing a cart.

'A condition of distress here met my eyes that I never saw before or since. The train was strung out for three or four miles. There were hundreds needing help. What could we do?'

Margaret Griffiths, back once again in the traces of her handcart, showing her granddaughters how she came to Zion.

Salt Lake City in 1853. An engraving from Piercy's *Route from Liverpool to the Great Salt Lake Valley*.

The ferry over the Loup in 1853. On the left are the wagons queuing to cross. On the right, the ferry is being pulled across, and in the foreground, the ferryman's quarters.

The enigmatic Elias Morris.

The Mountain Meadows Massacre. Mormonism's darkest hour.

The memorial, the wreath, the rose in the jam pot and a note of apology.

'We are "<u>forever</u>" sorry for this very tradgic event in Mormon history. A very sad L.D.S. Descendant.'

One of the stone houses built by Shadrach Jones in Willard.

Chimney Rock, the remarkable column of sandstone that rises 470 feet above the Platte and is visible for forty miles around.

a direct manifestation from the Most High that although we are driven by men, He has not forgotten us.' Every cooking pot was filled that evening and they all ate well. The next day, Ann and Joseph set out for the camp at Garden Grove, where they spent the rest of the winter.

It was a hard winter. Wave upon wave of sicknesses fell upon the camp – malaria, typhoid, dysentery, pneumonia. The inhabitants hung on, from crisis to crisis. Food was inadequate and fuel scarce. In the spring, they were moved to Winter Quarters, the Mormons' main camp on the Missouri. Here Ann and Joseph and 3,500 other Saints waited for Brigham Young to rescue them. Ann and Joseph had to wait for three years. Others had to wait five.

Life in Winter Quarters was no better than in Garden Grove. The camp had been built in the previous autumn when Brigham had realised that he had little hope of moving his people further west before winter. When Ann and Joseph arrived, there were 3,483 people living there, in 631 small cabins, some of brick, some of logs, but mostly of turf. They worked on clearing the surrounding land for crop growing and they looked after the flocks of sheep and herds of cattle left by those who had already crossed to the Valley. Occasionally they found work outside the camp which earned them a little desperately needed money. But, weakened by their constant labour and their inadequate diet, over a thousand of them died before the camp was finally emptied. In 1848, they were moved to other camps on the Council Bluffs side of the river. We know nothing of Ann and Joseph's struggle to survive during these years, but survive they did and, in the spring of 1850, there was hope that they might soon be back on the trail west.

In this year, the land of the Mormon settlers in the Salt Lake Valley became a United States Territory, the first step on the road to becoming a state. This new territory was to be called Utah. The Mormons succeeded in retaining control over much of the government. 'We wish to report what will be the cause of great rejoicing to all our brethren,' reported *Udgorn Seion*, 'namely that we have received a letter announcing that

Brigham Young has been chosen as Governor of the territory'. Brigham soon realised that the settlement's new status would eventually attract to Utah many who were not of the Mormon faith. He urgently needed to strengthen the Mormon community. 'We want men;' he announced. 'Brethren, come from the States, from the nations, come!' There was fertile land and water enough to sustain many more settlers and a good harvest had been garnered that year. 'Come to help us build and grow, until we can say, "Enough, the valleys of Ephraim are full!"'

On the Missouri, there were hundreds of Saints who, like Ann and Joseph, were eager to get to the Valley but who could not afford the journey. For them, and for thousands like them in Europe and in the United States, Brigham created The Perpetual Emigrating Fund, a fund from which the poorer members of the church might borrow to pay the cost of emigration. The wealthier brethren were expected to contribute generously to the fund and those who borrowed from it were expected to start repaying the loan as soon as they found work in the Valley. The experiment proved hugely successful and over the years, countless voyages to Utah, including many from Wales, were made possible by the fund. But, in 1850, it was used to help the poor Saints still stranded in Winter Quarters. Five thousand dollars were provided to buy oxen and wagons and food for them and Ann and Joseph and the children were among the first to benefit from the fund.

The trails that year were not only crowded, but dirty. They were cluttered with discarded rubbish, polluted by the waste of 50,000 people. What had, in previous years, been a trail of green grass and flowers was now one long dump. 'Sometimes' wrote one pioneer, 'feather beds, blankets, quilts and clothing of every kind was strewn all over the plains for miles, also wagon tires and irons of every description, gun barrels, stoves, etc.' The camp sites were filthy. Rotten food, dead animals, camp waste and sewage squelched under foot and fouled the air they breathed. The inexperience of the '49ers' was mostly to blame. They had no idea how much an ox could comfortably haul. They tended to overload their wagons and then discard inessentials as soon as the paths became boggy and their animals quagmired in clay. 'I thought I had before seen destruction of property,' wrote one emigrant, 'but this morning beat anything I have ever seen. To attempt an enumeration of what was thrown away would be useless and it could not be done. Trunks, clothes, mattresses, quilts, beef, bacon, rice, augers, handsaws, planes, shoes, hats, thread, spools, soap, mowing scythes. These are a few of the items I saw this morning.' Some of their surplus goods they kept until they reached Fort Kearny or Fort Laramie, in the hope of selling them or bartering them for lighter, more useful goods, but this usually proved hopeless. As a result, the trail beyond the forts was particularly foul. Joseph Berrien, one of the '49ers', arrived at Fort Laramie well before the height of the migration but says he saw about 20,000 pounds of salted pork rotting on the trail. Another bad place was 'The Valley of the Shadow of Death', between the Platte and the Sweetwater, where the poisonous alkaline waters were such a threat to the animals. Despite the best efforts of their guardians, many oxen drank from these contaminated pools and died, and when an ox died, not only did its carcass defile the path for weeks, but the wagon had to be lightened and more goods had to be dumped. A correspondent on *The St Louis Republican* counted over a thousand wagons abandoned on the trail, and hundreds of rotting carcasses, ripped open and half eaten by wolves. The strangest things were discarded, large numbers of anvils and ploughs, a diving bell, a heavy safe and guns galore. 'Lying by the wayside are a great variety of books, which their owners have thrown away to lighten their loads,' wrote one '49er'. 'From this extended library I frequently draw a volume, read it and return it.' Another found a handsome, brand new, Gothic cupboard. He soon put it to good use as firewood to boil a cup of coffee.

The wastefulness of the '49ers' proved a blessing to the Mormons. Out on the plains lay the very things that the Mormons most needed. 'Bar iron crowbars, drills, augurs, chisels, axes, lead trunks, boxes, spades, grind stones, bake ovens, stoves without number, cooking utensils of every kind, kegs, barrels, harnesses, many of which must have been very costly at home.' Things that were in short supply in the Valley were lying there by the wayside, waiting to be picked up. In late summer, when the main flood of emigrants was past, Brigham sent out his men to scavenge the trail and to reap this unexpected harvest.

Cholera was bad again at the beginning of the season. In their diaries, the Saints relate how they passed grave after grave. This year, they were organised into ten companies. Joseph Fish, in the first Mormon company, remembered his father trying to count the graves, but having to give up when he reached a thousand. The second company, led by Benjamin Hawkins, took an unusual precaution, which may have saved many lives. Most companies extracted their water either directly from the river or from the innumerable pits that were dug in the camp sites down to the water table. It was believed that the muddy water collected in these pits was cleaner and healthier than the river water because it had been filtered through sand and gravel. In fact, it was more polluted and more dangerous because the camping sites themselves were hopelessly contaminated, not only by the waste and sewage of the tens of thousands of '49ers', but by the decomposing bodies of their dead, buried nearby. The infections and germs seeped through the sand and gathered in these pits where, stewed in the heat of a Midwestern summer, they were brewed into a fatal cocktail. But Benjamin Hawkins' company listened to the advice of a man called Thomas Johnson. 'Don't go near the pits. Only drink water from the river,' was his counsel. 'And drink no water without boiling it first.' His instructions were adhered to and the company escaped the worst of the epidemic. Johnson was a man before his time. The research that proved that cholera was a water-borne disease was not published until 1854, although much of the research had been completed by 1850. Could he have known of the work and of its conclusions before leaving England?

The next five Mormon companies were not so lucky. The

diarist Franklin Langworthy saw many wagons stranded by the death of their owners. 'In some instances,' he writes, 'every person belonging to a wagon has died of the pestilence. Such carriages have been seen standing by the way, with all the clothing and provisions on board, and the cattle or horses wandering about the plains without owners.' He saw desperately ill people abandoned by their fellows. The fear of cholera literally drove people out of their minds. The fear was as contagious and as debilitating as the disease itself. 'I think I never saw a people so completely frightened out of their senses as the people comprising my ten,' wrote Gilbert Belnap. He also attempted to record every grave he saw but soon gave up. 'Graves are so numerous that to notice them all would make my narrative tedious.'

Behind the wagon trains, especially those trains with the heaviest losses, came the wolves. They would prowl around the camps at night, sniffing out newly buried cadavers. 'A pack of wolves, fierce and hungry, made the night hideous, from dewy eve till early morn,' wrote one of the Saints in the fourth company. 'When daylight came we found that we had camped where the creatures were expecting to banquet, it being in the centre of a spot where the remains of fifty or sixty persons had been interred. These we discovered, to our horror and dismay, were mostly unearthed.' One diarist, with his imagination run riot, wrote that he could hear hundreds of wolves skulking around his wagon, 'more probably than 500'.

In addition to cholera, the fifth company suffered a famous stampede – famous, not because of the damage it wrought, but because of the classic description of it that was composed by the company Captain, Wilford Woodruff. 'Our encampment passed through one of those horrid scenes today which are so much dreaded by all emigrating companies on the plains, which was a stampede of all the ox teams. No person who has not experienced or witnessed one of those dreadful scenes can form a correct idea of them, for to behold thirty or forty ox teams, with from two to five yoke of oxen in each team, attached to a family wagon of goods and women and children, all in an instant, like the twinkling of an eye, deprived of all reason, sense and government, and filled with a mad, frantic fright, all darting off with lightning speed, each running their own way, roaring, bellowing, rolling and tumbling over each other, wagons upsetting, spilling the goods, smashing their wheels, axles and tongues, women and children in the road for the next teams to trample under their feet as they roar and charge on their way with their yokes, bows and chains flying in every direction, is a scene not easily imagined or described.'

Most of the beneficiaries of the Perpetual Emigrating Fund travelled with the later companies. Ann and Joseph travelled in Shadrach Roundy's company, the last company but one. We know comparatively little about Roundy's company, its members having left but one unexciting diary and two skimpy reminiscences, both written sixty years or more after the event. By the time they were underway, the cholera seems to have run its course and there was only one death in the company. Finding feed for their animals was their gravest concern, which was to be expected, as they were amongst the last wagon trains of what had been the busiest season in the history of the trail. After leaving Indian territory, they split up into smaller units so as to spread their animals over as much of the available pasture as possible. We know they suffered a stampede, but it was small beer compared to Woodruff's.

Although little of Ann and Joseph's experiences on the trail have been recorded, we do know that they and their children arrived safely in Utah, eighty days after leaving the Mississippi, and eight years after leaving Wales. In the next ten years Ann had twelve more children, ten of them twins. Joseph died in 1860, when he was 44 years old, and Ann spent the rest of her life in Union, now part of Salt Lake City. When she died in 1895, she left fifty grandchildren and 21 great-grandchildren.

1851

THE RUSH ENDED as suddenly as it had begun. In California nuggets of gold were no longer found lying underfoot or shining in the gravel of the rivers. To get at them now meant digging deep and investing serious money in expensive machinery. The '49ers', in their letters home, many of which were published in local newspapers, all told the same story – that the rewards were no longer worth the risks and that the rush had run its course. The numbers of fortune-seekers going to California fell from 50,000 in 1850 to a few hundred in 1851. In their stead, many more women and children started moving west, most of them making, not for California but for the rich, empty farm lands of Oregon. Once again, peace returned to the trails. The scars and stains of the previous years were scoured clean and the flowers grew again.

It was a joy to be on the plains in 1851. There was good pasture and fresh camping sites. Cholera kept away and the emigrants, Mormons and 'Babylonians' alike, shared a happy camaraderie. 'At intervals we have been discussing together the possibility of making a custard pie for supper.' writes Mary Snow in her diary. 'I have the rolling pin, our stores afford the eggs, and the delicious milk of a large drove of cows belonging to Oregon emigrants, redolent of the odours of fresh grass, freely offered to us if we will but milk them, furnishes the remaining requisite. All that is wanting now is a place to roll the crust, but by placing two boards on the trunks used as seats in our baggage wagon, we have a fine table which is the envy of all our neighbours. It would almost seem as if this was a land flowing with milk when I state that without any cows of our own, we have had, since we started, plenty of good milk and cream. We have not yet been out of sight of emigrants who have generously shared these things with us.' It was unusual for the Saints and the 'Babylonians' to be so friendly.

Nearly half of the 10,000 people on the trail that year were Mormons on their way to Zion. The majority of them had been waiting in Winter Quarters, too poor to finance their own crossing. At last, the Perpetual Emigrating Fund had come to their rescue. It had been a good year for the new colony on the Great Salt Lake and the coffers of the Perpetual Emigrating Company were full. There had been a successful harvest but, more importantly, the thousands of '49ers' who had passed through Salt Lake City the previous summer had left an unexpected windfall. Some had wanted to trade their tired oxen for fresher, healthier animals; others wanted to get rid of their oxen and buy horses. Some were ill and in need of care, others were tired and wanted to be pampered. And some were just sick of the taste of salted pork and dried beans and wanted fresh meat, potatoes and peas again. And they were ready to pay. Brigham Young was not pleased to see so many 'Babylonians' in his city. His main purpose in coming to the Salt Lake had been to be done with 'Babylon' for ever. But with his usual pragmatism, he agreed to cater for their needs, at a price.

And what a price it proved to be! Soon after the 1849 harvest, 100 lbs of flour was selling in Salt Lake City for $10. At the beginning of June 1850, when the '49ers' started to arrive, the price had risen to $50 and before the end of the month, it was up to $100. Whilst the price of food and fresh oxen were shooting through the roof, the price of what the emigrants had to sell was falling fast. Wagons bought in St Louis for $150 were selling for $5.50, harnesses bought for $30 were selling for $2.

George Morris' story is typical of the Saints' dealings with the 'Babylonians' that summer. During the previous winter, two of George's young oxen had strayed, and when spring came, he set out to find them. On his return, driving his retrieved animals before him, he passed a '49ers' camp in crisis. They could hardly move their wagons, so tired and weak were their oxen. They offered George two of their fully grown, but tired animals, for two of his young, but fit ones. After some hard bargaining, George agreed to accept three of their animals and $10 in cash for two of his. He took his newly-bought animals home and put them to graze on the lush valley grass and, as soon as they were strong and fit again, he sold them to another company of desperate '49ers', this time for four tired oxen, $15 and a wagon that had cost $110 in St Louis. By the time the last of the emigrants had passed through the Valley, George owned ten oxen, four cows, a wagon, clothes, shoes and foodstuffs of all sorts, 'sufficient,' he said, 'to make us more comfortable than we had ever been before.' Recently arrived families were paying off their debts quickly and enough had been gathered into the coffers of the Perpetual Emigrating Fund by the spring of 1851 to pay for 2,500 poor people from Winter Quarters to come to the Valley. They were joined by another 2,500 who had paid for their own transport, making the season's migration one of the most successful in Church history.

But, once again, there were few Welsh emigrants amongst them, even though a fair number had set out from Wales. The *Joseph Badger*, announced *Udgorn Seion* on its front cover in October 1850, 'is scheduled to sail from Liverpool on the 18th of this month, under the presidency of John Morris, from Pembrokeshire. The ship will contain 148 Welsh Saints, and 76 English and 100 of the world ['Of the world' meant non-Mormon, 'Babylonians']… Another Welsh emigration will take place about the beginning of January, and let those who intend to emigrate at that time send their names and their deposits in without delay.' Eighty Welsh accepted the invitation to sail on the second ship. But, again, on arrival in America, hardly any of them chose to continue their journeys beyond the Missouri. They settled either in St Louis or in the Welsh settlement in Council Bluffs, tempted by the easy money and the comfortable life they found there.

One of the few Welshmen to reach Salt Lake City this year

was John Ormond, the son of the John Ormond who had abandoned his poor wife in Marloes in 1849. John Ormond Jnr, was a more attractive figure than his father. He was a determined, practical, hardworking young man and a bona fide, dyed-in-the-wool pioneer. He had received little education and had spent most of his life labouring. Nevertheless, he prospered in America, substantially improving the quality of his life and building a happy home for his wife and children. And he left an interesting diary.

He was born in Marloes, which is in the southern, English-speaking part of Pembrokeshire. His father carried the post, four times a week, between Dale and Haverfordwest. Before he was ten years old, John Jnr was in the saddle, carrying the post for his father. Then, in the early 1840s, the government nationalised the postal service and John Ormond Snr found himself out of work. He became a carrier, freighting goods over the eighty miles between Haverfordwest and Merthyr Tydfil. Once again, his son, by now thirteen years old, was expected to help in the family business. But John Jnr soon realised there was more money to be made in Merthyr Tydfil than in Pembrokeshire and he soon moved to Penydarren, on the outskirts of the town, to work as a coal miner. In that year, 1845, he joined the Mormons. There is little in the diary by way of explanation. 'I enjoyed myself with the Saints,' he wrote. 'They spoke with new tongues and prophesied, healed the sick and cast out devils. Those signs were a common thing in those days of the Church.' As described in a previous chapter, the family, without their mother and youngest brother, had sailed for America in 1849. Later that year, on the Mississippi, cholera had taken away two of his sisters.

The rest of the family continued up the Mississippi. In St Louis, they transferred to a smaller steamboat with a shallower draught, but just beyond St Joseph, with eighty miles still to go to Council Bluffs, the steamboat came to a stop. The river was in flood and she was unable to power her way further upstream. The captain decided to secure his vessel and to look for a comfortable lodging on land for the night. Before morning, he was dead, struck down by cholera. The passengers then decided to continue to Council Bluffs overland but the cost of oxen and a wagon was too much for the Ormond family. Instead, they went to look for work in the nearby village of Savannah. John Snr found work in a lodging house. John Jnr found work in a quarry. The two daughters began to sell confectionery, which they made themselves. By autumn, they had earned enough to buy the oxen and wagon they needed to continue on their way to Council Bluffs.

Having arrived, they rented a cabin and a patch of land and John Jnr buckled down to fencing and preparing the land for growing vegetables. His initial plan had been to sell his produce to the '49ers' as they passed through in the summer, but when he understood how large the rush might be, he had a better idea. He constructed a large log cabin, fourteen feet by eight and seven feet high. He then cut a tree trunk into four slices and shaped the slices into wheels and fitted them on to the underside of the cabin. He was building a mobile fast-food canteen, from which he intended to sell ready meals to the passing trade. He built a counter down the middle, separating his customers from where his father would dispense the food. He then borrowed two oxen and attached them to his snack bar, towed it down to the centre of Council Bluffs and parked it in the middle of the dusty track that was called Main Street. He and his sisters then started making pasties and meat pies which he filled with any game he could shoot – prairie hens, wild pigs, squirrels. And there were fresh vegetables from their garden on the side. The business was an instant success. 'Soon after, my father met me there with a basket of pies and cakes and I returned with the borrowed oxen and as soon as I was home father returned and said, "I have sold all the stuff." So my sisters and I went to work baking and we baked up a lot of stuff thinking it would be enough for the next day but it was not half enough. So we worked day and night for a while and father made money very fast as long as the emigrants stayed there... The third morning when father went to town we could not find the shop, for the boys had lots of fun that night with it and had left it out of sight, so we found it and got it back to the place.' Lest it should happen again, they took the wheels off the cabin and put it up on blocks, and from then on it stayed put.

When the flood of '49ers' began to ease, John Jnr gave up cooking. He worked as a sawyer for a while and then as a butcher. In the spring of 1851, he went to work for a cattleman called David Wilkin, who was preparing to drive a train of eight freight wagons and a herd of a hundred heifers to Salt Lake City. By the beginning of August, Wilkin was ready to leave. Only thirteen people travelled with him. There was a large family from Scotland, mother and father and nine children, there was John Jnr and there was a girl called Jane Lloyd Jones from north Wales. Jane had come to America on her own, although she could not have been more than nineteen years old when she left home. She was probably the only member of her family to have converted to Mormonism.

Young people who embraced Mormonism against the wishes of their parents were often turned out by their families. Elizabeth Davis, for example, was fourteen years old when her father threw her out of the family home in Eglwysbach, in the Conwy Valley. Her descendants say that she carried the scars of this treatment, both physical and emotional, for the rest of her days. A letter has survived which describes the anguish of a family torn apart in similar circumstances. It was written in 1855 in Victoria, near Ebbw Vale, by a David Bowen to his son, Lewis. Lewis and his wife were preparing to emigrate to Utah. 'My dear children and grandchildren. It has been a long time since we saw each other, though we are only a matter of seven or eight miles apart. You, Lewis, are sowing the weeds of Mormonism in the locality, which thing your mother and I scorn to the uttermost degree. Because of this, we cannot conscientiously ask you to our house. For one thing, your mother is too weak to stand the sorrow you have caused her, and you have received advantages to know better than to join such presumptuous, assumptive, deceiving, and vile people.' There follows a page or more of religious arguments and then the old father has this to say. 'All present wish you a share of all blessings, though we cannot associate while you remain Mormons... Whether I see you or not before my grave, I know not. If you live as long as us, you will probably feel very much the sorrow you have caused us in our old age, but I pray the Lord to forgive you all, I must now leave you, and place our burden before the Lord. David Bowen.'

The Mormon Trail was becoming easier to travel every year. Mormon pioneers were expected to improve the route wherever they could so as to ease the passage of those who were to follow. By 1851, the larger rocks and stumps had been removed from the trail and access roads had been dug down through the steep banks to the rivers. John Jnr found that bridges had been built over many of the deeper streams. They were often crude structures, sometimes no more than armloads of saplings thrown into the ditch, but they made the wagon train's progress infinitely easier.

It proved a wet summer, the rivers were high and the mud deep. They had constant trouble with their animals. Herds of buffalo would pass at night, exciting the oxen. Time after time, they stampeded. The Indians were also more of a problem than they had been in previous years. Now that cholera was not so much of a threat, they had returned to their old hunting ground along the banks of the Platte. The changes they saw there disturbed them. The pasture in the valley was being overgrazed by the thousands of animals in the wagon trains and, as a consequence, the buffalo were having to wander further and further from the river to find feed. Eventually, the herd split in two, one half keeping south of the river, the other north and the two halves never came together again. The Indians felt they had a right to demand compensation from every wagon train that crossed their hunting grounds for the damage being done to the pasture. This made the white man, in turn, nervous and distrustful. That summer, there was little love lost between them.

Wilkin knew his small company was an easy target for the Indians. He kept his guns at hand at all times. 'The Indians was very saucy,' wrote John, 'and said they would kill and plunder if

125

they could not have what they wanted in beef and flour and so forth.' Halfway across the plains they saw a band of Cheyenne approaching. 'We stopped and shook hands as was the rule to do with the Indians all along the plains. Pretty soon the road was blocked with Indians who came down from the hills on foot. They would have taken all they wanted but David Wilkin, being owner of most of the outfit, ordered us to close down the covers of the wagons. He, having with him two old pistols, put one in his shirt and the other in his belt so that the Indians thought we were all well armed. They was out of sight in a hurry and we started on our way rejoicing.'

Later the same day, they came across two white men who had been freighting goods to Salt Lake City. 'The Indians came down upon them,' wrote John, 'and just took what they wanted and left them alone there.' The same thing happened to Orson Hyde, one of the Apostles. He attempted to cross the plains that year with only a small company of seven men. They came face to face with three hundred Pawnees. Hyde wrote that he lost about eighty dollars' worth of blankets, guns, clothing, camp furniture, and provisions, besides his horse. What was 'looting' to Hyde was 'demanding compensation' to the Pawnees and, at least, no lives were lost. There was also a photographer on the plains in 1851, attempting to compile a photographic record of the early pioneers. He had travelled as far as Deer Creek, more than halfway to the Valley, when he ran into trouble, falling into the hands of the Crows, the most enthusiastic looters of all the tribes, and was found on the trail a little later, stark naked, apart from a pair of moccasins on his feet and a thong around his waist. His camera, all his equipment and what might have been an invaluable photographic record of life on the trail in the very early days were all gone, but at least he escaped with his life. The name of this intrepid cameraman was Jones. I like to think he was Welsh.

Faced with escalating distrust on both sides, the government decided to act. They called the tribes together for a powwow. Messengers were sent to every chief from the Arkansas River to the Canadian border, from the Missouri to the Green River, inviting them to come with their people to Fort Laramie by the first of September to bury the tomahawk and to smoke a pipe of peace. Over 9,000 of them turned up – Cheyenne, Sioux, Arapahoe, Crow, Arikara and Assinboin – the greatest powwow ever held on the Plains. The Shoshone came with Jim Bridger from their lands around Fort Bridger. The Mandans and the Gros Ventres came with Father de Smet, the famous Catholic missionary, from the upper reaches of the Missouri. They came in all their finery, festooned with eagle feathers and wolf skins and the small horn of the antelope, their faces adorned with white and vermillion, their long black hair streaming behind them. There was much parading in their colourful regalia, much feasting and dancing and, after the celebrating, they came to an agreement. On payment to the Indians of $50,000 annually, the white man was allowed to continue to make use of the trails and the forts he had built along them.

The Indians, in their finery, must have been a sight to behold. Although all the Mormon companies had passed Fort Laramie before early September, many of the diarists wrote excitedly about meeting tribal groups on their way to the powwow. Jean Baker, for example, was travelling with Brown's company alongside Wilkin and John Ormond. On August 28th, she wrote in her diary, 'Captain Brown passed the word for all the wagons to keep as close as possible as there were Indians in the vicinity. Looking forward, I saw a little army of them about a mile distant, coming down the side of the mountain. Our men at once loaded their guns so as to be in readiness in case of an attack, but on our approaching the Indians, they opened their ranks and we passed along without any trouble. The Government agent was with them in a buggy and sitting between his knees was the daughter of the chief; a pretty little creature of about three years old who seemed to be quite pleased at our appearance. The agent told us that these were some of the Shoshones, that 3,000 more were encamped on the banks of the Sweetwater, 20 miles from us, that those present were 90 of the principal warriors, with their families, going to a great counsel of various tribes to endeavour to settle their differences and bury the tomahawk. They made a grand appearance, all on horseback and very gaily dressed; some with lances, others with guns or bows and arrows; also a number of ponies carrying their tents; the men passed on one side of us, the women and children on the other; but all of them well mounted. Their clothing was beautifully trimmed with small beads; altogether it was quite an imposing procession.'

Wilkin's company must have also passed the Shoshone and their agent at the same time as Jean Baker's company. They probably also saw the other 3,000 members of the tribe camped on the Sweetwater further down the trail. But John makes no mention of them. He had other things on his mind. Wilkin's company was in trouble. Their clothes were in tatters, their shoes were worn through and they were running short of food. Getting Jane and the rest of the company safely to the end of their journey was now John's priority. 'We travelled along through sage and gravel,' he wrote, 'barefooted and half worn out in every respect. Our grub was very short and it gave out entirely before we came into Salt Lake so we had to do without for two days, when I was dispatched to the city on horseback to get some provisions and I made good time, you bet. I got some beef, potatoes and flour.' He returned to the company with the food and finished the rest of the journey with them, entering Salt Lake City on September 28th.

All that winter he continued to work for David Wilkin, looking after his heifers. But when spring came, he started his own business, making clay bricks, or adobes as they were called. 'As soon as the weather was warm enough to dry adobes, I went to work at adobe making and I had very good luck. I sold enough to pay my board bill and pay for a team to haul rock and other stuff to build a home on my lot.' For his services on the plains Wilkin had given him two oxen and $60 in cash. He used the money to buy land in the middle of Salt Lake City and sold the oxen to buy lumber to build his home. 'By July 20, I had a house built and finished in a rough state. The house was sixteen by twenty-eight. It was plastered, it had two rooms, three doors and two windows. I had the lot ploughed and planted with potatoes and corn. I accomplished all this and paid up all as I went along with my work. I done most of it myself. I made my furniture out of rough lumber and it answered the purpose.' And in August 1852, a year after he and Jane had arrived in the Valley, they were married.

And then, exactly a year after their wedding, Jane died in childbirth. 'The 25th of August, I was left alone again,' wrote John. 'But my father and two sisters came in the year before, so I had somebody to comfort me a little. I then sold out all I had and received nearly $500. Now what to do I didn't know, for if I remained single, all my money would go and I thought the best thing for me to do was hunt up another companion. I should not have done so so soon but young women were scarce at that time. They would all marry the first chance they had. So there came along a train with some young women in it and I thought I had better look up one, and again settle down. So I spoke to the first one I saw out of that train and in a very short time she said yes. And in a short time we were married.'

For the pioneers, there was urgency about finding a partner. As John noted, suitable unmarried women were scarce. A survey was made of the unmarried Welsh women aboard the *Josiah Bradlee* when that ship sailed from Liverpool in February 1850. Among the ninety Welsh on board, there were eight young women of marriageable age. One of them married on board the ship, within six days of leaving harbour, and a second married twenty days out. Another two were married on the Mississippi and two more were in lasting relationships before reaching St Louis. Only two of the party remained unclaimed and one of these was brutally murdered by a rejected lover one dark night on the Mississippi. More of her sad story later.

Quick courtships were especially common amongst widows and widowers with young children. John Williams of Denbigh lost his wife on the trail. His son described how 'expecting soon to leave for our new home, my father deemed it advisable to seek for someone to be a mother to the children, many of whom were quite small – scarcely able to dress themselves. And under these circumstances a household assistant was greatly needed. Father realized this and felt that to fail meant to him a miserable home the remainder of his life. But the all wise providence opened the way. Elizabeth Humphreys, whose husband died on the plains, was in the same fix as father. Both needed a home, so they married.' Margaret Richards wrote that when she married David Richards of Nant-y-glo, the marriage offered her security and safety, something, she said, that she had not experienced before. 'It was not,' she added, 'a matter of love'.

John Ormond's new wife, Martha Jenkins, was the daughter of a Fishguard family. Her father, Enos Jenkins, kept a shop in the town. She was 27 years old, a little past the marrying age of the time, and travelling on her own, probably because, like Jane, she alone in her family had accepted the Mormon faith. It is difficult to imagine how abandoned and unloved an emigrant like Martha would have felt on the plains. Susan Witbeck was seventeen and travelling alone. As she approached the end of her long journey to Salt Lake City, she realised that members of her company, who had been her companions over the past months, were preparing to part and go their separate ways. 'For days before we reached Salt Lake, relatives of some of our group had come out to meet them and take them to the homes of loved ones waiting for them. Our company was constantly getting smaller. As each happy load pulled on away from us, it began to slowly dawn on my mind that there would be no one to meet me, and no home to go to, when I reached my destination. The feeling of loneliness kept increasing, until, the last night we camped before reaching Salt Lake, I could control my feelings no longer. I wandered far away from the camp, threw myself upon the ground, and gave way to all my stored up heartache.' Martha Jenkins probably felt equally alone, unable to face her new life without a companion. Her company reached the Valley sometime between September 15th and 20th. She married John on the 24th.

A Mormon wedding on the trail was a simple affair. According to Dan Jones, 'a young couple could meet for the very first time at nine o'clock in the morning and, if they so wished, be husband and wife according to the laws of the land and the church, before midday.' John Gerber decided one morning that it was time he and his sweetheart, Mary, got married. He asked the captain's permission, which was readily granted. That evening, at the end of the day's trek, 'Mary and myself dressed up preparatory to being married. We attended the meeting in the centre of the corral about 8 p.m. After singing, the Captain made a few remarks concerning camp duties. Bro. Smith announced to the Saints my desire to be united in marriage to Miss Anna Mary Knapp and asked if there were any objections. There being none, he performed the ceremony making Sister Knapp and myself man and wife. After the meeting a number of the Elders and Saints congratulated us. We retired to our tent where Bro. and Sis. Schramm and Sis. L. Dolder took supper with us. I retired with my wife about 11 o'clock. The weather was fine.'

There is no evidence that the hasty weddings of the Wild West were any less successful than conventional ones. Charles Derry's wife died on September 7th, 1854. On October 25th, 'a young woman of a fair complexion and a lovable face passed me by. I caught a glance of her soft blue eyes and instantly the thought flashed to my mind that she would be my wife. I followed the fair-haired damsel to her wagon and without further ceremony I said, 'Sister, my name is Charles Derry; I have been in this valley three weeks. My wife lies on yonder mountains, having been dead seven weeks. I have two little children, one is sick. I have no home at present. I am a blacksmith by trade, and I hope to be able to make a living. If under these conditions you will consent to be my wife and a mother to my children, I will be a husband to you in every sense of the word.' The girl accepted his proposal and, three days later, they were married. 'Over forty-seven years have rolled away since that day,' wrote Derry, 'and that bond remains unbroken, not a thread of it shattered.'

The same is also true of John Ormond and Martha Jenkins. Their marriage proved long and happy. By 1851, only 5,000 of the 30,000 Mormons in Utah, were living in Salt Lake City. The rest were scattered along the foothills of the eastern range, from Ogden in the north to Parowan in the south. John and Martha settled in Brigham City, fifty miles from the Idaho border, in the shadow of the Wellsville Mountains, on the banks of Box Elder Creek, and there John built another home. He could turn his hand to many skills. He farmed, he worked as a builder, he ran a saw mill, he invested in a threshing machine, he worked on the railway, he became an engine driver. Seven children were born to them, six boys and a girl. Martha's upbringing as the daughter of shopkeepers in Fishguard prompted her to open her own furniture shop in Brigham City. When she died in 1904, in her 79th year, John took over the business with one of his sons. He died in 1913, in his 82nd year.

1852

IN 1852, THE Americans succumbed again to the enchantments of the west. 'Go west, young man!' was the slogan of the hour. 'Go west and grow up with the country!' Over 50,000 followed the Platte that year, not all of them bound for the goldfields by any means, and not all of them looking for land to cultivate or a farming life for their families. There were bankers and barbers, bookkeepers and builders, entertainers and entrepreneurs, merchants and market gardeners, all trades and all professions, from all walks of life. They imagined a good living might be made serving the needs of the 100,000 or more who now worked out west. They might have read of the two-acre field of onions in California which sold for $2,000 or the apples sold in the Sacramento Valley for $1.50 each. And they might also have heard that the continental trails were not as dangerous as they once had been, that bridges and ferries were becoming abundant and that it was now possible to buy food and other necessities at rudimentary trading posts scattered along the way.

Ten thousand Mormons joined them on the trail, the greatest number ever to have crossed the plains in any one year. Once again, the coffers of the Perpetual Emigrating Fund were full to overflowing. Brigham Young decided that one last push should be made to clear the camps along the Missouri and to bring the remaining poor to Utah. Between 1,300 and 1,400 of them were on the trail this year. Then he turned his attention to those Saints, many Welsh amongst them, who were postponing the last leg of their journey because life was proving so comfortable in Council Bluffs. Brigham Young was never afraid to harangue his people when he felt it necessary. He viewed it as his calling 'not to coddle, but to prod the Saints, not to praise them, but to warn, instruct, move them to greater effort.' 'You've all led comfortable existences, improving the quality of your lives as you've never done before,' he said, 'but now you're reluctant to give it up. What are you waiting for? Have you any good excuse for not coming? No! You have a far better chance than we had when we started as pioneers to find this place; you have better teams and more of them. You have as good food and more of it; you have as much natural strength as we have had to come; our women and children have walked here, and have been blessed in walking here, and barefoot too except when now and again they were given skins by the Indians to make moccasin; and cannot you do the same?'

Brigham Young was not a man to cross. The Welsh hurriedly prepared to leave Council Bluffs. One diarist noted, as he passed through the town that spring, that 'most of the Mormons were on their way to the Salt Lake' and that 'about one in three of the houses of the town were for sale.' In the *Frontier Guardian*, the Church's newspaper in Council Bluffs, there appeared regular notices of forthcoming auctions. 'Gentlemen, see here! A special Bargain! 160 acres, the whole lying above the wet land and without a single stump to be seen in the fields. It is to be offered at a very low price or exchanged for 4- to 7-year-old oxen or a sturdy wagon.'

But it was very much a buyer's market and the Welsh, like everyone else, had difficulty selling their properties. When Joseph Parry, the nephew of the John Parry who founded the Tabernacle Choir, had first arrived in Council Bluffs in May 1850, he had bought a small farm. Now, two years later, on Brigham's summons, he was preparing to leave for the Valley. He feared he would not be able to sell the property, but at the last minute he received an offer of one fifth of its value, which he gratefully accepted. Samuel Leigh was not so lucky. 'We could not sell our place when we left,' he wrote. Samuel was a school teacher from Llanelli, a reasonably wealthy man who had owned two houses in Wales. When he decided to emigrate with Dan Jones on the *Buena Vista*, he had sold both properties and with the money had bought George A. Smith's farm, one of the best in Council Bluffs. But he too failed to find a buyer. 'I left the house, yards and all the surroundings in the possession of a brother who had come from the old country. He gave me five dollars for what was left in the house. It required about five dollars to pay fares to ferry our teams and wagons across the river.'

The Welsh abandoned their settlement in Council Bluffs en masse. The meeting hall they had built together was washed away in a flood in the late Fifties. They travelled across the plains together, forming a Welsh company, one of the twenty companies that left the Missouri that year. In the company there were about 250 people travelling in fifty wagons. Although the Welsh were in the majority, there were some English and a few French also travelling with them. The most trustworthy and interesting diary describing the journey is the one written by the long-suffering and accident-prone David D. Bowen, he who arrived on the *Hartley* in 1849 and who, in St Louis that year, had lost his wife and daughter and mother-in-law in tragic circumstances. Since then, he had been working at numerous coal pits in the St Louis area, earning good money. He had married again, to Phoebe Evans, a Merthyr girl, who had also come out on the *Buena Vista*.

Nothing came easily to David Bowen. Wherever he went, he seemed to pull down hornets' nests on his head. In January, he had decided to obey Brigham Young's call to come to the Valley and had set out from St Louis, with Phoebe and their newborn baby, to join the Welsh company in Council Bluffs. He shared the cost of a wagon and oxen with an Englishman called Thomas Vargo, but, halfway to Council Bluffs, they had quarrelled. David, true to nature and stubborn as a mule, had refused to bury the hatchet and had walked away, selling his half of the wagon to Vargo. With the money he had bought a steamboat ticket to Council Bluffs for Phoebe and the baby. He had then followed them there on foot, driving his animals, a pair of oxen and a cow, before him. In Council Bluffs he bought two more oxen and with them made a deal with an American called Daniel Sherar, who had a wagon but no oxen. David agreed to haul his wagon, fully loaded, to Utah and, on arrival, to receive the wagon as payment. But in Deer Creek, a hundred miles beyond Fort Laramie, they quarrelled. Sherar denied that he had ever promised David the wagon and David refused to haul his wagon a step further. Neither could move without the other so they eventually had to agree to a temporary truce. But on arrival in the Valley, Sherar again refused to give him the wagon and David took him to court. The judgment was that the wagon should be shared, a half each. David sold his half to another man for a load of timber. Unfortunately, the timber was in San Pete, a hundred miles away, and David now had no wagon in which to haul it back to Salt Lake City. The diary is full of similar plans which, more often than not, unravelled messily. Who better than David Bowen, therefore, to describe the confusion of the Welsh company as they prepared to set out on that first morning of their trek?

'This morning the hue and cry was everybody to be ready for starting on our long journey. After breakfast all the men were yoking their cattle and the women preparing their cooking utensils in their respective wagons, which made our camp all alive. I had a deal of trouble with my cattle for they was not broken, but very wild and young. The day we started from winter quarters was very hot. I laboured so hard with the cattle and sweat so much that I had the headache that bad I was almost blind all day. Sometime in the afternoon Bishop Davies ran against another wagon and broke his axle. The camp had to stay that day and part of the next.' Not the most auspicious of starts and worse was to follow. A nine-year-old member of the company was killed in the cruellest fashion, run over by his own family's wagon.

This boy was the son of William Howell, a much respected Church member, who had himself died in Council Bluffs only a few months earlier. When Mormonism first came into his life, Howell was the owner of a draper's shop in Aberdare and an important figure among south Wales Baptists. He had apparently worked for a while as a Baptist missionary in Brittany, although he spoke little French or Breton. The Saints immediately put his experience to good use by sending him to Le Havre to establish a Mormon mission. He took with him a bundle of French and English tracts to be distributed in the town and harbour, but Howell and his pamphlets met with little success. The conservative Catholics of France proved much tougher nuts to crack than the radical Non-conformists of Wales. William returned to Aberdare to fetch his nine-year-old daughter, Ann. Quite what he intended Ann's role to be is not clear. Perhaps he believed that his enemies would be less likely to attack if he was in the company of a child. For the next months, Ann shared the trials and vicissitudes of her father's life, often fleeing from persecutors, often sleeping under the stars. They spent much of their time in Saint-Malo and there, in an old chapel in the town, William organised the first meeting of the Church of Jesus Christ of Latter-day Saints in France. Only six people attended the historic meeting. It could hardly be called a great success, but it was the first. At the end of 1850, three American missionaries relieved William. One of the three was John Taylor, the missionary who had converted John Bennion, a man who had previous experience of proselytising in difficult Catholic territory, having been a missionary in Ireland. Today, Taylor is recognized as the father of the Mormon Church in France, but it was William Howell who first pushed the door ajar.

Within weeks, William was leading a company of 245 Saints across the Atlantic. Such was the fervency and enthusiasm of his leadership that fifty of the non-Mormon passengers joined them and asked to be baptized. And all the deckhands and galley staff of the steamboat that took them up the Missouri to Council Bluffs also converted to the faith and left the ship. William, with Martha his wife, and their three children, chose not to go on to Utah that year but to remain with the Welsh on the Missouri. His intention, perhaps, was to allow his wife to give birth to their fourth child in relative comfort. Or perhaps he realized that his own health was a cause of concern. Towards the end of May, he opened a shop in Council Bluffs. In June, Martha gave him another son. In September and October, at Brigham Young's insistence, he began to prepare to leave for the Valley but, in November, he was dead – 35 years old, and a Mormon for only four years.

In accordance with his dying wishes, Martha and her children set out for the Salt Lake in the spring. She was a brave woman, but what happened next would have broken the strongest of hearts. William, her nine-year-old son, was crushed under the wheels of her wagon. It was a horrendously common accident on the plains. Children slipped and fell as they clambered aboard the moving wagons and there was no way of bringing the wagons to a sudden stop. Sometimes they would crawl under the wagons during the midday break, and fall asleep in the shade. And the wagon would start up again, without the driver realizing that a child lay beneath his wheels. And it was thus that William died. To add to her pain, it was probably Martha herself who was driving. But, like so many of these remarkable pioneer women, having buried her son, she pushed on.

In his diary, David Bowen mentions another brave Welsh woman who was on the plains that year. Her name was Rachel Rowland, 22 years old, from Hirwaun near Merthyr Tydfil. Two weeks before leaving Wales, she had married William, a puddler in the iron works in Hirwaun, and his children from his first marriage were with them on the voyage. Rachel and William had stayed three winters with the Welsh in Council Bluffs and by 1852 had produced two more children of their own. That spring they had all gone to visit William's brother who was working down in St Louis. They were on their way back to Council Bluffs, travelling on the *Saluda*, an old steamboat which had seen better days. On her deck, there were between two hundred and 250 passengers, all eager to get to Council Bluffs and none more eager than the captain himself. But the waters of the spring thaw were running off the mountains and slabs of ice were being washed down the river. For five days the *Saluda* tried, again and again, to round one particularly difficult bend near the village of Lexington. Time after time, she had been swept back by the current. On the morning of April 9th, the captain decided to give it one more go. He loaded as much wood as he could into her furnace and ordered as much steam as she was capable of raising. Gradually the *Saluda*'s bow pushed out into the stream. Slowly she began to make headway. Then, suddenly, forty feet from land, the boilers exploded and the old boat was ripped apart from stem to stern. The buildings around the landing shook as though an earthquake had hit them, and the debris of the explosion was scattered over the village in tiny pieces.

David Bowen heard of the accident whilst he and Thomas Vargo were making their quarrelsome way up from St Louis. 'Among the victims,' he wrote, 'was our old friend William Rowland and family from Hirwaun. He and one of his children were blown overboard and never were seen anymore. His wife, Rachel, was in bed with her own children when a piece of the deck fell on them and killed both children at once.' It was believed that about a hundred people were killed in the explosion, although the exact number was never known. Rachel survived, albeit with her leg badly broken. She remained a cripple for the rest of her days. Two of William's daughters by his previous marriage also survived, although both were badly burnt. Two and a half months later, all three were back on the plains again, most probably in the Welsh company.

Katurah Vaughan of Llangyndeyrn was also on the trail this summer. She, too, had lost her husband on the Missouri. Four months after he died, Katurah had given birth to their son, but the baby had also died. She managed, somehow, to get to Salt Lake City, and, like many widows in similar circumstances, found a new husband as soon as she got there. Today she is remembered as the great-great-great-grandmother of Lynne Cheney, wife of Dick Cheney, Vice President of the United States from 2001 to 2009.

There are so many of these women, intrepid and steadfast, survivors all. Gwen Lloyd from Llanfrothen lost her husband and one of her children to cholera on the Mississippi, within hours of each other. Gwen could not speak much English and the journey to Council Bluffs with her two remaining children and an eleven-month-old baby could not have been easy. Her family in Wales managed to contact her and begged her to return home but Gwen was adamant that she would finish her journey. She sold her husband's clothes to buy a cow and agreed to share a wagon with an old, half blind emigrant. When they reached the edge of the Valley, a deputation of Welshmen came out to meet them, bearing gifts of flour, melons and fresh vegetables. Amongst them was a man Gwen recognized from back home. He came to her and offered her a basket of fruit and then asked her to marry him. When she refused, he took his present back and insisted that she pay for the fruit she'd eaten. It was often said that the Wild West was kinder to dogs and men than to horses and women.

In this year, seventeen-year-old Ann Rogers, from Amroth in Pembrokeshire, was another who came to the Valley after a journey that would have tested the steadfastness of a saint. She was one of a large family, the youngest of nine children. The three eldest had refused to go because they were not believers. Another of Ann's sisters drowned two years before they set out. Then her mother had died and her father had married again and had one child by his new wife. A family of eight therefore boarded the *Josiah Bradley* in Liverpool in 1850. One of her sisters married on the *Josiah Bradley* six days out of Liverpool and, in St Louis, her brother Thomas decided to leave them to look for work. A few days later, as their steamer made its way up the river, Elizabeth, Ann's favourite sister, went on deck with a boy she'd met on the *Josiah Bradley*. He had asked her to marry him earlier in the voyage and she had turned him down. That night, he asked again, and again she refused. In a rage, he strangled her. Later that night, the steamboat pulled in to the bank and there, in the moonlight, Elizabeth was buried. Ann remembered it as the saddest day of her life.

The family was now down to five. Her father had not been well since leaving Amroth. He decided they should stay for a while with the Welsh in Council Bluffs. He bought a farm there but the work proved too much for him and, in August 1850, he too died. Then Henry, the last of her brothers, was offered a job in a wagon train bound for California. He stopped writing after a few months and they never heard from him again. Only Ann, her stepmother and her half-sister now remained to complete the journey. They were not on good terms, but Ann had little choice but to accompany them on the trail. They made a deal with another family to share a wagon but out on the plains, the two families quarrelled and decided to part. The wagon was sawn in half, each family taking a set of wheels and one oxen. Ann and her stepmother and half-sister struggled on. Soon after their arrival in Salt Lake City, the stepmother married again and left with her daughter to live in her new husband's home. Ann was alone. Six months later, she married her employer, a man 29 years her senior.

The Captain of the Welsh company was William Morgan, who had been in charge of the settlement in Council Bluffs. He wrote three letters whilst on the trail, which were subsequently published in *Udgorn Seion*. In these letters, he rhapsodises about their life on the plains. 'We would be glad if our brothers and our sisters were closer to us so that they might see the saying 'A land flowing with milk' become a reality. In our camp, plenty of milk is thrown out casually, as if it were the water that three or four Merthyr colliers had bathed in, for we have more than we can use, and no-one in need of it.' He tends to overegg the pudding, seeking, no doubt, to encourage more Welsh Saints to emigrate. 'Although the journey was long, I considered it nothing but enjoyment every step of the way.' Other descriptions of the journey are not so rosy. 'This trip was no pleasure trip, but a hard road to travel,' wrote Joseph Parry. 'We had several deaths. The Indians got away with some of our horses and cattle. We were three months on the plains.' They also had some difficulty in crossing the Platte and the alkali poison killed a number of their animals.

William Morgan filled many pages describing one particular story, a strange incident that doesn't quite ring true. 'One day, totally unawares, I happened to come into the midst of about three or four hundred Indians, namely the Sioux. As was my custom, I was on horseback, riding ahead of the camp to look for the trail and for a comfortable place to have lunch; and having gone ahead of the camp for about two miles, I saw two of them coming as fast as their horses could carry them to meet me. I was like king Henry, ready to say, "kingdom", but not "for a horse", for I had a good one under me, but "for being in camp". It was too late to turn back, it was better to go forward, and it was not long before their Indian majesty and myself met each another. He greeted me, "How do, Mormon good." I thought, by then, that they were not as bad as I had believed; I went ahead between the two chieftains, in their magisterial resplendence, till we arrived at their camp, which was about a mile and a half from the place where we had met... They behaved towards me in an extremely gentlemanly fashion. Their chiefs spread their blanket on the ground, motioning for me to sit down to smoke what they called the "pipe of peace", as I understood through the translator, Huntington. The manner of having the pipe handed around, in each group, is like the shilling jug in the taverns of the old country which is handed round to all the members of a group, and each one in his turn takes a drink. So it is with this pipe: the chief takes two or three puffs and then passes it on to the next one and so on round the circle until the chief has it again. Refusing to sit down with them to smoke is a sign among them that the one who refuses is envious... When the camp came, we took up a collection for them, such as a spoonful or two of sugar, cakes &c., and their majesties accepted our gifts... Although the red boys, from what I could observe, were completely harmless, yet I do not say that they will not steal if they have the chance; but I can say this much... nothing was stolen from us nor was an insult ever given to any of us.'

It is not a convincing tale. How did the Indians know William Morgan was a Mormon? And who is Huntington, who appears so suddenly? And how did Morgan's company know where to find him? The patronising tone ('red boys', 'their Indian majesty'), the weak jokes ('my kingdom for being in camp') and the over-elaborate language ('magisterial resplendence)' are irritating. The story doesn't quite add up, especially when one learns of the similar experiences of other companies that year. In William West Lane's company, for example, which had left the Missouri two days after the Welsh, Davis Clark was also captured by Indians. 'They were armed with bows and arrows, spears and tomahawks. They drew their weapons and made motions as if they were going to chop me to pieces... They took me five or six miles to their camp.' There he was pulled from his horse and thrown into a tepee. He was obviously very frightened, as William Morgan must have been. 'A strange looking man then entered the tepee. I did not know whether he was an Indian or White man. He looked a bit like both. He had on a buckskin coat, fringed and beaded, pants made of scotch plaid, a hat on his head and moccasins on his feet. He asked me in English how I came to be there. I told him the circumstances. He said he was part French and lived with the Indians.' He was probably the son of an Indian mother and a French-Canadian Mountain Man father. Huntington, the mysterious man in William Morgan's story, is likely to have been of a similar parentage. The Frenchman agreed to take Davis Clark back to his camp in exchange for a bottle of whisky. In the camp, he would have had a chance to assess the strength of the company. The next morning, fifty warriors, in war paint and fully armed, led by the Frenchman, descended on the camp and demanded salt, sugar, blankets, shirts and whisky from the emigrants.

Another similar incident occurred to John B. Walker's company that year. 'A hundred Indians took D.M. Burbank a prisoner. We thought he would be killed but the Chief gave him up to us if we would give them flour, sugar and coffee.' No doubt William Morgan's abduction was of the same order. He had been kidnapped so that he might be exchanged for the 'spoonful or two of sugar, cakes, &c.' He laughs off the incident, giving the impression that he had the situation well under control, but the Indians were dangerous and not to be taken lightly. 'Several nights ago,' wrote Davis Clerk, 'some

Indians crept close to camp to steal horses. The horses snorted, one of the guards walked toward the Indians, and got shot by them. He died after reaching the Valley.' William Morgan was lucky.

On the evening of September 26th, the Welsh company was approaching the end of their journey. As it grew dark, they heard the sound of a wagon coming quickly towards them. 'All were straining their eyes to see what was coming,' wrote William Morgan, 'and before long the lead watchmen shouted out, "Welsh from Salt Lake". To our great joy who were they but Thomas Jones, Hirwaun; Morgan Hughes, Pontyates; and William, son of Evan Jones, Mill Street, Aberdare. They had travelled thirty to forty miles to welcome us, with a load of the fruits of the Valley – watermelons, mush melons, potatoes, pickle cucumbers, grapes, etc.' On September 25th, the Welsh company entered the city, 'all healthy and our hearts thankful to our Father. We had travelled 1,130 miles, without a furrow of land on our path being owned by a civilized man.'

But they were not the last of the Welsh to reach the Valley that season. Behind them, still on the trail, there was one other Welshman. In time, this man would become the most powerful and the most successful businessman of all the Welsh in Utah. He would build an industrial empire that made him one of the richest men in the state. He would become one of Brigham Young's confidants. He would dominate the Welsh community. But he would also commit a crime so heinous that the memory of it continues to darken his reputation even to this day.

His name was Elias Morris. He was born in Llanfair Talhaiarn in Denbighshire, the son of a stonemason. His father worked for the Bamford-Hesketh family, helping to build the walls of their medieval fantasy, Gwrych Castle. Elias was an intelligent lad. As a twelve year old, he was sent to learn his father's trade with the master craftsmen of the construction industry in Manchester and Liverpool. But he often returned to Wales to undertake contracts with his father and, on one of these visits, in 1849, in Abergele, he heard another stonemason, John Parry, son of the John Parry who founded the Tabernacle

Choir, preaching Mormonism and was convinced. Two days later John Parry took Elias to meet Samuel Brookes, the lighthouse keeper of the Point of Ayr lighthouse on Talacre Beach near Holywell in Flintshire. It was there, in the sea at the foot of the lighthouse, that Elias Morris was baptized.

He launched himself enthusiastically into his work for the Church. 'From that moment, I never ceased testifying to the Gospel of Christ restored to the earth in these last days.' Within a year he had formed a strong branch of sixty members in Abergele. They would meet in a room in the Bull Hotel where there is today a plaque to commemorate those meetings. 'We were mobbed and persecuted much,' wrote Elias. 'The different sects united together so as to disturb our peace.' Typically, he retaliated, not with fists, but by bringing an action against his persecutors in the local Magistrates' Court. 'The mob party were fined, besides paying the cost. The magistrate reprimanded them for their un-Christian-like conduct towards us Latter-day Saints. From this time the public persecution ceased.'

This tough, talented, hardworking young man came to the notice of John Taylor, the missionary who later took over from William Howell in Le Havre. Taylor had been charged by Brigham Young to investigate the possibility of establishing a beet sugar industry in Utah. It was a crop that seemed to grow well in the Valley and one which, Brigham hoped, would make them self-sufficient in sugar. Taylor had studied the process and was now gathering a team of talented engineers and managers from among the British Saints to help create the new plant in Utah. One of those he recruited was Elias Morris, then 27 years old.

All the machinery needed to refine beet sugar was ordered from a company in Liverpool, over 125 tons of furnaces, presses, evaporators, boiling pans and piping. The man Taylor chose to oversee the transportation of this load, plus half a ton of sugar beet seed, to New Orleans was Elias Morris. Poor Elias! He had hoped to sail to America in the company of his seventeen-year-old wife-to-be, Mary Parry. Instead, he sailed with a sugar factory. They reached New Orleans safely and transferred to a steamboat which took them upriver to Fort Leavenworth, where the machinery was to be loaded on to wagons for the final stage of the journey. Elias then continued up the river to Council Bluffs, to collect the forty wagons that had been built there for this purpose. He probably also knew that Mary, his intended bride would be there. She had crossed the Atlantic a month earlier on the *Ellen Maria* with a group of about sixty Welsh. He found her, married her there and then and they both returned to Fort Leavenworth with the wagons. The next problem was to find oxen to haul the wagons. This proved to be more of a problem. Because of the weight of their cargo, over three tons per wagon, they needed up to eight yokes, sixteen animals per wagon. They eventually succeeded in buying four hundred but they were mostly young animals, not used to the yoke.

The man chosen to be Captain of the wagon train was a 29-year-old Englishman named Philip De La Mare. Elias was to be his deputy. De La Mare had only recently arrived in America and, like Elias, had no experience whatsoever of driving wagons or handling oxen. Things began to go wrong from the outset. 'The first day's travel was but four or five miles,' wrote Elias in his journal. 'In that distance four or five axles were broken, the cattle being very mild, we teamsters very green, the wagons very badly made with bad timber and green, and the loads very heavy.' The wagons proved totally inadequate for the task. They were given away to a company of poor Saints who were preparing to leave Fort Leavenworth for the Valley and forty stronger, heavier animals bought in their stead. To add to Elias' and Philip De La Mare's responsibilities and worries, the company of poor Saints attached themselves to their company and looked to them for leadership. Off they went again. 'On account of the long delay before starting we ran short of provisions before we got three parts of the way.' In truth, their own naivety and inexperience contributed more to the food shortage. They had been tricked into buying what they thought was flour but what turned out to be mostly Plaster of Paris.

Halfway to Utah a company of missionaries, on their way back to Council Bluffs from Salt Lake City, crossed their path and were perturbed by what they saw. They sent Brigham Young a message warning him that this company was in trouble. 'This appears to be the last company of saints on the route, and it is evident that unless a strong re-enforcement of team soon comes to their assistance, they must suffer with the cold, and will have difficulty to get to the Valley before the snows of winter meet them. The cattle belonging to this company are poor indeed; many of them can scarce stand on their feet and it appears to be with the greatest difficulty they can move along. Their loads generally are very heavy... The worn out condition of the teams proves that the teamsters do not understand the nature of cattle. If this company had been under the charge of an old Yankee farmer, the cattle would doubtless have been in a much better condition. Inexperienced Englishmen or Frenchmen are not the men to drive teams across the Plains as heavily loaded as these are... The gloom and downcast countenances, of both men and women, shows that they feel this a very severe hardship, and they are evidently nearly discouraged. This company generally are living on 4 ounces of flour each per day; and if they are not met soon with both team and provisions, they will undoubtedly suffer.'

Four ounces of flour a day! Four ounces hardly cover the bottom of a frying pan. No wonder they were 'gloomy and downcast'. But the missionaries were not told the half of it. Philip De La Mare and Elias had abandoned the heaviest loads back on the Sweetwater, on one of the bleakest and most exposed sections of the trail. The company had been caught there in a violent snowstorm some days earlier. Ten of the oxen had died, frozen to death, and eighty had strayed and could not be found. They did not now have enough to move the heaviest wagons, so they had left them on the far side of South Pass, with six men to guard them, and to continue the search for the lost animals. These unfortunate men were also expected to hunt for their own food, although what they could have shot 7,000 feet up in the Rockies with winter fast approaching is difficult to fathom. The remaining animals were used to haul the wagons of the rest of the company and the wagons of the poor Saints down from South Pass, and a rider was sent on ahead to get help from the Valley, two hundred miles away. Two days later, the six men in South Pass found some of the lost animals and the heavy wagons began to move again. But, at the crossroads where the Mormon Trail leaves the California Trail, they took the wrong turning and went forty miles out of their way. They survived by eating some of the oxen. Eventually they made contact with the rest of the train and the wagons came together again. Help arrived from the Valley, bringing fresh oxen. Most of these were given to the poor emigrants, allowing them to reach the end of their journey before winter set in. De La Mare and Elias remained with the heavy wagons. Winter was now upon them.

For another ten days, the heavy wagons struggled to make headway, forty teams slowly straining their way towards the Valley, cutting a path through the heavy drifts, the melting snow rising in steam from their flanks, their cumbersome loads lurching and slithering behind them, down Echo Canyon, where the trail crosses the river fifteen times, through Dixie Hollow, past Dead Ox Canyon and Little Dutch Hollow. Mary accused Elias of worrying more about his boilers than about her. 'My love', he replied, 'boilers rust, you don't.' Ahead of them was Big Mountain, the last great hurdle in their path. It proved one hurdle too many. They abandoned the wagons at the foot of the mountain. Cocooned in the snow, they would be safe enough. The following spring they were hauled out again to complete their journey and to finally be put to work. But the factory proved a dismal failure. There was too much alkali in the soil to grow the right variety of beet and not a grain of sugar was produced. After only a few months, the machinery was dismantled and adapted for use in the production of linseed oil and paper. For Elias Morris, Brigham Young had other plans.

1853

THE YEAR 1853 proved to be difficult for the Mormon pioneers, but for reasons that had nothing to do with conditions on the trail. Indeed, it appeared at first that 1853 was to be a golden year. Everything, both on the high seas and on the Plains, seemed to be conspiring to make the journey to the Salt Lake easier than ever before. Firstly, a new act had come into force in Britain, laying down higher standards of comfort and hygiene on British passenger ships. Hot food was to be prepared for the passengers each day. There was to be one cook for every hundred passengers, the cost of the food and of its preparation was to be included in the price of a ticket. Separate accommodation was to be provided for single men and women. Toilets and washing facilities were to be made available for all. To these, the Mormons added their own rules. Every morning, the passenger areas on the ship were to be thoroughly cleaned by the passengers. In good weather, every passenger, including the elderly and the sick, were to be brought up on deck into the fresh air. Every night they met to discuss the day's problems and to pray for help in solving them.

The trail, also, was becoming easier and safer to travel. There were now ferries on the Elkhorn and the Loup, the two tributaries of the Platte that had previously posed the greatest difficulties for the emigrants. More and more bridges were being built, even over the smaller rivers. Dozens of new trading posts were springing up. Even near Devil's Gate and Independence Rock, two of the remotest regions on the trail, the emigrants describe seeing two or three tepees where a few goods were for sale, admittedly at vastly inflated prices. One diarist wrote that he visited a trading post a few miles east of Raw Hide Creek. 'As the affair was made up of Frenchmen, Indians, squaws, horses, mules, oxen, dogs, trees, a shady bower, a sheep pen, a wagon, and a tent, it was most picturesque. Cattle in by no means good condition were from ninety to a hundred dollars per yoke. I noticed that nearly all these trading posts were kept by Frenchmen, who were mostly married to Indian women.' He was probably referring to French-Canadians.

One of these Frenchmen built a famous bridge over the Platte, close to where the city of Casper stands today. The toll for using the bridge varied according to the level of the water in the river. When it was in flood and there was no other way of crossing, the charges were at their highest. It was said that the owner spent $5,000 building his bridge and that he made $40,000 in 1853 alone. In addition to the bridge, he had a shop and a smithy nearby, where he would exchange weary animals for fresh, making a huge profit on every deal. Having spent a few weeks on the rich pasture around the post, the tired animals would soon be as good as new and ready to be traded again. Despite the emigrating season being short and hectic, the French-Canadian traders made a very good living. The daughter of one of them remembered her father pouring lumps of gold into her lap at the end of a season and the weight of them tearing her frock.

There was also the news that the cost of emigrating for the Saints was to be substantially lowered that season by two developments initiated by the Church. Firstly, funds from the Perpetual Emigrating Fund were to be made available to the poor of Britain. In the first three years the fund had concentrated on bringing in the refugees from their camp sites on the banks of the Missouri. Now that the last of them had been removed, Brigham Young called upon the various presidents of the conferences throughout Britain to choose worthy and deserving poor from their ranks to receive the help of the Fund to get them to the Valley. His letter was translated and published in Welsh in *Udgorn Seion*. 'Let your selection be made in wisdom,' he wrote, 'having regard to those who are faithful and have borne the burdens in the heat of the day; and also, in some measure, to their professions or trades, according to our need.' Four hundred British Saints took advantage of the offer in 1853. It is not known how many of them were Welsh, but in the following year we know that more than half of the 247 Welsh aboard the *Golconda* were travelling under the auspices of the Perpetual Emigrating Fund.

At the same time, the organisers of the British Mission in Liverpool had devised a new scheme whereby those who did not qualify for help from the Fund could travel to Utah more cheaply than ever before. It was known as 'The £10 Emigrating Plan', a sort of third-class, no-frills, budget-ticket to Zion. Everything was cut to the bone. Ten passengers were squeezed into every wagon. The daily food ration was reduced. All necessities were bought in bulk, many tons at a time. No one was allowed to bring more than a hundred pounds of personal possessions. By such methods the price of a ticket to Salt Lake City was pared down to £10, about half the usual charge. 'Let all come who can procure a bit of bread,' said Brigham, 'and one garment on their back. Be assured there is water, plenty and pure, by the way, and doubt no longer, but come next year.' The plan proved very popular and 957 British Saints travelled on the £10 ticket in 1853, 41 per cent of the season's emigrants.

The organisers of the Mormon emigration in Liverpool were eager that British Saints who contemplated travelling to Utah, should hear of the improvements on the high seas and on the Plains. They therefore hired an artist, Frederick Piercy, to travel on the *Jersey*, the main emigration ship of the season, to record his impressions of the journey to Salt Lake City. 'The steerage passengers were composed,' he wrote, 'of one half English and the other half Welsh, causing a confusion of tongues amusing until you were personally interested in what was said. They, however, managed very well, and most heartily and lustily helped each other in all kinds of work where more than one pair of hands were necessary for its accomplishment.'

Frederick Piercy was not a Mormon, but he wrote about

them with sympathy and understanding, and his sketches are the best images we have of the trail in the early years. They include sketches of a lighthouse on the mouth of the Mississippi, a buffalo hunt, a wagon train camping at Wood River, another approaching Fort Bridger and the view of the Valley from the top of Big Mountain, with the Great Salt Lake shimmering in the distance. He pictured the ferry over the Loup. It shows a log raft attached to ropes by which it was pulled backwards and forwards across the river. A row of wagons await their turn to cross and in the foreground is the untidy shelter of the ferryman. But the best of his illustrations is of Salt Lake City itself, six years after Brigham Young had drawn the first line in the dirt. On each side of the wide streets, fine buildings are beginning to rise, the Tithing Office and the President's Office and the Council House and the Tabernacle. The foundations of the temple have been laid but it would be years yet before this building was complete. Around them stand dozens of smaller buildings, public and private, some two storeyed and of stone, others no more than shacks. 'And now our journey, so full of interest and novelty to me, was nearly completed,' wrote Piercy, 'and we were about to exchange the rude, but bracing and healthful prairie life for the comforts and refinements of the city... By the time we entered Great Salt Lake City, darkness had enveloped it, shutting out from my straining and enquiring eyes all details. I could see the streets were broad, and hear the refreshing sound of water rippling and gushing by the road side. Occasionally a tall house would loom up through the gloom, and every now and then the cheerful lights came twinkling through the cottage windows – slight things to write about, but yet noticed with pleasure by one fresh from the Plains.' He profoundly enjoyed his experiences. 'When I return to the noise and smoke of the city,' he wrote, 'I shall have sweet memories.' His book was published in 1855, under the title, *Route from Liverpool to the Great Salt Lake Valley*.

By 1853, the emigrants had a better idea of what awaited them at the far end of their long journey. Letters from the early settlers appeared regularly in *Udgorn Seion*, declaring

152

how good life was in Utah. 'When I observe the temporal advantages of these valleys,' wrote Elizabeth Lewis, formerly of the White Lion, Kidwelly, 'my thoughts frequently escape back to compare the conditions of my fellow countrymen, and their poor land, their heavy rents and taxes... When I hear about the plagues, the cholera, and the sickness, the deaths, the robberies, and the murders that are destroying mankind there, and embittering the sweetest pleasures, I cannot but grieve that they are not here by the thousands.'

It was a theme that was constantly proclaimed in *Udgorn Seion*. 'Here in Wales, we have over-populated towns, unemployed men, poverty, wretchedness, theft and fraud of all kinds, the oppression of the poor, the neglect of the widow and the orphan; taverns, prisons, asylums and brothels all overflowing with occupants. War breaks out, men are swept away, sickness and poverty wreak their havoc, whilst squalor, prostitution, and the consequent diseases of this generation contribute to the depopulation of the earth... Over there is a spacious country, enough room for every family to raise their sustenance from the land. A healthy land, beautiful and pleasant. A free people, religious freedom, political rights. There are no oppressive tyrants, nor heavy taxes, nor low wages, nor hard taskmasters, nor unreasonable labour, nor any of the hundred and one complaints that we hear here.'

In truth, despite the gilded portraits conveyed in these *Udgorn Seion* letters, conditions in the Valley were often difficult and challenging. It was impossible, for example, to earn cash in Utah in the early days. The Saints had to survive by barter. In his memoir, Joseph Parry remembered the difficult times he endured when first he arrived in the autumn of 1852. 'During the fall and winter I worked on the Public Works. We were paid such products as the county produced. Neither money nor merchandise could be had. For it was not to be had in the country. We never had any during the whole of the winter... We had no groceries, but little meat, neither had we any fruit of any kind. But our bread and water was sure unto us, and we were thankful to our God for bringing us here.' But such tales did not make it into the pages of *Udgorn Seion*. They printed only the success stories.

Did these tales of an idyllic life in Utah and of cheap transport to America induce some people to take advantage of the Mormons and to join the Church merely to get there? Certainly, a missionary in west Wales was writing that people in his area were enquiring about emigration before they had even accepted baptism. John Haines Williams of Pembrey admitted that he was partly convinced of the truths of Mormonism after hearing descriptions of the good life in Utah. Dan Jones lost some of his flock on the Mississippi in 1849. 'They went away along the road to destruction at a gallop,' he wrote. 'I shall take greater care next time to refrain from bringing any but the faithful Saints with me.' But the numbers who took advantage were few. Whatever the rewards that awaited them in America, joining the Church in Wales was not a decision to be taken lightly. The derision and contempt in which the Saints were held often continued to flare into bloody violence. A letter to *Udgorn Seion* describes a mob attacking the doorman of a hall in Haverfordwest where the Mormons were gathering. 'They pushed him over the stairs to the street, and they beat him badly; he shouted out for his life and, when I reached him, several had hold of him on the ground, kicking him, &c., and he was covered with blood.' David, Thomas Jeremy's brother, was kicked so badly that he still felt the pain thirty years later. In Eglwysbach, in Denbighshire, the Mormon children were barred from the village school. In Mathry in Pembrokeshire, Thomas John kept his boys from school after they were beaten by the older pupils and cruelly whipped by the headmaster. No wonder that Thomas Jones of Rhymney, asked to be baptized secretly, at night, under a bridge, so that his neighbours might not know that he had accepted the Mormon faith. And no wonder that so many Mormons eagerly obeyed Brigham Young's exhortation 'to gather up to Zion and come while the way is open'.

Thomas Jeremy, the farmer from Glantren Fawr in Llanybydder, understood how remarkable it would seem to his readers that land was to be given gratis to every Mormon newcomer to the Valley. 'We are in our own house, on our city lot,' he wrote. 'The size of the lots is an acre and a quarter, which everyone owns without money and without price, apart from paying to have it measured and recorded, namely a dollar and a half. The Welsh chose to have their lots on the west side of the city on a beautiful plain... I believe that we have obtained the most fertile land in the city, although it is all extremely good.' In addition to the city lots, they could obtain farming land outside the city. 'All the Saints here get as much land to work as they wish, without paying anything to anyone, except to measure it, and record it.' Back in Wales, a tenant smallholder, oppressed by heavy rents and ruthless landlords, could only dream of owning his own land. But in Utah he could live the dream. 'In this river, there is an abundance of large fish, and also flocks of wild geese and ducks descend on it and on the small lakes along its banks. This is an excellent place for those who enjoy shooting game, with no reason to fear anyone. All are free to shoot as many as they wish.' Shooting game! Working-class men like themselves shooting game! Such a thing was unimaginable in Wales.

But despite all these promises and despite the improvements along the trail, all the way from Liverpool to the Salt Lake, 1853 had hardly commenced before a bolt from the blue shattered whatever hopes the faithful might have held of better times ahead. In the January edition of *Udgorn Seion* an article appeared which was to transform the Mormon world. 'We hope that our dear brothers and sisters will be reasonable in their judgment of it, and that they will exercise patience until they can receive more reasons in support of the subject.' The article described a conversation that was said to have taken place between God and the Prophet Joseph Smith some ten years earlier. Joseph had asked the Lord why Abraham and Isaac and Moses and the rest of the Prophets had been allowed to marry as many wives as they wished whilst he, Joseph, was only allowed one. God had answered that the ancient fathers had lived according to a covenant between man and

God 'instituted before the foundation of the world'. Polygamy, or plural marriage, had been a part of that covenant. It had flourished in the age of the Prophets, but in the following centuries, as the old order lost sway, it had been forgotten. Now God wished to re-establish it. 'If any man espouse a virgin, and desire to espouse another, and the first give her consent... then he is justified.' In other words, as long as the first wife agreed, a man might marry a second wife, and a third and a fourth, and increase his progeny greatly. God explained to Joseph that there were two forms of marriage, a marriage for life and a marriage for all eternity. By having his marriages sealed to eternity, a man might enjoy the company of his wives and his children in the afterlife. The larger his family, the greater his status and his importance in the next life. Indeed, a man had a duty to marry more than one wife. All who wished to be saved should observe this commandment and obey it, 'or he shall be damned, saith the Lord God'.

What William Law had published in *The Nauvoo Expositor* in 1844 proved to be true. It had been revealed to Joseph Smith at the start of the Forties, just as Law had written. Since then, a number of the Church hierarchy had secretly wed more than one wife. Before his death, Joseph had married about a hundred wives and, although Brigham maintained that he had wished to die when he first heard of the revelation, he had married fourteen wives before Joseph's death and about half a dozen afterwards. But these things had been kept secret from ordinary Church members, lest they should be misinterpreted and misunderstood. Now that the Saints had been gathered from Council Bluffs and were safe under his control in Utah, Brigham felt that the time had come to make public God's decree about plural marriage.

In the outside world, amongst the 'Babylonians', the revelation proved extremely damaging to the Saints. It engendered passionate hostility in America and Europe and the ferocity of the backlash was fearsome. What was worse was that the Saints were subjected to ridicule. Polygamy provided their enemies with a whole battery of new jibes and insults.

For the next forty years, it proved an insurmountable obstacle in the way of rapprochement with the rest of America and, even today, not all the smoke and confusion generated by it has totally cleared.

In Wales, the reaction to the revelation was furious. It would be difficult to conceive of a time and place less sympathetic to polygamy than mid-nineteenth-century Wales. The Welsh were busily trying to wipe away the mud with which they had been splattered by a government report on education, the so-called Blue Books of 1847, which had accused them, amongst other things, of lax sexual practices. Their wish now, above all things, was to be thought respectable by their English neighbours. Victorian prudery was rampant. The Queen (God bless her), was pregnant with her eighth child, and her marriage, with dear Albert at her side and her offspring at her feet, was a fine example to all her subjects of a pure and undefiled union. To the ordinary Welshman, the Mormons and their offensive, uncivilised practices were an embarrassment and a disgrace and the sooner they were brushed under the carpet and forgotten, the better. In 1876, The Rev. R.D. Thomas (Iorthyn Gwynedd), whilst on his coast-to-coast tour around all the Welsh settlements in the United States, refused to go anywhere near Utah. 'Their views and practices,' he said, 'are a mockery of Christianity and humanity.'

Within Mormon ranks, the revelation led to much doubt, uncertainty and loss of faith. During the first six months of the year, 1,766 British Saints, about six per cent of the membership, turned their backs on the Church. In Wales, *Udgorn Seion* prepared for a hard struggle, fearing the worst. 'However controversial this subject may appear to the minds of religious men of this country,' wrote the editor, 'only one in five of the world's inhabitants do not believe it… There will be time in our coming issues to present this matter in greater detail, and to prove it from the scriptures, showing that it is not sensuality that governs it, rather the perfect order of the Lord… We hope that all will be calm, until they can hear more.'

The feelings of the majority of the Welsh Saints are not

easy to gauge. They tended not to broadcast their opinions. For them, their leader's word was law and there was to be no argument. But some of their confusion and bewilderment is evident in the letters written to the editor of *Udgorn Seion*. 'Esteemed Editor – I have no doubt that the doctrine of plural marriage among Saints has caused an enormous surprise to some of the readers of your publication... And since that has, and does, strengthen the arms of prejudiced opponents to kindle more hatred and ridicule against the sect... I beg your help to clear the stones from the path.' 'Mr. Ed. – As a regular reader of your praiseworthy *Trumpet*, I humbly wish to receive clarification... It seems remarkable to me to see the same respected editor having changed his opinion so much... Now Mr. Editor, the question is which of your two *Trumpets* am I to believe.' The editor has no answer for them, except to urge them, time and again, to hold true to their faith and await developments. 'We believe every truth as it is revealed by God... The Latter-day Saints have implicit confidence in all the revelations given through Joseph the Prophet.'

In fact, the editor appears to be in as much a quandary as any of his readers. In previous issues of the magazine he had urgently denied rumours of plural marriages in Zion. A year earlier, he had written, 'There is nothing more obvious than that the Saints are greatly wronged by the publications of the country when they say that Polygamy is in their midst; for what alliance of people would publish that polygamy is a sin, while at the same time practicing it? All the books of the Saints forbid it, especially *The Book of Mormon* and *The Doctrine and Covenants*.' It is obvious that the editor, like his readers, had no reason to believe that polygamy was being practised amongst the hierarchy. When the news came that this was not so, and that the Church leaders had been practising polygamy in Nauvoo and Salt Lake City for a decade or more, it was as much a shock to the editor as it was to his readers.

'It caused quite a commotion in our branch,' wrote a Pembrokeshire member. 'One of the girls came to me with tears in her eyes and said, "Is it true that Brigham Young has ninety wives? I can't stand that, Oh, I can't stand it." I asked her how long it had been since I had heard her testify that she knew the Church was true, and I said, "if it was true then, it is true now". I told her I did not see anything for her to cry about. After I talked to her awhile, she dried her tears and carried on with her arrangements to get married and emigrate.' Thomas Giles, President of the Monmouthshire Conference, was also trying to calm his worried members. He had to lay hands on the wife of Edmund Jones of Abertillery many times, 'in order that she might be rid of jealousy towards her husband, that her mind might be easy as to plurality of wives. We found that she received benefit by so doing.'

In the spring of 1853, over 2,600 British Saints had paid a deposit on tickets to Utah, a figure which included about two hundred Welsh. What were their feelings now, confronted with this startling news from their home-to-be? Fanny Stenhouse wrote, as she crossed the Plains to the Valley, 'What living contradictions we were! Singing in a circle, night and morning, the songs of Zion and listening to prayers and thanksgiving for having been permitted to gather out of 'Babylon' and then, during the day, as we trudged along, in twos and threes, we were expressing to each other all our misgivings and doubts and fears and the bitterness of our thoughts against polygamy while each wife, confiding in her husband's honour and faithfulness, solaced herself with the hope that all might yet be well. How little sometimes do the songs of gladness reflect the real sentiments of the heart. How often have I heard many a heartbroken woman singing the chorus, "I never knew what joy was / Till I became a Mormon." I could never sing that song.' Not often does a Mormon wife so lay bare her feelings but Fanny Stenhouse was not a typical Mormon. She left the Church soon after reaching Salt Lake City and her aversion to plural marriage was the prime cause of her leaving.

Certainly, no Welsh woman on the Plains in 1853 expressed her feelings as candidly as this, but doubtless there were many who privately felt similar fears. William Henshaw and his wife and his four children emigrated to the States in 1851.

He was one of the pioneers of Mormonism in Wales, the first missionary to work in Merthyr Tydfil and Penydarren. They were living in St Louis, trying to earn the means to continue their journey to Utah, when they heard about Brigham's revelation. They refused to go one step further and soon left the Church. Isaak Brockbank and his mother heard the news in Council Bluffs where they were waiting, with a family called Thomas, for the wagon trains to be organised. 'The news of the public announcement of the doctrine of Plural Marriage, as a cardinal principle of the Church, reached us, and threw more consternation around the Saints, especially those who were not very firmly grounded in the faith, my mother and Mrs. Thomas being among that number. Mrs. Thomas went so far as to say that she would rather her daughters would die there than that they should go to the Valley and become the wives of a polygamist.' 'My two aunts stayed at Council Bluffs,' wrote another emigrant, 'having met some old Nauvoo Mormons who told them Mormons would marry them for plural wives. They would not go any further.'

In the *Flintshire Observer* on December 5th, 1862, was published a most painful account of a Welsh wife's fears, in a letter sent from Utah. 'As to polygamy,' the author writes, '<u>you</u> are without a dread of anyone claiming a share with you; this dread has made me so miserable in past times that I almost wished myself at the bottom of the sea instead of in Utah, but so far I have been spared that trial. Oh! A---, you cannot conceive what women have to suffer here with a view to obtain some great glory hereafter, which I for one am willing to forgo.'

In the autumn, *Udgorn Seion* announced that the Welsh contingent on the trail had had a pleasant passage. 'The best feelings blossomed in the camps, with no complaining and no sickness.' But the magazine is once again painting too rosy a picture. The crossing had not been as happy and as trouble free as the report implied. The only Welshman on the trail that year to leave a detailed description of the journey paints a very different picture. Indeed, so great was his disillusionment that he left the Church and Utah and the United States within the year and made his way back to Wales.

John E. Davis was a Cardiff man. He was 62 years old, a bachelor and half blind, not the best person perhaps to give a balanced account of the tribulations of the trail and the difficulties of life in a polygamous society. Nevertheless, when he got home to Cardiff he published his critical opinions in a book called *Mormonism Unveiled*. He appears to have been a tetchy, crotchety and grumpy old man. Many of his grumbles are about trivialities. He grumbles that conditions on the ship were not as good as the description given beforehand. He grumbles that the surplus food left over from the voyage was not shared between the passengers for use on the next leg of their journey. He accuses some of the organisers, without much proof, of profiting financially from the Saints under their care. He grumbles that his company was not given a worthy welcome in Salt Lake City. These are, on the whole, the petty bickerings of a querulous old man, but two of his grievances are of more serious concern.

Firstly, he writes that the '£10 Plan' proved unsuccessful. Despite the organisers having warned the Saints beforehand that the journey would not be easy, it is clear that, for many of them, including John E. Davis, the conditions proved to be much harsher than they had anticipated. Davis accuses the organisers of failing to supply the requisite number of oxen and that, as a result, they had to leave with fewer wagons than originally planned. Twelve people, instead of ten, had therefore to be accommodated in each wagon and some of their personal belongings had to be left behind. 'It had been promised to us in England that we could take a hundred pounds each across the Plains with us,' wrote one of the company, 'but before we left Keokuk, near Nauvoo, the leaders told us that we could not take that much. We had to throw away our trunks, boxes and some of our books and make bags for our clothes, so that I do not think we averaged sixty pounds each.' Another of John E. Davis' complaints was that the organisers had promised there would be two milking cows at the service of each wagon, but these had not materialised. It was a complaint made by many members of the company. 'We had one milk cow among thirty-six of us,' said one, 'and she died on the Sweetwater.' The organisers' defence was that there was a scarcity of oxen and cows·throughout the whole of the Midwest in 1853. It was said that 105,000 cattle from the Missouri basin had been taken to California that season and sold for fabulous prices. The owner of one huge herd of five hundred cattle, six hundred oxen, sixty horses and forty mules had said he would make a profit of six hundred per cent when he arrived in California, even were he to lose half his stock on the way. John Hackett, a Texan, drove a herd of 937 cattle from his home state to California. On the way, he managed to lose 755 of them, but still made a profit. No wonder cattle were scarce on the Missouri that year.

John E. Davis' second complaint was more serious. He accused the organisers of sending the '£10' company out onto the Plains with insufficient food. The daily ration, according to Davis, was a pound of flour, eight ounces of rice, eight ounces of salted pork, eight ounces of beans, eight ounces of sugar and three ounces of dried fruit. This adds up to about 2,200 calories, not enough for a man engaged in hard physical labour. According to Davis, the organisers' estimation of the time needed to get to Utah was also wildly optimistic. The wagon trains carried food for a hundred days, but on average it took them 105 days to complete the journey. The result was that many of the Saints were very hungry by the time they reached Salt Lake City.

The reminiscences of other company members confirm John Davis' charges. Some emigrants finished their salt and sugar and tea before they reached Fort Laramie, hardly halfway to the Valley. Others say their flour finished three weeks before the end of the journey and the supply of milk had ceased when the milk cows had to be put in harness due to the loss of some of the oxen. Travelling with the main Welsh contingent was an umbrella manufacturer from London, called Junius Crossland. He had been refusing food so that his family could have more and he told his friends that, should he die, they were to place the following words on his gravestone. 'I am murdered by the unwise procedure of the £10 Company.' And, sure enough, he died soon afterwards. John E. Davis' accusation that the organisers, in their eagerness to move as many people as possible as cheaply as possible, had cut the food ration too close to the bone, causing much unnecessary suffering, appears to have been true.

On arrival in Utah, life proved no easier for John Davis. He had to work hard to earn a living, cutting timber in the mountains. He believed that Brigham Young could work miracles and had tried to meet him in the hope that he might cure his incipient blindness, but Brigham refused to see him. After nine months in Utah, now disillusioned with Mormonism, Davis decided to return home to Wales. He took a wagon to California and from there worked his passage back to Britain in a ship carrying guano, the seabird droppings used as manure. These boats were infamous for their filthy conditions and the hard labour demanded of their crews, but somehow John Davis managed to arrive safely in Cardiff – not bad for a querulous, half blind, old man.

In his book, he devotes a whole chapter to polygamy. He knew his readers would be greatly interested in the subject and that the sales of his book would benefit. He claimed that it was meanness and miserly penny-pinching that enticed most men into plural marriages. Maid servants were scarce and expensive in Utah, he said, but if a man married his maid, he had no need to pay her thereafter and she couldn't leave. This, he claimed, made marrying the maid more attractive than employing her. He has stories about women being thrown out of their homes and left without a roof over their heads, with no legal redress whatsoever. He knew of a man, he said, who had married his own daughter and another who had married a mother and daughter on the same day. Brigham Young's blessing was an essential part of every wedding, for which, according to Davis, he extracted a considerable fee. And if, in time, a divorce was sought, only Brigham Young could grant that, again for another large fee. His book is a colourful concoction of truths, half-truths, gossip and lies, but of one thing, he says, he is absolutely certain. 'To the honour and virtue of the Daughters of Cambria be it said, that during the whole time I was at the Salt Lake, I did not hear of one Welsh girl having married, except as the only wife. Not a single instance came under my knowledge where a girl from Wales had married a man who had a wife already living!'

In this, Davis was wrong and he must have known it. In fact, he tells the story of Dan Jones' affair with Mrs Lewis, the Welsh 'Queen' and adds that 'Dan Jones and Mrs. Lewis got married in Salt Lake City, so that now Jones had two wives.' It was not difficult to find examples of other Welsh girls in plural marriages. Ann Rogers, the girl who lost all her family on the crossing, went to work for a man called William Snow after arriving in Utah. A few months after she had started working for him, he married her and on the same day he married another girl although he already had two wives. According to the family history, all four marriages were blessed with many children and all four families lived happily together. Thomas Jeremy, the farmer from Glantrenfawr, Llanybydder, married, as his second wife, a Dutch girl, Minnie Bosh. When Sarah, his first wife died, Minnie felt she had lost her dearest friend. Sarah's gravestone describes how her care for Minnie's children had been so tender and so loving that the children didn't know which of the two was their real mother. And this paragraph from the biography of the master-mason, Edward Lloyd Parry, from St George in Denbighshire, tells a similar story. 'When he came home from work one day he found his cousin, Ann Parry, visiting there and his wife, Elizabeth, said, "Edward, see your cousin, Ann, has come here to be your second wife." He said to Ann, "Is that so?" She replied in the affirmative.' The wedding duly took place. Ann's first child was named Elizabeth Ann, after the two wives. Ann gave the child to Elizabeth to mother as Elizabeth had been unable to have children of her own. 'The child was taught to call the first wife "mother" and her own mother "Aunty Ann". The rest of the children were taught to call the first wife "mother" and their own mother "ma" and did not really know which was their own mother until quite grown. Ann had eleven children.'

John D. Rees of Merthyr Tydfil and his wife, Mary, and their four children, arrived in the Valley in William Morgan's wagon train in 1852. Soon after their arrival, he married a second wife. The family history has it that Church officials had urged John to take this step and that Mary had given her consent, but only on condition that John married her sister, Jane. Jane was 28 and, in Mary's opinion, well on the way to spinsterhood. She died of cancer a year after the wedding. John was eager to find another bride but, this time, Mary would not give her consent. She walked all the way from Brigham City to Salt Lake City, a sixty-mile walk, to argue her case before Brigham Young, but to no avail. John was given permission to marry his third wife, a girl called Zillah Mathias from Abergwili, and Brigham Young officiated at the ceremony. Zillah was eighteen and John was 42.

Brigham believed it was a wealthy man's duty to father more than one family. It was with his help that Sarah Giles of Merthyr found a husband. One day, whilst on a visit to Ogden in the north of the state, Brigham called to see Lorin Farr, the mayor of the town. 'Lorin,' he said, 'you own half of Ogden and have plenty of money. I want you to take Sarah as your second wife.' And that was that.

Only a minority of marriages in Utah were polygamous, somewhere between twenty and forty per cent. And there was undoubted opposition amongst the women of some of the matriarchal families of the Welsh. In his autobiography, John Thain of Pembrokeshire wrote that the Church authorities urged him to take a second wife but that his first wife had come to him and said, 'If you marry again, you'll still only have one wife.' And the small village in the San Pete Valley called Wales, which had been founded by coal miners from Merthyr, was described as 'one of the few communities in Utah in which there were no plural marriages among the members of the Church'. The matriarch-in-chief of the village, Margaret Davis Rees, the first woman to be baptized into the Mormon faith in south Wales, urged her sisters to avoid such unions. She got to her feet in a meeting of the village wives and announced, 'Well, ladies, I don't know how you feel about the number of wives there should be in a marriage, but I tell you this; there's only room for one in mine.'

In the non-Mormon world, much publicity was given to the fact that, as often as not, there was a big age difference between a Mormon and his second or third wives. This was cited as proof of the moral depravity of the Saints. There certainly were examples amongst the Welsh of girls who were married to men old enough to be their fathers, if not their grandfathers. Poor Mary Jones, for example, who lost her mother and her father on the Mississippi in 1849, was married to a 62-year-old man, she being but a fifteen-year-old child. After a year of marriage she was allowed to divorce him because of his cruelty towards her. He was subsequently excommunicated from the Church.

Lovina Jones came to the Valley with her family from Pontypridd in 1853, when she was nine years old. Three years later she became the second wife of William Bailey Lake. He married a third wife on the same day. A year later, on Lovina's fourteenth birthday, William was killed in a skirmish with Indians. Whilst yet only fifteen, she was married again, becoming this time the third wife of her first husband's brother-in-law and, within the year, a child was born. Before she was sixteen therefore, Lovina had been a bride, a wife, a widow and then a bride again and a mother.

But these sorts of marriages were the exceptions. It was more common for the relationship between a man and his second or third wives to be unemotional contracts, more like business agreements than love affairs. Amongst Brigham Young's 55 wives there were numerous elderly ladies, eight of them having previously been married to Joseph Smith. These marriages were often driven by a sense of duty, the duty to obey the commands of the Church, the duty to produce children, the duty to look after the less fortunate in their community. At times, polygamy in Zion seemed akin to a welfare system. The marriage of Ann Parry of Llanasa in Flintshire is a case in point.

When she set out in 1849 to cross the Plains she was destitute and in considerable distress. She had sailed with her husband on the *Buena Vista*, but he had fallen victim to cholera on the Mississippi. She had one young son and another child on the way. Mrs Lewis, the quondam landlady of the White Lion in Kidwelly, took pity on her and paid for her journey to the Valley. Out on the Plains, within sight of Chimney Rock, her second son was born. Her first winter in Utah was spent in misery, freezing with her children in a wretched, one-roomed turf hut. Before another winter set in, an old friend from Wales called to see her. David Peters had been a successful businessman, owning a woollen factory in Llanfrothen, Caernarfonshire. He and his wife had crossed the Plains in the same wagon train as Ann. He took Ann as his second wife and moved her and the children into his home. Eventually, he designed and built a house for his two families, a wing for his first wife Laura and a wing for Ann and a central section where the two families mingled. Again, it appears that the two families lived happily together. Ann died when she was forty and Laura looked after her children as if they were her own.

But often, the life of a second, third or fourth Mormon wife could be lonely and hard, with a house full of small children, not much money to feed and clothe them, and a husband whom she saw only once or twice a week, if she was lucky. We shall look in greater detail at the difficult lives of Welsh people in polygamous marriages in later chapters.

1854

THE *GOLCONDA* LEFT the dock in Liverpool on February 4th, 1854, with 282 Welsh Saints aboard, the majority of them from Merthyr and the surrounding area. This was the largest contingent of Welsh to travel together since the voyages of the *Buena Vista* and the *Hartley* in 1849. There were small groups of Welsh on other ships that sailed that year, five on the *Windermere*, seven on the *John M. Wood* and eight on the *Marshfield* and so on, but, as usual, the Welsh preferred, if possible, to travel together. Their names are all neatly recorded in the ships' manifest which can be studied on Brigham Young University's 'Mormon Migration' website (**http:// mormonmigration.lib.byu.edu/**). In the document there are details of their trades and crafts. There were fifteen coal miners amongst them, and eleven who called themselves just 'miners'. There were five masons, five cobblers, and one or two of a number of other crafts including builders, tailors, compositors, weavers, clerks, accountants, engineers, carpenters, seamen, shopkeepers and gardeners.

They were a cheerful bunch. Some have left colourful diaries, others have been the subjects of lively biographies. Many of them recount the excitement of the religious gatherings that were held aboard the *Golconda*. They arranged such meetings five times a week, 'in which we were richly blessed with the gifts of the Spirit, in tongues, interpretations, visions, revelations and prophecies, which caused the hearts of the Saints to rejoice exceeding.' Others remembered less pious excitements. Two weddings were celebrated, 'and I do not believe,' wrote William S. Phillips in a letter to *Udgorn Seion*, 'that more merriment was ever before enjoyed in a wedding on land or sea. Everyone was searching for their boxes in order to reach for their best outfits and the wedding was celebrated in the manner of the old Welsh many years ago.' He doesn't explain what 'the manner of the old Welsh' was, but according to another diarist, John Johnson Davies, a 23-year-old weaver from Carmarthen, 'the bridegroom was carried around the ship in a chair by four bachelors. They made it for that purpose. The bride was tied to a chair and was hoisted up the mast quite a ways. The captain said: "What a brave woman!" Then she took her handkerchief and waved it in the breeze.' It seems to have been a very jolly occasion and a welcome break, no doubt, from the monotony of shipboard life.

John Johnson Davies, the weaver, was travelling with a brass band from Carmarthen. They provided the soundtrack to the merriment on board, giving concerts and accompanying the dancers. He was also a member of the choir and of the string band. Elizabeth Davis, of Ferryside in Carmarthenshire, remembered that they entertained themselves by staging mock trials. One of the cooks hauled before the judge was charged with stealing a rice pudding, but the judge failed to reach a verdict because somebody had eaten the evidence.

Some of the emigrants were wealthy. John A. Lewis had been the owner of a shop and twelve houses in Cardiff. Some were poor. Ann Williams was one of nine children left orphaned when her father was killed working on the railway near Llanelli. As an eleven year old, she was employed as a servant in Rhymney, working without pay, for her food and lodging only. In 1846, when she was 21, she married a collier, but, a year after the wedding, he broke his back in an underground accident and died four years later. A few months afterwards, Ann married again, to another Rhymney collier, William Morgan Richards. William was a Mormon and, when he and Ann married, he was preparing to leave on a mission to Machynlleth. Ann went with him, and at the end of his two-year mission they set sail for Utah, as poor as church mice. The oldest passenger on the ship was 84-year-old Esther Jones of Cardiganshire. The youngest was one-month-old Margaret Griffiths Lewis of Merthyr. Some travelled in groups, like George Munro, Watkin Rees and William Jones, three friends who had worked together at the iron works in Dowlais. And others, like Martha Morgan, thirty years old and unmarried, travelled alone. She found a husband in Utah within the year.

William S. Phillips, who had been President of the Welsh Mission after Dan Jones' departure, was in charge of the Welsh contingent on the ship. He was aided by his former secretary, Richard Vaughan Morris, Elias Morris' brother, and by a former missionary, Thomas Obray, who had only recently returned to Britain after a two-year stint in Malta. Even in these early days, the Mormons had already established missions in far-off places like Calcutta and Sydney, Valparíso and Hawaii. Obray had been chosen to open a mission in Malta because he was experienced in the ways of British naval dockyards. His father had been employed at the admiralty docks in Pembroke Dock and Thomas followed him into the same occupation. When his father was killed, falling off a scaffold, Thomas left Pembrokeshire and found work in the headquarters of the North Sea Fleet in Sheerness. It was whilst he was in Sheerness that he joined the Church, and when Brigham Young decided to open a mission in the Maltese dockyards, the headquarters of the Mediterranean fleet, Thomas, with his long experience of life in Her Majesty's dockyards, seemed an obvious choice as missionary. His path during the ensuing months proved to be rocky and tortuous and, when his term came to an end, he had only 29 converts to show for his efforts.

Another colourful character on the deck of the *Golconda* was Thomas Job. One of his acquaintances described him as 'a harmless, good man, but rather eccentric, with a turn for Mathematics and Astronomy'. In a lonely cottage called Ffosybroga (Frog's Ditch), high up in the Carmarthenshire hills between Llanpumpsaint and Pontarsais, with no teacher to guide him and no one to advise him, he had struggled to teach himself science and had published an ambitious pamphlet, entitled *The Fabric of the World Examined*, in which he attempted to explain the origins of the universe. In it he challenged some of the theories of Sir Isaac Newton. The preface to his pamphlet reflects the difficult circumstances in which it was written. 'I laboured under the greatest disadvantages, having no instruments to make celestial observations when necessary, but what I managed to frame myself, neither received I any instruction in Mechanics, Astronomy, or any other science in Natural Philosophy, but what borrowed books could procure; nor had I time to peruse them, but during the hours that ought to have been devoted to rest, after my hard and toilsome work during the day was over.'

The story of his life is recorded in a remarkable autobiography, written by him in Utah when he was seventy years old. It was never published but is available online at **http:// archive.org/stream/ThomasJob/ThomasJob_djvu.txt** It tells the story of a clever boy, struggling to educate himself, eager for knowledge and learning, but constrained by poverty. 'My parents were opposed to my learning,' he writes, 'not believing it would be of any benefit to me.' Nevertheless they sent him to the village school for two years. 'The schoolmaster was an old broken Welsh farmer... Many of the young men who attended school had great desire to learn how to read and write, yet under the circumstances it was impossible... To learn from English books was also a great difficulty for Welsh boys.' After leaving school, he worked as a farm labourer. He struggled to continue his education. 'At night I would be translating and writing, and during the day, wherever I would be at work, I had my writings along to be committed to memory.' He had always been interested in the movements of the stars and the planets. 'I can recollect that when I was very young, I was much enraptured with the appearance of the heavenly bodies and other natural phenomena. I asked my father endless questions.' He taught himself geometry and algebra and trigonometry, and he studied electricity and magnetism, but it was an aimless, ill-directed education, with no focus or plan. From this confused background grew an interest in astrology and soothsaying and magic. He made a name for himself as an astrologer and, from 1845 until he sailed for America, he published an annual almanac. People came to consult him about what the stars might have in store for them. He then graduated to being a 'dyn hysbys', an important figure in traditional Welsh country life. 'Dynion hysbys', or 'wise men', were the dispensers of cures and charms and the keepers of arcane secrets, which they recorded in mysterious tomes, some of which have found their way to the National Library of Wales. They were always suspected of being in league with dark forces. Now people came to Thomas Job to seek cures, to lift curses and to find lost cows for a small fee. The meandering route that led to this unusual calling is chronicled in detail in the autobiography – which books he read, where he went for advice, who helped him. Thomas Job was undoubtedly a hardworking man and a doughty fighter, but constancy and steadfastness do not seem to be qualities with which he was blessed. His religious life reflected the same restlessness. He'd been a Congregationalist, a Baptist and an Unitarian. Now he was a Mormon and was off to the New World to start all over again.

But the most interesting of all on the *Golconda* was John Silvanus Davis. Other than Dan Jones, no one had contributed more to the Mormon cause in Wales than this man. He owned and managed the press which had published all the Mormon literature in Wales since Dan Jones' return to America and he had been the author of much of its output. For five years, he had edited *Udgorn Seion* and, under his editorship, it had become a lively, informative magazine. In amongst weighty matters of theology and morality, summaries of the leader's speeches, reports on Church business and the like, John introduced lighter material. He regularly included letters sent by Welsh Saints in Utah to their relatives back home and they make fascinating reading. This, for example, from David D. Bowen to his parents in Llanelli. 'You, my father, have worked hard all the days of your life, to keep others rich and well off, and in spite of all your effort in the end you are yourself poor, not being in possession of a foot of land in your life, without paying a big amount of rent for it, or having a single animal either, except for an occasional pig... You believe me a fool for leaving such a place as you have there in Felinfoel, where we did not possess a single animal, and coming to this country where there is every fullness to be had. I have animals of every kind, cattle, oxen, pigs and geese; also I have houses and lands &c, and I do not owe a halfpenny of rent to anyone, and I can obtain what I want of land cheaply.' David hoped that his parents would eventually come to live with him in Utah but they were highly suspicious of his religion and refused to answer his letters. Still he persevered. 'Thus you see how much better is this land than the old country. I cannot describe the happiness I would have if you were to join with the Saints and immigrate to this Country. My wife Phebe, my little son Morgan, send their love. Morgan can speak three languages, namely Welsh, English and a language of the Indians, although he is but seven years and six months old.'

John Davis liked to introduce a little humour into his magazine. Some of the jokes are still funny today. A worthy Saint, for example, was pestered by a neighbour, who mocked him by constantly enquiring when he intended to leave for Zion. At Christmas, the Saint heard his neighbour singing the old Welsh carol 'Awn i Fethlem' ['Let us to Bethlehem'] and shouted to her, 'Why don't you call by my house when you leave and I'll accompany you as far as Jerusalem.'

He also delighted in publishing light-hearted verse in his magazine, usually disparaging the Non-conformists, to be sung to traditional Welsh airs. 'The Reverends' Complaint', for example, lists all the strongholds of Welsh Non-conformity which he claims are now under threat from the advance of Mormonism, to be sung to the old Welsh tune, 'Mochyn Du' ['The Black Pig']. Yet, despite the foolery and fun, this was a serious and influential periodical. 'I endeavoured to benefit you, while being no respecter of persons,' he declared. 'I did what I could to say and to write good things.' Unlike Dan Jones, who published *Udgorn Seion* as a monthly, John Davis eventually published every fortnight. Under his editorship, the circulation rose to over two thousand.

And yet the task of editing *Udgorn Seion* was of secondary importance to him compared to his other great labours for the Mormon cause. His *magnum opus* was the translation into Welsh of all the standard works of Mormonism, a task which he accomplished in a mere eighteen months. First, *Llyfr Athrawiaeth a Chyfamodau*, a translation of *The Book of Doctrine and Covenants*, a collection of the revelations and prophecies given to and by Joseph Smith. This appeared in 1851. In the following year, he published *Y Perl o Fawr Bris* [*The Pearl of Great Price*] – more revelations and a collection of translations, some from 'ancient Egyptian', made by Joseph Smith. And in the same year, *Llyfr Mormon* [*The Book of Mormon*] itself, nearly five hundred pages of fine print. This is the only Welsh translation ever made of *The Book of Mormon* and the only Welsh edition ever printed. Every ensuing edition is a facsimile of this work and on the title page of each one are the words, 'Published by and on sale from J. Davis, Georgetown, Merthyr Tydfil'. It remains a masterly translation. John sent a copy to the Baptist periodical *Seren Gomer*, asking them to review it. 'A pity so much trouble was taken,' they answered, 'to produce so perfect a translation of so worthless a text.'

John Davis' output was phenomenal. Yet, in 1851, when in the middle of his great work, he was only 29 years old, newly married, with the first child on the way. Though saddled with his publishing responsibilities and the cares of imminent fatherhood, he still found time to take Elizabeth to London to see the Great Exhibition at the Crystal Palace and to catch a play in Drury Lane. In an age when so many giants of Welsh culture were busily forecasting the death of the language, John Davis was fighting for its future. 'Never neglect your language,' he wrote. 'The Welsh language will not die presently as some imagine... We were sent to trumpet in our mother tongue, which is the common language of the country, and what turncoat would dare stand in our way?' In 1854, having finished his great work, he was released from his duties and given permission to leave for the Valley. He was told that there was room for himself and Elizabeth on the *Golconda* which would be leaving within the fortnight. They rushed to be ready, emptying the house, selling the furniture, packing their treasures and taking leave of their family and friends. John paid an advance of a hundred pounds to have two wagons waiting for him in St Louis, as he was travelling with nine boxes of belongings and a bed. He also paid the fares of two of his neighbours and their families.

The *Golconda* reached New Orleans in forty days and the Welsh were transferred onto the *John Simmonds*, one of the larger steamboats on the river – six boilers, 295 feet in length – which was to take them on the next stage of their journey as far as St Louis. John A. Lewis, the former shop owner from Cardiff, travelled with his family in first class. 'We had every comfort on the boat that could be desired and it was simply grand,' wrote one of his daughters. 'After we had been sailing for a day or two the boat was caught on a sand bar and we were detained four days, making it in all about two weeks before we arrived at St Louis, after a delightful journey. The steerage Saint passengers on this boat were very sick and we girls used to take them good things to eat nearly every day.' John Johnson Davies travelled in steerage, down in the bowels of the ship, up against the engine. 'The steamboat puffing and snorting and pushing hard against the stream, but oh what dirty water for us to use! We dip it up to settle it, but it doesn't get much better. Never mind, we will do the best we can with it. I must drink it anyhow, because I am very thirsty. And what a "rackity" noise; it made me shudder! The captain shouting and the water splashing and the band playing and some of us singing, and some of the sisters washing and the babes crying and the sailors talking, and many of them smoking. All of us trying to do something, and the boat tugging and snorting when travelling up the Mississippi River!'

Upon arrival in St Louis, they had to wait a few days, whilst another, smaller steamboat was found to take them up the Missouri. Watkin Rees, George Munro and William Jones, the three who had worked together in the same iron works in Dowlais, found work together in a local iron works. 'I had a job as a heater in the Bremen Rolling Mills,' wrote Watkin, 'they as puddlers, making good wages, but we did not stay long, for a boat was soon had.'

In St Louis, another Welshman joined the company. He was Samuel Obray, brother of Thomas, the Malta missionary. In the memoir compiled by his great-granddaughter in 1982, he is portrayed as a strong-willed, impetuous, rather ruthless man. Three years earlier, in February 1851, Samuel had left the family home in Pembroke Dock to join the Saints in Utah. He knew that his wife, Margaret, would not go with him. From the day he had married her, five years earlier, he had been urging her to accept his faith, but she had proved as strong-willed as he. He had decided therefore to go to America without her. Like John Ormond Snr, five years previously, he left without warning, without explanation and without saying farewell, taking his three-year-old son with him. Margaret went to the police and accused Samuel of kidnapping the child. The Haverfordwest police contacted the Liverpool police who quickly discovered that the only ship chartered by the Mormon Church that month was the *Ellen Maria* and that she was due to leave Liverpool Docks at any moment. They rushed to arrest Samuel and recover the child but when they reached the *Ellen Maria*'s berth, she was gone. She had sailed on the previous tide. Samuel must have uttered a long sigh of relief when he saw Liverpool slipping away over the stern, but the police had not given up. A strong north-westerly was blowing and the *Ellen Maria* was having a hard time of it beating her way out of the mouth of the Mersey. They chased after her and succeeded in boarding her, but Samuel was ready for them. His son had a distinctive mop of ginger hair and he had noticed another family whose children had hair of a similar colour. Hastily, he dressed his son as a girl and placed him in amongst the red-haired children. He managed to convince the police that his son was not on board and that his wife had fabricated the story in an attempt to stop him leaving. The police left the *Ellen Maria* empty-handed and Margaret never saw her husband nor her son ever again. Samuel and the boy had been in St Louis for nearly four years, trying to raise the money to travel on. Whilst there, he had married Louisa Bainbridge, one of the elder daughters of the red-haired family. Now, when he heard that his brother would be passing through St Louis in the spring, he had decided to join him.

In St Louis, the wagons ordered by John Silvanus Davis before leaving Wales were waiting for him. They were taken on board the *Australia*, the steamboat they had hired for the final stage of their journey, and lashed to the deck. John spent most of the voyage splashing water over them, lest the sparks from the funnels set them alight. The *Australia* took them to Kansas City, 'it being a new place, a Custom House and about half a dozen resident houses. We were landed in the woods about a half a mile above, where we put up our tents and camped for two or three weeks. This place was very unhealthy with tall timber covered with climbing grapevines so dense that we had to look straight up in order to see the sky. The cholera broke out again and many people died and, after camping here about two or three weeks, we were moved out to Magee's Farm several miles away from the river, and then again, soon after, further out, to a place near Westport on the edge of the prairie, where we camped for about three months, waiting for cattle and wagons.'

At the staging camp in Westport, the Welsh were distributed amongst the nine companies that were to cross the Plains that year. Perhaps the organisers felt that divided, they would be less troublesome than when they travelled together. John S. Davis and Elizabeth travelled with the first wagon train of the season. In his old age, John remembered how he had learnt to shoot whilst on the Plains and how he had brought many a rabbit and duck to his family's table. He had also tried his hand at shooting buffalo and had barely escaped with his life when the horse he was riding stumbled in front of an enraged beast.

As night fell on August 15th, John and Elizabeth's company approached a large camp of Indians a few miles east of Fort Laramie. John wrote that he saw 'thousands' of Sioux that night. 'They were friendly,' he writes, 'and eager to sell their wares.' If he had approached the same spot two nights later, he would have received a very different welcome. Unbeknown to him, he was skirting the fringes of one of the great tragedies of the West, a turning point in its history, which would sour life on the Plains for a generation.

The Sioux were waiting for the distribution of the annual payment of $50,000 which had been promised them two years earlier, if they did not attack wagon trains on the Plains. They were in good spirits. 'As we were making headway, we had intelligence that they were our friends,' wrote an Englishman called Hezekiah Mitchell in his diary. 'We camped amongst them. They gathered in their horses and oxen to make room for ours to feed. One Chief came and told us where we could get wood, after which another person of distinction came and told us where we could camp. We shook hands with one or two of them, went down to their large temple or what so ever name they may give it, and saw them dancing, singing, playing music, etc.' There was no trouble that night and it's clear from the diaries that the Indians were relaxed and friendly.

Two days later, a large company of Danish Saints arrived at the same camp site. They too had a diarist amongst them and this is what he wrote later that day. 'August 17th. We passed a large encampment of Indians before we reached Fort Laramie. They shot one of our cows that was lame and we let them have the meat.' The incident was obviously of no great importance to the Danes. There was little future for a lame cow on the trail and the Indians might as well have her. But when the Danes arrived at Fort Laramie, the soldiers there listened to their story with great interest. For weeks, they had been plagued by the constant pilfering of the Indians and were eager for any excuse to teach them a lesson. They seized this opportunity to send a company of soldiers to the Indian camp to arrest the killer of the unfortunate cow. This was the beginning of a course of events that led eventually to forty years of fighting.

Two more days passed before the next wagon train of Saints came by. Watkin Rees, one of the three Dowlais men,

178

was travelling in this one. He didn't quite get hold of all the facts, and one or two of the statements he makes in his diary are not quite correct, but he has the gist of the tale. 'We are now nearing Fort Laramie,' he wrote. 'A courier came into our camp from Fort Laramie, warning us to be careful of the Indians, for they were on the warpath and two thousand of them had had a fight with soldiers at the fort the day before, where they had killed thirteen soldiers. We passed that way the following day. The Indians were all gone. The ground they camped on, an extensive grassy flat, was smoothly trampled as if many people had camped there. The courier was going east for reinforcement, while the people at the fort had shut themselves up in fear lest the Sioux would return and kill them all. The trouble seems to have started over a lame cow belonging to a Danish Brother in the company ahead of us.'

John Johnson Davies, the weaver, was travelling with the same company and he obtained further details. 'The military Captain sent a few of his Soldiers to see the Indians about a cow and they got into a dispute and they fired at one another and they had a fight.' Watkin Rees takes up the story again. 'To intimidate the Indians, the soldiers fired a shot over their heads. As soon as they had done that, the Indians were upon them and cleaned out the whole platoon.'

Today the incident is known to historians as the 'Grattan Massacre'. Grattan was the name of the young, inexperienced officer who had led the platoon to the Sioux camp. He only had 28 soldiers with him but he had bragged in his drink that he could conquer the whole Sioux nation with only twenty men and one big gun. He believed the Indians were afraid of him and that he would have no trouble persuading them to give up the man responsible for killing the cow. But that was not to be. The Sioux Chief accepted responsibility and was ready to offer compensation for the cow, but he refused to give up the perpetrator of the deed, because he was a visiting brave from another tribe and therefore protected by the Indians' hospitality laws. Grattan was incensed and ordered his men to start shooting. Only one Indian was killed, but, unfortunately,

179

he was the Chief. This maddened the tribe and, as there were a thousand of them, and only 28 soldiers, the result was inevitable. All 28 were killed.

By this time, John Davis and his company were two days down the trail. They were awoken that night by a messenger galloping through their camp shouting that the Sioux were on the warpath. 'We did not know, but that their intentions were to molest us too,' wrote one of the company. 'In consequence, after mature deliberation, we deemed it wisdom to fix our wagons as soon as possible in the night and put out on our journey as soon as it was daylight and avoid them if possible.'

Three weeks later, the last Mormon wagon train of the season passed by the site of the Grattan Massacre. This company also had its diarist. 'It was at this place that the Indians killed the soldiers with their officers,' he wrote. 'They are buried close by the road. I have visited the graves & some of the men's heads are not even covered. There was a man's face lying on the bank with the teeth firm in the jaw bone, and the flesh appeared recently taken off. It was the settlers who buried them, as the remainder of the soldiers could not leave the fort, being few in number.'

Amongst the Sioux who witnessed the massacre that day was a child who was to become the greatest Indian warrior of them all – Crazy Horse. He was then a thirteen-year-old boy. Twelve years later, it was he who entrapped and killed Captain Fetterman and eighty of his men near Fort Phil Kearny in northern Wyoming. Ten years after that, he was at Sitting Bull's side when Custer and his men were defeated and massacred at the Little Big Horn. It was the Grattan Massacre that gave an edge to his lifelong hatred of the white man. The massacre also started forty years of fighting and killing which did not end until the Battle of Wounded Knee in 1890, when the last of the tribes that had fought so long and so bravely in defence of their way of life on the Plains was finally conquered. The clash between white men and Native Americans was probably inevitable, but the match that lit the conflagration was the shooting of the Danish Mormons' lame cow. Had John Silvanus

Davis' company passed Fort Laramie two days later, he would have stumbled upon the greatest scoop of his life.

John's intention, after arriving in Utah, was to farm, but Brigham Young had heard of his editorial prowess and had invited him to continue as a newspaper man on the staff of one of the Salt Lake City papers. His health was not good and, after a few years, he left the paper to keep a shop in the city in which he sold an alcohol-free beer of his own making. It came in two flavours, sarsaparilla and wintergreen, both very American flavours and both very popular with his customers. His beers kept him in comfort for the rest of his life.

Thomas Job, the self-educated scientist, did not remain long in the faith after arriving in Utah. Brigham Young refused him permission to publish his articles on astrology in Church periodicals, so he turned his back on the Church of Jesus Christ of Latter-day Saints. Instead, he joined a rival Mormon church, the Reorganized Church of Jesus Christ of Latter-day Saints. This Church, now named 'The Community of Christ', still flourishes, with its headquarters in Independence, Missouri. Its members believe that Joseph Smith's son was the rightful heir of Mormonism and that Brigham Young had illegally seized the leadership from him. They never sanctioned polygamous marriages and believe it was Brigham Young, not Joseph Smith, who was responsible for introducing the practice. They also believe that it was never Joseph Smith's intention to establish their holy city beyond the Rockies.

Most Mormons who quarrelled with Brigham Young returned to the Missouri to join the Reorganized Church. But not Thomas Job. Although he joined them, he refused to leave Utah. For the rest of his life he campaigned for the Reorganized Church in Utah, without the slightest success. He became an outcast, living alone far out on the empty plain beyond the small village of Goshen, but still he continued his fight. His last home was as poor and as lonely as his first in Ffosybroga, but Thomas Job never compromised and refused to run. He had found his cause, and stuck to it with a constancy and a steadfastness that had evaded him earlier in life. Today, the ruins of the wooden cabin, where he died in 1890, stubborn and intransigent to the last, are on the verge of disappearing back into scrub.

John A. Lewis lent much of the money he'd made selling his shop and his twelve houses in Cardiff to 25 Welsh families whose travel to Utah he had financed. Many of them took advantage of his generosity, leaving the Church after they had arrived and refusing to honour their debts. Before leaving Wales, John had also bought a farm in Utah from Dan Jones for $2,900, but when he saw what he had bought, the poor soil and the rudimentary buildings, he felt that Dan had also taken advantage of him. But he was not one to sit around bemoaning his fate. He still owned twelve oxen, two cows, two wagons, a good pony, a little money and four healthy children and he started over again. He never regretted his coming. 'John A. Lewis gave up his riches to live his religious convictions,' wrote one of his descendants. 'Even when he was taken advantage of by many individuals, he was able to differentiate between the failings of men and the teachings of Christ.'

The three friends, George Munro, Watkin Rees and William Jones stayed together. Ever since Parley Pratt and Dan Jones had discovered iron deposits and a coal seam in the south of the territory, Brigham Young had been planning to establish an iron works there. He was convinced that the cost of having to haul iron over the Rockies was holding back the young territory and that self-sufficiency in iron would lead to great improvements in the economy. A letter from him appeared in the pages of *Udgorn Seion* as early as May 1850. 'We urgently need men to set up a furnace – the coal and the iron are waiting.' By 1854, a new settlement called Cedar City was growing in the far south around the nucleus of an iron works and all immigrants with any experience of iron production were urged to go there. That's where the iron-workers George Munro, Watkin Rees and William Jones were headed. That's also where the poor couple, Ann and William Richards went, and the diarist David D. Bowen, and Samuel Leigh, the Llanelly schoolmaster and many others.

The success of the iron works in Cedar City would depend to a great degree upon the effectiveness of the smelting furnace. The man chosen to design and build this all-important structure was none other than Elias Morris of Llanfair Talhaiarn. Brigham Young described him as 'the foremost among the building contractors of the territory'. Elias could not have been given a greater challenge and he delighted in the responsibility. He was convinced that the furnace would make his fortune. He refused to take a salary, preferring to reinvest it in the scheme. In September, Isaac Haight, the general manager of the works, wrote to Salt Lake City saying, 'The furnace is completed, and is said by those who have seen it to be as good a furnace as they ever saw in England, or any other country. We are also building six coke ovens.' Elias Morris was put in charge of building the coke ovens as well. 'I heard that the iron works are in full operation,' wrote John S. Davis in a letter home to Wales, 'and that there is a call for one hundred and fifty more people to carry on the work. The furnace was working nearly two weeks ago and had been working for a whole fortnight and the fire went out only because of a lack of help to find fuel.' At the end of 1854, all seemed to augur well for Cedar City.

'There are plenty of ways for everyone to make a living in this valley,' John Davis added, 'and plenty of unclaimed land to support more than three times as many inhabitants, without counting the other broad valleys roundabout. After spending the first winter, the poor can be seen lifting up their heads, and coming into possession of houses, lands and oxen… The work of God is succeeding, knowledge is increasing, and the devil and his host are raging. Let the honest hasten to Zion in time, so they will not be left behind; for the dreadful day is drawing nigh.'

1855

'FOR THE DREADFUL day is drawing nigh.' John S. Davis had no idea how imminent the 'dreadful day' would prove to be. Locusts had threatened the harvests of the Valley in previous years. In 1848, swarms of them had arrived from their breeding grounds in the hills west of the city and had all but devastated the crops of the fledgling colony but, at the last moment, when all seemed lost, thousands of gulls had appeared from nowhere, and had eaten all the locusts. This was interpreted as a miracle, another example of God's care for his chosen people. The incident is commemorated by a striking sculpture in Temple Square and the native gull is now the Utah state bird. The harvests of 1850–1854, however, were particularly bountiful and the menace of the locusts was all but forgotten. But on the dank hillsides of the Nevada and Idaho uplands, under a light cover of sand, millions upon millions of eggs of the Melanoplus Spretus, the Rocky Mountain Locust, were waiting for the right temperature to hatch and the right conditions to swarm. In 1855, they got what they needed.

The first sign of the arrival of locusts was a darkening of the sun as the swarm filled the sky, a rustling in the yard and a light tapping on the windows. They would come over the mountains in their millions and, by nightfall, everything green for miles around would have been eaten and a wintery grey fallen on the fields. They would eat every blade of grass and every leaf of a tree. And then they would eat the green shawl on the clothes line and the green paint on the doors and the green curtains in the window. They would gnaw the furniture, chew the leather of the saddles and harnesses. They worked their way into the cupboards and destroyed the clothes that hung there. One farmer described seeing locusts more than three inches long. 'We killed dozens underfoot with each step we made and the squashed locusts were instantly gulped down by their voracious brothers.' The family would be sent out to beat saucepans and wave blankets in a desperate attempt to keep the swarm at bay. They tried sweeping them into water filled ditches. They tried laying mounds of straw in their path and setting fire to them, but all in vain. There were too many of them.

In 1875, Albert Child, a Nevada doctor, attempted to measure the size of one such swarm. To estimate its length, he gauged the speed of the swarm and multiplied it by the time it took to pass. Then, to estimate its breadth, he contacted friends to the east and to the west with the help of the new technology of the telegraph. He came to the conclusion that it covered an area of 198,000 square miles, about twice the size of Great Britain, that it contained 12,500,000,000 locusts and that they weighed 27,500,000 tons. The amazing fact is that the Rocky Mountain Locust, which was so numerous in the early days of the Mormon settlement, had disappeared and become extinct by 1885. By ploughing and planting their crops on the high meadows where the locusts laid their eggs, the early settlers unwittingly destroyed the breeding grounds of the species. But that was thirty years into the future.

In September, *Udgorn Seion* published a letter sent from Utah in May. 'There are not fifty acres of corn of any sort still standing in the Salt Lake Valley,' it said. 'There is not a green shoot of corn to be seen in the valleys of Juab, San Pete nor Filmore. They are still sowing in the Little Salt Lake, and in Cedar City also, but the locusts are there, ready to eat the crop as soon as it springs up. To the north, as far as Box Elder, the same is the story, and from the look of things, there is not the slightest sign that a single bushel of corn will be grown in the valleys this year.'

Before summer was out, there was famine in the land and people begging on the highways. Henry Bush of Newport remembered he had to eat 'thistles and red roots. At one time I remember we got so weak from the want of food that my brother and I could not get out of bed. I remember that I was even sinking away and was aroused back to consciousness by hearing my mother scream and cry, "Why do I have to see my children starve to death!" Father was somehow able to get some bran that had been already sifted twice. This saved us.' 'The grasshoppers destroyed nearly all the crops in the northern settlements, and bread stuff was very scarce,' wrote John Johnson Davies, the Carmarthen weaver. 'Many had to dig roots to sustain life; I had to do that myself. I went to the fields to water my corn and got very weak. I started for home and when I got to the house I met my little daughter, Martha, in the door, and she asked me for some bread, and there was no bread in the house. This was a trying time for us. I took a sack and started out and said, "I will get some flour before I come back." I went to Sister Marler; all she had in the house was twenty pounds of flour and one loaf of bread. She gave me half of what she had, and when I got home my wife smiled. Then we had a good breakfast.' What kept John Johnson Davies' family, and many other families, alive through the bleakest days were the bulbs of a small flower called the sego lily. They were edible and nourishing and grew commonly throughout the valleys. More importantly, the bulbs grew deep in the earth, deep enough to escape the locusts' devastation. That year, they were harvested by the ton. Today, unsurprisingly, the sego lily is the state flower of Utah.

The Welsh emigrants who were preparing to cross the Plains that spring knew nothing, of course, of the trials that awaited them in their new home. About a hundred of them had sailed for New Orleans on the *Clara Wheeler* in November 1854, hoping to be on the Plains early in the coming season. Their journey had followed the usual route – to New Orleans, then up the Mississippi and into the Missouri. But by the time the next party set out from Wales, Brigham Young had ordered a change of plan. As so many Saints were being struck down by diseases on the Mississippi, before they'd had a chance of being properly acclimatized, Brigham Young had decided that, from now on, they should avoid New Orleans and take a train across country from Boston, New York or Philadelphia. The ocean voyage to these eastern ports was a fortnight shorter than the voyage to New Orleans and, every year, the railway network was stretching further and further into the west. It was now possible to travel by train as far as Pittsburgh in only two days. Mormon Grove, which had been chosen as the site of the 1855 staging camp, was on the Missouri, another 800 miles beyond Pittsburgh, but they could reach it by riverboat, journeying down the Ohio to St Louis and then up the Missouri as usual on the final leg.

Before the end of July, thousands of Saints had gathered in Mormon Grove. Keeping them fed and healthy was an immense task, but one which the Mormons, with their usual order and discipline, were well capable of organizing. The leader of the first Welsh contingent to use this new route was Thomas Jeremy, the Llanybydder farmer who had come to the United States with Dan Jones on the *Buena Vista*. He had been sent back to Wales as a missionary in 1852 and throughout his time there and on his return journey to Utah, he kept an interesting diary.

'Mormon Grove presents a beautiful appearance,' he writes, 'with its pretty grove, its regular streets lined on each side by tents in regular order and the creeks on each side in the valleys below. The Saints here are kept in admirable order.' Most of the emigrants had to stay in Mormon Grove for the best part of six weeks, buying wagons and oxen, learning how to handle them, collecting the various goods and commodities deemed necessary for the journey and learning how to camp and cook and live on the trail. In Thomas Jeremy's opinion, no group was doing a better job of learning the ropes than the Welsh. 'We have succeeded admirably and with less trouble than some of the other brethren have had with theirs.' He was pleased that the Welsh, once again, were to cross the Plains together, in one company.

It was already a custom amongst the Mormons to celebrate

the anniversary of Brigham Young's arrival in the Valley. 'Tuesday 24th July,' wrote Thomas in his diary, 'we duly celebrated this memorable day by a grand procession in which the Welsh, as usual in everything, took the lead. All the Saints of the Grove following with firearms of all descriptions. Also flags, banners etc. and plenty of music to enliven the scene, with the shooting of guns etc. After the Grand March, we assembled the Saints together for the purpose of a meeting, at which many good toasts were passed and many happy addresses, and a poetical ode was delivered by Bro. Mills, composed for the occasion. In the evening there was dancing etc., etc.'

Thomas was a very patriotic Welshman. He loved to hear the Welsh being complimented and praised. 'I should here remark, to the credit of the Welsh company under my jurisdiction, they were addressed one evening by Bro. M. Andrews, President here at the Grove. During his lecture, he repeatedly said that the Welsh Saints under my charge, were "the best class of people individually that he ever saw, always willing, ever ready to do their duty. They have called on me," he said, and asked, "Bro. Andrews what can I do now? Is there anything to be done?" Such was the substance of his praise for the Welsh. I was truly glad to hear his remarks and to add them to the many others I've heard from others.' Even more than kindly words about the Welsh, Thomas loved to hear kindly words about himself. 'Many of the leaders at the Grove have frequently shown the warmest regard for me at the meetings and then in private. They have blessed me again and again, also telling me how much they loved me.' These last words were underlined. The following day, the Welsh started for Utah in Capt. Charles A. Harper's company. With them travelled English, French and Italian Saints. 'The Welsh,' noted Thomas, 'were the first company ready.' The diaries have little to relate of the first days of the journey. A little girl died, an ox gorged itself to death. At night, around the fire, three choirs, Welsh, English and French, competed in song.

Then came the first big hurdle in their path. 'Tuesday 7th. We came to the banks of Big Blue and found the river too high for us to ford over.' A river in flood could hold up a wagon train for many days, if not weeks. There was a ferry operating at the crossing but its cost was prohibitive. 'Thursday 9th. The river has fallen.' It was decided to seize the opportunity to drive the wagons through. 'We are passing the wagons over as quickly as possible, for the river is again rising and making it more and more difficult for us to pass over.' The river continued to rise and soon, with only half the wagons over on the western side, it became too deep to ford. Some of the young men attempted to swim over. 'The current is very strong,' wrote Thomas, 'and several persons have narrowly escaped with their lives. One young man swimming across was overwhelmed with the current and was found senseless on the water and pulled to shore. He soon recovered.'

Thomas Jeremy has no more to say about the crossing, but another Welshman picks up the story. He was Joseph Thomas Perkins. Perkins was a good swimmer. It was he, in fact, who had rescued the young man from drowning. In his autobiography, he describes the incident. 'While we were camped on both sides of the river, a brother in the Church, a Frenchman, started to swim the river – he was a good swimmer. He tried to swim straight across the stream with his clothes on but he sank in the water. Ropes were got and I plunged in the water after him. I had a rope in one hand and I grabbed him with the other and brought him out. After much trouble his life was saved.'

Joseph Perkins was a practical as well as a brave man. He made sure he had one hand on a rope before diving into the river. Despite his English surname, he was Welsh through and through. The family surname had been Peregrin until it was changed to Perkins sometime between 1849 and 1852 because it was thought to be more acceptable in America. The Perkinses came from Loughor where the grandmother kept a public house called 'The Trap'. Joseph was 34 years old, a strong, tough collier, who had worked down in the mines since he was eight. In his youth, he'd been a heavy drinker, unruly and wild, keeping company with bare-knuckle fighters and frequenting their secret, illicit meetings in the hills behind his home. In 1843, his brother William became a Mormon and then, in 1845, his mother and his father. For a whole year, Joseph withstood their attempts to convert him but when he saw an old drinking companion, who had once been a bare-knuckle fighter, down on his knees, praying for him, he could hold out no longer. 'This melted me,' he wrote. 'I went to breakfast with him, then to morning meeting and at 2 o'clock p.m. that day I was baptized.' Eight years later, his conversion had brought him here – to the banks of the Big Blue. 'Captain Harper went on his horse and tried the ford of the river,' he wrote. 'He came back and informed us we had to lift the wagon beds 10 inches to keep them out of the water.' This was common practice when crossing rivers on the trail. They would bind planks to the sides of the wagons, raising their height, sometimes a foot or more, and then caulk the gaps with rags. Sometimes, in really deep water, they would remove the wheels, lash four wagons together and float them across like rafts. But it was dangerous work. Between 1840 and 1850, over three hundred emigrants on their way west are believed to have lost their lives attempting to cross rivers in flood.

The first attempt to cross the river was to be made by the company Captain, Charles Harper. His wagon was eased gently down the steep, slippery slope into the water. The wheels had been locked by chains wound through the spokes and round the axle. A dozen men held on to ropes attached to the back of the wagon, lest it should roll away out of control. This task accomplished, they halted a moment on the water's edge to detach the chains and anchor ropes and to catch their breath and then a 'gee' to the leading oxen, a crack of the whip over their heads, and into the flood they went. Before the oxen managed to get their footing, they were swept away in the stream. 'The water took them and wagons downstream,' wrote Joseph. 'The Captain jumped off.' All would have been lost had it not been for Joseph. He swam out to the leading ox, grabbed it by the horns and led it to safety on the opposite shore. He then returned, bringing the Captain's oxen back with him, because they were the best trained and most docile in all the company. Soon he was back in the river again, leading another wagon over. 'I led twelve wagons across the river with the Captain's cattle,' he wrote. 'He called me out of the river and said that I had stayed in the water long enough. The thirteenth wagon, coming down the hill with twenty-two sacks of flour and other freight, tipped over into the river. Just as this wagon was got out of the river, the water rose 4 feet.' And that was the end of work for the day.

The next morning the river was still in flood. There were nineteen wagons yet to cross but, despite some hard bargaining with the ferry owners, they had still failed to agree a price. Just then a large cavalry unit arrived at the ford, seven hundred soldiers, half of them mounted, on their way to Fort Laramie to teach the Sioux a lesson for their attack on Grattan the previous autumn. According to John L. Edwards, of Cwmnant Farm in Llanwenog, another of the Welsh in Harper's company, the cavalry tried to swim their horses across, but gave up after one of their number was drowned. The Mormons realised that the army would probably want to use the ferry and that, if they continued to refuse the ferryman's price, they would have to wait until all seven hundred men and horses had crossed. So they paid the fee and quickly ferried over the remaining wagons. The cavalry, led by General William S. Harney, one of the heroes of the war with Mexico, passed them some days later. The Welsh were to meet them again, further down the trail.

In 1855, apart from the Saints, there were few other emigrants going west. Only about five hundred travelled to California and perhaps another 1,500 to Oregon. Everyone believed that a war against the Sioux was inevitable and they feared to venture on to the Plains lest they be caught up in it. Yet there were over 4,500 Mormons on the trail, 1,500 more than in the previous year. To keep the Sioux at bay, they put their faith in God and in the size of their wagon trains. But they were prepared for trouble. The old rule that all men should carry their weapons at all times was reinstated. They were ordered to carry at least two pounds of lead in their wagons for making bullets. No one was to walk too far ahead nor too far behind the wagon train. Every camping site had to be on open ground so that the Indians couldn't approach unseen. The animals were to be kept within the wagon circle throughout the night, with six men constantly on guard. As they approached the more dangerous stretches of the trail, every eye scanned the horizon, every finger tightened on the trigger. Two women were shot by accident and both died before the end of the journey.

Everyone was on tenterhooks. It was an edgy, uneasy time. Unfounded rumours of bloody massacres flew up and down the trail. Many newspapers in the east published stories of desperate battles, such as the attack by 2,000 Sioux on a Captain Doniphan's company of three hundred emigrants, all totally fictitious. Similar stories flew back to Wales. 'It is reported that the Sioux have taken a Mormon camp of twenty wagons, and that there are in their midst about twenty women and children,' wrote a correspondent to the *Udgorn*, but there was no truth in the report.

On September 28th, Thomas Jeremy wrote in his diary, 'While on the road today a large company of Sioux Indians met us. Some of them spread their buffalo robes directly in front of our leading wagon. They sat upon it and their design was to stop the train and make us pay tribute to them. I happened to be there at the time with my shotgun, so I immediately ordered the wagons to move on while I went forward towards them with my gun set ready. When they saw my mode of paying tribute to such rascals, they took up their robe and gave us the road. They continued following alongside all day, loading their guns and making many war like demonstrations. We heard that they tried the same game with the Andrews camp behind us with no better success.'

A little over a month after leaving the Big Blue, they once again met with General Harney and his seven hundred men. The General had attacked a Sioux village the previous day. In the history books, this bloody little scrap is remembered as the Battle of Ash Hollow and, at the time, it was celebrated as a great victory for the army. Harney boasted that he'd killed three hundred of the most ferocious Indian warriors in the West and had taken a hundred prisoners. They were brushed aside with ease, he claimed, and his cavalry swept through their village. But it was later shown that only 250 Sioux warriors had been present and that most of them had escaped. Eighty-six people had been killed, but most of them were women and children. The tepees were all burnt and seventy prisoners taken, but these again were mainly women and children. When this truth was revealed, General Harney earned for himself the soubriquet of 'Woman Killer'.

The Battle of Ash Hollow was another of the small fires that would soon burst into an uncontrollable blaze over the whole of the Great Plains and, once again, the Welsh had stumbled unwittingly into the margins of the history. From the overnight camping site, Thomas Jeremy could see the Sioux village burning. John L. Edwards remembered seeing soldiers burying their dead. According to Joseph Perkins, the emigrants were asked to leave early the following morning so as to be clear of the area, lest the Sioux should counterattack. A squad of soldiers travelled with them for three days until they were well clear of the danger area. Like extras in some great tragedy, the Welsh hurried across the stage.

On October 8th, Thomas Jeremy noted that a letter had been received from Brigham Young. A similar letter had been sent to every company still out on the trail. It warned them that food was very scarce in the Valley and that the crisis was worsening. Following the damage wreaked by the locusts, he said, there had been a crippling drought that had left pastures scorched and streams and rivers dry. The companies were urged not to waste any of their food.

That winter in Utah, thousands of cattle and horses were moved up to the mountains in search of better pasture but the plan went disastrously awry as the hardest, coldest winter yet faced by the young settlement fell upon them. More than half the animals died and the food shortage worsened. 'There are not more than half the people that have bread and they have not more than one half or one quarter of a pound a day per person,' wrote a correspondent to the *Millennial Star*, the Mormon paper that was published in Liverpool. 'A great portion of the people are digging roots.' The people suffered so much during the winter of '55/'56 that Brigham Young even considered abandoning Utah altogether and re-establishing his kingdom in the San Bernardino Valley outside Los Angeles. In the spring of 1856, the locusts returned. There were no harder times in Mormon history than in 1855, 1856 and 1857.

Amongst the Welsh who emigrated in 1855 there was one very peculiar figure whose strange story is well worth retelling. He, like Thomas Job, had lost his way after arriving in Utah and had left the Mormon Church. His name was William W. Davies and he was another in the long line of stonemasons who emigrated to Zion from the Vale of Clwyd. He was born in Denbigh in 1833 and was baptized into the Mormon faith in 1849 when he would have been sixteen years old. His name appears on no ship's manifest nor on any register of those who crossed the Plains, but it is believed that he travelled in 1855. He would therefore be 22 years old. A few weeks before leaving Wales, he had married Sarah E. Jones.

By all accounts, William was a deeply religious youth, but guileless and easily deluded, who heard voices and saw visions. Soon after arriving in Utah, he became convinced that Brigham Young was leading Mormonism astray. He believed that the Prophet was too much concerned with worldly matters and was neglecting his spiritual duties. In his opinion a Prophet's work was to prophesy and Brigham Young was not prophesying enough. It was then that he unfortunately met with a man of similar opinions, but of a more extreme temperament. His name was Joseph Morris. Morris also felt that Brigham Young was a problem.

Some say that Morris was a Welshman, but it seems likelier that he was born just across the border in Cheshire. He had worked in a coal mine somewhere in north Wales, possibly the Point of Ayr mine, and during his time there had been badly burnt in an underground accident. It was in Wales also that he was baptized into the Mormon faith, in the same year as William, when he was 26 years old. William and he therefore may have known each other before coming to Utah. Morris accused Brigham of allowing the rich to profit at the expense of the poor, of allowing polygamy to sour Mormonism and of not behaving like a prophet. That spring a bright comet appeared in the skies above Utah. It was a sign from God, said Joseph, a sign that the Seventh Angel, as described in the Book of Revelation, had come to earth to rule the world and that he, Joseph, was that angel. He then claimed that God had commanded him to take over as Prophet but to allow Brigham to continue as the Church's Head of Business. From 1858 onwards he sent a steady stream of letters to Brigham, explaining kindly that God wished him to resign, but that a job would be found for him. Meanwhile, he, Joseph, would take over the role of Prophet. The letters are still to be seen in the Church archives. Over them Brigham has scribbled 'Balderdash!', 'Twaddle!' and 'Bosh!' In 1861, having failed to convince Brigham of the urgent need for him to resign, Joseph Morris called on his followers to leave their homes and to gather with him in an old fort on the banks of the Weber River, thirty miles outside Salt Lake City. It had been built years earlier as a defence against Indians. Morris intended to wait there until God passed the reins of power into his hands. Brigham, meanwhile, ignored the whole tomfoolery.

William W. Davies was one of many Welshmen to join Joseph Morris. John E. Jones of Newport was another. He became one of Morris' twelve apostles. John Evan Reese of Llandeilo, formerly President of the Cwmaman branch of the Church, and his wife, Mary, from Llangyfelach, were also faithful followers. William and Sarah would have been at home in their company.

Morris prophesised that Christ's Second Coming was about to happen and that He would appear in the fort within days. So certain was he that the old order was passing and that the end of the world was at hand that he advised his followers not to bother with preparing the fields for next year's harvest. Instead, the faithful spent their time sweeping and tidying the fort so as to have it looking smart and at its best when the Lord arrived. About Christmas time, Morris received messages from Christ advising him that His arrival was imminent. 'You may possibly see me on Monday,' was one such message, 'but if I should not come on Monday, I shall surely come on Tuesday.' By this time, over ninety fit and able men, with their families, had gathered in the fort and their numbers were increasing. They were roused to fever pitch by a constant flow of prophecies from on high. Brigham Young could ignore them no longer. He called one of his militia officers to him and charged him with the silencing of the noisy prophet on the Weber.

The Morrisites were hopelessly outnumbered. A five hundred-strong unit of the militia came to the Weber, hauling two large cannons. They sent an ultimatum into the fort, giving the occupants half an hour to surrender. But before the defenders had time to read the message, the first shells fell amongst them, killing two women and blowing the jaw off another. The Morrisites fought bravely and for three days they kept the Church troops at bay, killing two of them. Throughout this time, they were eagerly anticipating the arrival of Jesus, who would surely lead them to victory. Eventually, they had to submit. The militia officers entered the fort and shot Morris and his deputy dead. And that was the end of the Morrisite Rebellion. Over a hundred of the fort's defenders, including William and Sarah, were taken prisoner and marched to Salt Lake City. Seven of them were found guilty of murder and received sentences ranging from ten to fifteen years in jail. But many people in Utah were disturbed by the heavy punishments meted out by the Church courts and the extreme violence directed against what they considered to be a harmless bunch of eccentrics. Brigham denied that he had ordered an all-out attack but was widely criticized, especially by the growing non-Mormon population of the territory. The federal courts ordered the immediate release of every prisoner, William and Sarah Davies amongst them. They were given a military escort out of the territory to the Idaho border and there they were left, leaderless and shelterless, with re-entry into Utah prohibited. Many of them lived together for a while in Soda Springs in Idaho and then in Virginia City and Deer Lodge in Montana, slowly moving further and further into the west. During his time in Montana, William Davies started seeing visions again and receiving revelations from God. He said that God had commanded him to go to Walla Walla in Washington Territory to establish there the 'Kingdom of Heaven' where Christ would return again.

About forty of the Morrisites agreed to go with him. The Wild West was a harsh and cruel place and they had become used to being members of a supportive and protective community. They had also become used to the concept of a man claiming to be God's representative on earth and addressing them on His behalf. It did not seem unbelievable to them, nor was it unwelcome. When they were offered the chance to continue that way of life, they gratefully accepted it.

They arrived in Walla Walla in 1867 and bought eighty acres of land and there they stayed for the next fifteen years. Like many utopian and egalitarian communities at that time in North America, they shared everything, each according to his need. William was their leader in all things, be they of this world or of the next. His name was on all deeds, he signed all the contracts. But the legal owner of the 'Kingdom of Heaven', the land and the farm buildings and all their contents, was the community as a whole.

William proved to be a good leader to his people. He kept a tight grip on his flock and never betrayed their trust in him. He built a church and a school in the 'Kingdom of Heaven'. 'The houses,' said the *Walla Walla Statesman* in 1878, 'are built in a cluster, all neat and tiny. The women and children are scrupulously clean, with the men and boys all wearing long hair. They have the latest agricultural equipment with ample sheds for cattle and hay. They grow sugar cane and have a mill to make sugar and molasses. Hemp is grown to make rope and cordage, and in the winter the young men make brooms from broom corn.' William had pamphlets published expounding the beliefs of the community and sent missionaries to distribute them as far south as San Francisco.

Soon after they had settled in Walla Walla, Sarah gave birth to a baby boy and he was called Arthur. 'Thus,' said William, 'was God's promise made flesh.' Christ had returned to them, he said, not in an earthquake and a pillar of fire, but, as He had done in Bethlehem long ago, as an innocent child. When Sarah understood that she had given birth to the Messiah, such was her awe of him that she feared to touch the child. But William explained that God would not have chosen her to be the mother of His son had He not considered her worthy.

Arthur grew to be an attractive child. He was intelligent and friendly and was much loved in the 'Kingdom' and in the surrounding communities. Preserved in the records of Walla Walla County is a photograph of him, clothed in a white cloak that falls to his feet, displaying a curious dignity and authority. He was happily accepted as the reincarnation of Christ and he became known far and wide as 'The Walla Walla Jesus'. The membership of William Davies' community grew to seventy.

The following year, a brother was born to Arthur, who proved, according to William, to be God the Father made flesh and, at about the same time, William declared himself to be the Holy Ghost. This was not considered implausible in the 'Kingdom' and the greatest respect was shown to all three. Indeed, it was the certainty that God was amongst them that preserved 'The Kingdom' for nearly fifteen years.

It could have lasted longer had the community not been devastated by an outbreak of diphtheria. Sarah died in the autumn of 1879. On February 15th, 1880, the younger boy died and, exactly a week later, he was followed to the grave by his brother Arthur. The death of their Christ was the end of 'The Kingdom'. They had invested all their hopes in him and, when he died, the community immediately began to unravel. Before the end of 1880, three of the faithful had decided to leave, but before they left, they demanded to be given their share of the value of the land and buildings. Short of selling the 'Kingdom of Heaven', William had no means of paying them. They took him to court to make him pay.

In the dock, William defended himself with honour and dignity. He humbly described how the Spirit of the Lord had fallen to earth one day in January 1866, and how it had landed on him, not as an honour, but as a terrible duty. He explained that he had encouraged his people to live moral lives and that he had tried to banish alcohol from the community. Many of the faithful appeared in the dock to vouch for his integrity. 'I know of no other God except Mr. Davies and his two sons,' said one. 'If the Davises were God, it was all right with me,' said another. But William lost the case and had to sell the 'Kingdom of Heaven' and the community was broken up and scattered. William Davies was no Brigham Young. He possessed none of his charisma nor his drive nor his administrative skills nor his intelligence, but there is something strangely appealing about his credulous ways and his pathetic but honourable devotion to his followers. In an age when many self-styled messiahs sucked their followers dry, William left Walla Walla and the 'Kingdom of Heaven' as poor as on the day he arrived.

By this time, many of his followers felt more able to face the challenges of life in the West. John E. Jones, the Apostle, and Rachel Jones, his wife, had remained with William until the end, but now they left Walla Walla and moved, with their family, over the border into Oregon. There they managed to buy land, raise a family and farm successfully. They remained a religious family throughout their lives, continuing to respect the Sabbath, but they never again joined an organised church nor followed any messiah. Today, Jones Butte, a low hill behind the farm, still carries the family name.

We also know what happened to John Evan Reese and his wife, Mary. They had decided not to follow William to Walla Walla. After they were released from jail in Salt Lake City, they went to the goldfields of Alder Gulch, near Virginia City in Montana. There Mary made a fortune taking in laundry and washing the miners' clothes. She came away with $1,100 hidden in the folds of her dress, enough to buy land in the

Gallatin Valley, near Bozeman in Montana and to stock it with cattle. For the rest of their days, John Evan and Mary remained faithful to the son of Joseph Smith and the Reorganized Church of Jesus Christ of Latter-day Saints. The stream that runs by their property and the small village that grew in the valley are both called Reese Creek in their honour and today John and Mary lie in peace in the Reese Creek burial ground.

As for William Davies, the details of his life after he left Walla Walla are vague. He is thought to have married a Mrs Perkins and moved to California, where it is believed he joined a conventional church. But he returned to Walla Walla to die, and there he was eventually buried.

1856

THE STAGING CAMP of the 1856 season was situated seventy miles west of the Mississippi, in Iowa City, at the terminus of the Rock Island Line. For the first time, it had been possible to travel all the way to the staging camp by rail, without having to use the steamboats. Although this meant an extra leg of about 250 miles in the wagons to get to the Missouri, it was considered a quicker, cheaper and infinitely healthier route. As usual, the camp was meticulously ordered. Captain Dan Jones, who was returning that spring from another stint in the Welsh mission, bringing with him 560 converts, the largest contingent yet to leave Wales, sang its praises in a letter published in *Udgorn Seion*. 'Everything is kept so clean and spotless that we might well be in a gentleman's park. People travel hundreds of miles here to see if what they had heard about us and our camp was true.' It was laid out with fastidious care. In the centre were rows of large, circular tents, each one with its number above the entrance. These were surrounded by rows of square tents. And a new feature this year were the large pens of what seemed to be outsized handcarts that clustered around the tents. These two-wheeled vehicles were to play a central role in the drama of the coming months.

Despite the apparent order in the camp, the strategy for the season's migration was in turmoil. For a multitude of reasons, Brigham Young knew he had to bring more Saints to Zion. Firstly, he worried that there were so many of them still out in 'Babylon', so many who wanted to come but were without the means to do so. He felt an urgent need to gather them, for the Latter Days were at hand. He worried also that Zion was far from ready to receive the Lord, that the temple was unfinished and that much building work remained to be done. 'Strength of arm and shoulder will be necessary to carry the work forward,' wrote Thomas Jeremy in a letter to Wales that year, 'for the time is short and the labour is great, and it is as much as we can ever do to get ready before the Lord Jesus comes to visit this earth.'

Then Brigham was also worried about the financial health of his new settlement. If the economy was to grow there had to be a corresponding growth in the workforce. He wanted to see as much as possible of the West settled by his own people before other groups, who were not Mormons, arrived. He had been sending out communities of Saints to settle wherever there was good water and fertile soil, far beyond the borders of present-day Utah, into the Carson Valley in western Nevada, for example, and into the San Bernardino Valley in California and Fort Bridger in Wyoming and Lemhi in Idaho. His empire covered more than a sixth of the territory of the United States and to defend it and develop it, he needed more Saints in Zion.

At the back of his mind also was the growing possibility of war with the United States. The Mormons were an anathema to the people of the East, their faith considered un-Christian and their polygamous marriages uncivilized. The government in Washington regarded Brigham Young as a dictator and feared that his aim was to carve out an independent kingdom within the borders of the United States. In the presidential election of 1856, the Republican Party had promised, if elected, to do away with what they described as 'the twin relics of barbarism – Polygamy and Slavery'. The relationship between Washington and Utah deteriorated month by month and, whilst the threat of invasion hung over him, Brigham Young wanted more men to defend his state.

But money was scarce. Brigham had been spending heavily on constructing the temple. He'd built a canal to bring down the huge blocks of granite that were to be its walls from the quarries in the hills. He had irrigated the Valley and built roads. He had spent heavily on projects such as the iron works in Cedar City, where Elias Morris laboured. He'd spent on coal pits and lead mines, on a paper mill, woollen mills and a large commercial pottery. He was attempting to make Utah self-sufficient, so that she no longer had to depend on trade with the 'Babylonians', but these projects had as yet only swallowed up large chunks of capital without producing much in return. To crown all his other worries, the harvest of 1855 had failed again.

One consequence of the worsening financial situation was that the coffers of the Perpetual Emigrating Fund were emptying. During the three years since its inception, the Fund had been a great success. In addition to financing the removal of the poor from the camps on the Missouri, it had paid the costs of over 4,000 Saints travelling from Britain to Utah. But so tough were the times and so taxing the struggle to settle their families in their new home that many of the newcomers were finding it difficult to repay the loan. The fund's capital was leaching away. That summer, William Lewis, one of the 1849 pioneers, wrote to a friend in Wales about the difficulties of bringing his daughter over. 'The way appears to be closed at present, since the Public Works have been idle since the last part of last year, which was brought about by the scarcity of food because of the grasshoppers and the drought. If the work had continued I would have paid into the Fund before now, and then I could send for her by next season.'

For all these reasons, Brigham urgently needed a more efficient means of bringing his people across the Plains. Somehow, he had to increase the number of immigrants and decrease the cost of their journeys. He reasoned that the most expensive element of their passage was the purchase of oxen and wagons and it was here that he determined the greatest savings could be made. His new plan was certainly cheaper, possibly faster, but it was also much more dangerous. Before the summer was out, it would lead to the deaths of hundreds of people and at the heart of this impending tragedy were the two-wheeled handcarts.

At the beginning of the December 1855, whilst on a visit to the headquarters of the British Mission in Liverpool, Dan Jones had been shown a letter from Brigham Young to the head of the mission, Franklin Richards, explaining the new plan. When Dan arrived back at his editorial office in Swansea, he hurried to publish in *Udgorn Seion* an account of what he'd learnt. 'When we were in Liverpool last week... we declare having seen a letter from President Young encouraging the Saints to come on foot... carrying their tents and their provisions for a few weeks, and a few clothes with them, on light two-wheeled wagons that will be purpose built for the journey and which will be pulled by the men.' Brigham Young intended for them to walk from Mormon Grove all the way to the Salt Lake, over 1,200 miles, hauling behind them all their worldly goods and every necessity for the journey in some sort of glorified wheelbarrow. 'Fifteen miles a day will bring them through in 70 days, and after they get accustomed to it they will travel 20, 25 and even 30 with all ease.'

The idea of pulling carts halfway across the continent and of walking twenty miles a day through the heat of the Great Plains and the cold of the Rockies, did not immediately appeal to the faithful, but Dan hurried to quieten their fears. 'We believe the emigrants could go to the end of their journey in two-thirds, if not half the time, and do so without having to walk much more or any more than they do with the oxen... They can rest now in the time that was taken earlier to watch over the oxen at night, or search for them after they escaped by stampeding or through the Indians stealing them. There would be no need for half the camp to guard against their getting poisoned by drinking the alkali waters... without mentioning the making of bridges, getting up out of the mud holes and the ditches, and the time taken to repair wagons that were always breaking down... It is thought that the journey to Zion in this manner will not cost much over half the cost of going with oxen.' He estimated the cost of the journey to be £8 for adults and ten shillings for children.

To travel to Utah for £8 a head! A sum well within their

means. An £8-ticket to Zion! The faithful began to dream and to believe. Little did they know of the trials that lay ahead, of the stifling heat, the dust, the mosquitoes and the constant weariness. Little did they know of the nameless graves that lined the route. Little did they imagine that before the year was out, some of them would be crawling towards Zion. They put their trust in their Prophet, Brigham Young, and in their leader, Dan Jones, men who knew the conditions that awaited them on the Plains. If they were in favour of the plan, then that was good enough for them. 'Let not anyone be frightened at this plan, for to us, and to everyone who has been back and forth along the entire way to Zion, many advantages appear very obvious in using this way over the old oxen way.' Dan added that an ox-drawn wagon would accompany every twenty emigrants, in which extra food might be carried and where there would be room for the sick and infirm. There would also be cows travelling with each company so that fresh milk and butter would be available every day. Wagonloads of food would be sent from Utah to meet them at Fort Laramie and at South Pass and, furthermore, he promised that he, personally, would ensure that the journey would start in plenty of time for them to get to Utah before the winter snows. 'There is no danger,' he wrote 'that either President Richards or your own servant will start any of their brethren at a time inappropriate for the journey.'

Only a few weeks remained before the first Mormon ships of the season would leave for Boston and New York. Arrangements for the new scheme had to be hurried. In the next edition of *Udgorn Seion* Dan described his visits to a number of the south Wales branches to whip up enthusiasm for the plan. 'The first questions that comes out of the mouths of many of the brothers, and sisters also, are, "Well, well, how will we carry our bonnets, umbrella, parasols, and silk gowns; and our expensive shawls will be damaged by carrying them in bags! Oh dear, I cannot think of going without them." "Yes," says another, "we cannot take our looking glasses, our ornaments, our china, or all our new clothes we have prepared for the journey."' His answer to them was, 'Away with the old pictures off your walls... away with the clocks and the watches, the adornments, the rings, yes and even the splendid clothes intended for the coming years; let it all be sold... to gather the £8, instead of remaining behind as prey for the plagues, and Babylon's dogs of war.' By early spring, the names of over seven hundred would-be Welsh emigrants had been collected and, a few weeks later, on April 19th, Dan Jones left for America on the *Samuel Curling* in the company of 560 of them. The rest were to follow in a number of different ships over the ensuing weeks.

Dan Jones and his entourage sailed into Boston harbour five weeks later, and eight days after that, they arrived at the Rock Island Line terminus in Iowa City. Although speedy, the train journey had not been uneventful. To keep costs down, they had travelled at times in cattle wagons, in filthy conditions and foul air. Dan wrote that he had had to fight 'all the blasted fiends of hell' to preserve the virtue and the honour of Welsh maidenhood on the journey. 'In several towns, such as Buffalo, Toledo, Chicago, and Rock Island, especially the last, we were obliged to mount an armed watch on the carriages, on Saturday night, and fight with crowds of hounds such as those that were once in Sodom throughout the Sunday with arms, clubs, pitchforks, and swords in order to keep them from rushing on the sisters, and indeed all the brethren fought well until victory, and although we had very little help from the Sheriff and his army, he was kind enough to give us the freedom to defend ourselves, and no sooner was that obtained than the little Mormon army rushed into the middle of the throng, outing a swathe before them as wide as the road, and guess who was leading them. The next day it was proved before the Mayor that these bloodhounds had sworn allegiance to each other in order to help each other to steal the fairest of our women to serve their own devilish purpose, and it was thanks to the power of arms and the bravery of my fellow soldiers that they did not succeed.' No mention is made of 'The Battle of Rock Island' in any other diary or biography.

The likelihood is that most of the excitement was conjured in Dan's own imagination.

He was not now a healthy man. He complained in his letters of the heavy responsibility of overseeing such a complicated itinerary for so many people. It was weighing him down and sapping his spirit. As the Welsh contingent dashed from train to train, Dan would have had to find food for them, arrange toilet and washing facilities and supervise the transfer of the baggage. Most of them couldn't speak English and few of them would have previously travelled far from their home parishes. It could not have been easy. 'By the time I reached here,' he wrote from the camp in Iowa City, 'I had hardly enough strength in me to live any more, and it was not for nearly three weeks that I, nor anyone else, knew in which world I would be the next day.'

Meanwhile, the Welsh were being introduced to their handcarts – wooden boxes, five feet long, perched on two wheels and an axle. The axles were the same width as the axles of the ox wagons, allowing the wheels to run easily in the ruts of the trail. Nailed to the sides of the boxes were two shafts, joined together at their ends by a wooden crossbar. It was against this bar that the two strongest members of the family would push to move the cart along, the rest of the family helping either by pulling on ropes attached to the bar or pushing from behind.

The carts were very flimsy. The wheel rims were bound, not with iron hoops, but with straps of leather, and the wooden wheels turned on wooden axles, with no metal parts to smooth the action or to prevent chafing. Often, the only metal in them were the nails which held the box and the shafts together. They were built in haste, often before the timber was dry. In the oppressive heat of the Great Plains, as the green wood dried and twisted, one handcart after another would warp and fall apart. Their only virtue was that they were light, weighing only about sixty pounds.

After arriving in Iowa City, the emigrants were told they would be allowed to take only seventeen pounds of personal belongings with them on the handcarts. Clothes, bedding, cooking implements and other travel necessities would make up most of this allowance. For people who had paid dearly to bring family treasures with them across the Atlantic, who had lugged them from train to train and who had succeeded in holding on to them through the confusion of the journey so far, this must have been a bitter blow. Priscilla Merriman Evans, of Monkton in south Pembrokeshire, wrote that she had to leave behind 'my feather bed, and bedding, pillows, all our good clothing, my husband's church books, which he had collected through six years of missionary work, with some genealogy he had collected, all had to be left in a storehouse. We were promised that they would come to us with the next emigration in the spring, but we never did receive them. It was reported that the storehouse burned down so that was a dreadful loss to us.' Nathaniel and Jane Edmunds had brought enough clothes with them from Merthyr Tydfil to last them ten years but they all had to be left behind in the camp in Iowa City. Another emigrant wrote of the 'many things left on the camping site for anybody to take or leave at his pleasure. It was grievous to see the heaps of books and other articles thus left in the sun, rain and dust.' Much of what was left behind were irreplaceable treasures, keepsakes which would have made separation from their loved ones a little easier to bear.

Sixty-four handcarts were shared out between the Welsh, one for each family. The single men and women were then allotted to the carts with the weakest families. Some families were very weak indeed. They had been chosen, not for their fitness for the task, but for their dedication to the cause. As a consequence, many unlikely pilgrims had arrived in Iowa City. Ann Thomas, for example, was 78 years old and nearly blind. She and her husband, Evan, had been the first Mormon converts in the village of Rhymney back in 1843. In his seventieth year, Evan had died, whilst working as a collier in the Pennsylvania coalfields, trying to raise the money to bring Ann to America. Now she had been given her reward.

Thomas D. Evans had only one leg. A railway wagon had run over his left leg, cutting it off below the knee, when he was a nine-year-old lad in Merthyr. Walking long distances was extremely painful. His stump chafed against the wood, causing it to fester and bleed. On wet days, the leg sank deep into the mud of the trail and he would have to heave it out to take the next step. This wooden leg, until recently, occupied a place of honour in the Church History Museum in Salt Lake City. His wife, the aforementioned Priscilla, was in her fourth month of pregnancy. Every night she would help her crippled husband and the ten other emigrants to erect the tent they shared together. Thomas was not the only disabled traveller amongst them. 'In our tent,' Priscilla wrote, 'there were my husband with one leg, two blind men, a man with one arm, and a widow with five children' – not the ideal team to be pushing a handcart over the Rockies. But as Dan Jones said, 'their trust in the Lord was unshakeable and their faith greater than any obstacle in their path'.

By the time Dan had recovered, two of the handcart companies had already left for the Missouri and the third, an all-Welsh handcart company of 320 people, was ready to set out. These first three companies of the season had relatively trouble-free passages. Priscilla's chief complaint was that there was so few in her company who could converse with her. Coming as she did from below the Landsker Line in Pembrokeshire, she could not speak Welsh and it frustrated her that she was one of the very few in the company who were not fluent in the language. 'Don't you think I had a pleasant journey travelling for months with 300 people of whose language I could not understand a word?' she wrote. 'The widow, her children, and myself were the only ones who could not talk Welsh.' The Captain of the company, Edward Bunker, an American from Maine, also felt the same frustration. 'The Welsh had no experience at all and very few of them could speak English,' he wrote. 'This made my burden very heavy.'

Bunker's company left Iowa City on June 23rd. 'They left in the midst of loud shouts of Hosannah and rejoicing,' wrote Dan Jones. 'I escorted them the first day and their only concern was that I would not be allowed to go with them.' He had been asked to stay behind to look after the remainder of the Welsh in the staging camp.

Amongst the handcarters in Bunker's company, there were a number of large family groups, such as the twenty members of the Parry family from around Abergele in Denbighshire, the seventeen members of the Lewis family from Swansea and the thirteen in Thomas John Rees' family. Thomas was a collier, the son of a collier and the father of colliers. He had been born in Merthyr, he had married there and he had lived there all his life until he emigrated. He was illiterate when he married, marking his marriage certificate with a cross, but Margaret, his new wife was a teacher, and she soon taught him to read and to write well enough to be elected President of the Merthyr branch of the Church. In Merthyr were born the eight children that sailed with them for America. John, the eldest son, brought with him his fiancée, Margaret Jenkins, and she brought her father and mother, Henry and Martha Jenkins. Henry died as the company was passing Fort Laramie and Margaret remembered how they buried him in the middle of the trail and lit a fire over his grave in an attempt to put the wolves off the scent. The rest of the family arrived safely in Salt Lake City. Thomas John Rees must have enjoyed himself on the trail, for a year later he was off again, this time setting out with his son, Henry, for the goldfields of California. Margaret and the rest of the family were left behind in Utah to fend for themselves. The men were back within eighteen months, no richer but probably wiser.

Meanwhile, coal had been discovered in Utah. The Indians had led the Mormons to 'the stones that burn', a seam of coal that surfaced on the slopes of a hill in the valley of the Sanpete, some two hundred miles south of the Salt Lake. It proved to be a workable seam of good coal and soon, fifteen families had been moved to the area to work it, most of them originally from Merthyr. Amongst them was Thomas John Rees and five of his sons. After having enjoyed the freedom of the trail and the adventure of prospecting for gold, it's hard to believe that John and his boys were happy to knuckle down to life underground again, but it had not been their choice. They had received a call from Brigham Young, and when Brigham Young called, he was not to be denied. The pit thrived and a large village soon grew around it, which they called Wales. In 1875, the mine was sold to a London company and the proceeds shared between the villagers. Thomas and his sons continued to work for the new company, each one of them now the owner of a fine house and an acre and a half of land in the middle of the village and there Thomas remained for the rest of his life. When he died, in 1882, there were over six hundred people living in Wales.

Today, little over two hundred remain. The coal pit has long since closed. The shops, the petrol station and the library have gone. On the hill above the village, however, the cemetery is still busy, still with Reeses amongst its clientele. The weathering stones reveal how the memories of home faded as the years passed. On the earlier ones, the spelling of the place names are precise and the geography is accurate. Thomas Rees was born in 'Merthyr Tydfil, Glamorganshire', Thomas Davis in 'Rhigos, Glamorganshire, South Wales' and Dan Williams in 'Brecon, South Wales'. But later they become more vague and blurred. Mary Harries was born in 'Merthyr Tydfil, Glan Morgan Shire', Ann Price Rees in 'Merthyrtydvill, Wales', and Henry Thomas in 'South Wales, Great Britain'.

Spring came late in 1856, but when it came it was worth the waiting. Iowa was no longer an empty land. Newly settled farms dotted the landscape. On the road to Des Moines small villages grew. 'As we travelled through the places, many made fun of us for walking and pulling our carts,' wrote Priscilla, now five months pregnant. 'But the weather was fine, the roads good, and although I was sick and weak and we were all tired out at night, still we thought it a glorious way to come to Zion.'

They reached Florence, a fast growing community on the west bank of the Missouri, on July 19th and ten days later, having repaired the carts and replenished their food stocks, they were off again on the final leg of the journey. To keep costs down, food was rationed from the start. Everyone was allocated a pound of flour a day which was generally used to make pancakes of fried dough. During the first weeks, a little bacon and coffee were also distributed, but the supply soon ran out. 'After months of travelling we were put on half rations,' remembered Priscilla, 'and at one time before help came, we were out of flour for two days. We shook the flour sacks in the water to make gravy, but had no grease of any kind.' Many of the company complained about the diminishing rations, but in the opinion of John Parry, the deputy Captain of the company and the son of John Parry, the founder of the Tabernacle Choir, their complaints were unwarranted. 'Several grumbled because there was not an abundance of food given out, and some stayed behind because of it; but I lived on what was given out, and worked as much as any man in the camp, and you understand that I am alive, and looking better and healthier than I ever did before.' John Parry enjoyed every moment of his passage to Utah. 'America is a beautiful and attractive land, with an abundance of everything except for inhabitants. I have not seen anyone who is repenting for having left the old country, rather they praise God for their deliverance from it... I wish for you to remember me to all the Saints in Wales, especially my brothers and sisters in the north. I would really love to see them receive redemption from the cruel captivity of Babylon to the glorious freedom of the children of Zion.'

Bunker drove his company hard and refused to allow the old and weak to travel in the ox carts. According to Priscilla, the only option when one fell ill was to be carried on the family handcart. 'Strong men would help the weaker ones, until they themselves were worn out, and some died from the struggle, and were buried by the wayside.' But Bunker knew that they had to be over the Rockies before the first heavy snowstorms fell. Even before they had reached the foothills, they experienced the first intimations of winter. 'Some thirty miles this side of Laramie, we woke up one morning to find six inches of snow on the ground,' wrote Robert D. Roberts. 'We remained in camp until the sun had melted the snow a little, and then resumed our journey, feeling very down hearted, as the road was very muddy, which made the carts hard to pull.' Bunker pushed the company harder than ever.

One of the blind men who shared the tent with Priscilla fell seriously ill. His name was Thomas Giles and he was possibly the most interesting of all the Welsh Saints who pulled a handcart to Utah. He had been a miner. He had worked underground with his father when he was eight years old. Twenty years later, he was blinded in an accident at the coalface. By then, married and with three children, he had become a much respected Mormon elder and the President of the Monmouthshire Conference. Despite his blindness, he continued his work of visiting the brethren in their homes, preaching to them, counselling them and comforting them. His diary, kept by a secretary who went with him everywhere, records the details of his visits, to Fleur-de-Lis, to Argoed, to Tredegar, to Blackwood, to Sirhowy, to Pen-y-cae (the old name of Ebbw Vale), to Pontllanfraith and beyond, to Merthyr, Newport and Swansea.

'24th October, 1852. Went to the Rasa branch, and was teaching the Saints to prepare for emigrating to Zion. In the evening at six I preached first on the establishment of God's kingdom, then on the person of God, that he possesses a body, parts and passions, and thirdly on the gathering to Zion. I laid hands on Sister Mary Davies according to her desire, that she may receive health, and on another boy to the same purpose.'

'19th March, 1854. Attended a prayer meeting at Bro E. Rees' and administered the ordinance for healing the sick upon three persons and went about 2 miles to a public baptism and afterwards to Cwmtillery, a distance of about 3 miles to a meeting. In the evening I preached to a large and attentive audience.'

He was very fond of music. '11th October, 1852. In the evening we went to the concert, and had very much amusement, through hearing the brethren and sisters singing, and also the harp.' He had a good voice and was often invited to sing at these meetings. He sang Welsh Mormon hymns such as 'Daeth yr awr' [The hour cometh] and 'Pa beth yw'r arwyddion' [What are the signs].

'24th July, 1852. Went with the mail to Llanelli. I had the privilege of addressing the Saints, and at the president's request I sang two songs, the first on the persecution at Nauvoo, in Welsh, and the other on the signs of the Last Days, also in Welsh.'

Giles was an enthusiastic supporter of the language. In the meetings of the Monmouthshire Saints, he made sure that the language received the respect he felt it deserved. In the Nant-y-Glo Conference of 1848, for example, the officers addressed the assembled Saints first in Welsh and then in English, showing, says the clerk, 'the same respect to the English brothers and sisters'. In the larger towns – Tredegar and Ebbw Vale – there were separate Welsh and English branches, and in the smaller communities the meetings were bi-lingual. September 8th, 1852, was a red-letter day in Thomas' life. 'Went to Llantrisant, and Elder Hodge came there to meet me, to buy the Harp, a present given to me by the Saints.' References to the harp and to learning to play the harp abound thereafter in the diary. 'I practiced playing upon the harp.' 'Had some lessons in Musick from W. Williams.' '23rd November. I was at Brother Williams' practicing to play the harp today & likewise the 24th & 25th.' By the time he left for the Valley in 1856 he was an accomplished harpist.

He sailed with his wife, Margaret, and his children, Joseph (8), Hyrum (6) and Maria (1). With them travelled the harp. In a cattle wagon, on the train journey to Chicago, Maria died. The only evidence we have of this is a passage in the diary kept by John Parry, who was travelling on the same train, describing his own child's death. 'My little boy had the measles,' he writes. 'He was very sick. In just a few hours he died. We buried him in a Chicago burial ground, along with Thomas Giles' little girl.' Margaret was pregnant again, which may have eased a little of the pain of losing her daughter.

Thomas was not short of money. In Iowa City, he paid for his wife and the two boys to travel in a wagon to Utah. But he himself chose to travel with the handcarts. Why this should be, why he should leave his family at this, the most dangerous stage of their journey, we don't know. The missionaries often preached that to pull a handcart over the trail and to use the money thus saved to finance another family's crossing was 'a glorious way to come to Zion'. Perhaps this is what Thomas did.

Towards the end of the trail, somewhere in the region of Fort Bridger, Thomas Giles was struck down by a serious illness, so serious that Bunker despaired of his life. He ordered two men to remain with him to dig his grave. But Thomas Giles was not ready to die. He knew that an old friend, one of the great men of the Church, the Apostle Parley Pratt, was on his way from the Valley to the east and likely to pass within a few days. He strove to keep alive until he should arrive. When he came, Parley Pratt anointed Thomas with the holy oil, blessed him and laid hands on him and Thomas, so the story goes, arose from his deathbed and continued triumphantly on his way.

The Welsh entered Salt Lake City 64 days after leaving Florence. Theirs was the fastest crossing of the season. On average, they had walked sixteen miles a day. 'My dear brother and sister,' wrote Hopkin Matthews in a letter home to his family in Treboeth, Swansea, 'I am happy to be able to inform you that my family and I arrived safely at the end of our journey on the second of this month, at which time we were welcomed with a sumptuous meal prepared for us, which contained a variety of delicious fruits of the Valley… We had an unusually successful journey across the Plains and through the mountains, and the weather was splendid… Alma and Joan were with me and my dear wife to pull the entire way: Elisabeth, Mari, and Margaret walked the entire way. Sometimes we travelled 30 miles per day.'

Not every family was as fortunate. Samuel Brookes had been the keeper of the lighthouse on the Point of Ayr near Talacre in Flintshire for more than thirty years. His small cottage in the dunes near the light had been a rendezvous for the Saints of north-east Wales for many years and some of the early converts, including Elias Morris, had been baptized in the sea at the foot of the lighthouse. In his 65th year, Samuel had set out for Zion, accompanied by his wife, Emma, and their three children, Mary (17), George (11) and Frank (5). The family left Iowa City with Samuel and Emma between the shafts of the cart and Mary and George pushing from behind. Frank was a crippled, disabled child and he was carried in the cart the whole way. The strain of pushing the wagon proved too much for Emma and Samuel. She died before they had left the Missouri and was buried in the burial ground in Florence. Mary took her mother's place between the shafts. Samuel died a few days after reaching Salt Lake City. The orphaned children waited in the camp in Union Square for someone to offer them work and a home. With them were the other newly arrived emigrants who had no relatives and no friends to welcome them. Mary was taken to be a maid by a family from Ogden, 35 miles to the north, and crippled Frank was taken to live with a philanthropic family in Salt Lake City. George was left in the square by himself. He spoke little English and didn't know how to ask for help. He waited there for six days, surviving on gifts of bread and fruit from passers-by. Then, a member of the Parry family of Abergele recognized him and took him home, to raise him as their own son.

But the Bunker Company's losses were no heavier than would have been expected on a normal ox wagon crossing. Amazingly even the half-blind, 78-year-old widow, Anne Thomas, arrived in Salt Lake City no worse for her ordeal. They had proved that Brigham's plan was feasible, that it was possible to pull a handcart to Zion. 'We were tired, weary, with bleeding feet, our clothing worn out, and so weak we were nearly starved,' wrote Priscilla, 'but thankful to our Heavenly Father for bringing us to Zion.'

October had already come and the winter snows would soon be upon them. In Salt Lake City it was assumed that the Bunker Company was the last of the season. But, far back on the trail, unbeknown to them, two companies of handcarters and two companies of ox wagons were still struggling towards the Valley. James Willie's handcarters were approaching Fort Laramie, more than five hundred miles from the safety of Salt

Lake City and about a hundred miles behind them was Edward Martin's company, also pulling handcarts, and then came the ox wagon companies of Hunt and Hodgetts. These last three companies were travelling together, sometimes Martin up ahead, sometimes Hodgetts, with Hunt nearly always bringing up the rear. A fortnight later, on October 14th, when the first blizzards struck the Rockies, there were still over 1,300 Saints up in the mountains, hundreds of miles from the Valley, without blankets, without warm clothing and their food running out. Amongst them, there were between sixty and seventy Welsh, most of them with Hunt.

There had been a serious hitch in communication between the British emigration office in Liverpool and the American ports, and between those ports and the camps in Iowa and Nebraska. The last two Mormon ships of the year, the *Thornton* which left Liverpool on May 4th, carrying 764 emigrants, and the *Horizon*, leaving on the 25th, carrying 856, should have been on the Atlantic weeks earlier. No one in Iowa was expecting another complement of migrants. When they suddenly appeared, food and tents and other necessities had to be bought at short notice and 250 handcarts hurriedly assembled. The organisers, usually so efficient and competent, must have known that they were cutting things dangerously fine. Willie's company didn't reach Florence on the Missouri until August 11th. The other three companies were not there until August 22nd. They knew that to leave the Missouri after the beginning of July was dangerous. Willie called a meeting of his company to decide their next steps. There and then, they should have postponed their journey until the following spring, but it took a brave man to challenge the plans laid down by Brigham Young. Only four in the company had travelled the trail before, and all four were returning missionaries, eager to be home. Three of them, including James Willie himself, were returning after long missions in Britain. All three spoke powerfully in favour of continuing the journey despite the lateness of the season. Willie declared that he intended sticking to Brigham's plan until he heard from the Prophet himself. The Church did not have the means to support 1,500 Saints in Florence over winter, he said. Faith was what was needed, faith and prayer and trust in their leaders. God would watch over them and lead them safely through the storms, if they would but be obedient to His commandments.

But the fourth missionary was cut from a different cloth. When Levi Savage was called on a mission four years earlier, he was still grieving over the death of his wife. But he immediately answered the call, leaving his baby son in the care of his sister. Unlike the other three, who were sent to the comparative comfort of the British Mission, Levi was sent, all alone, to open a mission in Thailand, or Siam as it was then called. Because of some administrative confusion, he failed to gain entry to the country and went instead to Burma. There, he spent three unprofitable and frustrating years, not being able to speak the language and failing to make a single convert. Consequently, he was not as ready as his fellow missionaries to submit without question to the instructions from the Valley. He urged the emigrants to consider what was ahead. 'I told them that we would have to wade in snow up to our knees, and at night wrap ourselves in thin blankets and lie on frozen ground without a bed. The handcart system I do not condemn. I think it preferable to unbroken oxen and inexperienced teamsters. The lateness of the season was my only objection to leaving this point at this time.' In tears, he pleaded with the company to acknowledge the huge risks that lay ahead, but he pleaded in vain. The majority voted to follow the three leaders. Levi Savage, despite his fears, felt that his place was alongside them. 'Brethren and Sisters,' he announced, 'what I have said I know to be true, but, seeing you are to go forward, I will go with you, will help you all I can, will work with you, will rest with you, will suffer with you, and if necessary, I will die with you.' Dan Jones' promise, that they would not be allowed to leave unless there was ample time to reach Utah before the snows came, was forgotten.

A fortnight after leaving Florence, Willie's company was already in trouble. Their oxen joined a herd of stampeding buffalo and thirty of them were lost. These were the animals that hauled the five food wagons. Without them, it was difficult to move on. 'We hunted for them three days in every direction, but did not find them. We at last reluctantly gave up the search, and prepared to travel without them as best we could. We had only about enough oxen left to put one yoke to each wagon; but, as each wagon was loaded with about three thousand pounds of flour, the teams could not move them. We then yoked up our beef cattle, milch cows, and, in fact, everything that could bear a yoke – even two-year-old heifers. The stock was wild and could pull but little, and we were unable, with all our stock, to move our loads. As a last resort we unloaded a sack of flour on to each cart.' This meant an extra hundred-pound load on every handcart. And it also meant the end of the fresh milk supply, because no cow could pull in the shafts all day and give milk at night. Another disappointment awaited them in Fort Laramie. There was no sign of the food that was supposed to have been sent from the Valley. The daily ration was therefore reduced from a pound of flour a day to three-quarters of a pound and soon afterwards to ten ounces.

They had now left the Platte Valley and were travelling past the Rattlesnake Hills, along Poison Spider Creek. Ahead of them was the Sweetwater Valley, one of the remotest, most desolate regions in all America, 6,000 feet above sea level. Spring is of short duration on the Sweetwater, summer even shorter, and when summer turns to winter it's a dangerous place to be. Certainly, it was no place for old people and children, without adequate shelter, without sufficient food and without warm clothing. 'We had not travelled far up the Sweetwater,' wrote one of the company, 'before the nights, which had gradually been getting colder since we left Laramie, became very severe. The mountains before us, as we approached nearer to them, revealed themselves to view mantled nearly to their base in snow, and tokens of a coming storm were discernible in the clouds which each day seemed to lower around us… Cold weather, scarcity of food, lassitude and fatigue from over-exertion, soon produced their effects. Our old and infirm people began to droop, and they no sooner lost spirit and courage than death's stamp could be traced upon their features.'

In the week before the snows came, a number of deaths are recorded in the official journal. 'Thursday, Oct. 9th, Samuel Gadd of Orwell, Cambridgeshire, 42 years old. Monday, 13th, Paul Jacobson of Lollard, Denmark, 55 years old. Wednesday, 15th, Caroline Reader of Linstead, Suffolk, 17 years old. Thursday, 16th, George Curtis of Norton, Gloucestershire, 64 years old, John Roberts of Bristol, 42 years old, and Lars Julius Larsen, born in the camp in Iowa City. Life went out as smoothly as a lamp ceases to burn when the oil is gone. At first the deaths occurred slowly and irregularly, but in a few days at more frequent intervals, until we soon thought it unusual to leave a camp-ground without burying one or more persons.'

October 19th was the day on which the first snowstorm struck them. It was also the day upon which the last ration of flour in Willie's company was shared out. Only six scraggy beef cattle and four hundred pounds of dried biscuits now remained between the four hundred handcarters and starvation. On the same day, a hundred miles behind them, the Martin and Hodgetts Companies were at the Last Crossing of the Platte River, preparing to cross the freezing water. The chunks of ice in the stream and the blinding snow made it a daunting prospect.

Martin's company was one of the largest ever sent out by the Mormons, 575 people pulling 145 handcarts with eight wagons supporting them. Apart from the 1847/48 companies, there had been none larger. Few of these emigrants would have had any idea of what these mountains held in store for them. Miners and colliers, their spare frames evidence of poor diets and lives spent in darkness; clerks and office workers, unused to hard labour; farm workers and house maids who had hardly strayed beyond the boundaries of their home parishes before coming to America. It was only five weeks since they had left their homes and now they were alone in this empty, wintry land, dirty, tired, cold and hungry, hauling behind them in their rickety carts everything that had survived from their previous lives;

preparing to wade through this freezing river; four hundred miles from the nearest settlement and night falling.

Alongside them were the 150 members of Hodgetts' Company. Most of these had paid the full fare for the journey. They travelled in 33 wagons, enjoying considerably more comfort than their neighbours. They could have left Florence much earlier in the season and be now approaching the end of their journey, but they had agreed to stay back to keep an eye on Martin's handcarters and to help them, if necessary. They would need help themselves before this journey was out.

These two companies came together to the bank of the river. The water was high and running fast, ice rolling down in the current. It was hailing hard as the carts, one after another, ventured into the stream. In some places the water was up to their knees, in others, up to their armpits. Their reminiscences must have been painful to recall. 'We drifted out of the regular crossing and we came near being drowned. Poor Mother was standing on the bank screaming. As we got near the bank I heard her cry, "For God Sake, some of you men, help my poor girls!" When we were in the middle of the river I saw a poor brother carrying his child on his back. He fell down in the water. I never knew if he was drowned or not. I felt sorry that we could not help him but we had all we could do to save ourselves from drowning.'

No family was spared. 'My husband had only gone a short distance when he reached a sand bar in the river, on which he sank down through weakness and exhaustion. My sister Mary waded through the water to his assistance. She raised him up to his feet. Shortly afterward, a man came along on horseback and conveyed him to the other side of the river and left him there. My sister then helped me to pull my cart with my three children on it.'

They emerged from the river soaked to the skin. 'After we got out of the water we had to travel in our wet clothes until we got to camp and our clothing was frozen on us. That night we had no dry clothes to put on.'

After leaving the ford, the company had struggled through

snowdrifts for five weary miles before making camp. 'I was detailed to wheel the dying Aaron on an empty cart, with his feet dangling over the end bar, to camp, and after putting up our tent, assisted his wife in laying him in his blankets, the last time on earth. I was awakened at midnight to go on guard again till 6 or 7 in the morning. Passing out in the middle of the tent, my feet struck those of poor Aaron. They were stiff and rebounded at my accidental stumbling against them, and reaching my hand to his face, I found that he was dead, with his exhausted wife and little ones by his side, all sound asleep. I did not wake them.'

That night more snow fell. Aaron's wife slept until just after midnight, and then she awoke. 'I was extremely cold. The weather was bitter. I listened to hear if my husband breathed – he lay so still. I could not hear him. I became alarmed. I put my hand on his body, when to my horror I discovered that my worst fears were confirmed. My husband was dead. He was cold and stiff – rigid in the arms of death. I called for help to the other inmates of the tent. They could render me no aid; and there was no alternative but to remain alone by the side of the corpse until morning. Oh! How those dreary hours drew their tedious length along. When daylight came, they prepared the body for burial. And oh! Such a burial and funeral service. They wrapped him in a blanket and placed him in a pile with thirteen others who had died, and then covered him up in the snow.'

For the next nine days, the company was too weak to move. With each passing day, they became weaker, colder, hungrier and more helpless. Every morning there were more dead to be buried.

'Captain Martin stood over the graves with his shotgun in hand, firing at intervals to keep the crows from hovering around in mid-air. It is very sad indeed to see the graves, not deeply dug, the brethren being so weak for want of food. From five to ten and upwards to twenty a day buried with a little earth and brush upon them. In the early morning the loved ones see them scratched up by large grey wolves and eaten, a skull bone here, a leg, hip and arm bone... on the hills in a bloody condition... in the snow, the wolves howling all around.'

These are the days remembered in the record as the darkest days on the Mormon Trail. The companies faced a fate that appeared inevitable. But they were also days of compassion and great stoicism. In the history of the western trails, there are numerous examples of men and women who, under similar stresses, bent and cracked, attacking each other to save themselves, resorting even to cannibalism to survive. But not the Mormons. They continued to support each other, to share what little they had, to obey their leaders and to trust in God.

Fifteen miles behind the Martin and Hodgetts Companies squatted the 269 members of Hunt's company, similarly stranded in deep snow, but having not yet reached the last ford on the Platte. They, like Hodgetts' company, were also travelling in ox carts and they had also agreed to keep an eye on Martin's company. Dan Jones had originally been the captain of this company but he was no longer with them. After two weeks on the trail, he had been released from his duties as Captain and had joined an elite company of returning missionaries who had gone ahead at speed in horse-drawn carriages and were already safe in Salt Lake City.

The emigrants in Hunt's company, like those in Hodgetts', were paying the full fare for their passage. They came from reasonably comfortable backgrounds, being mostly small business owners, shopkeepers and skilled workers. Such a man was Elias Jones, son of the landlord of a public house and owner of a number of small shops in Swansea. He and his family travelled in two wagons, with eight oxen, two cows, a horse and a trap. They had plenty of warm clothes and blankets, they carried their own food and they had shelter from the worst of the weather.

David Bowen, another of the party, had been saving for years to pay for a place in a covered wagon for himself and his family. He had been employed by a company manufacturing anchors and chains in Llanelli. Two years previously he had finally saved enough to be able to start his journey but, out on the Atlantic, as he leant over the ship's side, his purse had slipped from his grasp and all his savings had spilled into the sea. He and his wife and his three children had therefore to remain in Pennsylvania to raise more funds. After a year working in a coal mine, he had saved enough to be on his way again.

But although they travelled in comfort compared to the Martin Company, their journey had not been without hardship. The official record kept by the company scribe tells of many trials along the way. 'Sunday, 21st September. Bro. Elias Davis aged 44 years died. He was highly respected by those who knew him. The disease which laid him low was diarrhoea. He was buried the same evening at the road side.' 'Tuesday 23rd Sept. A cold frosty morning. An accident occurred to Sister Ann Davis whose husband died two days ago. After crossing Skunk Creek, she was in the act of getting out of the wagon when her clothes caught in the tongue of the wagon and she fell. The wheels passed over her thigh and shoulder but luckily the road was soft sand and the injuries received was not so great, but she was able to walk a few hours after.' 'Friday, 7th November. Weather continues extremely cold. Ann Davis died.'

'Sunday, 7th September. Esther Walters, wife of John Walters of Cardiff, was delivered of a daughter. Both doing well.' 'Tuesday 7th Oct. Bro Richard Griffiths had an ox giving out. He unhitched the pair from the wagon and drove on with the one yoke of oxen, leaving the loose pair for Bro. Samuel Evans to drive on. While driving them, one of the bow keys broke, by which means the oxen became separated, and the one that had the yoke hanging to the neck ran off and so frightened some of the other oxen that it caused them to leave the trail and go at high speed. Wagon after wagon were now seen going in different directions at a terrible rate and general consternation prevailed in the last half of the train, so many being in danger of being knocked down or crushed between the wagons. In a few minutes they were brought to a state of rest, some ten or twelve wagons having left the track. We have to lament that Sister Esther Walters was knocked down and so injured that she expired in a few minutes afterwards, leaving a babe of four weeks, which at the time was in the wagon.' 'Wednesday, 5th November. Jane Walters, daughter of Esther Walters died at 9.30 a.m.'

They kept a careful watch for any signs of Indians. One morning they came upon the scene of a murder, bits of a woman's dress scattered on the sage bushes and a shirt covered in blood and a child's skull and what they thought was human hair. 'We saw the blood-stained garments of Thomas Margett's wife and child, who had been murdered by the Indians,' wrote one of them. According to *The Deseret News*, a Mormon paper published in Salt Lake City, Thomas Margett and James Cowdy and his wife were killed by the Cheyenne on September 4th, and Margett's wife had been taken and never seen again. 'They are committing depredations behind and before. After dark all the men were called out to form a line around the camp, as it was supposed that Indians were lurking around. About 11 o'clock a double guard was set for the night.' 'Our captain was hard on us. We had to herd at night and pull carts during the days and many times I have been kept up until midnight and then stood guard until morning and then start again and it was this everlasting guarding that killed people.'

It was with Hunt's company that Margaret Giles, wife of Thomas Giles, the blind harpist was travelling. (Thomas by this time had arrived safely in Salt Lake City.) Soon after leaving Florence a child had been born to her. It was a difficult birth. The little girl lived for only two days and, soon afterwards, Margaret also passed away, leaving her two boys with no one to care for them. Travelling in the company was a woman called Hannah Evans, who had at one time helped Thomas Giles find his way to his various appointments around south Wales. She undertook to look after the boys. Four days after Margaret's death, the snowstorm was upon them, closing the trail ahead. Hunt's company, like the three others, came to a standstill.

Meanwhile, no one in Salt Lake City had any reason to suspect that there were still Saints out on the trail and that a tragedy was unfolding in the mountains. There would have been no hope of rescuing the four companies had it not been for one fortuitous circumstance. On October 4th, a fortnight before the snows came, Dan Jones and the small company of returning missionaries in their fast vehicles had arrived in the city. They had completed the journey in thirty days. In a letter to *Udgorn Seion*, Dan described how they had travelled, 'at a gallop always, through everything that meets us – often fifty miles or more in a day and ten or a dozen of those before daybreak, and as many or more at night. The Indians are so hostile along the route we followed, that we scarcely dared stop at night, for fear they would fall upon us and kill us. We rested, for the most part, in daylight, when we could see from afar those who approached. By doing that, we escaped many a danger.' They had passed all four companies on their way and they brought to the Church leaders in Salt Lake City the startling news that somewhere in the Rockies there were still over 1,300 Mormon souls on their way to Zion.

Even though the snows had not yet fallen, Brigham Young grasped the seriousness of the situation immediately. One of his most impressive qualities was the speed at which he reacted in times of crisis and the inspirational leadership he showed at all such times. Realising what was about to happen, he called a public meeting for the following day and immediately set about organizing a rescue mission. 'That is my religion. It is to save people. We must bring them in from the Plains.' He began listing what would be needed. 'Sixty good mule teams, fifteen wagons, twelve tons of flour, clothes of all sorts and forty teamsters, men who had experienced the worst possible conditions.' These were needed immediately, he said, and it was only a beginning. Much more would be needed before the rescue was done.

The following day, he repeated his message to an even larger crowd, adding that if his demands were not met by nightfall, he intended to start for the mountains himself. Promises for all he had asked for were given before the meeting ended and on October 7th, only three days after the Saints in Utah had first heard of the imminent crisis in the mountains, and nearly a fortnight before the first snows fell along the Sweetwater, the rescue train set off.

In the evening of October 19th, upon the very day in which the last of the flour was shared out to Willie's company and the storm burst overhead, before they had fully realised how desperate was their predicament, the forward scouts of the rescue party found them. One of the emigrants described the first sighting of the rescuers as 'a shimmering miracle in the sunset'. 'The news ran through the camp like wildfire and all who were able to leave their beds turned out en masse to meet them. Shouts of joy rent the air; strong men wept till tears ran freely down their furrowed and sunburnt cheeks and little children partook of the joy which some of them hardly understood, and fairly danced around with gladness.' Three days later, the first of the heavy wagons carrying the flour arrived.

But their trial was far from over. Their only hope of survival was to keep moving. There was little room in the wagons for the sick and the weary. The majority had to keep walking. Their rescuers drove them hard. Michael Jensen remembers his mother mourning his father, who was newly buried. 'Mother sat on a large kettle turned upside down, weeping bitterly. One of the men who was helping to manage the company came along just then and he had a walking stick in his hand. He struck Mother across the back with his stick and said in a sharp voice, "Get up and go on, you cannot sit here crying. We have to go at once or we will all die."

During the first night after the rescuers had arrived, nine of the emigrants died. The next night, two more. The worst day was on Rocky Ridge, the highest point on the trail. They started early in the morning, having a seventeen-mile trek before them. The whole company, 350 people or more, pulled their handcarts along the craggy ridge all day and most of the following night. A freezing wind from the north-west blew in their faces. They suffered frostbite on their hands and their feet and their faces. Maria Linford, realizing that her husband was weakening, took off her slip and wrapped it around him, but couldn't save him. He died before dawn. James Kirkwood was eleven years old. He had carried his young brother on his back for most of the night. Neither his mother nor his elder brother could help because they were carrying another brother on their cart. Upon reaching the camp, James laid his brother down and fell dead. Twelve-year-old Elizabeth Cunningham fell unconscious into the snow and no one had the strength to lift her. She was lapped in a blanket and left lying by the trail. Hours later, her mother discovered she was missing and returned to look for her and discovered her still alive. She managed to revive her and get her to the camp and she survived. The last of the carts struggled in at five the following morning.

'There were so many dead and dying that it was decided to lie by for the day,' wrote John Chislett. 'In the forenoon I was appointed to go round the camp and collect the dead. I took with me two young men to assist me in the sad task, and we collected together, of all ages and both sexes, thirteen corpses, all stiffly frozen. We had a large square hole dug in which we buried these thirteen people, three or four abreast and three deep. Two others died during the day, and we buried them in one grave, making fifteen in all buried on that camp ground.' They were buried in the clothes in which they had died and the graves were covered with willow and large rocks to keep the wolves from getting at the bodies, but to no avail. 'I learnt afterwards,' wrote Chislett, 'from men who passed that way the next summer, that the wolves had exhumed the bodies, and their bones were scattered thickly around the vicinity.'

The next day, they were driven on by their rescuers. They came to detest the handcarts. A week later, at the Green River, more rescue wagons came to meet them, bringing food and clothing. There, at last, room was found for all in the wagons, and the carts were abandoned. There were so many of them, one piled upon another, that there were fears those on the bottom might be suffocated. Their clothes were infested with lice and they stank to high heaven. But they were alive. The worst of their nightmare was over. The exact number of Willie's company that died is not known. Historians estimate that about 65 lost their lives, but this figure does not include those that died in the weeks after reaching Salt Lake City.

There were still three other companies in the mountains. Having found Willie's company and led the main rescue wagon train to them, the scouts went on to search for the Martin, Hodgetts and Hunt companies. Nine days later, when they were close to giving up, they saw footsteps in the snow. They followed them to a ridge of red rock and there, under cliffs known today as Red Buttes, they found the Martin and Hodgetts companies. The descriptions by members of the beleaguered companies of that first glimpse of the scouting party convey something of the miracle of their rescue. The leader of the scouts rode a white mule which was hard to make out against the background of snow. As he trotted down towards them, his black cloak rose and fell like great black wings. It appeared to the watchers below that he was flying towards them. 'I was playing in front of Sister Scott's wagon,' remembered John Bond. 'All at once Sister Scott sprang to her feet in the wagon and screamed out at the top of her voice. "I see them coming! I see them coming! Surely they are angels from heaven." A general cry rent the air. "Hurrah! Hurrah!" Some of the voices choking with laughter and with tears. "Hurrahs!" again and again as the broken hearted mothers, clasping their emaciated arms around the necks of the relief party, kissed them time and time again.' The leader of the rescue party was a man called Daniel W. Jones. His book, *Forty Years among the Indians*, is a valuable record of the rescue. 'Many declared we were angels from heaven,' he writes. 'I told them I thought we were better than angels for this occasion, as we were good strong men come to help them into the Valley, and that our company and wagons loaded with provisions were not far away. I thought this the best consolation under the circumstances.'

The company had not moved for nine days. Their food had very nearly run out and the weather was worsening. It's unlikely that they could have restarted had help not arrived. But the main rescue party was still many days away, and even when they arrived they would have no great store of food to share out. The scouts could do little except raise the emigrants' hopes and prod them back on to the trail again. 'The only salvation was to travel a little every day. There was danger of starvation before help could arrive, unless the people made some headway toward the Valley.'

The scouts had one more task to perform before they returned to bring up the main rescue wagon train. 'We started full gallop for John Hunt's camp fifteen miles further back.' Hunt's company, with its contingent of Welsh Saints, seemed in better order. 'Their tents were pitched in good shape, wood was plentiful, and no one seemed concerned. These people were just on the eve of suffering, but as yet had not. Quite a number of their cattle had died during the snowstorm which had now been on them for nine days.' It was made clear to them that their only hope was to start moving again. The next morning, after making sure that the company was striking their tents and loading their wagons, Daniel Jones and his men started their journey back to the main rescue party to inform them of the positions of the three companies. On their way, they overtook Martin's company, painfully struggling up a steep hill. 'A condition of distress here met my eyes that I never saw before or since. The train was strung out for three or four miles. There were old men pulling and tugging their carts, sometimes loaded with a sick wife or children, women pulling along sick husbands, little children six to eight years old struggling through the mud and snow. As night came on, the mud would freeze on their clothes and feet. We gathered up some of the most helpless with our lariats tied to the carts, and helped as many as we could into camp on Avenue Hill. This was a bitter, cold night and we had no fuel except very small sage brush. Several died that night. There were hundreds needing help. What could we do?' They did the only sensible thing, which was to hurry back for more help.

On the last day of October, a fortnight after the first snow, the main rescue party at last made contact with the Martin, Hodgetts and Hunt companies. They had all gathered into the shelter of Devil's Gate, a deep canyon cut by the Sweetwater five miles west of Independence Rock. There they would have had a little shelter, out of the worst of the wind. There they tried to decide what to do next. 'Imagine between five and six hundred men, women and children,' wrote George Grant, the leader of the rescuers, in a letter to Brigham Young, 'worn down by drawing handcarts through snow and mud; fainting by the way side; falling, chilled by the cold; children crying, their limbs stiffened by cold, their feet bleeding and some of them bare to snow and frost. The sight is almost too much for the stoutest of us; but we go on doing all we can, not doubting nor despairing. Our company is too small to help much, it is only a drop to a bucket in comparison to what is needed.' But Brigham had foreseen this and had arranged for a further 250 wagons to follow the first rescue train. However, it would be a many days yet before they arrived at the Sweetwater. Grant's letter continued, 'I think that not over one-third of Br. Martin's company is able to walk. This you may think is extravagant, but it is nevertheless true. Some of them have good courage and are in good spirits; but a great many are like children and do not help themselves much more, nor realize what is before them.'

Amongst the pitiful throng in Martin's company was John Griffiths and his family. John was born in Bangor, north Wales, in 1810, and, as a young man, not yet twenty, had found work as a boilermaker in the Liverpool Docks. There is a record of his being baptized there in January 1840. He worked for the same foreman throughout his time in Liverpool and, when the foreman moved to a new job in the Royal Naval Docks at Woolwich, John and his family went with him. John was then comfortably settled, with a good job, a happy marriage and a growing family. But some time later, things began to go badly awry. Thomas, the eldest son, was sent out to Utah by his father, partly, according to the family history, to avoid having to fight in the Crimean War, and partly to prepare the way for the rest of family to gather to Zion. After arriving in America, he disappeared. No more was heard from him and his family never discovered what had become of him. Then

Margaret, John's first wife, died. Still his enthusiasm was not quenched. He had to borrow from the Perpetual Emigrating Fund to pay for his family's passage and, like all who used the Fund, he and his family were expected to travel in a handcart company. A few months before leaving for Utah, he married again. Six of the family therefore sailed on the *Horizon*, the last of that year's chartered ships – John, his new wife Elizabeth, and the children – Margaret who was sixteen, John who was eleven, Jane, eight, and Herbert, five.

John and Margaret were between the shafts of the cart when the family left the staging camp in Iowa City. John suffered badly from rheumatism. Soon the constant strain of pushing, day after day, wore him down and he became unable to do his share of the work. His place between the shafts had to be taken by his eleven-year-old son, John. It was John who was helping his sister to push when they waded through the icy Platte. The cold proved too much for him and he was the first of the family to die. 'I shall never forget the last time we crossed the Platte River,' wrote Margaret, years later. 'I was the only female that drew a handcart through the icy waters at the last crossing of the river. The next morning, when we awoke, the mountains were clad almost to their base with a white mantle of snow and the storms of winter were gathering. It almost seemed that we would perish. In fact, many of our company froze to death, my twelve-year-old brother among them, and we buried him there in the desolate wilderness.' Her father was also in a bad way and getting worse. 'He could not keep up,' she wrote, 'as he had rheumatism so bad he could not walk.' One day, he tried to grab the tailgate of a passing wagon to help himself along. 'The teamster saw him and lashed his long whip and struck father on the legs and he fell to the ground. He could not get up again. As I was pulling a handcart I did not know anything about it till we got into camp, for the handcarts had gone on before, and then I went back about three miles, but could not find him. I was nearly wild. I thought the wolves might have him.' But the Hodgetts company was camped nearby. 'My father saw their tracks and crawled on his knees all the way to their camp. He was so badly frozen when he got there, they did all they could for him. Two of the brethren brought him into our camp about eleven o'clock that night.'

It was so cold at the Red Buttes that women, waking in the morning, were unable to raise their heads because their hair was frozen to the ground. Death was commonplace. One morning, Jane, the younger sister, was watching her stepmother eking out a meal from their meagre supplies. 'She was baking some griddle cakes on the camp fire and one old lady looked so pitiful my stepmother handed her a cake before she had finished baking all of them. Shortly after, she looked again at the old lady, who had not moved, and found her to be dead, with the cake in her hand. She had not tasted it.' Somehow, with the help of their rescuers, the family succeeded in pushing their cart to the Devil's Gate camp. There they were engulfed for days by further storms and there they lost another member of the family. 'One morning when I awoke, my brother John lay dead by my side,' remembered Jane. 'Two weeks later my brother Herbert, age six years, died the same way. He died of starvation and cold.'

They stayed in Devil's Gate for over a week. Everybody, both wagoners and handcarters, had to leave everything they owned there, so as to make room for more of the sick in the wagons. As soon as the storms abated, they pushed on again. More wagons came from the Valley and, finally, they were able to abandon the last of the handcarts. 'We reached the valley of the Salt Lake on the 30th day of November 1856,' wrote Margaret, 'after two months of the most indescribable suffering and hardships, the worst we thought that any company of men, women and children was ever called upon to endure. My father, John Griffiths, was ill most of the way with rheumatism and died the next morning after reaching Salt Lake City, from the cold, exposure and privations of that terrible journey.'

The number of deaths in the Martin Company is estimated at between 135 and 150, out of the 350 or so who left Florence. Most of the survivors suffered from frostbite. Many lost fingers and toes, some lost both legs up to the knee. Jane Griffiths lost the first joint of six of her toes. Margaret was unable to walk for nine weeks. But both survived the ordeal and lived to a fine old age. A family photograph shows Margaret, in her eighties, back again between the shafts of her handcart, showing her grandchildren how it was that she had walked to Zion.

The last company to reach Salt Lake City was Hunt's. David Bowen and his family arrived safely. Hannah Evans, with Thomas Giles' sons, also survived, although Hannah suffered frostbite on her feet and on her face. Eight months later, she married Thomas Giles.

We know a good deal about Thomas Giles' subsequent career. He made a name for himself as an entertainer and musician. He called himself 'The Blind Harpist of Utah' and was much admired by Brigham Young who often invited him to play for his guests at the Beehive House, his official residence. For the rest of his life, Thomas and his sons, Joseph and Hyrum, held concerts in villages and towns throughout the territory, the boys playing the fiddle and Thomas, of course, the harp. After the concerts, the floor would be cleared, the carpets raised and the evening would end with some lively country dancing, with Thomas or one of his sons calling the dance figures. Throughout their lives, the family remained proud champions of Welsh culture. Another son, Henry, was born to Hannah and Thomas and he became a famous exponent of 'cerdd dant', the uniquely Welsh art of singing poetry set to improvised melodies that harmonize with traditional airs played on the harp, and he regularly competed in eisteddfodau throughout Utah. Eventually, he became the first head of music at Brigham Young University in Provo.

One mystery concerning Thomas Giles remains. We know that he brought his harp with him across the Atlantic and that he still had it with him in Iowa City. One of the emigrants noted in his diary that he had listened to him play it in the camp. We also know that his harp reached Salt Lake City safely because it is to be seen there today, in the Museum of the Daughters of Utah Pioneers. It's a triple harp, made by John Richards of Llanrwst. The mystery concerns the transport of the harp over the last part of the journey, from the Missouri to Utah? It could not have been left in Iowa City with the bulk of the pioneers' excess baggage because we know that the sheds in which these goods were stored were burnt to the ground and everything in them destroyed. Could it be that the harp travelled in his wife's wagon, and that Hannah Evans looked after it after Margaret died, making sure that it was safely stored in Devil's Gate over winter and duly delivered to the Valley the following spring? This is possible, but I find it hard to believe that Thomas would have entrusted his harp to anyone. This instrument was to be his livelihood. It was also his chief comfort and his delight. There was absolutely no means of replacing it in Utah if it was lost or damaged. The only way he could be sure of its safe arrival was to assume the responsibility for it himself. He had succeeded in looking after it on the ship and during the countless train changes on the railway journey. Would he not also have wanted to look after it on the trail? Brigham Young and the emigration organisers encouraged musicians to bring their instruments with them. They liked to see dancing and singing around the camp fires and believed in the power of music to ease the toil of the day. We read of many examples of fiddles and concertinas and fifes in the wagons and it seems probable that Thomas would have been given permission to bring his harp also. The triple harp is a much lighter instrument than the classical harp. It does not have the metal parts that add to the weight of the latter. The triple harps at St Fagans National History Museum, made by the same John Roberts, weigh between twenty-five and thirty pounds. And there are numerous illustrations and descriptions of the old Welsh harpists wandering from village to village, carrying their harps slung across their shoulders. Thomas Giles was a strong man, 36 years old, a miner until his accident. It is true that he was seriously ill on the trail near Fort Bridger, but by that time the food wagons supporting the Bunker Company would have been emptying and there would have been room in them for the harp. There is one other piece of evidence. Margaret Davis Rees, who also travelled with Bunker, used to tell her grandchildren 'about the evenings crossing the Plains when they would group together and sing to the music of the harp'. Whose harp could that have been if not Thomas'? There is certainly no evidence of any other harp or harpist travelling with the company. It seems likely, therefore, that Thomas Giles, despite his blindness, carried his harp or pushed it in his handcart for a thousand miles over the Plains and across the Rockies. That's certainly what his descendants in Utah believe today. 'A glorious way to come to Zion!'

1857

IN 1844, WHILST passing through the arid hills of what today is the south-west corner of Utah, the explorer John Frémont came across a pleasant valley of fresh, green grass, watered by many springs. 'All refreshing and delightful to look upon,' he wrote. Six miles long and six miles wide, surrounded by low hills, the valley lies thirty miles to the west of Cedar City, where, in 1857, Elias Morris, with a workforce which included many Welshmen, was struggling to produce iron. They called the place Mountain Meadows and it became a popular camping site on the southern route from Salt Lake City to San Bernardino and Los Angeles. Little of that beauty remains today. Much of the soil was washed away by a great storm in 1866. What little pasture remained was destroyed by overgrazing. The springs failed and the lush grass withered and a grey scrub of wormwood and sagebrush invaded the valley floor. Some say God's curse lies on Mountain Meadows.

When a platoon of federal soldiers came to the valley in May 1859, searching for evidence of some rumoured murders, they found ripped fragments of children's clothing hanging from the thorns, bones scattered in the scrub and strands of women's hair blowing in the wind. They gathered these fragments of human remains, torn and mangled by wolves, and buried them by Magotsu Creek under a cairn of stones. On the cairn today appear these words: 'Mountain Meadows Massacre Grave Site Memorial. Built and maintained by The Church Of Jesus Christ of Latter-day Saints out of respect for those who died and were buried here and in the surrounding area following the massacre of 1857.' But these are not the words that were originally cut on the grave by the soldiers in 1859. They read then: 'Here 120 men, women and children, were massacred in cold blood in Sept. 1857.' And the soldiers were under no illusions about who was responsible for the massacre. They knew that the Mormons of Cedar City were to blame.

Mountain Meadows is a lonely place, shunned by the majority of Utahns today. On the morning I visited the valley, there was no one else there. A red plastic rose had been placed in a jam jar on the cairn, and alongside it, in a childish hand and with childish spelling, were written the words: 'We are <u>forever</u> sorry for this very tradgic event in Mormon history.' And it was signed, 'A very sad Latter-day Saint descendant'. This very 'tradgic' event, even after 150 years, still stirs painfully in the Mormon conscience, and for those who wish to denigrate the Mormon Church, it has been a constant source of ammunition. Research papers, academic tomes, films and novels regularly re-examine the evidence, attempting to explain the events of September 1857 and to apportion blame. The facts are still disputed, but one thing is certain. Under this cairn lie the bones of some of the 120 defenceless men, women and children, members of a pioneer wagon train, on their way from Arkansas to California, who were shot down in this valley, in cold blood, by the Mormons of Cedar City and their allies, the Paiute Indians. This, without doubt, was Mormonism's darkest hour. Until quite recently, the Church refused to allow researchers access to the relevant documents in their archives and, as a result, myths and slanders festered around the tragedy. But eventually the archives were opened and, in 2008, 150 years after the event, a version of the history was published which included the evidence of those archives. It proved to be an ugly story, the story of a community, under terrible pressures, buckling and breaking and betraying the values it most cherished. And at its centre, one of the three who shared the responsibility for triggering the slaughter, was a Welshman, Elias Morris.

The story starts on the Mormon Trail in the early spring of 1857. Abraham B. Smoot, Mayor of Salt Lake City, was on his way east on business. He noticed a surprising number of heavily laden wagons passing him, going west, many of them hauled by eight and even ten yokes of oxen. He couldn't make out who was freighting so many and such heavy loads towards Utah and, when he attempted to find out, he was given no credible answers. On arrival in Kansas City, he went to the office of the haulage company and, slowly, the whole astonishing truth came out. The wagons were carrying the equipment and supplies of an army of 2,500 soldiers who would soon be on their way to Utah to attack the Mormons. Secretly, without any public declaration, James Buchanan, the newly elected President of the United States, had gone to war with the Saints.

James Buchanan was, arguably, the most ineffective president in American history and the decisions he took at the start of his term of office seem particularly questionable. Utah's relationship with the rest of America was worrying him. They seemed to be travelling along diverging paths. When Brigham Young was appointed governor of the newly created territory in 1850, lawyers and civil servants were sent from Washington DC to help him govern in the American way. But Brigham preferred the Mormon way and refused to delegate any power to the federal officials. The people of Utah still preferred to take their troubles to the Mormon Church courts, rather than to the federal courts. Utah remained a theocratic autocracy. One federal officer after another gave up the struggle of trying to Americanize Brigham and resigned, reporting back to Washington that it was impossible to govern Utah whilst he was still in power. They accused him, on very questionable evidence, of constantly failing to comply with federal law and insinuated that he was on the verge of declaring Utah an independent state, no longer part of the Union. This touched a particularly sensitive nerve in Washington at the time because the southern slave states were also threatening to break away. Buchanan presumably felt that a show of firm and vigorous action was essential. Recklessly, he decided to send the army to Utah. He insisted they leave forthwith, even though his generals warned him that they were far from ready to wage a war and that they would probably have to spend a winter under canvass in the Rocky Mountains. To complement a series of rash decisions, Buchanan sent out his battalions without attempting to negotiate or even to contact Brigham Young. Today, this strange war has been more or less forgotten, but it was, in effect, the first American Civil War. No one was killed on the battlefield. Nothing was achieved that could not have been achieved through negotiation. But it was instrumental in the deaths of 120 innocent people in Mountain Meadows.

When Brigham Young eventually heard that an army was on its way to invade Utah, he sprang into action with characteristic energy. The 3,500 men of the Mormon militia were put on stand-by. He ordered the Saints in the outlying settlements, in Nevada, Idaho and California, to return to the Valley. He called the missionaries back from all the scattered Mormon missions around the world. His intention, he said, was to avoid an all-out battle but rather to hit and run, to fight a guerrilla war. And if the enemy should ever force him to retreat, he would leave a scorched and deserted land behind him, the towns and villages burnt to the ground, the crops cinder in the fields and the people retreating to the mountains. From there he would continue to harass and sabotage the enemy. 'God Almighty helping me, I will fight until there is not a drop of blood in my veins,' cried Heber Kimball, one of Brigham's closest counsellors, 'Good God, I have enough wives to whip the United States.'

Meanwhile, oblivious of the rumours of impending war, the annual migration from Liverpool was underway as usual. It might have been thought, after the terrible experiences of the previous season, that the Saints would have had enough of hauling handcarts through the Rockies, but two of the companies on the trail that year were again handcart companies. Brigham had announced in the annual conference the previous autumn that, despite the losses of the Willie and Martin companies, this was the way ahead for the Saints. He claimed that 'the Saints who have come in this way have been healthier, more contented and happier, and have encountered less trouble and

Independence Rock, 'rising from the plains like the capstone of a huge Neolithic burial mound'.

Elias Morris' name and that of his wife carved by him on the summit of Independence Rock.

A group of 'down-and-back boys' sent by Brigham Young to bring the immigrants across the Plains.
(Courtesy of Church History Library of The Church of Jesus Christ of Latter-day Saints)

A wagon train from Utah on its way up Echo Canyon.
(Courtesy of Church History Library of The Church of Jesus Christ of Latter-day Saints)

The statue of
Martha Hughes
Cannon outside
the Utah Capitol
Building.

Martha Hughes Cannon with Gwendolyn.

William Ajax, the last editor of *Udgorn Seion* and the owner of the strangest store in Utah.

An advertisement for William's underground store, the 'Eighth Wonder of Utah'.

Ajax Underground Store

The Pony Express greeting its great rival, the telegraph.

When the Mormons needed music to celebrate or to mourn or to glorify God, they turned to Evan Stephens.

Titus Davis' grave in Willard, also commemorating his wife, Mary Gwenllian, 'buried at Tally, Carmarthenshire'.

Benjamin Jones' grave, also in Willard, also commemorating his wife, Esther, 'interred at Pencareg churchyard, Wales'.

One of the saloons in Hell-on-Wheels. 'Everybody seemed to be safe, so long as they didn't get into the paths of bullets.'

The end of Big Steve Long and his half-brothers, Ace and Con Moyer.

'Afar down the river could be seen the harbinger of another day – a large body of men laying the railroad that was to cross the continent.'

A mile of track was being laid in a day, often through remote and difficult terrain.

Here was born Olive Davis, the mother of 'The Osmonds'.

Members of 'The Osmonds' sitting outside their mother's home on the day it was reopened as a museum.

Ben Perkins of Llangyfelach lived the Mormon life at a time when it was not easy to do so.

Mary Ann Williams, his wife, appears as brittle as an autumn leaf but was in fact as tough as bog oak.

Sarah Williams Perkins, Ben's second wife, standing in front of her nine daughters. Her only son gazes from the veranda, rather left out of things.

A group of Mormon polygamists in jail. Ben Perkins is sitting on the left.

Hole-in-the-Rack. A fifty-foot passage blasted through rock, wide enough for a wagon to pass through.

Top of the trail. South Pass City, population, about seven.

Every summer the youth of the Church are sent to trek the hills as their forefathers did, pulling handcarts and sleeping under the stars.

No-one remembers like a Mormon and what he or she likes to remember is the struggle and sacrifice of the Pioneers.

On July 24th, every year, they celebrate Pioneer Day. This is the day upon which Brigham Young first entered what was to become Salt Lake City.

Hauling handcarts, they march through the towns and cities of the state, celebrating the achievements of the Pioneers.

Marchers from Taylorsville-Bennion, a district named after the Bennion family, the first pioneers from Wales.

'The Spirit of the Past is the Strength of our Future.'

The Welsh Weekend in Malad City, celebrating the Welshness of the Valley.

Malad City, where, apart from in Wales itself, there are 'more people of Welsh descent per capita than anywhere else on earth'.

vexation than those with teams.' The dead were forgotten, although Brigham did admit that there were lessons to be learnt. The carts needed to be more solidly built, their loads more equally shared and there should be better arrangements for the elderly and the ailing. He advised everyone to buy a pair of strong boots before setting out and, most important of all, he declared that 'no company must be permitted to leave the Missouri River later than the first day of July… By observing these suggestions it is believed that, with one food and support wagon for every two hundred persons, the emigration will be much facilitated at a still lessened expense.'

There was a good Welsh diarist by the name of Evan Samuel Morgan in one of the two handcart companies. He was a young, unmarried, 23 year old, from Cadoxton, outside Neath. In the diary, we learn about his life before he left Wales. As an eleven year old, in 1844, he'd started working underground. Five years later, his elder brother brought a copy of *The Book of Mormon* home with him from the pit, which Evan 'read with great delight and pleasure, believing the doctrines it contained to be true'. He was baptized in 1851 when he was 18 years old and in 1854 he began preaching. He left his work and went on a six-month mission to Carmarthenshire, 'without purse or scrip', living on the generosity of Church members until he eventually found work at an iron works in Ystalyfera. After work he would join the Saints of the Ystradgynlais branch, preaching and bearing witness up and down the Swansea Valley. Then, in March 1855, he went to Liverpool with his brother-in-law, John, to look for work on one of the transatlantic ships chartered by the Saints, but without luck. There they met Dan Jones, who sent them to Anglesey to spread the gospel. At that time, there was coal being mined in Anglesey along the Cefni River, near Llangefni. Evan and John found work in the Pentre Berw mine. When the workers were laid off in Pentre Berw, they moved to another pit near Malltraeth. Then to Holyhead harbour, to work on the new sea wall. 'Altogether, there were about 2,000 men working there, tearing the side of the mountain down and hauling it to the sea to build a breakwater to protect the shipping.' Then to a slate quarry in the Nantlle Valley near Caernarfon. They moved from place to place in the north-west so as to visit as many branches of the Church as possible. At night, they would preach and distribute tracts and copies of *Udgorn Seion*.

On August 3rd, 1856, he noted in the diary that he had addressed a meeting in English. Speaking English did not come easily to Evan. 'It was at this meeting that I made my first attempt at speaking in the English language in public. It was for the benefit of Sister Hughes, who was an English woman and did not understand the Welsh tongue.' Remarkably, he had been preaching and teaching all over Wales for more than two years without having need of English. In March 1856, still only 22 years old, he was appointed President of the Anglesey and Conwy Valley Conference. But he yearned to emigrate and in July of that year the diary entries suggest that he was already preparing to go. He visited Llandudno, Conwy and Ffestiniog in the company of an American named Benjamin Ashby. Ashby was coming to the end of his term as a missionary in Wales and intent on returning to Utah as soon as he was released. Later in the month Evan met Evan Griffith Roberts, of Capel Garmon, President of the Denbighshire Conference and his wife, Jane, from Llanddulas. They also were planning to emigrate. On August 5th, he was staying with Sister Grace Jones, and writing a letter on her behalf to her daughter in Utah. On September 7th he was in a Quarterly Conference in Eglwysbach, in the Conwy Valley, listening to Israel Evans, another American missionary and counsellor to Daniel Daniels, the President of the Welsh Mission. He also would soon be going home. In all these meetings and conferences, Evan must have been planning his departure because, in the following spring, the six of them, Ashby, Griffith and Jane Roberts, Grace Jones, Israel Evans and Evan, left Liverpool together, sailing for Boston on the *George Washington*.

He arrived in America without a penny to his name. He'd spent all his savings in coming thus far. The Perpetual Emigrating Fund, drained dry by the huge migration of the previous year, was making no loans in 1857. 'After I paid for a meal in Boston my money was gone,' he wrote, 'rather an unpleasant condition to be in, in a strange land among strangers.' He needed £3 for a train ticket to Iowa City, and for food on the journey. 'Sister Grace Jones loaned me enough money (Five Dollars), which I paid back to her after reaching the Valley.' He then needed another £3 to pay for his share of the handcart costs – the food, the tent, the cart itself. He was lucky again. 'There was a sister in the company, rather sickly she was, who got discouraged about crossing the Plains to Utah with a handcart, which she would have had to do if she had gone on. She had paid for her handcart fare in Liverpool. She stayed in Boston, and as she was not going, she gave me the opportunity of going in her stead.' One can but wonder at the mettle of these people, strangers in a strange land, a war on the horizon, not a penny in their pocket, but not a whit discouraged! From the Missouri onwards, the six travelled together in a company of 149 other emigrants. Israel Evans was appointed Captain of the company, Benjamin Ashby his deputy and Griffith and Jane and Grace and Evan shared a handcart.

The winter of 1856/57 was again hard and cruel in Utah and, when spring came, the locusts returned to devastate the spring shoots once more. Once again, food was in short supply. The confidence of the young territory was further shaken by the collapse of many of the enterprises by which Brigham had set so much store. Not only did the sugar plant fail, but a scheme to mine lead also went to the wall, as did a paper producing plant and a large industrial pottery. And now there were even whispers that the iron works in Cedar City, the most ambitious of all Brigham's projects, was in trouble.

Many unforeseen technical problems had arisen in the works. The coal contained too much sulphur. The firebricks were of poor quality and the inner walls of the furnaces cracked as a consequence. The blast bellows stopped working when the river fell below a certain level and when the river rose again, the works were flooded. In the spring and summer, when the workforce left to sow or harvest their own fields, there was a shortage of labour. And, most importantly, the scale of the enterprise was too small. A far greater investment was needed to ensure a successful future. It seemed that everything was conspiring against the success of the iron works and that the experiment was failing. As it faltered, life began to drain out of Cedar City. Two or three years earlier, when the future seemed rosy, nearly a thousand people lived in the town, making it one of the largest communities in Utah. But, by 1857, much of the population had drained away, and it was the poverty of those who remained that now caught the eye of passing visitors. 'Never before had I seen,' wrote one, 'such dirty and ragged people among the Mormons as here.' Even before the events of the summer, life in Cedar City was already difficult.

In Salt Lake City, Brigham was becoming convinced that God was displeased with his Chosen People, and that they were being punished for allowing the fire of their faith to burn less fiercely than of old. 'I have felt like weeping since I have been in this territory,' he preached, 'on beholding the ungrateful feelings of many of this people and their ingratitude towards their God.' To breathe new life into the Church, he instigated a religious revival, calling on his people to confess their sins and to repent. It was not what we in Wales would regard as a revival. Brigham whipped his people to repentance. He approved of spying and of passing on gossip to the authorities. He urged the brothers to enter each other's houses to search for evidence of spiritual failings. It was more like Mao's Cultural Revolution of the 1960s and '70s, a merciless, cruel inquisition. Dark undercurrents of suspicion and distrust flowed like poison through the towns and villages of Utah. In his diary, David D. Bowen, the Llanelli mariner, wrote, 'Every person, men, women and children had to be re-baptized into the church or they were considered out of the church. A poor disaffected Mormon had but a small chance of his life or to live among them. However I was very slow to comply with their request. Teachers visited me daily, wishing me good and desiring very much on me to be re-baptized. At last I thought it would be better for my safety to go through the ceremonies. Subsequently I did. All winter there was nothing but preaching and teaching the Celestial Principles of Polygamy. And every man was counselled to take another woman no matter whether he be a good or bad man, whether he was a rich or unrich.' 'The Spirit of God is like a fire purifying and consuming all refuges of oppression,' wrote Dan Jones in a letter to Wales, 'and I believe that soon purer wheat will be seen on the threshing floor of pure-hearted Zion than was ever seen before… He who does not live his faith in all things will be excommunicated.'

Church officers visited every Mormon home, bearing a list of questions to be put to the head of the family. 'Are you paying your tithes regularly? Do you pray with your family, night and morning? Do you preside over your household as a servant of God, and is your family subject to you? Have you betrayed your brethren or sisters in anything? Have you committed adultery, by having any connection with a woman that was not your wife? Have you committed murder?' 'Every person is required to answer them,' explained Richard Williams in a letter to his relatives in Wales. 'If he lies, the curse of God will be upon him.' They were anxious times in Zion.

In the white heat of the revival, Brigham preached some ugly and fanatical doctrines. 'There are sins that men commit for which they cannot receive forgiveness in this world, or in that which is to come,' he said. 'And if they had their eyes open to see their true condition, they would be perfectly willing to have their blood spilt upon the ground.' He seems to suggest that some sins are so terrible that only by taking their own lives can the sinners find forgiveness and that, if they refuse to do so, then they should allow themselves be murdered. It's not clear whether these words were commandments or conjectural speculations, not to be taken literally – the historians continue to argue the point – but whatever they were, they ensured that 'a duty to murder' and 'spilling blood for redemption' were concepts that were being hotly debated in Utah that summer, and that violence was never far below the surface.

George A. Smith, the Apostle who had led the Welsh company into the Valley in 1849, came to Cedar City in mid

August to prepare the people for war. He was a fiery orator. He repeated some of the more sensational and shocking rumours – that the troops intended to kill 300 of the leading men of Mormonism, including Brigham Young, and that a scum of despicable riff-raff was following in the wake of the army, 'the worst descriptions of men, picked up on the frontier, who were making great calculations for booty and beauty.' 'Prepare for the worst,' was the message, 'including, if necessary, laying down your lives in defence of the Kingdom of God.' A dark streak of fanaticism burnt within Mormonism that summer and nowhere did it burn more fiercely than in Cedar City.

Some believed an apocalyptical doomsday was imminent. This, they believed, was Satan's last attempt to destroy the Kingdom. The Latter Days were surely upon them. 'The dogs of war will be released into the field, accompanied with pestilences and ruin,' thundered *Udgorn Seion*, 'for the Lord Jesus cometh and the fate of those who deny his Gospel is sealed.' Nerves in Cedar City were strung as tight as bowstrings. At the slightest provocation they were ready to let fly.

Evan Morgan's company was the first to leave Florence that year. When they left in May, there was no talk of war, but as they passed Chimney Rock and Fort Laramie and the Last Crossing of the Platte, rumours about the crisis in Utah were spreading like wildfire along the trail. Brigham Young was said to be killing apostates by the dozen. It was whispered that he had panicked and fled. They said a mighty army was on its way to crush the Mormons. They said that when the army arrived, jail and death awaited every man with more than one wife. Then, in the middle of August, when Israel Evans and Evan and Jane and Grace were a day or two west of Independence Rock, hard news arrived from the Valley that war was indeed in the offing and that the U.S. army really was on its way to invade Utah.

For the rest of the summer, the emigrants and the soldiers played hide-and-seek along the banks of the Platte. On the right bank, the Mormon trains hurried by, anxious to keep out of trouble. On the left, scattered units of the army made their way slowly along the California Trail, unsure how to react were they to come face to face with a Mormon train. No one wanted to be the first to fire. No one wanted to start a shooting war. 'I remember some travellers overtaking our company,' wrote one of the Saints, 'and telling us to "hurry up or Johnston's Army will get you, for they are just behind a little way." We hurried and they did not overtake us.' 'They used to try to scare us by saying they were going to subdue Utah,' wrote one Mormon. 'But we didn't scare.' Three days later, in South Pass, Evan Morgan's company passed units of the Mormon Militia guarding the approaches to the Valley, and everybody breathed a sigh of relief. At the end of his account he added, 'Behind us, in the distance, was Buchanan's army. Some distance in advance of us was the noted company of [Arkansas] emigrants to California who were massacred at the Mountain Meadows... It was a large, rich company.'

Most of the emigrants to California that year took the northern route out of Utah, north of the Great Salt Lake, and then down the Humboldt River Valley to San Francisco. The Arkansas company was the first to take the old Southern Road to San Bernardino, Los Angeles and San Diego. They were a boisterous crew, rowdy, unruly, easily upset and quick to anger. They were contemptuous of the Mormons and never slow to show it. On their way down the Jordan Valley, they had been constantly accused, without much proof, of poisoning Indian cattle, of slandering Mormon women and of pasturing their animals on Mormon land without permission. They made enemies easily. Now they were approaching Cedar City, a maelstrom of distrust and suspicion.

A young man named Edward Parry remembered them coming down the main street. 'A man riding a large grey mare seemed to be the spokesman. He tried to get some of the crowd to buy him a gallon of whisky but none would do it. He became abusive, swore at us all, said that he had the gun that killed old Joe Smith, and that his company would go on to California and get an army and come back and wipe out every ***** Mormon.' Elias Morris said that his own mother was insulted by members of the wagon train. A loudmouthed fellow 'addressed her in a very insulting manner, brandishing a pistol in her face and making use of the most insinuating and abusive language.' The Saints refused to sell them corn and this infuriated the Arkansans further. The Cedar City marshal attempted to arrest one of the young Arkansan troublemakers but his friends quickly gathered around him and he got away. They appeared to the Mormons to be harbingers of the coming storm, a warning of what to expect when the American army arrived. Some believed they were spies in the pay of the enemy. Others believed they were demons sent straight from hell.

The head man of Cedar City was Isaac Haight. Not only was he the boss of the iron works, but he was also the mayor of the town and the chief officer of the militia. His counsellor and deputy was Elias Morris, an unpaid post but one that added greatly to his responsibilities. There were other small towns, apart from Cedar City, in the iron fields, each one with its leader and counsellors. The most powerful of these men was William H. Dame, mayor of Parowan, twenty miles to the north. The most fiery and bellicose was John D. Lee, the militia leader in Harmony, about the same distance to the south. Lee and Haight were both enraged by the Arkansans' behaviour and wanted revenge. Dame's advice was that the emigrants should be allowed to proceed unmolested. A message was sent to Salt Lake City, asking for Brigham's guidance, but, long before an answer returned, the situation in Cedar City was out of control. Lee is blamed for starting the fighting, inciting the local Paiute tribe to attack the wagon train. He told them of the wealth of the Arkansans and of the rich plunder that would be theirs. As the sun rose, on the morning of September 7th, the Indians swept down upon the camp in Mountain Meadows, killing six of the defenders. But the emigrants fought back bravely. Recklessly, John D. Lee and other white men joined the fray alongside the Indians and they were seen and recognized by the defenders, thus complicating the situation and deepening the crisis. If the Arkansans were now allowed to reach California, they would spread the story of the Mormons' participation in the attack and revenge would surely be taken on the people of Cedar City. For three days, the emigrants held their ground. Other emigrant companies were approaching from the north. Something had to be done, and done quickly. Late on the third night, Haight and his deputy, Elias Morris, came to Parowan to meet the city council. At two o'clock in the morning, they voted to accept the consequences and allow the Arkansans to move on. But Haight and Morris were unhappy with the decision. They sought out Dame and urged him to reconsider. The approaching wagon trains would soon be upon them. It was now or never. In a rising panic, sometime in the early hours of the morning, they came to their fateful decision. The whole company should be wiped out.

Haight and Morris got back to Cedar City early the next day and, before nightfall, the first units of the militia were on their way to Mountain Meadows. As in all Mormon militias, obedience to their leaders was unquestioned. Most of them were members of Morris' unit, although neither he nor Haight nor Dame were with them. The following morning, under a white banner, there was a meeting between the Mormons and the Arkansans, and it was promised that, if the Arkansans placed themselves into the hands of the militia, they would be safely escorted between the lines of the Indians. The emigrants had no choice. For four days, they had been without water. Their ammunition was low and many of them were injured. Under heavy Mormon guard, they laid down their arms and left the camp. Then, without warning, the killing began. The militia turned on them, shooting the men dead, leaving the Indians to kill the women and children. They spared the lives of seventeen children under the age of six, who were later shared out between Cedar City families. Elias Morris may not have been there, nor Isaac Haight nor William Dame, but their fingers were on the triggers of every gun.

A more brutal and cowardly act is difficult to imagine. Life in the Wild West had always been exceptionally barbaric, savage and lawless. Lee, for example, before coming to Utah, had fought in the Battle of Bad Axe in Wisconsin in which the whites had killed between four and five hundred Indians – men, women and children – then skinned them, and used their skins as straps to sharpen knives. But none of this alleviates a jot of the horror of the Mountain Meadows Massacre.

Although the purpose of the massacre had been to keep secret the Mormons' role in the attack, it did not succeed. Within weeks it was common knowledge in California and soon afterwards throughout the rest of America. Yet years passed before any individual was brought to trial. In 1877, John D. Lee was convicted for his role in the killings and condemned to death. He was taken back to Mountain Meadows, to the very spot where he had shot so many innocent men and women, and was shot there himself. Haight spent the rest of his life on the run, protected by remote Mormon communities in the Arizona and Mexico outback. Dame was released because of the lack of evidence. But Elias Morris, somehow or other, managed to avoid scrutiny and to slip quietly back into his old life. His role in the massacre was never properly understood until historians were allowed access to the Church archives and until *Massacre at Mountain Meadows*, the first scholarly history based on these archives, was published in 2008. Few realised that he was present at the meeting which sealed the fate of the Arkansans. Admittedly, he was a very junior member of the triumvirate, having only recently been appointed counsellor to Haight and, as such, had probably little voice in the final decision, but it is still remarkable that he avoided even being cross-examined and that he was not summoned to appear before any court of law. In 1865, when things quietened down, Brigham Young sent him on a very successful four-year mission to Wales. He spent the rest of his life in Utah, becoming one of the richest men in the state. 'He is a great and good man,' said his obituary in the *Deseret News*, 'and it would be hard to name another who has done more for the community... In the field of industrial activity, he was one of the most energetic and best known of Utah's citizens.' He built many of the iron works of Utah, and developed many of its mines. He owned tanneries and soap factories, cement works and quarries and he tried, once again, to build a sugar industry and, this time, succeeded. He became a pillar of the establishment. He was the mainstay of the eisteddfod and of all things Welsh. Brigham Young turned to him for counsel. Everything that has been subsequently said or written about him suggests a conscientious, considerate, wise and responsible man, held in high regard by all. Yet the deep shadows of that nightmarish week in Cedar City a century and a half ago continue to hang over him and he was too good a man ever to have forgiven himself.

1858

As a consequence of the impending hostilities, few migrants were on the Mormon Trail this year. Brigham Young actively discouraged them. No ships were chartered to take them over the Atlantic and no companies organised to bring them over the Plains. Six small groups of Saints set off for the Valley, all, except one, with less than fifty members. Most of them were returning missionaries, anxious to be with their families again and eager to help in the coming struggle with the United States. Amongst them were five Welshmen, one of whom was Daniel Daniels, the ex-President of the Welsh Mission, and the ex-editor of *Udgorn Seion*. He had originally left Wales on the *Buena Vista* in 1849 and had returned with Dan Jones and Thomas Jeremy three years later. They were the first Welshmen to return as missionaries. But now, after six years of hard labour in the mission field, he had been recalled by Brigham Young. Daniel Daniels' diary was lost in a fire, but other diaries, kept by members of his company, give a clear picture of what happened to them on their journey. 'War having been declared against our people,' wrote one of them, 'and knowing that our enemies were eager to exterminate us, I armed myself and put myself secretly en route with several missionary elders who were returning to their homes.'

Although they came to fight, they carried few weapons. Eight rifles and six swords had been confiscated by customs officers in Liverpool. Arriving in New York, they were anxious to buy more, but New York was not a comfortable place for a Mormon in the spring of '57, especially if he was buying arms. 'The feeling was very bitter against our people in New

York, the winter the army lay near Fort Bridger and suffered so much,' wrote James Crane, a young Mormon from Penally in Pembrokeshire, who was living in New York at the time. 'I was working in a factory in New York and the men swore that if there was one soldier killed by the Mormons, they would kill every Mormon in New York.' Daniel Daniels and the returning missionaries managed to buy one crate of rifles, which they dispatched by sea to New Orleans, accompanied by one of their number. From thence, the crate and its minder were to go up the Mississippi, to rendezvous with the main party in Iowa.

Daniel Daniels and the other missionaries crossed Iowa without trouble, but on the Missouri they faced growing hostility and they feared that they might not be allowed to continue. Letters were appearing in the local press demanding that the Mormon Trail be closed. 'We learn that a number of Mormons just returned from England, left this vicinity for Salt Lake one day last week,' wrote one correspondent to the *Council Bluffs Bugle*. 'What will Col. Johnson do, will he let them pass on, or will he stop them?' It was claimed in another letter to the *Omaha Times* that a 'large number of enthusiasts, all well supplied with guns, pistols, and ammunition' was passing through Omaha. 'I think that if the attention of the President was called to this matter, a body of U.S. troops would be stationed at this point immediately.'

Daniel Daniels' small wagon train slipped quietly out of Florence one morning in late May, every man now armed to the teeth like so many revolutionary generalissimos. 'We are all, with the exception of 3 or 4, well-armed with good pistols and knives,' wrote one of them. 'I carry constantly a brace of pistols, a large bowie knife & a U.S. yauger.' A yauger was a type of rifle. 'I despise to carry deadly weapons but under present circumstances I am obliged to do it in order to defend myself in case of an attack which may happen.' Another member of the group carried 'a new double gun, a colt revolver, a sword, and a bowie knife.' The impression given in the diaries is of a band of inexperienced youths charged with a touch more recklessness than common sense. But it was not so. Only a dozen were in their twenties, half were in their forties and ten were over fifty. One of these was Daniel Daniels. He had lived the quiet life of a country stonemason, deep in the heart of Carmarthenshire, until well past his fortieth birthday. After being baptized into the faith, his life had been one adventure after another. Here he was now, 51 years of age, a man of sober sense and serious ways, throwing himself into a war against the United States, risking his life smuggling guns across the continent.

Up in the Rockies, the American army had had a hard time of it. Over 1,800 of them had spent the winter shivering in a bitterly cold camp a hundred miles from Salt Lake City. Others were scattered in the forts along the trail. The first hurdle in the path of the Mormon wagon train was the army base at Fort Kearny, halfway between the Missouri and Fort Laramie. The company was not likely to be attacked because the fort was on the opposite of the river and the river was running high, but they knew that, if seen, a warning that they were on their way would be passed to other units further upriver. They had at first decided to wait until nightfall so as to go by in darkness, but the weather suddenly worsened and a heavy mist fell over the valley. When it lifted they were past the fort and well clear of danger. This was interpreted, of course, as a miracle, the Hand of God guarding them against their foes.

Five miles beyond Chimney Rock, seven men came down the trail towards them. One of them was Thomas L. Kane, a good friend to Brigham Young and to the Saints and a man who knew his way around the corridors of the Federal Government in Washington. He had been sent to Salt Lake City by President Buchanan to discuss peace terms with Brigham Young. Now he was on his way back to Washington DC, bearing an answer which, he told the missionaries, was likely to lead to peace. One of his party brought a letter from Brigham advising the missionaries, even though peace might be imminent, not to trust the army. He wrote 'that there are between two and three thousand U.S. troops on Green River & that they are very hostile to all Mormons & are making prisoners of them wherever they can find them.' 'President Brigham Young,' wrote one of the missionaries, 'advises us to avoid if, possible, any collision with the troops. In case we are met by the troops we are ordered not to fight them, for he is anxious that they should strike the first blow.'

The missionaries were also given the astounding news that Brigham had ordered a total evacuation of the north of Utah, including Salt Lake City. 'Rather than see my wives and daughters ravished and polluted, and the seed of corruption sown in the hearts of my sons by a brutal soldiery,' he said, 'I would leave my home in ashes, my gardens and orchards a waste, and subsist upon roots and herbs, a wanderer through these mountains for the remainder of my life.' Everyone was to leave their home immediately and move south. They were to load the contents of their barns into their wagons and drive their animals with them, leaving nothing that could be of use to the enemy. One or two were left in each street and village to set them alight if the soldiers came. The bulk of the population obeyed immediately, a remarkable demonstration of Brigham's authority over his people. At his command, 30,000 people abandoned their homes and set off for the south, beyond Provo and Spanish Fork, with no idea of where they were going nor how they would survive once they got there. No arrangements were made to feed or to accommodate them. They were expected to make do as best they could, staying with friends or family, living in caves or tents or in their wagons, waiting for Brigham to give the 'all clear' for their return. It was a powerful demonstration to his enemies of the unity and the determination of the Mormon people but it was also Brigham's purpose to give the world the impression that poor Mormon folk were being unnecessarily bullied and abused by the army. In this he succeeded brilliantly. Brigham was a master of 'public relations'.

The command to move caused havoc. 'The roads from the highest settlement to as far south as 200 miles below Salt Lake City were lined with teams and people and loose cattle,' wrote John Edwards of Hirwaun. 'Men, women, and children footing for miles through dust up to their ankles and all but naked to the world. Ladies that had been bought up well, trudging along with their little ones, leaving their homes, sweet homes built at considerable trouble.' John Parry was in Echo Canyon, preparing to face Buchanan's army when he heard that his family had to move south. 'I arranged with Richard Griffiths to take my wife and child, born to us while I was in Echo Canyon, with them southwards. I did not know where they were going, but understood afterwards that they had very stormy weather. My wife and baby had to shelter under the wagon in the mud for most of the night, then went some distance to beg for shelter near Pond Town. The people got up and made a fire and were very kind to her.' John A. Lewis remembered that 'the cows and steers were hitched to the wagon and the few articles of furniture and clothes piled in. Then straw was carried into the house and some placed around each tree so that the guards who were to remain could set fire to the straw and burn the house and the trees to the ground. Then, if the Army took possession, all they would find in the whole of Utah would be ruin and waste. We journeyed to Spanish Fork and made a dugout in a hillside on the south-east corner of town and lived there.' 'There were hundreds of people in Spanish Fork,' wrote David D. Bowen in his diary, 'and all the other settlements were the same, crowded with strangers in every direction. All had to move with their herds of cattle and their flocks of sheep, their pigs, geese, and chickens, all they had that could walk, leaving behind them their fine farms and their excellent houses, to be destroyed by Indians or anybody else that felt disposed to do so.'

Out on the Plains, Daniel Daniels and the returning missionaries were preparing to pass the next fort in their path, Fort Laramie. They had already been spotted from the other side of the river by a troop of soldiers, therefore they knew the garrison had warning of their approach. But, once again, the elements came to their assistance. When they were within three miles of the fort, a most violent storm broke above them, thunder, lightning, hail, wind and rain. It lasted for three hours and, in that time, they passed the fort and were clear of the soldiers. 'This storm was sent by our Father in heaven to preserve us from the hands of our enemies,' they wrote. 'Praise the name of Israel's God, oh ye Elders! For he has this day wrought out a great deliverance for you.' They were convinced that these timely storms were part of a divine plan and that they were marching under a heavenly banner to some great pre-ordained victory. They believed that they were the host described in *Doctrine and Covenants* as 'coming forth out of the wilderness of darkness, and shining forth fair as the moon, clear as the sun, and terrible as an army with banners.' They went on their way, exulting.

By 1858, a weekly mail coach, carrying about a dozen passengers, was travelling regularly between Independence on the Missouri and Salt Lake City and then on to Placerville in California. It took 22 days to get to Salt Lake City and another 16 to reach Placerville. Every twelve miles mail stations had been built where the coach could take on fresh horses and in some of them there was food and drink available. Whenever the river was low, Mormons on the northern bank would cross to these stations to pick up the latest news from the west. They learnt of the progress of the talks between Brigham and Alfred Cummings, the man appointed by Buchanan to be the next Governor of Utah. It appeared that Brigham was prepared to accept Cummings as Governor on condition that the army built its main barracks well outside the boundaries of Salt Lake City. They also learnt of the movement of the enemy. A company of Saints going east had passed the enemy camp a few days previously and had noticed that their supplies were replenished, the ranks reinforced and that they were preparing to move.

On June 13th, Daniel Daniels and his company were approaching Simpson's Hollow on the far side of South Pass. A year earlier the Mormon militia had attacked an army supply column at this place, burning 74 wagons and seizing 2,000 cattle. This eventually proved to be the only skirmish of the war. 'Went past the remains of the burnt wagons,' wrote Bullock in the official company journal, 'and we could not help saying, "So may James Buchanan and all who abet him in his wicked deeds perish", and "Amen" was responded.' Then an eastbound coach brought news that the army was on the move. The missionaries, mindful of Brigham's advice, decided to turn off the trail and follow old paths across country in an attempt to get ahead of the soldiers. They pressed hard, starting each morning at four and continuing their march until the moon went down. There were two rivers to cross, the Green and the Bear. They found an old ferry raft on the Green, in terrible condition, but repairable. On the Bear, they lashed together two wagons, removing the wheels and stuffing bits of old shirts and sacks into every hole and crevice to make them waterproof. On one crossing this makeshift craft capsized, the cargo was lost and so, very nearly, was the ferryman, but eventually the whole company scrambled to safety on to the opposite bank with most of their equipment intact. Six days after leaving the trail, they came back on to it again, twelve miles ahead of the main army. God, once again, had looked after his own and brought them safely through. 'We were miraculously guided to this place through our enemies, troops and Indians,' wrote the official scribe, 'for which the Lord be praised for answering the prayers of the Saints.'

Then they rounded a corner and suddenly, a few yards ahead, there was a troop of enemy soldiers blocking their path. It was hard to say who was the more surprised and who had the greater fright. But there was no retreat as the main force of the enemy was coming up behind. So they advanced. 'The soldiers seemed perfectly paralysed and struck with amazement at our boldness and impudence in driving past them without saying a word, doubtlessly thinking we were only the advance of a large army.' Fortunately, these were not fighting soldiers but an unit of sappers, strengthening the bridges for the army that was approaching.

On the evening of June 21st, Daniel Daniels and his fellow missionaries arrived in Salt Lake City. There was no one to greet them. The whole town was empty. In eerie silence, they walked through the abandoned streets, marvelling at

258

the dreamlike scenes that confronted them. 'It presented a grand and imposing appearance from the abundant foliage and extraordinary amount of fruit with which the trees were loaded. No language can adequately describe the reflections we had while going through such a city under such circumstances. The stillness of death reigned supreme; neither man, woman nor child could be seen, all having left and gone south, with the exception of a few brethren left as a guard.' But it was not a place in which to linger. The missionaries soon departed, following their families to the south.

Five days later, on the 26th, the army entered the city and, in accordance with the terms of the peace, they marched through without stopping, building their fort forty miles outside the city. Brigham acknowledged the Washington-appointed governor and his staff of federal civil servants and, on the 30th, the people started to return to their homes. The Utah War was over.

Daniel returned to farming. He claimed a plot of land up north, just over the Utah/Idaho state line, in the valley of the Malad River, a valley that became, soon afterwards, the home of dozens of Welsh families. 'No grasshoppers are to be seen here,' he wrote, 'and the creek channels are well supplied with water, indicating the Hand of God. If you should get short of breadstuff in consequence of grasshoppers, you will know where to come.' Mary, his first wife, had come with him when he first left Wales and in his new home he married three further wives. He was President of the Malad branch of the Church and of the Malad branch of the Co-op until his death in 1879. His greatest pleasure was playing his fiddle.

1859

IN THIS YEAR, gold was discovered on Pike's Peak in the Colorado mountains and, during the next three years, 100,000 prospectors found their way there, following the California and the Mormon trails up the Platte as far as the confluence of the North and South Platte and then following the South Platte towards the embryo city of Denver. As a result, the number of trading posts in the hundred miles between Fort Kearny and the confluence increased dramatically. By 1859 there were fourteen of these sod cabins on the route, part store, part saloon, with usually a few fields attached. Their presence made the Plains less lonesome.

More and more pioneering families were venturing out onto the prairie, erecting their simple turf homesteads, turning the rich soil for the very first time, garnering good harvests. Small villages were springing up at astonishing speed. Buchanan, for example, thirty miles from the Missouri, was home to a hundred people at the start of 1859, and Genoa, forty miles further out, home to another hundred. The first family to settle in Shell Creek, 170 miles up the Platte, arrived there at the beginning of May 1859. By the time the Mormon wagon trains passed through at the end of June, there were four families and seven single men living there, with over a hundred acres ploughed and planted, growing potatoes, corn, peas, beans, pumpkins and melons.

During the year the weekly postal service between Independence and Salt Lake City was upgraded to a daily service. Many of the Mormon diarists mention the stagecoaches rolling by, with maybe half a dozen passengers inside and the same number outside, bouncing their way across the continent. In an emergency they would take messages from the wagon train Captains to Brigham Young in Salt Lake City, asking for an extra ton or two of flour perhaps or ten more yokes of oxen to be sent to meet them further down the trail. Every year, the trail became less frightening and the journey easier.

At the annual Church Conference in the previous autumn, Brigham had announced that, now that the war was over, Utah was open for business again and that a warm welcome awaited all migrants. He said he would like to see 10,000 Saints arrive in the Valley in 1859. After the trials of the past three years, the extreme cold, the locusts, the famine, the Reformation, the move south and the war itself, things would be better in 1859, he said, and so they were. In this year much was made in the Mormon diaries of how pleasant life could be on the trail. 'Everything was ordered and carried out with military precision. Tents were pitched, preparations for the evening meal commenced and every one was busy. My business, along with the rest of the youngsters, was to gather sagebrush and "buffalo chips" for fires.' They wrote about the care of their Captains, the friendships forged in the camps, the peace that prevailed and the constant protection of God. 'I don't think anything ever tasted as delicious and appetizing as those sagebrush cooked meals, in the cool of the evenings; and the setting sun was heavenly. After the suppers were over and everything was cleared away as spick and span as army quarters and a long evening before us, the camp fires giving light and warmth, there would be prayers and discourses by the Elders and Teachers, singing with the accompaniments of guitars, violins, cornets and such musical instruments. Those evenings recall memories of the most spiritual and soul-inspiring religious sentiments I ever experienced, the stillness, the vastness, the moon and stars shining over us, was all so overwhelming in its beauty.' After three years of miserable fortune, it seemed that a new chapter of hope and optimism was unfolding along the trail.

Shadrach Jones, a 26 year old from Llanelly in Monmouthshire, exemplified the spirit. He was a loveable and a loving man who contributed greatly to the fun and good fellowship on the trail. When he was fifteen his father had gone to America to work in a mine in Pennsylvania. He wrote regularly to his family, assuring them that his savings were mounting and that he would soon have enough to buy them each a ticket. Then, suddenly, his letters had ceased. In the meantime, Shadrach and his brother, John, now converted to Mormonism, had managed to reach America under their own steam. They went looking for their father and found he had been killed in a pit accident. The money he'd saved had disappeared.

After arriving in Utah, Shadrach settled in Willard, a small village to the north of the territory, where many of the Welsh had chosen to live. He loved music and enjoyed singing in choirs and playing in dance bands. He formed his own band and had a loft in his house adapted as a community dance hall. Whilst still comparatively young, his hearing began to fail, but his love of music persisted and, despite his deafness, he continued to conduct the village band and host the dances. He had married a girl from Carmarthen but they had no children. They welcomed young people into their home, many of whom were newcomers from Wales, lonely and without a family. These youngsters often lived with Shadrach and his wife for extended periods. Some were even adopted by the pair and raised as members of the family.

Today, Shadrach is remembered in Willard as a house builder. His houses were built of stone, unlike the turf and wood and brick houses more common to the area. It is said that their walls were two feet thick and that Shadrach's mortar hardened to the consistency of concrete. 'The most beautiful old homes possibly of early days were rock homes,' wrote Levi Edgar Young, a prominent Mormon historian. 'It is said that the best and oldest of those are at Willard. There was a humble old Welshman in early days who used to build rock houses. His name was Shadrach Jones.' Many of Shadrach's houses are now listed on the State Register of Historic Sites as examples of the skill and craftsmanship of the early pioneers.

In 1883, he returned to Wales on a mission and, whilst there, he suddenly died. Some say he was killed by a bad cold that worsened into pneumonia, others that he blew out a gas lamp, without realizing that the gas also had to be turned off. His grave is in the cemetery of the old Calfaria Baptist Chapel in Ravenhill, Swansea.

Another interesting family travelling with Shadrach in the same wagon train were the Hugheses from Merthyr Tydfil. They were seven children, without a parent, the eldest being Maria (17), then Taliesin (15), Gomer (13), Mathew (8), Lewis (7), Daniel (5) and the youngest, Sarah Ann (2). Shadrach would certainly have befriended them. Three years earlier, their parents had brought them as far as Pennsylvania where their father had gone to work as an engineer in a pit in Pottsville. Then the mother died and the father lost heart and didn't want to go on. He decided to return home. But the children were made of sterner stuff, especially the two eldest, Maria and Taliesin. They decided to continue and to take their younger siblings with them. Their mother's brothers, Daniel and William, were out in Utah already and they came to the Missouri to meet them and to escort them to their new home. Having arrived there, Taliesin seems to have looked after them all, until the last of his sisters married and left home. They never saw their father again.

The wagon train with which Shadrach and the Hugheses travelled was no ordinary train. It had been formed, not as an immigrants' train, but as a heavy goods train. Its main cargo was machinery for the printing office of the *Deseret News*, Utah's leading newspaper. They were also hauling paper and ink and type and driving a herd of 450 cattle.

Possibly the most interesting of the wagoners, certainly the most energetic, was James Crane, from Penally, in the south of Pembrokeshire. The tales told about James suggest that he was extremely cheerful and good-humoured. His wife, in her diary, describes how, one day 'the company all seemed to have the blues, they all felt so down-hearted. My husband asked them if they were Mormons. They replied, "Oh yes, we are Mormons." My husband then asked them what was the matter with them. "Well," they said, "we have been driving cattle all day and have had nothing to eat and we're not likely to get anything." He asked the old cook if he had anything to cook. He said yes, but he had not had time to cook it, it having been raining all day and was still raining. He said he had flour and bacon, tea, coffee, and molasses. My husband said, "What, you have all them things in your wagon and all going hungry?" He asked them if they had a camp kettle and they handed him one that would hold about three gallons. Also some flour. In about fifteen minutes my husband had made them a kettle of mush and they had molasses and butter. They all had a good supper. We fixed up the two tents and sat up and sang and talked until midnight.' James' high spirits were infectious and his unflagging energy a blessing to any company.

Yet he'd had a hard life. He was born into Victorian poverty at its most grinding. All he knew of his father was that he came from Brighton and that he'd disappeared before he was born. His mother was too poor to keep him and, before he was three weeks old, he'd been placed on the parish in Pembroke and farmed out to a husband and wife on Caldey Island, who were paid two shillings a week to look after him. For four years, James lived on Caldey. His foster father was drowned in a maritime tragedy that's still remembered by Tenby people. It was the day of the Tenby Fair, two days after Christmas, in 1835. A strong sea was running and it was blowing a stiff gale but fifteen islanders were determined to go to the fair. They were advised not to venture on such a sea, but venture they did and a few hundred yards from the safety of Tenby bay, a wave broke over their rowing boat and she capsized. Everybody on board was lost. Seven wives on Caldey were made widows and 33 children made fatherless. One of the children was James. His earliest memory is of his foster mother, maddened by grief, running through the streets of Tenby, wailing for her husband. She died when James was six, and he was then farmed out to another widow. She sent him to school, where he learned to read the Bible.

The cost of supporting the poor had risen so steeply after the Napoleonic Wars that the Government decided to seek cheaper means of dispensing relief. In 1834, they passed the New Poor Law which stipulated that workhouses should be built throughout the land to accommodate the poor, but that conditions within their walls should be so rigorous, comfortless and harsh that only the desperate would seek help there. James was sent to the Pembroke Workhouse where he remained for the next five years. He ran away twice and, each time, he went looking for his mother. At the second attempt he found her and was allowed to stay with her for a few weeks but it was not a happy time. She had married and become a mother again and had lifted herself out of poverty. She would not let James sit at the table with her new family. He had to eat by himself in a corner. He remembered her telling him that she felt no love for him, no more than she felt for a stranger in the street. Eventually, he agreed to return to the workhouse. He felt, he said, that the workhouse treated him better than his mother. Indeed, his memories of the workhouse are surprisingly warm. 'The Governor of the house, Mr. Large, was very kind to all and I believe did his duty well, as he was very much liked by all. But the rules of the house required him to be very strict, which, instead of injuring me, I found to be very good for me throughout my life. I learned to write a little. I also learned a little arithmetic.' Strange that such a spirited and attractive man should have emerged from so hard and unloving a childhood. After leaving the workhouse, he worked as a cowman on a nearby farm for seven years, until one day he heard a Mormon missionary preach that the end was nigh and that escape to America was the only hope. That was in 1851, when he was 21. Now, here he was, eight years later, on the road to Zion.

In 1859, very few of the Welsh Saints on the Plains had come directly from Wales. James, like most of them, had spent time in the eastern states, financing his onward travel. He had emigrated in 1856, accompanied by Joseph Cadwallader

Davies, the brother of his fiancée, Alice, and they had worked on a farm on Long Island, then on a building site and then in a factory in New York. Within a twelvemonth, James had earned enough to pay for Alice's passage. She came out to join him in 1858 and they were married in Iowa City. But, to get to Utah, they needed more money, and in Iowa they were desperately unlucky in their employers.

They first went to work for a man who was experimenting with growing sugar cane. He had invested most of his money in a steam press to squeeze the sugar out of the canes and had promised his workers that they would all be well paid once the sugar had been sold. But 'they have very cold, severe winters in Iowa,' wrote Alice in her diary, 'and that fall the frost came a little earlier than usual and his cane got frozen, so his molasses business proved a failure and he could not pay his hands.' After two or three months of hard work, they had to leave empty-handed.

They then went to work for a farmer called Barling, Alice as a house servant and James in the fields. Having been there a few months, they heard that a freight wagon train, preparing to leave for Utah, was looking for teamsters to drive the wagons. Each man taken on would be allowed to bring his wife. James and Alice immediately decided to go. 'We told Mr. Barling we would like to get our pay as we had not drawn any of our wages all winter. He said if we would stop and work all summer, in the fall he would pay us, but if we left then he could not pay us. They let us have a little flour and corn meal and a few pounds of butter.' Once again, James and Alice had to leave empty-handed.

But they were on their way to Zion and, better still, Joseph, Alice's brother and James' best friend, was coming with them. Best of all, Joseph brought his new wife with him, Maria Williams from Llanfair Talhaiarn, Elias Morris' niece. She had crossed the Atlantic on the same ship as Joseph, travelling with four friends, all four of them members of the Church. But in New York, all four had decided to abandon the Church and go on to California instead of Salt Lake City. Maria had refused to join them and, instead, had stayed on in New York, with no companions and not much English. She found work as a maid in a Mormon household and it was probably during this time that she got to know Joseph well. Two years later, he sent for her from Iowa City, telling her that there was a spare berth for her in the wagon and asking her to marry him. If she wished to accept, he said, she would have to jump on the very first train. They were married the day before the wagon train rolled out and they joined James and Alice in what must have been a very merry wagon. 'I never felt better and had better health than I did crossing the plain,' wrote Alice. 'We had plenty of provisions and had a good time.'

Their good spirits are reflected in many entries in James' journal. The day they came to the Skunk River, for example, on their way across Iowa, was a day of hard work, but James remembers it with pleasure. 'When we got there the river had overflowed its banks and had filled the bottom for two miles across. We arrived there about nine o'clock in the morning. We stood and looked despairingly at the situation, wishing we were on the other side.' James started to chat with two other travellers standing beside him on the bank of the river, and they explained to him how to convert wagons into a raft, as Daniel Daniels had done on the Bear the previous year. 'Some of the company objected to our crossing in this way. I could see no other way than this. I called on those that were willing to join me, and those that were not could take their own course. The unwilling ones, seeing that they were about to be left behind, finally joined in without any bad feelings. We had to cross this stream three times until we were all used up pretty badly, and the last trip it snowed on us all the way. We were so numbed with the cold that we hardly knew what to do. There was a house close by where we hired a room and stove for the night, and in half an hour we were merry, singing, and chatting one with the other.'

They arrived in the Valley in 72 days, a very fast crossing for a train of heavy goods wagons. 'Considering the length of the journey, we had a good time,' wrote James. 'Plenty of provisions, once in a while short of water and an occasional quarrel with the unruly teamsters, nothing but what might be expected on such long, hard journeys.' *The Deseret News* announced their arrival 'in good condition, no accident worthy of note occurring during the trip, though they lost about sixty head of cattle, principally or wholly from disease, out of 448, with which they left Florence.'

Although James kept a diary throughout long periods of his subsequent life in Utah, nothing he later wrote has the same edge and excitement as the paragraphs he wrote on the trail, and with good reason. The journey across the Plains was for him, as for many other young Saints, a rite of passage, a crossing from the old, difficult world of his mother country into a better life in the New World, a second chance, a new beginning. With him were the people he loved most in the world, his wife and his closest friend. Around him he had the support of like-minded people, Shadrach and the Hugheses and suchlike. Together they faced the challenges of this new land in all its variety and beauty. Walking the trail was the most exciting, the most significant event in all his days and his life would never be the same again.

'When we came out of Emigration Canyon and saw Salt Lake City,' he wrote, 'Oh! How thankful we did feel to the Lord. And none but those that experience it can tell the heavenly feeling that possess a Latter-day Saint when they first see the City of the Saints. The tears of joy coursed down my cheeks and I thanked the Lord that I had been preserved thus far to receive of his blessings. We drove our teams into President Young's yard and his family made supper for the whole company. This was the first time I had ever seen President Young. He had on a large straw hat, home-made. The feelings of my heart were drawn out towards him and I am thankful to say it continued thus with me all the days of his life.'

1860

THIS FAMOUS, BUT probably apocryphal poster, which heralded the start of a glamorous new postal service, is part of the legend of the West. On April 3rd, the first 'Pony Express' rider left St Joseph, Missouri, and ten days later, having crossed the Great Plains, the Rockies and the Sierra Nevada, arrived at his journey's end, in Sacramento, California. He is still one of America's favourite images – the dashing horseman bestride his galloping steed, the speeding loner on his perilous path through wild Indian country, the bearer of the mail, uniting the scattered communities of the West in the dark months before Civil War. For the pioneers on the trail, a glimpse of the Pony Express whirling past was truly memorable. They wrote about it with a sense of wonder and awe. 'I was on guard,' wrote Ira Hayward. 'About midnight I heard the clattering of the hooves of a horse a long distance off. Our wagons were in a circle each side of the road. The night was still as death. When in hailing distance, I shouted, "Who comes there?" the clatter stopped immediately. A voice was heard, "Pony Express." "Come on." The clatter started afresh. He rode on a gallop through the camp, many wondering what was up.'

The most famous description is by Mark Twain. He saw the Pony Express in the following year, through the window of his stagecoach as he journeyed to Nevada. "'Here he comes!'

Every neck is stretched further, and every eye strained wider. Away across the endless dead level of the prairie a black speck appears against the sky, and it is plain that it moves. Well, I should think so! In a second or two it becomes a horse and rider, rising and falling, rising and falling – sweeping towards us nearer and nearer – growing more and more distinct, more and more sharply defined – nearer and still nearer, and the flutter of the hooves comes faintly to the ear – another instant a whoop and a hurrah from our upper deck, a wave of the rider's hand, but no reply, and man and horse burst past our excited faces, and go winging away like the belated fragments of a storm. So sudden is it all, and so like a flash of unreal fancy that but for the flake of white foam left quivering and perishing on a mail-sack after the vision had flashed by and disappeared, we might have doubted whether we had seen any actual horse and man at all.'

Mark Twain also noticed, in complete contrast to the furious speed of the Pony Express rider, a company of Mormons, tramping wearily along. 'Dozens of coarse-clad and sad-looking men, women and children, who had walked, as they were walking now, day after day for eight lingering weeks, and in that time had compassed the distance our stage had come in eight days and three hours – 798 miles! They were dusty and uncombed, hatless, bonnetless and ragged, and they did look so tired.'

Another famous author who passed a Mormon wagon train on the trail in 1860 was the explorer, traveller and journalist, Richard F. Burton, on his way to Salt Lake City in the stagecoach, to research his next book, *The City of Saints*. His description of what he saw was a little kinder. 'Though homely in appearance, few showed any symptoms of sickness or starvation; in fact, their condition first impressed us most favourably with the excellence of the Perpetual Emigrating Fund's travelling arrangements.' He mentions that the company he saw was being led by a Mr John Smith. This was on the morning of August 23rd, on the way to the Muddy Creek station. Burton and his carriage arrived at the station at midday that same morning, some four hours later. John Smith and his company didn't arrive until the 27th, four days later, and, by then, one of the Welsh emigrants in his charge, a Mrs. Catherine Jones Bennett of Connah's Quay, Flintshire, was dead.

Muddy Creek is a small, insignificant river in the south-west of Wyoming. It is not easy to find the ruins of the old staging station on its banks. Approaching from the east on Interstate 80, the main highway to Salt Lake City, you turn off, just before crossing Muddy Creek, on to an unpaved country road. A dirt track leads up the valley for about four miles and then the car has to be abandoned. A path winds down to the Muddy, which, if it isn't in flood, can be cleared in a running jump, and there, in a cluster of trees on the far side, are the stone foundations of the old wooden station where the Pony Express rider and the stagecoach passengers grabbed a bite to eat whilst the horses were changed. Many of the Mormon companies also stopped here to overnight, being assured of good water, ample pasture and the company of the station agent and his wife – 'a miserable old English woman' according to Burton. Close by is a low fence surrounding a small plot. This is Catherine Bennett's grave.

She was so very near her goal. A hundred miles more, another week, and she would have been there. She was travelling with her husband, Benjamin, and her daughter, Elizabeth. She was 67 years old, seven years older than her husband. They were a family of fishermen and mariners. Benjamin, like his father before him, had been a pilot on the Dee. According to family tradition, it was a visit by Brigham Young to Hawarden in the autumn of 1840 that led to their conversion. We know nothing of Catherine's journey to Muddy Creek nor why, nor how she died. The only reference to her are a few words in the diary of one of the company. 'Thursday, September 27th. Started before breakfast. Travelled 8 or 9 miles to the station on the Muddy near some springs where we camped for the balance of the day and night. At this place we buried Sister Bennett, an aged Saint from England who died the day before.' Even her nationality was incorrectly recorded.

The gravestone is modern. It was erected by the Bennett family in 1998, and a plaque on it commemorates their great-great-great-grandmother. On the bottom are the words: 'Placed by her American and Welsh descendants.' It is not certain that this was the exact spot where she was buried as no trace of the original grave has survived.

In fact, not many pioneer graves have survived along the trail and only in a very few cases are the names of their occupants known. It is estimated that somewhere between 300,000 and 500,000 used the trail before the coming of the railway, to travel either to California or Oregon or Utah and, out of these hundreds of thousands, between four and eight per cent are believed to have died on the journey, most of them from cholera in the early days. This means that there are, on average, between six and twenty people buried on every mile of the route between the Missouri and the far west but, today, hardly any graves are to be seen. In the whole of Wyoming, for example, only forty are known. Many disappeared because the families deliberately made them indistinguishable from the surrounding scrub lest the Indians should find them and open them, to steal the clothes and the few valuables that would have been buried with the bodies. Other graves were lost because of the climate. They were mostly little cairns of stone, hastily thrown together, with a few words roughly carved on a piece of wood or a buffalo skull and placed on the cairn. They wouldn't have withstood the freezing cold and the ferocious winds of a single winter. 'Many a father, mother, brother, sister, look back with their mind's eye to that lonely spot,' wrote one diarist, 'but they will have to wait till the resurrection day before they will see those bodies again, for those mounds have become the same as the other surface of the earth around, so that to find the place is next to impossible.'

Today, searching the trail for the lost graves of the pioneers and attempting to identify those buried in them has become a popular pastime, and the Mormons are amongst the keenest practitioners. When a new grave is discovered, it creates quite a stir, especially if its occupant can be identified. For example, in 1862, two years after Catherine Bennett's death, a woman called Charlotte Dansie died in childbirth on the western slopes of South Pass. Seventy-seven years later, two of her descendants went looking for her grave. They knew roughly where she had died. They also knew that Charlotte and her baby had been buried together in the same grave and that her husband, on the day of her funeral, had ripped off the lid of an old chest and laid it over her body. The lid, they knew, had been decorated with brass figures of lions. They also knew that, as she was lowered into her grave, her husband had slipped her favourite necklace of blue beads around her neck.

They had dozens of acres to search but luckily they chanced upon a shepherd who knew the area well. He told them of a mother and child's grave which had recently been found, but which had been plundered by those who found it. He led them to it and in it they found the remains of the rotted lid of the old chest decorated with brass lions. Later, the shepherd confessed that it had been he who had desecrated the grave and he handed over a necklace of blue beads which he had found amongst the bones. The site of the grave was given to the family in perpetuity so that it could be properly maintained and protected and today a granite stone marks the spot.

But although only a small fraction of the migrants on the trail were Mormon and only a small fraction of the Mormons were Welsh, yet, remarkably, three of the forty graves in Wyoming that contain identifiable remains are the graves of Welsh Mormons – Catherine and two others.

It was only in this century that one of them was found. Bill Lehr's hobby was studying scorpions. Mr Lehr was, and probably still is, a science teacher in Big Piney Middle School, about fifty miles from the trail, west of South Pass. On a September day in 2001, he was out looking for scorpions in the neighbourhood of the trail when, on turning over a large rock, he spotted a name and a date on its underside: 'L.M. Edwards. Aged 4 years. 1861.' 'Remarkably,' said one of the experts of the Oregon-California Trails Association, 'it appears that this grave has not been disturbed. Apart from the stone falling on its face, it is in the same condition as when the Edwards family left it on that sad day in 1861.'

But who was L.M. Edwards? There is no record in the Church archive of a family called Edwards crossing the Plains that year. But this is not unusual. The names of many of the pioneering families have been lost. However, there is a family of Edwardses, with a young child with the initials 'L.M.', listed amongst the passengers on the SS *City of Manchester* that sailed from Liverpool on September 16th, 1861. The family is described as John Edwards, labourer, from Abergele, his wife, Eleanor, and four children, John (7), Eleanor M. (6), Leah M. (3) and William, who is a baby. Sometime between boarding in Liverpool and her death near South Pass, Leah had celebrated her fourth birthday. That's all we know about her. But today, her gravestone, and the place where she died, are looked after with as much, if not more care than she might have received whilst she was still alive.

But it's the third Welsh grave that is the most moving, mainly because of its location. This again is the grave of a young girl. Her name was Annie Jane John, only child of David and Mary John. She was eight months and five days old when she died on August 20th, 1861. Her father came from Little Newcastle in Pembrokeshire. No one amongst the early Welsh Saints had been better educated than David John. He was brought up to be a Baptist minister, sent to a private tutor as a boy and then on to an academy in Haverfordwest, where he was taught Latin and Greek, to prepare for the pulpit. But whilst yet only fifteen, he was converted to Mormonism and was baptized without his parents' permission. Out of respect for his father, he agreed not to leave the Baptist Church until he attained his majority. On his 22nd birthday, in December 1856, he dreamt that an angel came to him and showed him all the mountains of the west and said that those were the mountains of Eternity, through which the Saints passed to Zion. A month later, these verses, written by him, appeared in *Udgorn Seion*.

Mi gollais fy holl ffrindiau gynt
Pan unais gyda'r Saint.
Er hynny, elw yw i mi.
Rhyfeddol yw fy mraint.
Gadawaf Babilon cyn hir.
Mi af i Seion draw
Ac yno caf addoli'm Duw
Heb erlid, ing na braw.

[I lost all my former friends
when I joined the Saints.
But it was still of great profit to me.
My privilege is remarkable.
I shall leave Babylon ere long
and go to Zion yonder
and there I shall worship my God
without persecution, pain or fear.]

Five years passed before he could fulfil his ambition. He had, by that time, married Mary Wride and Annie had been born. They sailed in the spring of 1861 but even before they had arrived in America, Annie's health was already worrying them. 'Severe cold possessed many, among others my babe Annie Jane (being my firstborn),' wrote David in his diary. 'A young lady by the name of Mary Ann Thomas took her in her arms up on deck. When I found her, her face and forehead were turned blue with the cold, water running freely from her eyes and nose, the cold settled on her lungs.' The cold never left her lungs thereafter. By August 19th, they had arrived at one of the remotest parts of the trail, a mile and a half west of the place where the Sweetwater rips through the cliffs of Devil's Gate. In the camp that night Barry Wride, David's brother-in-law, watched his small niece sicken. 'Annie Jane John, my sister's daughter, was very ill this night and had been for some days previous.'

David was not in camp that night. It was his turn to be guarding the stock. 'I was called on guard at 2 A.M. I felt reluctant to go because my child was sick, but knowing it to be a duty to share the burden of care and responsibility, I obeyed and hastened to release the guard. I left my wife and baby deep asleep in the wagon, seemingly enjoying a sweet sleep, so I left them without saying a word, lest I should disturb them. I walked about 1 mile to the cattle, found them lying down and still. I thought there was no danger of Indians, neither any sign of the cattle going astray, so I laid my buffalo robe on the ground, put my pistol by my side, and laid down, my roof being the wide canopy of heaven. Not then knowing that the Angels of God were with me on guard, I soon fell in deep sleep and dreamed the following dream.' Like many Mormons, David believed there was meaning to his dreams, that God was communicating with him, so he took careful note of them. 'I saw my wife walking towards me with a smiling face dressed in a white, rather short dress, 'till I could see that her hose were white and that she had on black silk slippers. Her face and neck were as the driven snow. As she approached near me she smiled. Her smile offended me. I rebuked her, saying that it was wrong for her to be so merry, seeing me in such great pain. She replied that she was not aware that I was sick. I told her to look at my right leg which was naked. It was covered with sores, dark and gloomy, and above them all, high on the thigh, was a large black gathering from which dark, thick blood ran profusely. The blood as it ran, covered my leg, foot, and toes and from the end of the toes dropped to the ground and as it fell to the earth it sank out of sight so that we could perceive no trace of it left behind.' What would Freud have made of such a dream? 'When my wife witnessed this scene of pain, she wept bitterly and said, "I must go, Annie Jane is quite sick." And she left quite mournful. I awoke, left the herd at 6 A.M., went to camp. After arriving, the first thing I heard was that Annie Jane had been very sick from 3 to 4 o'clock. My dream was before me so strong 'till all my strength and faith was taken from me. She died in her mother's arms at 8:30 A.M. Hundreds and thousands of Saints have laid down their lives between the Missouri River and Salt Lake. They died martyrs to fatigue and worn out constitutions in the wilderness. Among those martyrs is my first born.'

It started to rain early on the morning Annie died and it continued to rain all day. Her body was placed in one of the wagons and carried to the next camp, fifteen miles to the west. There Brother John Turner made a coffin for her and Brothers Benjamin Evans, William Howells and David P. Thomas opened a grave. The Sisters prepared the body for burial. 'August 21. She was buried at 7 A.M.' wrote her father. 'The bearers, to convey her remains to the last resting place, were 12 young men. We placed her name at the head of her grave and heaped a pile of large stones on it to protect her body from wild beasts. It would be useless here to portray the feelings of parents in being compelled to leave their only child.'

The description of the funeral is followed by detailed instructions on how to find the grave, in case, perhaps, they should ever return. 'This grave is about 15 miles west of Devil's Gate, where the river crosses between two high rocks nearly touching each other. This place is known as Little Devils Gate. She is buried on the side of a small hill, 600 yards east of a high rock and about the same distance south of the Sweetwater.' Although the headstone bearing her name has long since gone, the small cairn remains exactly where David John describes.

It is not a pretty place. Nearby is one of the salt pools, with its white collar of poisonous alkali. Precipitous rocks surround the site. Little grows here except sagebrushes. But this is sacred ground for the Mormons. In Devil's Gate nearby, Martin's company of handcarters sheltered from the storms of '56. Six miles back to the east is Independence Rock, the Register of the Trail, where generations of travellers have carved their names in the granite, thousands upon thousands of them, trappers, merchants, missionaries, farmers, miners and Saints. To the west is a stupendous prospect. A broad plateau stretches away as far as the eye can see, slowly rising in the far distance to Rocky Ridge, where so many of Willie's company lost their lives. From this plateau, jagged mountains rear skywards.

And in this strange, forsaken land there's nothing stranger

and more forsaken than the nearby township of Jeffrey City. Nothing moves in Jeffrey City. No one plays on the public playing fields, no one swims in the Olympic-sized swimming pool, the school for six hundred pupils is empty, and the modern blocks of flats are unoccupied. Walking the empty streets, I felt like Daniel Daniels walking through the streets of Salt Lake City. Jeffrey City is a modern ghost town, built in the 1970s to house the workforce of a nearby uranium mine. When the Cold War was at its height and there was need for more and more nuclear bombs, the population rose to over 4,000. But when the Cold War thawed, the mine was quickly bankrupted and the 4,000 disappeared almost overnight, leaving Jeffrey City to its ghosts.

And in this alien, pitiless landscape is the grave of Annie John. 'She was left,' according to one witness, 'where no flowers grow and where nothing breaks the silence but the ceaseless wailing of the wind and the wolves howling in the darkness.'

1861

AFTER 1860, THE glamour of the trail begins to fade. In their old age, those who crossed in later years might still tell epic tales to their grandchildren of the obstinacy of the oxen, the ferociousness of the wolves and the heroism of the pioneers, but they knew, in their heart of hearts, that the real hard times had passed and that the Mormon Trail, after 1860, was considerably less dangerous than it had once been.

Up until 1860, the Mormon pioneers had to buy their oxen and the wagons that they drove across the Plains. They bought them at the staging camps. They had to be taught how to handle them, how to yoke up in the mornings, how to crack whips over the heads of the leaders, how to 'gee' and how to 'haw'. There were many frayed tempers and many accidents. The oxen and wagon were the costliest element of their migration, more expensive than the fare across the Atlantic and the train ticket from New York put together. In Iowa, thousands of oxen were bought every season, not only by the Mormon pioneers but by other emigrants on their way west and, as a consequence, the cost of the animals in the east was artificially high. In Utah, on the other hand, at the end of summer, there was always a glut of oxen and the value of the animals fell sharply. And if, as seemed likely, war was to break out between the northern and southern States, things could only get worse. Thousands more oxen would be needed by the armies. Their price in the east could only rise. Brigham was again having to look for a cheaper method of bringing the faithful to Zion.

He took great interest in the experiments of his nephew, Joseph W. Young. Joseph had set out for the Missouri from

279

Salt Lake City early in 1860 with a train of 29 wagons, carrying foodstuffs grown in Utah. Along the route he left caches of food, enough to feed his men on the return journey. He arrived in Florence within 65 days. The spare food he sold. He then loaded 22 tons of freight into the empty wagons and set off for home, replenishing his food wagon from the caches left by him on his way down. He was back in Utah on October 3rd having not spent a cent – indeed, having made a decent profit. This was the first time a wagon train had gone 'down-and-back' in a season.

Brigham was quick to see the possibilities. There would be no need to buy wagons in the east and to kit them out. There would be no need to buy food. Most importantly, there would be no need to buy oxen. He ordered each settlement in Utah Territory to contribute an ox or a wagon or harnesses or food to the following year's 'down-and-back' wagon trains and to bring them to Salt Lake City by the middle of April. Their contribution would be deducted from their tithes. He called on each ward to supply teamsters to drive the wagons, young farm hands with no great family responsibilities, proficient in the skills of trail. Obedient to his call, 250 drivers volunteered, and 2,000 oxen and two hundred wagons were put at the Church's service; 150,000 pounds of flour were donated and enough food to provide for the drivers and the emigrants on the journey.

The new arrangement depended on painstaking planning and careful timing. If the wagons had to wait in Florence for the emigrants for any length of time, they would be late crossing the Rockies on their return journey and liable to be caught in the winter storms. On the other hand, if the emigrants arrived in Florence too soon, they would incur heavy food and accommodation costs whilst they waited. In Europe, the clock on the operation had started ticking months earlier. Back in March, George Q. Cannon, president of the Church's European Mission, had hired a ship in Scandinavia to bring to Hamburg the Swedish and Danish Saints who were emigrating that year. From there they caught another ship to Hull, then a train to Liverpool in time to board one of the ships hired by the Church to take them to New York. At the same time, the British emigrants would also be converging on Liverpool. The *Manchester* sailed on April 16th, carrying 378 Saints, the *Underwriter* on April 23rd, carrying 623, and the *Monarch of the Seas* on May 16th, carrying 955. Then, in New York, over a thousand American Saints joined the party. The staging camp this year was outside Florence, where today the city of Omaha stands. They travelled by train from New York to Quincy in Illinois via Chicago, often changing trains so as to get the cheapest rate possible. From Quincy, there was a twenty-mile journey down the Mississippi by steamboat, then a train to St Joseph, followed by two days by steamboat up the Missouri to Florence. They timed it just right, arriving at the staging camp a few days before the wagons arrived from Utah. On June 25th, the first wagon train back was on its way.

Once the 'down-and-back' boys came to meet them on the Missouri, the demands made on the emigrants became much less onerous. They no longer had to learn how to control 4,000 lbs of mean beef. They no longer had to grease axles or tighten the iron hoops on the wheels. They no longer had to worry about the scarcity of water between the Platte and the Sweetwater or the dangers of the alkali water along Poison Spider Road. There were experts at hand to look after these matters, experienced young men hardened by a lifetime of such work on their family ranches.

Relieved of their duties, the pioneers began to take on a more light-hearted tone in their journals. 'Aug 24th.. We resolved to make a mountain ascent, so off we jogged at a good pace.' It's hard to imagine the emigrants of previous years jogging off en route to climb a nearby mountain for fun. 'It appeared to be only about a half mile from the roadway. We passed through a river bare footed & tramped towards the mountain which we found to be further away than it appeared. After sundry slips we reached the top which was about 500 feet high. We had an excellent view of the scenery in the distance. The train looked small as it rolled along in the Valley below.' This is not the pioneer stuff of old, pitting themselves against the wilderness, hard-pressed to make it through another day. 'Aug 9th. Read *Davidson's Grammar* with Frank Raybould. Frank is a good & intelligent companion. We think of improving each other whilst going over the Plains in the study of Grammar.' 'Delighted with the scenery,' adds another. 'The breezes blow upon us & strengthen us for our exercise.' The epic adventure was becoming an excursion, the journey a trip. 'Enjoyed currant pudding for supper – quite a relish!' How much had changed in ten years!

Many young Welshmen worked as teamsters in the 'down-and-back' trains. Most of them were in their teens and early twenties. Evan Samuel Morgan, the boy from the Swansea Valley who had gone looking for work in the coal mines of Anglesey, was one such. Taliesin Hughes, the elder brother who had looked after his young siblings, was another and Henry Davis Rees, son of Thomas and Margaret Rees, founders of the coal village of Wales, yet another. A job on a 'down-and-back' train was much sought after. What young man would not prefer six months of adventure in places he had long wished to visit to six months of hard, monotonous work on some remote family farm? Working on a 'down-and-back' also gave them the first choice of that season's migrant girls. Many a tryst was sealed, many a troth plighted, before the train reached the Valley.

Despite their high spirits, they were all extremely hard workers. John Jenkins had lived in Cowbridge in the Vale of Glamorgan for the first five years of his life, and then near Council Bluffs until he was sixteen. He had been thoroughly 'westernised' in the five years since he'd arrived in Utah. He went 'down-and-back' to the Missouri three times. On his third journey, in 1866, he kept a diary and in it he describes how he helped to swim eight hundred cattle and oxen over the Platte. 'The Captain called for volunteers to swim the cattle across. Eight men volunteered, I being one of them. After about four hours of hard labour by the entire company we got the cattle started through the water and we eight volunteers followed them, swimming behind them to keep them going. To do this we would take hold of the tails of the cattle that were behind and swim with them. When the ones we had hold of would swim into the bunch, we would let go and grab a fresh hold on another animal as it was unsafe for us to go into the bunch of swimming animals. Had we done so, we were in danger of drowning. We were in the water about six hours before we got them across.

Another Welshman on the trail this year was Amos Jones of Ruabon, near Wrexham. Amos was 24 years old. He'd arrived in the States on the *Samuel Curling* five years earlier and since then, like John Jenkins, had been working in Iowa. In 1861, sensing that the Civil War was soon to break out, his family had decided to continue their journey to the Valley, and the names of his father and mother and his six brothers and sisters are duly listed in the records of Homer Duncan's company. But Amos' name is not amongst them. He had been recruited by the Pacific Telegraph Company, one of four hundred men hired to work on the first transcontinental telegraph that was being strung out across the continent that summer. The Federal Government laid great store in getting the telegraph operational as soon as possible. The outbreak of the Civil War was imminent and they saw the telegraph as a means of binding the west more closely to the rest of the Union. There were clauses in the contract of the Pacific Telegraph Company which penalised the company heavily if the work was not completed on time. They had sub-contracted the task of supplying the poles on which the wire was to be strung from the Missouri to Utah to Brigham Young. This he had accomplished in so efficient and orderly a fashion that Edward Creighton, the superintendent of the work, was keen to hire more Mormons. He went back to Florence, looking for further recruits from amongst the Saints who were preparing to leave, promising them half their wages there and then, and the other half once the wire had arrived in Salt Lake City. They would be released at the end of their contract in Salt Lake City where they could rejoin their families. One of the men who accepted the offer was Amos Jones.

The excitement generated by this great advance in long distance communication is evidenced by the frequent references to the telegraph in the diaries of the emigrants. They write about 'the telegraph poles recently erected on the other side of the river,' of mule teams passing them 'laden with telegraph wire', of the Pony Express stations which 'have now, through the exertions of Mormon boys who are employed by the government, become telegraph stations.' The wire followed the trail along its whole length, one pole every seventy yards, the gangs leap-frogging each other across the continent. In stony ground, they would plant three miles of poles a day, in sandy ground it would be twelve. Every fifteen miles, if a stagecoach station or a Pony Express station did not already exist, they built one. The wire arrived in Salt Lake City, with Amos in tow, on October 17th, having crossed eight hundred miles of mountains and desert in two months. Six days later, the wire from Carson City in the west arrived. That night, the ends of the two wires were joined together and a message sent from California to President Lincoln in the White House 'The people of California desire in this, the first message across the continent, to express their loyalty to the Union and their determination to stand by its government on this, its day of trial.' There was to be no future now for the Pony Express. It took the telegraph only a few seconds to accomplish what the Pony Express needed eight days, eighty men and a hundred horses to achieve. Two days after this first telegraph message was sent, the Pony Express filed for bankruptcy. Its thrilling, dashing ride was over.

Over the next decade the Saints made constant use of the telegraph. Not a day passed without Brigham Young receiving messages from his Captains out on the Plains, detailing where they were, reporting on their companies' condition and giving an estimated date of arrival. He made sure that these messages were passed on to the newspapers. It was another big step in the civilizing of the trail.

Of all the Welsh who crossed in 1861, no one distinguished herself more in her later life in Utah than Martha Maria Hughes. Few in Wales know of her today, but in Salt Lake City she is warmly remembered. Just off Temple Square, in the centre of Salt Lake City, a plaque commemorates her achievements with the words: 'In memory of Doctor Martha Hughes Cannon. Pioneer doctor. First woman state senator in the U.S. Author of Utah sanitation Laws. Member of the first state Board of Health.' The main building of the Utah Health Department is named after her, 'The Dr Martha Hughes Cannon Building'. In the centre court of the Utah State Capitol building, an eight-foot statue of her celebrates her trailblazing service to the state, and soon a greater honour is to befall her. The Utah Senate has voted that a statue of her should be unveiled in the National Statuary Hall in Washington DC. To this hall, every state in the Union sends statues of two of its most famous citizens. Representing Virginia, for example, are George Washington and Robert E. Lee. Sam Houston is there from Texas, Thomas Edison from Ohio, Andrew Jackson from Tennessee and so on. And from August 2020, the people of Utah are to be represented by Brigham Young and Martha Hughes Cannon. And yet in her home town, Llandudno, few have ever heard of her.

She was born there in 1857, the daughter of a carpenter. Her parents, Peter and Elizabeth Hughes, were members of a small community of Mormons that met in the old village on the Great Orme, high above the town. Thomas Williams, in his description of life in the old village, *Atgofion am Llandudno* [*Memories of Llandudno*], describes their weekly meetings in the gardens of the old Tŷ Coch farmhouse to which non-believers from the village often came to argue and heckle in friendly banter. When Edward Parry, the leader of the Mormons claimed he could speak with tongues, they brought him a Greek Testament and told him to read, and when he failed to do so they said he could no more speak in foreign tongues than old George Williams' cow could knit socks. But when Edward Parry spoke of the importance of being in Salt Lake City to meet the Returned Christ, there were some who listened, amongst them Peter and Elizabeth. The family set off for the Great Salt Lake in 1860 when Martha was just four years old. It proved a harrowing experience. Her elder sister, Annie, died on the Plains. Her father died three days after arriving in Utah. When she came of school-leaving age, Martha had decided that her career should involve caring for the sick. Out on the Plains, the only methods of treating the sick had been folk remedies and the power of the holy oil, but Brigham Young's ideas about medicine had undergone radical change and new, modern, scientific ways were being introduced into Utah. A maternity hospital was being planned and it was thought proper that women's ailments should be treated by women practitioners. Martha was called by the Church to follow a course in medicine, one of the first three women in Utah to be so chosen.

In 1878, she entered the University of Michigan to study for an MD degree. She paid her way, working as a maid in the student dormitory and offering her services as a secretary to wealthier members of the university. In addition to the basic curriculum, she took optional courses in bacteriology and electrotherapeutics, a new science which taught the use of electricity in medical treatments. She embarked on a postgraduate degree at the University of Pennsylvania, completing a thesis on Rocky Mountain Fever, the scourge of the early settlers. She showed it was a form of malaria which could be relieved by quinine. At the same time, she was taking a course in pharmacology and, as a cherry on this impressive cornucopia of qualifications, she finished her education with a course in public speaking, receiving a Batchelor of Oratory degree from the National School of Elocution and Oratory in Philadelphia. It was as if she foresaw, even at this early date, that, one day, public speaking would be important to her. On her return to Utah she was duly appointed to the staff of the first maternity hospital in the state and it appeared that a useful and distinguished career lay before her.

But it was not to be. After four successful years at the hospital, she suddenly abandoned her career, turned her back on Salt Lake City and fled to Europe, taking with her a seven-month-old baby daughter, Lizzie, and leaving behind a husband whom she had secretly married eighteen months previously. Life was never going to be easy for Martha Hughes. She was a complicated, driven woman, torn this way and that by her deeply conservative faith and her fiery radical politics. This is what makes her so interesting and modern a figure.

The husband she had left behind, Angus Munn Cannon, was one of the directors of the hospital, a prominent Mormon citizen and the brother of one of the Quorum of the Twelve Apostles. He was Martha's senior by 23 years and the father of seventeen children. Martha was his fourth wife. It would be a mistake to believe that Martha was pushed into a polygamous marriage by an oppressive, patriarchal society. She was an intelligent, enlightened and spirited woman whose determination to educate herself and whose subsequent career reflects a resolutely feminist and independent spirit. She knew what lay ahead. She knew she would not have a conventional home life. She knew she would only have fleeting visits from her husband. But they were in love. 'You have been loved as much as a woman has been, is, and yet will be loved,' he wrote. 'I am thankful to our Heavenly Father that I have you for my husband,' she declared. 'I would rather spend one hour in your society than a whole lifetime with any other man I know of.' But, more importantly, she believed with all her heart in the teachings of her Church and the holiness of plural marriage. 'Plural marriage,' she wrote 'would be unendurable without a thorough knowledge from God that the principle for which we are battling and striving to maintain in its purity upon the earth is ordained by Him.'

She could not have entered into a polygamous marriage at a more unfortunate time. A wave of anti-Mormon sentiment was sweeping through the United States. The Federal Government in Washington was determined to rid the nation of a practice it considered barbaric. Although a federal law banning plural marriages had been in existence for over twenty years, there had been few convictions, partly because, in Utah, the control of the courts and the right to pick juries had been left in Mormon hands and partly because the Civil War had intervened. But now that the war was over, the government hardened its attitude. Civil and criminal cases were put into the hands of federal courts and were argued before juries often chosen for their anti-polygamous opinions. Detectives were set to watch some of the more influential citizens and one of the first to be arrested was Angus. Martha was subpoenaed to give evidence against him and against other men whose wives had been in her care at the maternity hospital. Lest she incriminate them, she fled abroad, taking her newborn child with her. 'I would rather be a stranger in a strange land,' she wrote, 'and be able to hold my head up among my fellow human beings than be a sneaking captive at home.'

With her sickly child in tow, her 'little pale-faced baby, greatly in need of home comforts', she came to Britain, first staying with her mother's relatives in and around Birmingham. She felt unable to reveal to them that she was in a polygamous relationship and they, in turn, regarded her, a single mother, with deep suspicion. There was a journey to Llanddoged, near Llanrwst in Denbighshire, to search out her father's family. She travelled on to France and Switzerland and Germany, increasingly miserable and lonely, always longing for home and for Angus. She wrote to him with revealing candour. Angus kept all her letters and, at his death, they found their way into the Church archive in Salt Lake City, where they may be read today. In them is to be found a unique and painful record of the life of a Welsh woman in polygamy.

There is no suggestion that her husband's first three wives were a problem to her. She expresses no jealousy towards them. All three were so much older than she. Angus had married his first wife when Martha was only one year old. He had been given permission to do so by Brigham Young, on condition that he also married her sister who was much older and had failed to find a husband. His third wife, Clarissa, was a widow, with two children of her own to support and two adopted children. There is reason to believe, therefore, that Angus married two

288

of his first three wives more from a sense of duty than love, something that was not uncommon in polygamous marriages. Martha appeared to be friendly with all three.

But, a few days before she left for Europe, Angus, in great secrecy, married for the fifth time. This marriage proved more difficult for Martha to accept because Maria Bennion was six months younger than her. Angus wrote that 'he had put his devotion to the Church above everything'. Martha replied, 'I wish we could look at the divine part of these things only, but with so much earthiness in our nature this is not always easily accomplished.' For the first time, flashes of jealousy punctuate the letters. 'How I despise the name Maria – but I never did admire it [even] before I had any occasion to be jealous.' Angus continued to declare his undying love. 'You may doubt it with your own soul, but you are loved by the man you have gone through everything for and sacrificed everything on earth for.' But she was finding her exile increasingly difficult. 'Were it not for Lizzie and the religion of our God, I should never want to see Salt Lake again but seek some other spot and strive to forget what a failure my life has been.' Angus, apparently unbeknown to her and to the other wives, then took a sixth bride. Joanna was 38 years old, and perhaps another example of the 'humanitarianism of polygamy'. Finally, in December 1887, the warrant for Martha's arrest expired and she returned home.

At this time, she became active in the women's rights movement. She had absorbed the spirit and the beliefs of the movement at an early age. In her teens she had worked as a typesetter in the printing shop of the *Woman's Exponent*, a magazine for Mormon women which enthusiastically advocated both plural marriage and women's suffrage. The women of Utah were in a peculiar situation. For seventeen years, from 1870 to 1887, they had been allowed the vote, an entitlement largely won through the efforts of their enemies. Anti-polygamy lobbyists in Washington had reasoned that, if Mormon women were given the vote, they would surely use it to break free from the shackles of polygamy. But this is not what happened. The sisters voted 'en masse' for the 'status quo'. To be seen standing shoulder to shoulder with their men in defence of their faith was more important to them than overthrowing polygamy. They pointed out that only about 25 per cent of the women of the Church were in polygamous relationships and that it was of their own choice. They argued that if a woman was unhappy in her marriage, a divorce was easily obtainable in Utah. And they insisted that it was a religious matter, a matter of conscience, and that the government had no right to intervene. Their opponents eventually conceded defeat and consequently, having allowed Mormon women to vote for eighteen years, summarily disenfranchised them. This sparked a fierce reaction and a vigorous campaign to win back the vote into which Martha threw herself enthusiastically. Two campaigns were being fought simultaneously, intractably bound together, yet no two causes could have been more different. The Women's Suffrage Campaign was a modern, fashionable, progressive movement that was fast making great headway in the nation at large, whilst the campaign in support of polygamous marriages appeared, from outside Utah, to be a step back into darkness, restricting the freedom and the rights of women. Yet Martha was passionately involved in both.

Throughout the 1880s, the Federal Government tightened its grip on the polygamous Saints, squeezing them mercilessly. Many hundreds were jailed, hundreds more were heavily fined. More and more Church property was confiscated. Eventually, in 1890, thirteen years after Brigham Young's death, the Church capitulated and Wilford Woodruff, the incumbent Prophet, declared that God had instructed him there was to be one wife only for every Saint from now on. The Mormons promised that they would not sanction further polygamous marriages and that, although men in plural marriages were expected to support all their wives and children, no man should continue to co-habit with more than one wife. Legally, therefore, Angus and Martha's relationship should have ended but it was soon evident that it had not.

On her return to Salt Lake City in 1888, Martha had embarked on a new career. She had established a training college for nurses, the first in Utah, an adventurous, ambitious project. But no sooner had she embarked on her new career than, once again, it came crashing down about her. Once again, she was pregnant. Once again, to protect Angus, she had to abandon her goals and flee the territory, this time to California, where she gave birth secretly to a baby boy. 'Oh for a home, for a husband of my own and a father for my children,' she wrote, 'and all the little auxiliaries that make life worth the living. Will they ever be enjoyed by this storm-tossed exile?'

After a while, she returned quietly to Salt Lake City and resumed her private practice. In the grand scheme of things, she was still unshakable in her conviction that 'a plural marriage would enable her to associate with the elect in eternity'. But in the here and now, the road ahead often seemed rocky and wearying. 'Dear One, do not think that I am dissatisfied with my lot. On the contrary, I am thankful that God so ordained my destiny to embrace the celestial principle of marriage when I did, and now in it, my energies shall be bent towards its continuance, but I greatly feel my weakness at times and know not how long I shall hold out in the great cause.' 'That Martha and Angus loved each other is evident,' wrote one of Angus' grandsons, 'but equally manifest were their disputes. Theirs was a bittersweet relationship. Love letters and valentines interspersed with complaints about neglect and threats of divorce.'

She became a prominent member of the Utah Women's Suffrage Association and made a name for herself as an orator, not only in Utah, but in the country at large. She was invited to speak in the 1893 World Fair in Chicago and the *Chicago Record* noted that 'Mrs. Dr Martha Hughes Cannon... is considered one of the brightest exponents of the women's cause in the United States'. Utah at this time had yet to be made a state but it had been promised statehood if it formally abandoned polygamy. In 1896, the promise was kept and in the constitution of the new state a clause was included that sanctioned the re-enfranchisement of women. It would be another 25 years before women's suffrage became general throughout the United States. Having won this battle, Martha looked around for another fight.

She had been aware throughout her career that medical standards in Utah were not high. Salt Lake City was growing fast, perhaps too fast, doubling its size between 1880 and 1890. It became one of the dirtiest towns in the West. Diseases such as cholera, TB, whooping cough and measles were rife. There was a need for cleaner water, cleaner streets, better sewage systems and an improvement in the working conditions of the labour force. In the first election of the new legislature, Martha was one of the five Democrats campaigning for one of the five Salt Lake City seats in the state senate. Standing against them were five Republicans, one of whom was Angus. As might be expected, much was made in the press of the duel between husband and wife. Angus was offered reams of advice on how to rein in a frisky mare or how to clip a queen bee's wings. But Martha also had her supporters. *The Salt Lake Herald* declared, 'Send Mrs. Cannon to the State Senate and let Mr. Cannon remain at home to manage home industry. Mrs. Mattie Hughes is the better man of the two.' When the day of the election came, it was Martha and the Democrats that swept the board. She was the first woman to be elected to the state senate of Utah, which is why her statue stands today in the court of the Utah Capitol building. But she was also the first woman to be elected to any senate in the nation, state or federal, which is why another statue of her is soon to grace The National Statuary Hall in Washington DC.

She proved a great success as a senator. As might be expected, her best work was done in the field of public health. In her first month in office, she successfully introduced a bill to establish a public health authority which was instrumental in improving the water supply throughout the state, controlling infectious diseases and imposing higher hygiene standards. Martha was voted to the board of the new authority. At the same time she guided an 'Act to Protect the Health of Women and Girl Employees' on to the statute books and an 'Act Providing

292

for Compulsory Education of Deaf and Dumb Children'. She sponsored a bill to establish better hygiene standards in food production and another to establish a fact-finding agency to gather statistics and undertake research on behalf of the government. In 1899, there was a move to nominate her for a seat in the United States Congress, but it was not to be.

Once again, when her career was about to take off, she was dragged back down to earth, her plans scuppered by another pregnancy. This time it could not be kept secret. Ten years after the Manifesto that had made plural marriages illegal, here was a prominent public figure brazenly flouting the law. It became a national scandal. Martha must have realised what the consequences would be, but she chose the child before her career. Gwendolyn was born in April 1899. Angus was duly arrested and was fined $100, but Martha paid more dearly. Her political career was over. She had to give up her seat in the Senate and although she was yet only in her early forties, she retired from public life. She continued in private practice and made a study of nervous diseases, becoming an authority on narcotic addiction, but more and more of her time was spent with her children. Her relationship with Angus withered to little more than demands for money and petty quarrels. 'Dear Angus, Please send remittance. Children must be fed and clothed.' 'Dear Angus, The Building Society wants us to move out of the house because there are $255 due.' 'Dear Angus, I feel disgraced to be obliged to ask for butter.'

The evidence of the letters suggests a growing despondency. Despite her confident public image, in private she suffered pangs of self-doubt. 'People have said I had no feeling when in reality my pent-up feeling like a cankerous worm was gnawing me internally.' Her husband could give her neither the home she craved for nor the emotional security she needed. She was often tired and depressed. One senses her last years were unhappy. Eventually she left Utah and settled with her son in Los Angeles and there she died in 1932. One of her last wishes was that her diaries and all her personal papers be burnt.

For many years, her name and her career were more or less

forgotten, but her star rose again when she was seen to have been fighting many of the battles that young Mormon women, and women everywhere, are fighting today. Her cause was championed by various feminist groups seeking to remind the people of Utah of what she had achieved, how she had fought for better opportunities for women at work and in the home, 'Give me a woman who thinks about something besides cook stoves and wash tubs and baby flannels, and I'll show you, nine times out of ten, a successful mother'; how she had fought for the right of women to pursue the career of their choice, 'There are many scientific truths to be discovered, many arts to be perfected, which require the hearts and minds of women'; and how she had fought for gender equality. 'All men and women are born free and equal.' Throughout her life, she fought for the right of women to lead more enriching, rewarding and fulfilling lives. Yet for her, it was a fight made all the more difficult by her belief in plural marriage and her faith in the Mormon way.

1862

ONE MORNING IN 1979, Professor Ronald D. Dennis was on his way to St John, a small village on the far side of the Oquirrh Mountains, fifty miles south-west of Salt Lake City. He had heard that Benjamin Evans, an early Welsh emigrant to the area and one of the editors of *Udgorn Seion*, had settled there and was said to have brought with him from Wales a copy of the Welsh translation of *The Book of Mormon*. Professor Dennis believed that the copy was still preserved by the family. He also hoped that he might find there more of Benjamin Evans' papers.

No one knows more than Professor Dennis about the emigration of the Welsh Saints to Utah in the nineteenth century. He is a professor emeritus of Portuguese at Brigham Young University but is also the father of Welsh Mormon studies. His dedication to this field of research derives, he says, not from academic but from religious motivation. In 1963, a few months after completing a two-year mission to Brazil, he remembers being in a Sunday school class in Provo. 'When the instructor read to us the sixth verse of the fourth chapter of the Book of Malachi, about Elijah the Prophet being sent by God to "turn the hearts of the children to their fathers", I felt a burning desire to turn my heart to my ancestors, a desire that has continued with me to this day… Turning the heart of the children to the fathers' says Professor Dennis, 'means more to a Latter-day Saint than simply researching the biographies of his ancestors. It also means performing on their behalf the saving ordinances in one of the 153 temples throughout the world. We place a literal interpretation on "baptizing for the dead" (1 Cor. 15:29) and we perform and record baptisms on their behalf in our temples.'

As a young man, Professor Dennis had been aware that Captain Dan Jones was his great-great-grandfather. In 1976, he came to Wales to perfect his Welsh so that he could sift through the catalogues of the National Library of Wales and other libraries, searching for Welsh publications by his ancestor and his fellow missionaries. He uncovered a rich store of documents pertaining to the early days of the Church in Wales, bringing to light facts about the nineteenth-century mission to Britain which Mormon historians had not known. Later he did the same research in other libraries in the U.S., in Yale and Harvard, and of course in Utah itself, discovering a wealth of further treasures. He published his findings in a series of books, the first of which, *The Call of Zion*, told the story of the first large-scale emigration from Wales under the leadership of his great-great-grandfather. Forty-three years later, he is still at work, having recently finished a translation into English of all 4,500 surviving pages of *Udgorn Seion*. The fruits of his labour he has put on-line, **http://welshmormon.byu.edu** 'It's a way of sharing the drawers full of research and pictures that I had accumulated over the previous four decades, making them available to anyone in the world who can access the internet.' From this wonderful resource comes much of the information in this book. There is no page to which Professor Dennis has not contributed.

But disappointment awaited him in St John. When he arrived at the home of the Benjamin Evans' family, he found that the Welsh copy of *The Book of Mormon* was in poor condition, many of the pages missing, many more damaged. Nor were there any other documents of historical interest in the house. He learnt, however, that there was another manuscript in the village, a manuscript which might be of more interest than a dozen Welsh *Books of Mormon*. It was a diary, said to have been kept by another early Welsh settler, containing entries written in Wales before leaving and on the voyage across the Atlantic and over the Plains. The diary was in the care of a local man called Paul Stookey.

Professor Dennis went to call on Mr Stookey and was shown the diary. The cover was worn but the pages within were clean and in good condition. Mr Stookey explained that it had been written by his grandfather, William Ajax, a name which meant very little to Professor Dennis. He began to read and was immediately struck by the candour of the writing. 'March 13th, 1862. This is my birthday. I was born on the 13th of March, 1832, in the town and parish of Llantrisant, Glamorganshire, South Wales; therefore, I am 30 years old to-day. My father's name was Thomas Truman Ajax, and my mother's name was Rebecka Darcus. They were never married, and yet my father had three children by my mother. My father was a clerk. He was of good repute, and seemed to be well respected, but he had two rather great failings: He was much addicted to drink, and he had children by several females besides my mother. My mother was the daughter of an excise man, and, from all that I heard concerning her, she seemed to be an honest and an industrious person. She had this failing, it is true. She has been in the habit, within the scope of my memory, of washing &c., in gentlemen's houses. I was brought up since a babe by William and Frances Maxwell, whom I call father and mother.'

Professor Dennis was surprised and impressed by what he had found. 'It had obviously been written by a well-educated person who was as comfortable in English as he was in Welsh.' The author describes his childhood, his five years of schooling and ten years drifting from job to job across south Wales, carrying bricks for the builders of the Taff Vale Railway and stone for the craftsmen employed in widening the Old Bridge in Pontypridd. He worked for Crawshay in his Treforest iron works and in a mine called Gough's Pit in Pen-y-cae (Ebbw Vale). There, in Pen-y-cae, in 1853, as a young man of 21, he joined the Saints. He was sent on a mission to north Wales, working in the gold mine in Dolfrwynog, near Dolgellau, and in a slate quarry in Ffestiniog. During these years he set about educating himself, reading widely and studying Latin, Greek and French in his few spare hours. When he was 27 years old, he was made a clerk in the Welsh Mission's head office in Swansea. Professor Dennis was surprised to read that, from the spring of 1859 to the spring of 1862, his duties included editing *Udgorn Seion*. Why had he not come across this man before?

It was a time of great change within the Welsh Mission. The excitement and the fervour of the early years was fading. From the middle of the 1850s there had been a steady decline in the membership, from 4,318 in 1854 to about 1,900 in 1859. The best and most active members of the Church had left for Utah and there were fewer young members coming to take their place. Now the bad news from Utah was filtering back to Wales, news of the famine, of the fierce reformation, Buchanan's war, the Mountain Meadow Massacre, of polygamy and of the Civil War. In Wales itself, on the other hand, the news was good, wages were rising and the living conditions of the common man were improving. The economic advantages of gathering to Zion no longer had the appeal of earlier days.

The circulation figures of *Udgorn Seion* reflected the falling membership. According to William Ajax, the magazine was barely selling five hundred copies a week whereas, at the start of the 1850s, it had been selling 2,000 and more. One consequence is that no copies survive today of many of the later editions; in fact, not one copy from the last six months of the magazine's existence has survived and only seventeen of the more than two hundred editions published between 1858 and 1862. The months during which William Ajax kept his diary coincide with this dark period in the history of the Church in Wales. Often, his diary is the only surviving commentary on all-important decisions that were taken at that time. The bald facts were known, that the Mission's office in Swansea was closed, that the press was moved to Liverpool, and that the British Mission had decided not to continue publishing a Welsh magazine, but the reasons for these decisions were unclear and the campaign Ajax had led to try to save the *Udgorn* was unrecognised.

In January 1862, William was already worried about the

future of the magazine. He knew that the higher echelons of the Mission in Britain were doubtful of its benefits. For some years the leaders in Liverpool had been urging their Welsh members to abandon the Welsh language. In 1856 they had announced in *Udgorn Seion* that English was the chosen language of God and that the Welsh should recognize this fact. 'From the diversity of languages, God has seen fit to choose English as the means of revealing the truth of his Gospel. This is the common language of the Saints in Zion.' Or as Brigham Young remarked to a group newly arrived settlers in his own succinct way, 'Your first duty is to learn to live; that is, how to plant a cabbage, how to feed a pig, how to build a house and plant a garden. The next duty is to learn English, the language of *The Book of Mormon,* the language of the Latter-days and the language of God.' Three who had been most active in promoting the Welsh language in Salt Lake City – John S. Davis, Thomas Jeremy and Dan Jones – were persuaded to renounce their support. Being associated with the letter that made this decision public must have been difficult for all three. John S. Davis was chosen to pen it. He who had called on his brothers in 1851 'never to neglect their language', and who had written, 'The Welsh language will not die. We were sent to trumpet in our mother tongue… and what turncoat will dare prevent us?' now wrote, 'We urge the Welsh to learn English, and not to use the Welsh language as that hinders people from learning English. It would please me to hear that the Welsh in the old country were doing the same.' So great a change after only ten years in America.

But William Ajax refused to accept this counsel and fought fiercely to save the *Udgorn*. 'The Welsh,' he wrote 'like all other nations, pride themselves in their language; and a person can do nothing worse to arouse the feelings of a Welshman than to speak disparagingly of his language and his ancestors. There is no language that can reveal the principles of religion so well to a Welshman as Welsh, unless he be a thorough scholar. He may manage to converse freely in the English Language and to transact any business in it; but there is no language that reaches his heart as well as Welsh. And inasmuch as that religion has to do more with the heart than anything else, it is of immense importance that the principles of salvation should be revealed to him in that language that is nearest his heart. Because of these reasons, and many more I could name, the discontinuing of the printing of the *Udgorn* would, in my opinion, materially affect the work of God in Wales.'

His efforts were in vain. In April 1862, after 469 issues, *Udgorn Seion* ceased publication and William and his wife, Emma, were released to emigrate to Utah. They had a fortnight's notice, a fortnight to sell all they owned and to buy all they needed for their new life, and to say a final farewell to family and friends. On May 19th, they joined a small company of 36 Saints on board the *Antarctic*, the last Mormon ship of the season.

The Civil War was now into its second year and the fighting was intensifying. It disrupted the journeys of many of the emigrants. On her way to Utah, Elizabeth Davis of Eglwysbach in the Conwy Valley lost most of her possessions when her train was attacked by Confederate soldiers. Everything of value was stolen and the rest burned. 'After we left New York State,' wrote William Probert, 'we were often stopped by Union men to see if we had any arms on board, or any rebels.' As he made his way through the eastern states, Edward Edwards, a young man from Merthyr, donned a bonnet and shawl lest he be pressed into the Union ranks. The Missouri steamboat on which David William Davis of Aberaman travelled was stopped and ordered to fly its flag. They had two flags on board, a Union flag and a Confederate flag. Unfortunately, they raised the wrong one and everybody, crew and passengers, spent three weeks in a Yankee jail as a consequence. But most Mormon emigrants managed to slip quietly between the two armies without trouble.

The war caused many of the Saints, who had tarried in the eastern states, to hurriedly decide to continue their journey to Utah. One of them was Thomas John, a shoemaker, formerly of Mathry in Pembrokeshire, more recently of Williamsburg, across the East River from Manhattan. Anyone who worked in leather was in great demand during the Civil War. Thomas found ample work making belts and leather packs and cartridge cases for the army. 'It was a very prosperous time for all who could use the awl and thread,' wrote his son, Henry. He earned enough in a year to bring his wife and all eleven children to Williamsburg. Then the war broke out and, at first, much to the surprise of the northerners, the Union army was badly savaged. 'After the battle of Bull Run was fought between the Union Army and the Secessionists,' wrote Henry, 'the people were very much agitated and alarmed lest the enemy invade the city of Washington and take the Treasury of the United States.' Thomas and his family decided they would be safer in Salt Lake City and they left for Utah in the spring of 1862.

Another who hurried to Utah to escape the war was John Evans, originally from Llandovery. When he was eight years old, John had run away from home and had walked all the way to Merthyr to look for his father and had succeeded in finding him there. By the time he was nine, he was working in the Penydarren iron works, stopping trams full of ore by jamming wooden blocs under their wheels. When he was 25 years old, he had emigrated to America with his wife, Elizabeth, and had found work in the iron works and coal pits of Missouri, Iowa and Nebraska but, by 1861, they had left the smoke and had settled far out on the Plains in a lonely cabin on the Mormon Trail, about 170 miles from the Platte's confluence with the Missouri, a little to the north of a cluster of cabins known as Wood River City. William Ajax, when he passed later that year, noted in his diary that there were no more villages after Wood River City. John, therefore, was living on the very edge of the settled territories.

Around his lonely cabin he grew fruit and vegetables and made a good living selling them to passers-by on the trail – soldiers, prospectors, miners and Mormons. He worked for the company building the telegraph, he served as a county sheriff and he became an accomplished builder of sod cabins. The only education he ever had was in a Sunday school in Mathry where he had learnt to read his Bible, yet he wrote an interesting journal. Here is his description, in his own hopelessly misspelt words, of the morning when he first heard that the country was at war.

'we lived on Wood River when the war broke out betweene the north and the south of the united states thare was a companey of souldears came that vearey same day from fort carney on foot 15 miles Distance about ten a clock am and stopt at my house for Bracfast and I was vearey much surprise to see them for I new saveararal of them so I asked them whare ware thay going and thay answard to the war then said I what war then thay said to the south thay have commence fiteing thar this morning and we got a telegram from thare this morning at four a clock to come down imedeatly and so thay eate Bracfast close By my house and thay drank all the milk that we had and all the watter that was in the well and after Bracfast thay ware off agine and so we said good By to ech other and now after this I went down to wood river Centre about three miles from my place to see Broather Joseph E Johnson to try to find out what we better do in the future and he answard me like this what so evear you do don't you make eney Calcultion to stop in this countrey a nother winter for this war is the verarey war that the prophet Joseph Smith predicted 29 years ago I have hurd all about it maney time and this is the vearey same war and now thes indans will know all about this that the nashon is at war with ech other and fiteing one ageinst the other and thay will take advantage of it and take the law into thair own hands and Do thinges just as thay plese and it wont be safe to live hear eney longer I would not live hear another winter for all I am werth and so I made up my mind to go to Utah this summar.'

And off they went, John and Elizabeth and their three sons, Moroni, Madoc and Gomer. John became one of the stalwarts of the Welsh community in Utah. He organised many eisteddfodau in Brigham and Willard, the villages around his home. He and Elizabeth sang together in duet competitions and were a popular act in the numerous Welsh concerts in the area. He played the flute and danced the clog dance in the annual meetings of the 'Cumbrians' and 'The Sons and Daughters of

Wales', and he was a member of the famous Tabernacle Choir for nearly thirty years.

By the beginning of August, two and a half months after leaving Liverpool, William and Emma Ajax were also on the trail. His diary has lively descriptions of what they saw and did.

'Friday, August 8th. The whole of the day almost was spent in ferrying the wagons across the Loup Fork. Volunteers were called for to assist in pushing the wagons' ferry-boat, which call I obeyed, and was, consequently, in the water from 9 a.m. to 5 p.m. It was hard work, for the water was sometimes up to our arm-pits. Yet, we felt well while at our post. We ferried the mail-coach across in the afternoon. Grapes were in the woods here, but, as the ripe ones had been gathered, we were not much better of them. There was a tolerable good quantity of black currants, but I could not gather them, on account of being engaged in the ferrying business. Many gathered considerable quantities of them, and had, that way, the chance of having some nice tarts. We left about sunset and reached our camping-place about 12. We saw a meteor in coming on, which had much the appearance of a sky-rocket.'

'Tuesday, September 16th. A cold day, and a very cold morning. It blew so hard that our tent came down in the night. Passed by some rocks very much resembling the domes of cathedrals, with nothing growing on them but fir and cedar trees, and them very much apart from each other. Passed by the grave of a murderer when within about 1 mile of the first of the three crossings of the Sweet Water, on which was, as far as I can recollect, the following inscription: – "Charles R. Young, aged 43 years, was tried by jury on the 7th of July, 1862, for murdering George Scott on the 6th of July, and was found guilty and executed on the 8th, by being shot. R. Kennedy, Captain of the emigration company did the execution."'

An impressive example of the speedy and summary justice of the Wild West!

The first few days of the journey had appeared to William to be one glorious adventure – swimming in the Platte, inspecting the tepees of some friendly Pawnees, visiting acquaintances in other companies and delighting in the scenery which, he said, was 'very similar to the country west of Swansea'. Soon after first reaching the banks of the Platte, the emigrants looked forward to seeing 'The Lone Tree', one of the wonders of the Plains, an old cottonwood giant that grew by itself where no other trees grew. It was an important milestone on their journey. On his very first crossing of the Plains, Brigham Young had carved his name into its bark and every passing Saint endeavoured to do the same. As a consequence, by the time William arrived, the old tree was in dire health. It was in a much worse condition when he left, because William carved a whole 'englyn' on it. An 'englyn' is a four-lined poem in strict meter, conforming to rules formulated in medieval times, each line incorporating complicated internal rhymes and alliterations known as 'cynghanedd'. William's 'englyn' is not a particularly distinguished example.

Er maint yw trwch y llwch a'r llaid – a fwriwyd
  Ar fawredd Mormoniaid,
 Da yw ein ple – Duw o'n plaid
 Er hyll floedd yr holl fleiddiaid.

And he then carved an English translation, which, had it survived, might have read thus: 'Despite the depth of dust and dirt thrown at the illustriousness of Mormons, righteous is our plea, God is on our side, despite the ugly howling of the wolves.'

Today an equally uninspired and pedestrian creation stands where the Lone Tree stood in 1862. It's a ten-foot-high concrete pillar representing a tree trunk. The concrete on its surface is curiously wrinkled in an attempt to represent bark. Out of it grow strange concrete protuberances which possibly represent branches. It was raised to commemorate the Lone Tree, which, in the year after William carved his poetry, had failed to put forth leaves and two years later had keeled over in a storm. William's 'englyn' was possibly the straw that broke its back.

That night in the Lone Tree camp, the adventure lost its magic. One of the children in the company died. The next day, at Grand Island, another died. The day after that, two more. Before the journey's end over 25 had been buried, a twentieth of the company, many of them children. The disease which killed them remained undiagnosed and therefore untreatable.

Somewhere between the Missouri and the Rockies they met an old friend travelling with another company, a man called David Bevan Jones, or, to give him the bardic name by which he was better known – Dewi Elfed. Before leaving Wales, Dewi Elfed had led a complicated if not chequered career. Perhaps the most memorable of the many sagas of his colourful life was 'The Gwawr Chapel Affair', in which all the drama of an O.K. Corral shoot-out was enacted in the main street of Cwmaman, in the Aberdare Valley. The details of this drama have been chronicled by the historian D. Leslie Davies (see 'Sources'), but it's a story well worth retelling.

Dewi Elfed began his career with the Baptists. He was the minister of Gwawr Chapel when he converted to Mormonism. It appears that the majority of his congregation converted with him and, as the chapel buildings of Welsh Baptists were owned by their members, Dewi thought they had a right to continue to worship in Gwawr Chapel. But the Reverend Thomas Price, the fiery and powerful leader of the Baptists in the Aberdare area, thought otherwise. To see a congregation of his old members marching away to eternal damnation under the banner of a cock-eyed, foreign faction was painful enough, but to see them doing so in a building he himself had helped to build for the Baptist cause was more than he could bear. Dewi accused him of being more concerned about the wool on the backs of his flock than the lives of the poor sheep themselves, but Thomas Price had decided, come what may, that the Baptists should retake Gwawr. So, battle was joined. Dewi locked himself into the chapel with one of his faithful followers, shoring up the windows and bolting the doors. As the Reverend Price strode up Regents Street, 2,000 people fell in behind him, all eager to see him clobbering the Mormons. He was accompanied, on one side, by the Sheriff of Glamorgan, there to ensure fair play all round, and on the other, by a stonemason with his bag of tools, ready, if necessary, to smash his way into the chapel. Dewi refused to open the doors but the mason managed to force open one of the windows and the Reverend Price squeezed his considerable bulk through the opening. The assembled throng heard the hubbub of a wild chase, heavy boots stomping down the gallery, bellows of wrath echoing up from the vestry. Suddenly, the doors burst open and there stood the Reverend Price with a Mormon under each arm. 'You've heard of the casting out of devils,' he roared. 'Well, here's a modern example.' And with that, he kicked them down the steps of the chapel to the thunderous applause of the multitude. This, of course, is the Baptist's version of events. History, as usual, belongs to the victors.

Dewi Elfed undoubtedly had an unfortunate tendency to rush into confrontations and to raise hackles. He quarrelled with Dan Jones and Daniel Daniels. He was expelled from the Church because fifty pounds had disappeared from the account of his Conference, but he always bounced back, contrite, full of remorse, and was always forgiven. In the case of the missing money, he apologized, repaid it and was re-baptized into the faith.

What he gave to the cause was hard work and devotion. He was a tireless preacher. 'I am determined,' he said, 'to preach and bear witness in every town, village, valley and corner where I have not yet been.' He strove to visit the Saints all over Wales, 'to teach them and instruct them and to build up the Church in every way possible to me.' He organised a Mormon Eisteddfod in the pages of *Udgorn Seion*. He was a good poet and many of his poems were published.

> *Trwy holl drablith fy helyntion,*
> *Tystiolaethais 'nol fy nerth*
> *Am wirionedd egwyddorion*
> *Pur efengyl – mawr eu gwerth.*

Methodd trais a hudoliaethau
Dynnu hwn o'm hysbryd byw;
Methodd byd a'i demtasiynau
Ladd fy nghariad at fy Nuw.

[Through the chaos of my troubles
I bore witness, according to my ability,
To the truth of the perfect principles
Of the gospel – so great its worth.

Brute force and beguilement have failed
To tear this from my living spirit;
The world and all its temptations
Failed to extinguish my love for my God.]

But he also desired, one day, to emigrate.

Doed, O doed y ddedwydd awr,
Caf fod yn rhydd o Fabel fawr;
Ar Seion draw, a'i llwyddiant hi
Mae tynfa serch fy nghalon i.

[Come, Oh! come, the happy hour
When I shall free of Babel be;
To Zion yonder and her success
Is the love of my heart drawn.]

In 1862 his wish was granted. His departure for America, and William Ajax's departure soon afterwards were a considerable loss to the Welsh Church. They were the last of their kind. Never again during the nineteenth century would strong leaders be raised in Wales from within the ranks of the Welsh Saints. From now on, it would be the missionaries from Utah, many of whom might originally have been Welsh but had long since emigrated, that ran the show in Wales.

On October 5th, about four and a half months after leaving Liverpool, William and Emma reached the end of their journey. 'We pitched our tents and unloaded our wagons immediately after our arrival at the Public Square. It was then about 4 p.m. and the people were coming from a meeting. Interrogations beyond number were now put to almost each emigrant, respecting friends that were in our own and other trains, by the hosts of besiegers that were on our camping-ground. Several languages were used as mediums to convey the said interrogations; but principally English, Danish, and Welsh. Nearly all the questions put to me, which were by no means very few, were put in the latter, to speak which I could find scores around me. I never expected to meet half as many Welsh in this city as I did; or expect to find them half as kind.' William then lists the names and birth places of every Welsh speaker who had crossed the Plains in his company. Thomas Williams, formerly of Sirhowy, with his wife and child; David Williams, James Gough and Elizabeth Williams from Victoria and Daniel Jones from Pen-y-cae (both places that today are part of Ebbw Vale); Jane Jones and Catherine Thomas from Trinant, further down the Ebbw; Phebe Davies and Sarah Humphreys, Tredegar; David Todd, Cwmtillery, with his wife and five children; John Evans, Pembrokeshire; Hannah Treharne, Carmarthenshire and John Davies of Bethesda in north Wales – seventeen adults in all, twelve of them from the valleys of Gwent and six of them single women.

During his first months in Zion, William took labouring jobs, carrying bricks, building walls. He was not frightened of hard labour. He then disappears from the record for a while. He was possibly called to fight in the Black Hawk War, an ugly, bloody squabble between the Mormons and the Ute Indians. But in 1868 he reappears as a partner in a company called Watt, Sleater and Ajax that was preparing to open a large store in Salt Lake City. The partners had invested in a fine central site and had spent lavishly on a wide range of goods. They intended to specialise in kitchen and garden ware, in wagons and coaches, and in oil, coal and wood burning stoves. Watt seems to have been the major financier of the project, Sleater had the business contacts, especially in Chicago, where the goods could be bought at the best prices, and William was to look after the shop. But it was not a good time to set up such a business. They found themselves in competition with the most powerful force in all Utah – Brigham Young himself.

As usual, Brigham was seeking ways to advance his people. He saw that more and more merchants, who were not Mormons, were arriving in Utah, opening up businesses, doing very well and taking substantial profits out of the Mormon community. To remedy the situation, he announced that the Mormon Church intended to open a chain of stores throughout Utah and that the faithful would be expected to shop at those stores only. He then invited the owners of existing shops to sell their businesses to the Church for shares in the new chain, to be known as Zion's Co-operative Mercantile Institution. But Watt, Sleater and Ajax had heavy debts to repay and they knew that shares in the Z.C.M.I. would not be acceptable to their creditors in Chicago. They decided, therefore, to challenge the authority of the Church and to continue in business. The doors of their new shop opened at the beginning of 1869 and, about a month afterwards, the first of the new co-ops opened in the centre of Salt Lake City. Before the end of the year there were co-op branches in every village in the state and seventeen of them in Salt Lake City alone. But William continued to keep the doors of his shop open, selling his goods cheaper than the Z.C.M.I. The end was inevitable. One morning, he arrived at work to find a warning in Brigham Young's name plastered over the door, forbidding the faithful from shopping there. Within a few weeks, Watt, Sleater and Ajax were bankrupt and, to rub salt into the wound, Brigham Young excommunicated all three. William's name was washed clean from the slate of Mormon history, which is why Professor Dennis had never heard of him.

There was no livelihood for William now in the city. Once more, he and Emma and the nine children that they had now to feed, moved further west, out to the banks of Faust Creek in a remote valley called Rush. He began cutting hay in the surrounding grasslands to sell to the miners of a nearby goldfield. The Z.C.M.I. had little interest in what he did out in this wilderness. The business grew, William prospered and he began to think of opening a small shop to attract the occasional traveller that passed through the valley. Because of the heat and the dust he decided to build his shop underground and, with his barrow and shovel, he set to work digging out a large hole which he roofed with pine beams, over which he laid a mix of juniper branches and clay, with a layer of turf on top. Every year he increased the size of his hole. It became an obsession with him. Barrow after barrowload were brought out, leaving him with room after room of retail space. Eventually, he had dug out an area the size of four tennis courts, over a quarter of an acre of underground shopping. He built a subterranean eating house in similar style and above ground a comfortable hotel to sleep fifty. A small village, which became known as Ajax, gathered about his remote enterprise. There were stables for over a hundred horses, pens for three hundred cattle, folds for 6,000 sheep. In his shop William sold everything, farming equipment, gold mining equipment, clothes, food, harnesses, halters, drinks, books, carpets, tobacco, household goods, furniture, jewellery, even chandeliers – a greater variety of goods than any store in Salt Lake City. People came on trips to his shop, were entertained by the family brass band, feasted in his eating house and, at the end of the day, slept in his hotel. The underground store became known as 'the eighth wonder of Utah'. After William's death in 1899, the children ran the enterprise for a while until they were put out of business by the growth of catalogue shopping, the collapse of the local gold mine, and the coming of a railway line through the valley that made the shops of Salt Lake City much more accessible. Today, the village of Ajax has completely disappeared. A plaque raised on the site by the Sons of Utah Pioneers and the descendants of William and Emma explains a little of the extraordinary history of the place. Nothing besides remains. Only a small hummock where the hotel had stood and a rusty fence and a slight hollow where so much business had once been transacted.

1863

WITH EACH YEAR'S passing, the pace of life on the trail quickened. John Woodhouse first walked the trail in 1852. Ten years later he walked it again, making a note of the changes he saw. In 1852, the buffalo pats were everywhere and it was an easy matter to collect enough to light a fire and cook a meal. By 1862, such was their value as a fuel, one had to search hard and collect diligently to build the smallest fire. In 1852, the bones of dead buffalo lay scattered everywhere along the trail. By 1862 they had disappeared, having been collected and transported to the east to be processed into fertilizer and glue. In 1862, the Homestead Act was passed, granting 160 acres of land to those who were prepared to build a farm and a home on them within five years. As a result, there was a surge of small farmers settling in the Platte Valley, although it did not become a flood until after the end of Civil War. The Pacific Railroad Act was also passed in 1862, the act that brought the Union Pacific and the Central Pacific railroads into being, the former to build a line west from Omaha and the latter east from Sacramento. The Union Pacific announced that their track would follow the Platte River for the first three hundred miles of the route. This ensured further growth in the valley, a rosy future for the numerous villages and settlements that lay in its path and a boom in the price of land.

In this year, members of two families, those of Benjamin Jones and Titus Lazarus Davis, left their homes in Wales and set out for Utah. They were probably not acquainted when they left, but their histories would gradually intertwine. The heads of both families were born in Carmarthenshire, Titus in Llangeler and Benjamin twenty miles to the south-east in Llanfynydd. Both men were cobblers, Benjamin working in Lampeter and Titus in Llanwenog and later in Drefach Felindre and in Cwmdu, near Talley. Both men married farmer's daughters and both raised large families. Ten children survived childhood in Benjamin's family and seven in Titus'. To make ends meet, both Titus and Benjamin moved to more populated, industrialised areas to look for work, Titus to Dowlais, near Merthyr, and Benjamin to Cadoxton in the Neath Valley.

In February 1849, Captain Dan Jones passed by Benjamin's home. He stayed to preach a sermon, sowing the seed that eventually led to Benjamin's conversion. Benjamin chose to be baptized at night, but, despite the secrecy, his neighbours soon came to know of his conversion and his work consequently began to ebb away. Esther, his wife, was unwilling to accept her husband's new faith. She tried to persuade him to accept the job, which had been offered, of parish clerk in the village church, a job that came with a salary, but Benjamin turned it down. For a while, things were bad between them.

In the meantime, Titus Davis had also accepted the new faith and his marriage was also put to the test. Mary Gwenllian, his wife, did not follow him to Dowlais. She stayed at home to farm their smallholding in Cwmdu. The children, however, were drawn, one after the other, to the smoke at the head of the valleys. David, the eldest son, was the first to go in 1857, when he was sixteen, to work in a grocery in Merthyr, lodging with an English-speaking family. Then went Timothy to work in the iron works at Dowlais and then Thomas to work alongside him. Then Gwennie, the only sister, to keep house for her father and the boys, and finally one of the younger brothers, John. After arriving in their new home, the children, one after another, accepted their father's new faith and were baptized. Mary Gwenllian was left in Drefach with her two youngest, Jenkin, the five year old, and Henry, the baby. Some five years passed. Then Titus started thinking about emigrating.

In Cadoxton, Benjamin had also set his mind on Utah, but, once again, Esther was proving difficult. For some years they had observed a truce in their religious differences, but now old tensions surfaced again. In 1863, Mary, the eldest daughter announced that, come what may, she was leaving for Utah in the spring and her parents agreed that she might go. 'My parents and sisters and brother, and many of my friends came to the wharf to bid me good-bye,' she wrote. 'I cried pitifully, for I knew that some of them I would never see again. This was true, for there I gazed for the last time on the faces of my dear mother and my baby brother Johnny. To make the parting easier for me, my little brother Joseph was placed on a barrel so I could see him, and across the water came the clear, musical tones of his sweet voice as he sang, "We are coming, Sister Mary, for the time is drawing nigh." Oh, how sweet the tones of his boyish voice and how assuring were the words of the song.' The next day she arrived in Liverpool and transferred to the *Cynosure*, joining nine hundred British Saints for the Atlantic crossing. Benjamin had already decided that he would soon follow her with however many of his family as wished to accompany him. Esther refused to countenance the possibility. The rift in the family widened.

In the meantime, Titus and some of his children were also making plans to emigrate, but back in Drefach Felindre, Mary Gwenllian knew that she would not be with them. She could not face saying goodbye to her parents and her brother and the four small graves in Llanwenog churchyard where her babies lay. Nor was she happy about leaving the Baptists, the cause into which she'd been born. She turned for advice to the minister and to the chapel members. Mormonism, they said, was a dangerous cult, the Saints deluded. Titus and the children tried everything to make her change her mind, but she was adamant. 'She said would rather go about the country begging than to go with us to Utah.'

In the spring of 1863, therefore, Titus and his children prepared to depart without her. Jenkin, the seven year old was left to keep his mother company; Henry, the baby, went with his father. 'I remember mother came up the narrow lane to the road with me,' wrote her son, Thomas, 'and there said goodbye. That was the last I ever saw of her in this world. I was too young to realize the situation, too excited with the thought of going on a trip from home, that I never thought that I was parting with my mother forever.' She quietly bade them farewell, took little Jenkin by the hand and walked away. Poor woman! After her husband and her children had left her, she sank into debt and abject poverty, failing to make the small farm pay. Jenkin proved to be a good son, caring for her for the rest of her days. He, also, had a hard life, often sick and always poor, but throughout it all, he strove to keep in touch with his father and his siblings in Utah and to preserve some semblance of family unity.

Titus, meanwhile, had left Dowlais early one morning in May and walked with his children to Merthyr railway station to catch the Cardiff train. At the last moment, David, the eldest son, was called away on a mission and had to stay in Wales for another year. He was greatly missed, for only he could speak English fluently. The next day, the family travelled by train to London and then on by horse-drawn wagon to the Shadwell Dock in Wapping, where they boarded the *Amazon*, one of the very few Mormon ships that sailed from London. Aboard her were 882 passengers, all Mormon and 118 of them were Welsh.

The morning before they sailed a journalist came aboard the *Amazon*, intent on writing an article for his magazine, *All Year Round*. The article he wrote that day was subsequently published in *The Uncommercial Traveller*, a celebrated collection of his essays. The journalist's name was Charles Dickens. It's clear that Dickens' original intention was to write a disparaging article about the Saints, a people about whom he had heard many uncomplimentary things, but with whom he had never, until then, come into contact. 'I went aboard their ship to bear testimony against them, if they deserved it, as I fully believed they would.' He very soon changed his mind. 'These people are so strikingly different from all other people in like circumstances whom I have ever seen, that I wonder aloud, "What *would* a stranger suppose these emigrants to be!"

The vigilant, bright face of the weather-browned captain of the *Amazon* is at my shoulder. "What indeed! Most of these came aboard yesterday evening. They came from various parts of England in small parties that had never seen one another before. Yet they had not been a couple of hours on board, when they established their own police, made their own regulations, and set their own watches at all the hatchways... Nobody is in an ill temper, nobody is the worse for drink, nobody swears an oath or uses a coarse word, nobody appears depressed, nobody is weeping... Before nine o'clock, the ship was as orderly and as quiet as a man-of-war." Dickens writes of their 'steadiness of purpose' and their 'undemonstrative self-respect' and their 'aptitude for organisation'.

Unfortunately, he was not as generous in his description of the Welsh passengers. He had no kind word to say about them. 'The faces of some of the Welsh people, among whom there were many old persons, were certainly the least intelligent. Some of these emigrants would have bungled sorely, but for the directing hand that was always ready. The intelligence here was unquestionably of a low order, and the heads were of a poor type.' He wrote in an equally racist vein about the Jews that he saw that day in Wapping. 'Down by the Docks, the children of Israel creep into any gloomy cribs and entries they can hire, and hang slops there – pewter watches, sou'-wester hats, waterproof overalls – firtht rate articleth, Thjack.' Dickens was nothing if not a child of his time.

Whilst aboard the *Amazon*, he heard a choir sing and enjoyed their performance greatly. He looked forward to hearing the brass band that was also on board but in this he was disappointed. 'There was to have been a band,' he wrote, 'only the Cornet was late in coming on board.' It was not uncommon for a brass band to emigrate en masse to Utah. William Pitt and his band had arrived in Salt Lake City with the first companies. In 1854, as we saw, many members of a Carmarthen band had emigrated together aboard the *Golconda*, contributing greatly to the good spirits that prevailed on that ship. In 1856, a Birmingham band had walked with Ellsworth's handcarters all the way to the Valley and now, here was another band on its way. This band came from Cardiff. The cornet player who had not arrived was a Mr Toozer (a splendidly Dickensian name), and, although only 23, he was the most experienced of the members, apart from the conductor, George Parkman, who played the trombone and Rice Hancock, base tuba. The rest were all young men from the Cardiff branch of the Church. In 1862, the Bishop of the Ogden Stake, on a visit from Utah, had heard them play and was delighted with what he heard. The city of Ogden had no band, he said, and there was a warm invitation for them all to come over and fill the vacancy. Most of the band had agreed to go.

Mr Toozer, the missing cornetist, duly arrived later in the day, in time to ship out with his fellow bandsmen. 'Finally the time was fixed for sailing,' wrote Titus' son, Thomas A. Davis, 'and father went and took a stroll for the last time on the soil of his native land. The next morning we were pulled out into the Thames River and the great locks closed behind us. The band was playing "Star Spangled Banner" and "Yankee Doodle". The docks and the river bank were lined with people; some cheered, some groaned. We were assisted downstream by a steam tug. She took us far enough so the breeze could take effect upon the great sails. After this the tug left us.' From the Thames estuary, they steered down the Channel, around Land's End and up the Irish Sea, past the west coast of Wales, affording them one last glimpse of their homeland hills and then to Liverpool, where they picked up more passengers. Finally, five days after Mary Jones had left on the *Cynosure*, Titus Davis and his five children in the *Amazon* followed her out into the Atlantic.

Six weeks later, the band played again as the ship entered New York harbour. The Civil War was now at its height and the Battle of Gettysburg had been fought a fortnight earlier. Warships were anchored on all sides and as the *Amazon* was nudged into her dock with the band playing, numerous other bands joined in from the decks of the surrounding ships. A small boat rowed across to the *Amazon* and an officer came aboard to offer every member of the band a place in his crew.

But the Cardiff band refused. They had their sights set on Utah.

Meanwhile, Mary Jones, Benjamin's daughter, was in the train, crossing from New York to St Joseph on the Missouri. She was now only a day or so ahead of Titus, her ship having lost time on the Atlantic crossing. She was lucky not to lose more time when she jumped off the train to rescue a small child who had strayed from his family. By the time she got to the child, the train was leaving. She dashed to the station master's office and in her broken English explained her predicament. A place was found for her and the child on an express travelling the same route, and when the desperate parents stepped from their train in St Joseph, Mary and their child were there waiting for them on the platform. 'Our company remained in St Joseph two weeks,' remembered Mary. 'Then our next move was to Florence, Nebraska, by boat up the Mississippi River. When we landed at Florence, I was met by my cousin John L. Edwards. This brought me great joy, for I had not expected to see him.' John L. Edwards now becomes one of the principal figures in the story. He and Mary were not only of the same age, they were also cousins. He had left Wales with his parents six years earlier, when he was eighteen. They had probably been writing to each other ever since. 'He took me to an eating house to dine, then we went back to the wharf and he loaded my luggage into his wagon and started for camp, which was ten miles away. We reached there an hour after sundown. When I got out of the wagon, supper was ready and my cousin introduced me to the cook, George Harding.' George was John L. Edwards' closest friend. They lived in Willard, the village where Shadrach Jones had been building the best houses in Utah and holding the best dances. In her memoir Mary wrote, 'George later became my life companion.'

In a day or two, Titus and his family arrived in Florence. They had had a long and difficult journey to the Missouri, having been diverted through Canada to avoid the war and then down to St Joseph, from where they had taken a steamboat to Florence. 'We were glad to get there and rest for a few days,' wrote Thomas, one of Titus' sons. 'We received rations which consisted of some fat bacon and a little flour with a package of saleratus (a form of baking soda). With these we tried to do some cooking. Our bread was a complete failure, as we were inclined to put too much saleratus in it, but we learned to use sour dough by and by, and in that way were able to make a better article. A couple of days after our arrival at Florence we were taken to the camp of the Utah boys, some five or six miles out. It happened that among the young men sent to take us and our few articles of baggage out to the main camp, my father recognized one John L. Edwards and was exceedingly happy in meeting one whom he knew.' John L. had been brought up in Llanwenog, the village where Mary Gwenllian had lived before her marriage. Titus and he must have known each other well. It was agreed that Titus and the children were to travel with Mary Jones in John L.'s wagon. This was the first time, as far as we know, that members of the Titus Davis family and the Benjamin Jones family had come into contact.

The wagons in which they travelled were not the rough-and-ready vehicles of the early years but larger, heavier wagons, designed primarily to carry freight, hauled by four or six yokes of oxen. Each was filled with crockery and saucepans, food and clothing, cooking implements and agricultural tools, stoves and machinery, all sorts of merchandise and utensils to be sold in Utah. There was not much room in them for passengers. Most of the company would walk most of the way. At night, the men and boys slept under the wagons and the women and children slept on mattresses spread along the top of the load, hard up against the canvas roof canopy. Mary and Gwennie slept together in John L.'s wagon, with little Henry between them. A warm friendship grew between the girls. They had plenty to talk about because, as Mary was falling in love with George Harding, Gwennie was falling in love with John L. Edwards.

They had a joyous passage to the Valley. In each of the three big forts along the trail, Fort Kearny, Fort Laramie and Fort Bridger, the band gave a concert and the emigrants formed a choir to entertain the soldiers. To supplement their meagre diet, they went fishing in the Platte. They took the cover off one of the wagons and used it as a Seine net, pulling it through the river and catching over a ton of fish. But they had no salt to preserve their catch, so the whole lot was eaten in one big feast. Their company lost only one member on the trail, a little girl who had eaten poisonous fruit which she had picked along the way.

At the end of the journey they decided to parade into Salt Lake City in style, with the Cardiff band at their head. William Ajax came down to see them arrive and wrote a lively description of the scene in his diary. 'October 24th. The last Church train, with emigrants, arrived here on the 15th, another arrived on the 13th, and three arrived on 4th, and one on the 3rd. There were quite a number of Welsh in each of these trains, making, in the aggregate, some three hundred; and there was a band in one of the companies that had come from Cardiff, which played remarkably well. They were sixteen in number, many of them well known to me. The company in which they travelled formed a procession on entering, at the head of which Brother Samuel Evans carried a banner, having the motto "The Kingdom of God or Nothing" inscribed on it. The band played in the same, and, after taking a little rest on the camping ground, played for about an hour before President Young's house. The whole band left on the following day for Ogden.' As soon as the wagons were unloaded, Mary Jones and Titus and his children were taken to Willard by George and John L. There they lived for the rest of their lives.

In November, Titus' son, David, still on his mission, received a letter from his father to say that the family had arrived safely in Utah. In December, he went down to Cwmdu to read the letter to his mother. She already knew much of the news that it contained. Two months earlier a man, newly arrived from the Great Plains, had stopped to talk to her in Llandeilo market. He had passed Titus on the trail, he said, some six hundred miles from the Missouri, somewhere in the region of Chimney Rock. He said all the family were well and that they sent their best wishes to her. David tried once again to get her to come with him to Utah, but to no avail.

In March 1864, he went down to Cwmdu again, bearing another letter from his father. 'Read unto her my father's letter,' he wrote in his diary. 'She was glad to hear from him, but the same spirit of unbelief manifested itself.' On April 28th he visited his mother for the last time. 'On the following morning, I bade her adieu. She lost some tears as we parted.'

John L. and Gwennie were married in November. The following July, Mary and George Harding were married. Mary's father, Benjamin, emigrated to Willard in 1865 and lived with them for the rest of his days, but Esther, his wife, refused to accompany him, although seven of her children followed their father in subsequent years. She, like Mary Gwenllian, felt that she couldn't leave Wales, and, as in Mary Gwenllian's case, one son, John, along with a daughter, Eliza, were left to look after her.

The younger generation of both families flourished in Utah. Titus' sons became conspicuous Utah citizens. David Davis ran a very successful grocer's store in Salt Lake City. He grew rich and used his money to finance his love of sailing. He became the Commodore of the Salt Lake City Sailing Club and his two catamarans, *Cambria* and *Cambria II*, were the pride of the Great Salt Lake. Thomas, his brother, made a career in politics and was elected to the State Senate like Martha Hughes Cannon. Gwennie and John L. farmed all their lives, owning a large cattle ranch in the hills of the Promontory, the neck of land that jutted out into the northern waters of the Salt Lake, where the Union Pacific and the Central Pacific lines eventually met. They later moved back to Willard, into a house that had been built by Shadrach Jones before he left on his last fatal visit to Wales. John L. was twice mayor of Willard. Mary and Gwennie are remembered as leaders in all village enterprises, from beekeeping and candle-making to breeding silkworms. One year, Mary produced 150 yards of silk, enough to make a splendid frock for each of her seven girls.

Utah was not so generous to the older generation. Titus

continued to work as a shoemaker and repairer, but he had large debts to repay to the Perpetual Emigrating Fund. He looked for a wife to help raise his younger children and for a while he lived with a woman called Zenobia Weeks, but the relationship did not last. In his old age, he moved into a small, one-room home built on the back of his daughter's house. In February 1879, he received a letter from Jenkin, the son he'd left behind in Wales. 'Dear Dad, I am taking pen in hand in order to send you a few lines. It has been some time since I have written to you, and never has been as sad an occasion as this writing to you, telling of my grief, in the passing of our dearest and kind mother. She died on Wednesday at ten minutes after ten, the 29th of January. The funeral was held the following Saturday. We buried her in Talyllychau graveyard. She had asked to be laid to rest there.' His wife's wish to be buried in Talyllychau (or Talley as it's known in English), would have stirred bittersweet memories in Titus. He would have remembered the night, many years ago, before Mormonism had driven a wedge between them, when Mary Gwenllian and he had passed through the village on their way home to Cwmdu, carrying between them a hive of bees. They were travelling at night so as to disturb the bees as little as possible. When they arrived at the graveyard, by the ruin of the old abbey, they rested awhile amongst the gravestones. In the soft moonlight, the loveliness of the valley filled them with wonder and they were both deeply moved. Titus gave her his solemn promise that if she died before he did, he would bury her in this churchyard. And if he were the first to die, he asked that she should bury him here also. There they would lie, side by side, for all eternity in the shadow of Cynros Mountain. Jenkin finished his letter with these words. 'Dear Dad, it is time to say – Farewell! I'm running out of paper and if you are well off in this world, and I am poor, I ask you something I have never done before, for you and my Aunt, to send a little help financially for me to pay my debt here. I took care of my Dear mother while you were far away, and I hope you'll say, "Well done, thou good and faithful."' Poor Jenkin. He had looked after his mother faithfully and had striven, to the best of his ability, to keep in touch with his father and his brothers and sisters on the other side of the world. He deserved to be well rewarded by them.

Instead of lying alongside his wife in Talyllychau, Titus rests half a world away in Willard. But although they are separated by 5,000 miles and sixteen years, it was Mary Gwenllian's name that Titus wanted carved on his gravestone, with the words 'Buried at Tally [*sic*], Carmarthenshire' added below. Benjamin's grave is in the same cemetery, a few yards away. Although he married again in Utah and had three children by his second wife, it is Esther's name and Esther's name only that is carved beneath his own on his stone. 'Esther, wife of the above, intered [*sic*] at Pencareg [*sic*] churchyard, Wales.' Hiraeth for Wales throbs painfully through both inscriptions and the two men are united in a sense of loss and perhaps of guilt for having abandoned their wives when they answered the call to Zion.

1864

AFTER THE GRATTAN Massacre of 1854 and the Battle of Blue Water of the following year, there was little love lost between Plains Indians and white men. 'We had to keep a sharp lookout as you never can tell what an Indian is going to do next,' was Ebenezer Crouch's opinion. 'As we travelled along past their villages, they would dress themselves in all their war paraphernalia, mount their war horses and come charging across the prairie as though they intended to attack us, but they seemed to only want to show off and give us a scare, which they succeeded in doing every time.' One old woman recounted how she had tried to make friends with an Indian. 'I was making lemonade which I offered to one who had watched the process of preparing and to whom I had handed a chair. He seated himself with great dignity and took in his hand the cup I offered but would not touch the drink until I would drink with him. I began to drink from another cup but he handed his to me as much as to say "Drink from this". I took it, drank and returned it. He drank and said "Good squaw!" with many gestures of satisfaction.'

The Mormons, at least, made some effort to be friendly. They still believed that the Indians were their brothers in the faith, brothers who had strayed from the righteous paths but who, one day, would to be gathered in again. 'One of our sports,' remembered John Jenkins of Cowbridge, 'was to stand a dime in the split end of a stick, place the stick on end at about 25 paces, and then let the Indians shoot the dime from the stick with their bow and arrow. The dime belonged to the Indian that could hit it. It was remarkable how often they hit the target.'

'We have come across quite a few Indians who have been very kind to us,' wrote another diarist. 'Yesterday, for example, we had a heavy hail storm and some of the sisters had gone ahead of the company when the storm rose. Some Indians were near them and they took off their hats made with tarpaulin and held them over the heads of the sisters. We camped near their camp in the evening; they came over to us and got some bread and flour and pork, and were very much satisfied.'

In the east, close to the Missouri, lived the Pawnee, a tribe that had been in contact with white men for many years and had learnt their ways. They often stood in the paths of the wagon trains, scrounging and begging, demanding payment for the right to cross their hunting grounds and usually receiving more derision than charity. There was a down-at-heel, demoralized air about them. For a small payment they allowed the emigrants to inspect their camps. William Ajax had taken advantage of this offer. 'Nine Pawnee Indians, 2 Indians, 5 squaws, and 2 male papoose, appeared near our camp, to view whom Brother J. Davies and I repaired immediately. I handled the tomahawk the young one had in his hand, and shook hands with the younger of the two children, who was about one year old. The other was about 5 or 6 years old, and both were almost naked. The others had blankets and other articles of clothing to cover themselves. Our stay among them was about 20 minutes, during which they flayed a hawk ready for cooking, and placed a few feathers in the head of the bigger boy. When they finished flaying the hawk, they went to the camp, where they all, especially the children, received the greatest kindness from the Danish Saints, who made up quite a number of our company.'

On the whole, the emigrants ignored the Pawnee, but the Sioux and the Cheyenne were another matter. Nobody ignored them. Their hunting ground lay in the west, between Fort Kearny and the Rockies, where the white man's law did not extend. They were still a confident people, proud and untrammelled, but they had come to realize that their way of life was at risk, that there was to be no end to the long lines of ox trains that snaked through their hunting lands every summer and that the small homesteads, with their 160 acres of land, were creeping further and further up the Platte every season. Now was their opportunity, whilst the soldiers of the western forts were being drained away to fight in the Civil War. There were only about thirty men in each of the small forts that guarded the 130 miles of trail from Fort Laramie to the Platte Bridge Fort, where the city of Casper now stands – about 120 soldiers against the combined might of the Sioux and Cheyenne nations. In the spring of 1864, the number of Indian attacks on soldiers and settlers increased dramatically.

The Saints were confident that their own migration was not greatly threatened. Their trains were too large and too well armed and the Captains too experienced for it to be worth the Indians' while to attack them. But occasionally, far out on the Plains, they might see a band of Cheyenne or Sioux ride by, brilliant in their war paint and feathers, off to attack a Pawnee village in the east or perhaps some small, isolated company of white men on the Plains.

Just such a company was the Kelly/Larimer Train, made up of only five wagons and two small families, far too weak to defend themselves. One family consisted of Josiah and Mary Kelly, their eight-year-old daughter, Mary, and two black servants. The other family was William and Sarah Larimer and their eight-year-old son, Frank, with a driver named Noah Taylor. Accompanying the families were the Reverend Sharp, who was an old man, very nearly blind, and a man called Wakefield. There were therefore only eleven people in the company, including two children and two women. They were on their way to the Montana goldfields when they were attacked by between eighty to a hundred Indians.

The first people to hear of the attack was the small garrison in Deer Creek Fort, halfway between Fort Laramie and the Platte Bridge Fort. One of the soldiers based there was a young farmhand from Ohio named Hervey Johnson. His letters home have survived, describing this incident amongst many others. He vividly conveys the growing tensions on the Plains that summer. 'I would have written sooner,' he writes, 'but have been too busy to do anything not connected with a soldier's calling, having been out scouting after Indians almost every day since I wrote last, sometimes twice and three times a day. Emigrants are collecting in large trains for the better protection of themselves and their property. A great many have been killed, their wagons plundered and property burned. Dead and wounded men are picked up every day and buried by the soldiers and emigrants.' One such plundered train they 'picked up' was the Kelly/Larimer Train. 'The road was strewn for miles with arrows, clothing, beds, flour, bacon, salt and other plunder, four dead men, one of them a negro, all of them killed by arrows. The Indians were piling the plunder together and burning it. Three men, two of them badly wounded, one by three arrows in the back, the other shot through the thigh, are the only male survivors of the train. There were only two women and two children, a boy and a girl, in the train. They were all captured and carried off by the savages.'

Sarah Larimer and her son managed to escape the following night and succeeded in making their way to the Deer Creek Fort. Then Mary, Fanny Kelly's daughter, also escaped and found her way back to the trail. She was seen there in the morning by a small detachment of soldiers from Deer Creek Fort but, before they could rescue her, the Indians returned and they had to flee. 'A party of our company were out again yesterday,' wrote Hervey, 'and found the body of the little girl with several arrows in it. A large grey wolf was eating the child when they found it… I have often thought before I became a soldier that I would never kill or take the life of anyone, but I have got over that notion now. I could shoot an Indian with as much coolness as I would a dog.'

What made this incident infamous throughout the States were Fanny's sufferings whilst a prisoner of the Sioux. She was held prisoner for four and a half months, but was eventually freed, as a result of lengthy negotiations between the tribe and the military. The book she wrote, *Narrative of my Captivity among the Sioux Indians*, describes in lurid detail the barbaric treatment she received at the hands of her captors. 'Many persons have since assured me that, to them, death would have been preferable to life with such prospects, saying that rather than have submitted to be carried away by savages to a dark and doubtful doom, they would have taken their own lives. But it is only those who have looked over the dark abyss of death who know how the soul shrinks from meeting the unknown future.' Her book became a bestseller, making Fanny famous and wealthy.

At the beginning of July, a group of Welsh emigrants arrived at the organising camp on the Missouri. They had to kill time for three weeks before their wagon train was ready to depart and in that time they heard many wild rumours about the troubles on the Plains. Over a hundred of them, members of William Warren's company, left for Utah on July 21st, nine days after the attack on the Kelly/Larimer Train. Everyone was on edge, imagining a Sioux behind every sagebrush and a Cheyenne in every cloud of dust. Despite there being 65 wagons and 330 people in the train, Warren decided to wait for another company to come up, so that they could all travel together, doubling their numbers. He ordered every man to carry a weapon. 'The Indians were very bad at this time,' wrote one of the teamsters from Utah, 'attacking many of the emigration companies, who were going to Montana and California in search of gold and silver, but the Lord preserved us, his Saints. We travelled in a company of 110 wagons, which reached 5 miles in length when all in motion and had a double guard out every night.'

During the first fortnight they saw no sign of Indians, but then, on August 8th, they saw ahead of them a small homestead burning fiercely, with the body of a man lying in the roadway before it. 'The ground was dusty where the corpse lay, and it was so besoiled that it was difficult at first glance to tell whether it was a white man or an Indian, but by a little closer examination it was seen to be the body of a white man and we took it for granted that it had been the owner of the house which now was burning... The Indians had ripped open the feather beds and the contents were being blown around in the breeze. Whether the rest of the family was murdered and were lying somewhere in the weeds or the burning house, or if any of them had been carried away by the Indians, we did not learn.'

That night, a troop of cavalry galloped up to warn them that the Indian war party was still in the vicinity and that a wagon train had been attacked further up the trail. The next morning Warren's train arrived at the scene of this second attack, a mile and a half from a ranch called Plum Creek. 'It looked like there had been an awful fight,' wrote Elizabeth Edwards of Merthyr Tydfil. 'The wagons were still burning,' wrote Catherine Roberts of Eglwysbach in the Conwy Valley. 'I was permitted by the Captain to see the massacre,' wrote Thomas Cropper, who was one of the 'down-and-back boys' in charge of the train. 'The wagons were on fire, some of the horses were killed by being shot full of arrow. The soldiers buried the victims in one grave. A woman was taken alive. There were fifteen bodies.' The woman taken alive was Nancy Morton, the nineteen-year-old wife of Thomas Morton, the owner of the train. They were on their way to Denver, taking supplies up to the miners on the Pike's Peak. Amongst the wagon drivers was Nancy's brother, William Fletcher, and her cousin, John Fletcher. Years later, Nancy wrote a description of the attack and of her capture. 'This terrible and unsuspected apparition came upon us with such startling swiftness that we had no time to make preparations for defence. Soon the whole band of warriors encircled us and gave the war whoop, which I shall never forget. With wild screams and yells, they circled around and around which frightened our teams so that they became uncontrollable. Thinking there might be some faint hope of escape I sprang from the wagon, when my husband called "Ah, my dear! Where are you going?" Those were the last words I heard him say. With all the strength I could muster I started for the river, where I met my brother and my cousin and they said we had no hope of escape as the Indians had encircled us and the air was full of arrows. At that moment an arrow struck my cousin which proved fatal and he fell dead at my feet. In another instant three arrows penetrated my brother's body; he too fell at my feet and his last words were "Tell Susan I am killed. Farewell my dear sister."

'My first impulse was to kneel by my brother, when, upon kneeling, I discovered two arrows lodged in my side. Just as I went to remove them, an Indian chief came up and ordered me to go with him. When I immediately answered "No! I'm going to stay with my brother," he drew a large whip from his belt and, before I could utter another word, began whipping me severely. But I soon made an effort to escape and started to run when two warriors came up and ordered me to stop or they would kill me, and before I could make another resistance they tossed me on an old pony… As we were leaving I took one look back at those so dear to me lying dead on the ground, perhaps to be devoured by wild beasts. In my ears the war whoops resounded until I was nearly deaf. I could not suppress my emotions and I began to scream and cry.'

Nancy was held prisoner by the Cheyenne for five months. She was badly treated and tortured. She tried to kill herself. She later said that many white people, men and women, were executed before her eyes. But she survived. Eventually, she was sold to a French trader for four horses, three sacks of flour, forty pounds of coffee, 75 pounds of rice, a sack of salt, a sack of black powder, one harness, two reels of thread, three packs of needles, one rifle, one revolver, one sword, two coats and thirty necklaces of various coloured beads. He brought her back safely to Fort Laramie.

The Plum Creek Massacre was not the only Indian attack on August 8th. On that day, the Sioux and Cheyenne burnt numerous ranches and telegraph stations up and down the Platte Valley, from Fort Kearny in the east to Julesburg in the west. They ambushed other small wagon trains and killed many of their defenders. This was a carefully planned offensive, intended to instigate panic in the white community and to create havoc on the trails. It proved very effective. Every business that used the trails came to a halt. The stagecoaches stopped running, the telegraph line was cut time after time, and the homesteaders abandoned their isolated farms and sought shelter in the forts. For a while, no trains, however strong, were allowed to leave Fort Kearny and the flood of wagons on the Plains dried up. But William Warren and his company of Welsh and Danish Saints were too far into their journey to return to seek safety in the east. Turning back was no longer an option for them. Their best hope was to push on west with all speed, day and night, so as to be out of Sioux and Cheyenne lands as soon as possible. 'As we were travelling along at night,' wrote Scott Edwin, 'we could see the homes burning on the horizon.' A few nights after leaving Plum Creek, Thomas Cropper, the 'down-and-back' teamster, was on watch when he suddenly saw Indians approaching. 'I counted in the moonlight fourteen Indians crossing the river not far from our camp.' He shouted out a warning to the camp and the Indians, possibly because they realised they'd been seen, turned away. But the emigrants were badly frightened. 'As I passed some of the wagons,' wrote Cropper, 'I could hear the people's teeth chattering with fear.'

One of the young girls sitting in her wagon that night, teeth chattering as she listened to the night noises around her, expecting a burly Indian brave to leap into her wagon at any moment and to carry her off in his arms to a fate worse than death, was Elizabeth Edwards, the daughter of a Merthyr miner. She was fourteen years old and the owner of a very lively imagination. A year earlier, her father had died of typhus whilst planning his family's journey to Zion. His last words had been 'Go, and the Lord will protect you, and will be pleased with you.' Faithful to his wishes, his widow and his five children were now on their way to Utah.

Six days after leaving Plum Creek, Elizabeth was frightened out of her wits once again, although it's not clear from her account what exactly happened. 'We saw a drunken Indian come shooting his gun in the air. It just went to my heart so. There was a big band of Indians after him to capture him. The man with us said, "Don't be afraid. They are trying to capture him. He is drunk." I fainted away, and dropped right down. A man came by and said, "This child is scared to death." So he helped me along. Mother and the rest of our family had gone ahead with the wagons and they did not see the Indians.'

Elizabeth's memoirs, from which these lines are taken, were written down by her granddaughter in 1944, seventeen years after her death and eighty years after she had crossed the Plains. Often the memory plays tricks, making it difficult to disentangle the truth from the embellishments. It happens that another version of the drunken Indian story has survived, this one written by Thomas Cropper, the 'down-and-back' teamster. He was 22 years old, a native of Texas and experienced in Indian ways. His version is detailed and plausible and seemingly written whilst the incident was still fresh in his mind. 'As we drove along, four Indians came toward the train at full speed on horseback, one in advance of the other three. Every man grabbed his gun, thinking it might be an attack. The lead Indian had a short shotgun. He dashed into the train, snapping the gun at the women and girls, making them scream. I had my gun levelled on him and called out to James Jenkins, the teamster ahead, "Shall I shoot him?" He answered, "Don't shoot. His gun didn't go off." The other three Indians came up and grabbed him and took him away. The fellow was drunk.'

Elizabeth Evans' version compares very favourably with that of Thomas Cropper. A few minor details vary but the main events are consistent with his version. Not all memoirs are as dependable. Margaret Reese of Merthyr Tydfil, for example, was nineteen when she crossed to Utah in the same company as Thomas Cropper and Elizabeth. Like Elizabeth, her reminiscences were not written down until after her death in 1917, over fifty years later. Here is one of her stories as recorded by her family. 'At one time on the Plains the leaders saw a band of Indians coming. The leader prayed that the company would be spared. After the prayer he said: "If you will follow my instruction no one will be hurt." He then told all the women and children to get in the wagons and cover over, and all the men to have their guns ready but not to say a word but to look straight ahead. When the Indians got near them they lined up on each side of the trail with long spears in their hands. For three miles they marched with the Indians on each side. Every once in a while Indians would stab the oxen and the blood would squirt out, but no one was hurt. But three miles further they came to a terrible scene. A company of people going to California were massacred. Their wagons were burned and everyone in the company was murdered. My grandmother helped bury 39 people in one long grave. Those same Indians had done this terrible thing.'

Some things in her story ring true – a whole company being massacred, all the bodies placed in one grave – these might perhaps be a confused memory of the Plum Creek incident. But the long lines of Indians stabbing the oxen as they pass is more problematic. No other diary or memoir mentions a similar incident and the Indians' purpose is hard to fathom. Her story is probably a good example of how time distorts the truth, but the one thing that remains constant throughout all the diaries and memoires of 1864 is the unremitting fear of Indians and the sound 'of teeth chattering in the night'.

Having passed Fort Laramie, the worst was over. There were fewer buffalo and, consequently, fewer Indians, as they depended on the buffalo for food and for many other needs. The company began to relax. On September 7th they came to Deer Creek Fort where Hervey Johnson was stationed. Hervey had mentioned in his letter home that month that Sarah Larimer was staying at the fort. She was the woman who had been taken from the Kelly/Larimer Train with Fanny Kelly but had escaped. She was still there when Elizabeth and her family arrived and Elizabeth was very eager to see her. She writes in her journal about the horrors that Sarah Larimer had survived. 'Her husband and two boys had been killed and her two girls had been stolen. Her mind was completely broken and she was nearly dead. She didn't want anything. She was right out of her head. We could look at her through the window of a cabin. I thought it was the most pitiful sight I had ever seen.' In fact, Sarah Larimer had got over her abduction very well. She had escaped after only one night of captivity, her husband had recovered from his injuries and her only child was at the fort with her. But in Elizabeth's over-romantic imagination, she had been tortured and misused and injured for life.

After arriving in Utah, Elizabeth had to grow up very quickly. A year later she was married; a year after that, she was a mother. She put all her sons through college and she learnt to write when she was 53. Her granddaughter wrote in the memoir, 'I asked her once whether she loved her husband when she married him. She was 16 and he 32. She answered that theirs was not a love match, but that, as the years rolled by, she came to love him more than her own life.'

In November, after the last of the wagon trains had long since passed, a detachment of the Colorado Militia, over seven hundred soldiers, under their leader, Colonel John Chivington, set out to punish the Indians for their onslaught that summer and to teach them a lesson they would never forget. They attacked a village of Cheyenne and Arapaho in a place called Sand Creek in eastern Colorado and killed about 130 of them, thirty men and more than a hundred women and children. The soldiers vented their fury on the dead bodies, ripping out organs and skinning them with inhuman barbarity. It was said that most of Chivington's men were drunk and that he was in as bad a state as any of them.

The Indians were maddened and their offensive against the white man intensified. In January over a thousand attacked Julesburg, one of the largest communities in Nebraska, burning the telegraph office and destroying the stagecoach station. Sixty of the soldiers defending the fort were killed and about fifty civilians who had joined them. Then the Indians rampaged for a second time through the Platte Valley, burning every farm and building that had not been burnt the previous year. In February, they returned again to Julesburg, burning down everything they had failed to burn in January. It was not a good time to be a white man on the Plains and it did not augur well for the 1865 emigrants.

1865

THIS YEAR, BRIGHAM Young decided not to send the 'down-and-back' boys to meet the emigrants at the Missouri. The official reasons for the decision were spiralling costs, a scarcity of oxen in the Valley and the reluctance of the immigrants of previous years to repay their loans. Brigham said he preferred to put all his resources and effort this year into speeding the work of building the temple. He had chosen the site for the temple within days of arriving at the Salt Lake in 1847, but by 1862 only the foundations had been laid. Then Brigham decided he was not happy with the standard of the work done thus far and ordered everything to be torn down and rebuilt, and he entrusted the responsibility for re-laying the new foundations to the enigmatic Welshman from Llanfair Talhaiarn, Elias Morris. The temple was a heavy drain on the resources of the state.

But, in truth, Brigham had other reasons for discouraging emigration to Utah in 1865. He knew the ox train was soon to be displaced by the steam engine. Railway building had commenced that summer, from Omaha in the east and Sacramento in the west and although, at the eastern end, only forty miles of line had been laid, the prospects were extremely encouraging. When the Civil War ended in April, thousands of men looking for work were released from the ranks and millions of dollars of capital was diverted from the war effort. That autumn, the occasional grey long-coat of a Confederate soldier was to be seen working shoulder to shoulder with the blue coats of the Union, speeding the process of uniting the country by means of the railway, both figuratively and literally. When

Lincoln was assassinated, five days after Lee's surrender, the project lost its most resolute friend, but, by then, the railway had built up a head of steam so powerful that nothing could stop its progress to the end of the line. Brigham knew that, within a season or two, the faithful would no longer have to walk through the dangerous lands of the Sioux and Cheyenne and that a safer and cheaper alternative was at hand.

The Indian threat also remained very real although Brigham tried to deny it. 'The Saints,' he said, 'in their organised companies, led by responsible and experienced men, will not meet with any molestation.' But the truth was that the Indians that summer again created havoc and panic from one end of the Great Plains to the other, and Mormon or no, it would have been folly to encourage people to cross the Plains unnecessarily. The army refused to allow trains of less than fifty wagons to leave Fort Kearny and the trail had to be closed for a while at the end of May. At the end of June, about 3,000 Indians, under the leadership of Crazy Horse, amongst others, swept down on the small fort at Platte Bridge at the foot of the Rockies, killing 29 of its 150 defenders. A vicious war also broke out in Utah where the Ute tribe, under their leader, Black Hawk, raided and killed throughout the southern half of the territory.

Few Saints were therefore to be seen on the trail in 1865. According to Church registers only three companies crossed to Salt Lake City, and these were comparatively small – two hundred with Henson Walker, 245 with Miner Atwood and about 215 in the last company with William Willes. Only a handful of Welsh travelled with them, most of them joining William Willes' company. The names of a dozen or so of them have found their way into the record books. David Morris Davis and Hopkin Jones and their families from Neath, John Morse and his family from Llanelli, and George Stokes, who had been President of one of the south Wales branches. No diary or memoir was left by any of these. We know that they had a difficult crossing. It was a stormy and wet season and severe flooding held up their departure. Although Brigham had declared that no company should leave the Missouri after the beginning of July, it was August 15th before Willes' company left the organizing camp. They lost time on the trail. The emigrants, without the help of the 'down-and-back' boys, proved to be incompetent and inadequate. Willes sent a telegraph message to Brigham from Fort Kearny, grumbling about the uselessness of his company. 'Dear Brother, We have arrived thus far after a very tedious journey of 23 days having completed 184 miles in consequence of heavy rains and raw teamster and mostly wild cattle, as only about one third of our teams are broken in. The reason why we have been so long is chiefly owing to our teamsters being composed of old and decrepit men, entirely unaccustomed to handle cattle. Brother Waylett is the only man that is of any assistance in yoking and hitching up and he took sick with an intermittent fever, which left me the yoking and hitching up, selecting camp-ground, driving across broken bridges, mud holes and up hills, as we had not a teamster that would move whenever he come to a slight obstacle.'

Along the Platte, all the way to Julesburg, they walked alongside heavily protected gangs of surveyors who were marking out the line of the railway. These were followed by hundreds of labourers, moving tons of sand and gravel in barrow after barrow, raising or lowering the bed of the railway to the level marked by the surveyors. The line of the track was being levelled across the prairie and, as it entered the small settlements along the route, it created seismic upheavals in land values. Speculators and profiteers, tycoons of all sorts, descended upon the guileless villagers.

One of the foremost amongst them was George Francis Train. George had already made one fortune, buying and selling land in Omaha and Council Bluffs. Now he saw the chance to make another. He learnt that a station was to be built at Columbus. Columbus was an insignificant cluster of half a dozen cabins, but what was special about it was that it was located right in the very centre of the United States, exactly halfway between the Atlantic and the Pacific oceans. George believed that, one day, the government would surely establish an administrative office in Columbus. It might even be the future capital of the nation. With this in mind, he bought the whole village. But he had competition. A few miles down the line, there was another cluster of sod cabins, called Cleveland, which also claimed to be the dead centre of the United States, and also thought it might have a bright future as a home of government. But Cleveland had done something about it. They had built a grand hotel, right in the middle of town, so that the businessmen and the politicians of the future would have a comfortable home from home. Build it, they believed, and they will come. George couldn't stand by and allow such advantage to the competition. Soon after the hotel was completed he bought it, lock, stock and barrel and, that summer, travellers on the trail saw a remarkable sight – the Cleveland Grand Hotel, set on wheels and towed by hundreds of mules and horses, rolling down the trail to Columbus. In the end, George's efforts were in vain. His dream was never realised, the administrators never came and his second fortune was never made, but he comforted himself by spending some of his first fortune on a mad dash around the world, which he chronicled in frequent newspaper articles. Jules Verne read them and was inspired to write *Around the World in Eighty Days*.

The Indians continued to be a thorn, again literally and figuratively, in the flesh of the emigrants, especially in the region between Fort Kearny and the Last Crossing of the Platte. 'We were told by the soldiers here,' wrote one emigrant, 'that the Indians were mad, and that they would kill us on the way and that we would never reach Salt Lake. They advised us to stay until the next spring, but of course we wouldn't listen to them. We believed the Lord would protect us, for we were on His business, and would not let the Red Man kill us.' One morning, a day or two beyond Fort Kearny, Willes' company came across a buffalo skull lying in a prominent position on the trail. On it was a message, scratched in charcoal. 'Captain Miner G. Atwood's company camped here a few nights ago and were preparing camp when two of the women went to the spring for water. One of the women was carried off by the

Indians and several of the men were wounded trying to rescue her. They never recovered her.'

More information about the incident can be gleaned from a telegraph message sent by Atwood to Brigham Young. 'At noon, day before yesterday, the Indians stampeded our cattle and tried to drive them off. In the attempt they wounded seven Danish men, and captured and took away one woman, but got no cattle.' 'We had just unyoked,' wrote another member of the company, 'and the mules and oxen were being driven to water when about fifteen Indians came riding down amongst the cattle from the hills, hooting and yelling. Some of them had fire arms and some arrows. They fired at the herders, trying the while to stampede the cattle but the cattle all ran for the corral, the mules leading the way, and the Indians did not succeed in driving one away. Seven Danish men were wounded and one sister taken away; what her fate is none of us can tell. Her name is Jensine Grundtvig. This all occurred in less time than it takes to write it.'

The best description of the raid is by Albert Wesley Davis. Albert's family had emigrated from Wales generations earlier. He was an experienced plainsman, having lived in Utah since 1851. He was now on his way home after accompanying an uncle to the railhead at Omaha. When the Indians struck he was guarding the grazing animals. 'They commenced whooping their war whoop to stampede the cattle and get them away from me. I ran rapidly back and forth between the cattle and got them on a dead run up the hollow towards camp. At that, six Indians came into the herd and tried to turn them away from camp. I had on two navy revolvers and, as the Indians came into the herd, I drew one of them and commenced shooting at them. By the time I had emptied the revolver, I had driven the Indians out of the herd. I got every animal into the corral, not one being lost. There was a man back down the road that had been walking behind the Indians that I drove out of the herd. They surrounded him and he broke through between their horses and ran for camp. As he did so, I saw them shooting with arrows. One

338

arrow with an iron spike went into his cheekbone. In trying to pull it out, the arrow was pulled off of the spike. Miles Romney and Winberg, both returning missionaries, got a pair of horseshoe pinchers and tried to pull it out. They couldn't do it. After I got things quieted down, they came to me and wanted to know if I would go into the corral and pull the spike out of the man's face. I told them I would go. So I went and laid an ox yoke on the ground and had the man sit down on the yoke. Then I said to Miles Romney and Brother Winberg, "You both take him by the head and hold him solid for I am going to pull." I got hold of the spike with the pinchers and pulled with all the force I had. The spike came out and the man rose to his feet and took me by the hand and thanked me for pulling out the arrow. They anointed him with oil and administered to him and it wasn't long before he was well.' Albert was a useful man in a crisis. Strangely, he does not mention the abduction of Jensine. The company register shows that she was 28 years old, travelling with her husband, Frantz, and her seven-year-old son, Severin. She was never seen nor heard of again.

Because Willes' company had started so late in the season and had travelled so slowly, it was late October before they arrived at the Last Bridge over the Platte. They were four hundred miles from their destination and winter was closing in. Nine years earlier, Martin's company of handcarters had got into trouble in this exact same spot. It was here that the blizzard had struck them and it was here that they had stalled and suffered for nine days, without food or shelter, until their rescuers arrived from Salt Lake City. Willes' company seemed to be in worse trouble. Not only was their food running out, but they had arrived at Platte Bridge a week later in the year than Martin's company and, on the day they arrived, eight inches of snow had fallen. But they had two big advantages – the wagons in which they could shelter, and, most importantly, the telegraph.

The wagon trains were hardly ever out of touch with Salt Lake City. There was a telegraph station every fifteen miles along the trail and the messages, sent from those stations to Brigham Young, were regularly published in the *Deseret News* and *The Semi-Weekly Telegraph*. The whole of Utah knew, for example, that Willes would need his food stocks replenished somewhere along the trail, for he had already notified Brigham Young's office of this and the telegram had already been published in the *Deseret News*. 'To Brigham Young from William Willes, Fort Kearney, Nebraska Territory, Sept. 8 1865. We are only provisioned to the South Pass or Green River, and Brother Taylor has promised to meet us with provisions and teams.' Brother Taylor was Brigham's Emigration Manager. A month later, they could read Brother Taylor's message to Brigham, from South Pass, where he was waiting for Willes. 'To Brigham Young, by Telegraph from South Pass, Oct 18th, 1865. The teams that are along are out of feed. We ought to have oats for thirty teams sent to South Pass. We shall also want forty sacks more of flour, equal quantities each to South Pass, Hams Fork, Bear River and Weber and fifty pounds bacon to South Pass. T. Taylor.' Resupplying the wagon trains 'en route' was now common practice. It meant that the oxen had less of a load to haul and that there was more room in the wagons for passengers. Nine days later, the storm fell on Willes' company and all Utah was able to read about it in *The Semi-Weekly Telegraph*. 'We are enabled to lay the following telegrams before our readers, through the kindness of President Young. "Platte Bridge, Oct. 27, 1865. W. Willes' train passed here four days ago. Stock seemed to be in tolerable condition. People seemed to be standing the trip very well. We hear that they are now camped at or near Willow Springs, twenty-five miles from here. It appears that they have been caught in a severe snow-storm, and will have to remain in camp until it passes off."' The paper quickly checked the weather conditions from various telegraph stations along the trail. 'Platte Bridge, It has been storming very hard here all morning; snowing now.' The same day, the telegraph office on the Sweetwater Bridge reported that Taylor was on the move, going east to meet Willes. 'Sweetwater Bridge, Oct. 27. Taylor's train passed here two days ago. Stock looking well. Was making thirty miles a day.'

In South Pass, they were little more than six days away from where they believed Willes' company to be. A rescue party had been sent ahead as soon as they heard of the storm. One of the party, a young man called Heber McBride, wrote an excellent account of the whole rescue. Nine years earlier, Heber had been a member of Martin's handcart company and had survived conditions very similar to those that now faced the Willes' company. One of the deaths recorded in Martin's company was that of Robert McBride, Heber's father. Heber was a twelve-year-old lad at the time and his sister was four years older. Between them, they had managed to carry their mother and their two younger siblings to safety in Devil's Gate. It must have been harrowing to find himself now reliving those terrible days.

'Oct 24th. Very cold this morning. Went down and camped at Devil's Gate on the Sweetwater. It seems to be getting colder and the wind blowing harder.

'Oct 25th. Very cold this morning. When we started out it began to rain very cold and the wind blew almost a hurricane. It rained about an hour, then turned to snow and so cold that a man could not stand in it to drive the animals for very long, for it blew right in our face. One would drive as long as he could and the others walk behind the wagon. It snowed so hard and fast that we could not see where to go. Just had to guess at it. At last it got dark and we lost the road entirely and got away down a deep hollow and could go no further but the wind did not blow quite so hard. Then we took what blankets and quilts we could spare and put them on our horses and mules to keep them from freezing to death, for they were very warm, for we drove them very hard. Then we got as many as could get into one wagon with what bed clothes we had, and settled in for the night the best we could, without any supper, but it was a long cold night.

'October 26th. It was clear and very cold and when we got up the snow was about 16 inches deep in the ravine where we were. I was told to go down and see if it did not lead to the Platte River or perhaps to the road, and if I found the road to fire my gun. As the ravine took a turn to the right, I soon lost sight of the wagons, but as I went farther down the snow was not so deep. After walking about one half mile I came to the road, as I could see the sagebrush on each side. I then gave the signal and waited till the wagons came down. Then we went down about 12 miles to the Platte River to the place where my Father was buried in October 1856. And then we saw the emigrants in the snow, and they did not know what to do as they were all from the Old Country and were not used to this kind of life and they were very glad to see us.' Herber and the rescue party had come upon the Willes' company at exactly the spot where Martin's company had been found in 1856 and where his father had died. But Willes' company was never in the same danger. The difference was the telegraph.

The constant chatter of the telegraph, passing on messages, exchanging information, keeping an eye on developing situations and calling for help when necessary, made the trail a much safer place. On November 8th, Brigham Young received the telegram he'd been waiting for. 'South Pass, Nov. 8th. Our train will camp within five miles of this place to-night. We have all the supplies now that we shall require, also teams. A thousand thanks. Willes.'

1866

'I FIND MY mind wandering off now, and I can see myself the first day I started across the rolling country. I was too elated to walk, so I would run ahead and then would stop and wait for the crowd... The pioneer trip across the Plains, the emigrating trip from the Old Country, forms a background for my life.' No one has described the journey to the Valley with greater enthusiasm than Evan Stephens. Evan was twelve years old when he emigrated with his family in 1866, an ill-educated child from a poverty-stricken background but possessed of a happy disposition and a bounding exuberance. 'Born and raised in a quaint Welsh town of surrounding beauty, of course I hadn't seen much of the world when we started for Salt Lake City. The journey across the Plains was such an experience of pleasure to me, that I found it difficult to sympathize with the pioneers who thought it a hardship.' These joyous days on the trail coloured every aspect of his subsequent career and a surprising career it turned out to be. Evan developed a musical talent that raised him to the forefront of Mormon life. When the Saints needed music with which to celebrate or glorify or remember, they turned to Evan. He composed 84 out of the 421 hymns in their hymnal, he composed the music to celebrate the completion of the Temple, he composed the majority of the songs in the Utah schools' songbook and wrote the words and the melody of 'Utah, we love thee!', the state anthem for the first hundred years of its history. He was also the man who led the Mormon Tabernacle Choir to concert platforms throughout America and on to a world stage.

Evan was born in Pencader, Carmarthenshire, the son of a

farm labourer, the last child in a family of ten children, clinging to the bottom rung of the social ladder. He was given little education. Before he was ten, he was working as a shepherd. It seems that Dan Jones was responsible for the family's conversion, although they were not baptized until July 1849, five months after Dan had left for America on the *Buena Vista*. Since then, for fifteen years, the family had been dreaming of following him but with little hope of raising the fare. Then, at the start of the 1860s, Thomas, the elder brother, went down south to work in the coal mines and by 1863 he had saved enough to buy one ticket to Salt Lake City. His original intention had been to go himself and to bring the rest of the family over later. But, at the last minute, he had cold feet and gave his ticket to Ann, his eldest sister. We know she arrived safely and that she worked for a while as a seamstress in Brigham Young's home. Thomas then returned to the coalface and within a year had earned enough to buy a second ticket and this time he went himself. Together in Utah, Ann and Thomas raised the money to bring their parents and one child out to join them in 1866. The parents then borrowed to pay the fare of another child and, at the end of May, Evan, his brother Deio, and his mother and father were off to America. With them travelled one of his elder sisters, Mary, with her husband and two children and, later, another brother and sister followed.

It appears that the family had left all their travel arrangements to the last minute. When they arrived at the dock in Liverpool, they found that the Welsh contingent had left a month earlier and that there was no room for them on the *Arkwright*, the last ship the Mormons intended to charter that season. But they were eventually squeezed into a deck cabin, which turned out to be one of the choicest berths on the ship. They had a tortuous and complicated journey from New York to the staging camp on the Missouri. The Mormon travel agents, as usual, bargained hard for every cent of discount on the railway tickets, with the result that the emigrants spent a fortnight travelling from New York to Chicago via Montreal, constantly changing trains and often in cattle wagons. On board the steamboat that took them up the Missouri, Evan made himself ill by eating leftover scraps from the kitchen and when the family reached the small village of Wyoming, where that season's wagon trains were being organised, they found there was no room for them in the British train and that they would have to travel with a Scandinavian company. But nothing perturbed Evan. 'Of course I was a very young man. As I was going to have a walk between two or three hundred Danish girls, I ought to have been content and happy... I couldn't talk anything but Welsh. One thing I missed by not coming over with an English company was learning the language. Coming over with Scandinavians, I learned more of their language than English.'

In the summer of 1866, the focus of the whole American nation was on the two 'End-of-tracks', the furthest points to which the Central Pacific line in the west and the Union Pacific in the east had been laid. Gangs of Chinese sweated in the former, gangs of Irish in the latter, laying mile after mile of iron across the continent. The Central Pacific line was now close to the top of the Sierra Nevada and the Union Pacific was steadily pushing up the Platte Valley towards the Rockies. The two 'End-of-tracks' moved slowly towards each other, aiming to meet somewhere in the middle of the continent in two or three years' time. After the ravages of the Civil War, this was the opportunity for America to show the world that she still possessed the skills and the ambition, the confidence and the capital, to build something stupendous, with style. The hearts of all Americans swelled with pride when they read in their daily newspapers of the heroic exploits of their railway builders. The *New York Times* reporter wrote that he was witnessing 'the genuine American genius – the genius of the West especially, which welcomes obstacles and looks on impossibilities as incentives to greater exertion.' A mile of track was being laid in a day, often through remote, difficult terrain, far from supply centres.

Every thirty seconds, twenty men lifted two rails from the wagon behind them and ran forward to the end of the track at a foreman's command. On a further command, they laid them on the sleepers and before they had turned back for the next, the spikers would already be spiking the rails into place. Two rails every half minute, four every minute, 240 every hour. To keep this rhythm beating constantly for months on end, hundreds of support workers were needed. A continual flow of rails and sleepers and spikes, train after train loaded with essential supplies, steamed up to 'End-of-track' and unloaded their cargos. Armies of clerks kept track of the supplies, ensuring that they arrived at the right place, in the right order, at the right time. Another army of engineers and blacksmiths, stonemasons and carpenters maintained and repaired the equipment, more armies of cooks and bakers fed the men, doctors kept them healthy, guards looked out for Indians, cowmen looked after the herds of cattle that followed the camp, a moveable pantry of fresh meat, hunters shot buffalo to augment the store, all to keep 'End-of-track' moving steadily onwards, a mile a day, faster and faster as the men perfected their skills and became more proficient in their work. Out ahead, gangs of graders prepared the bed of the railway, levelling hills and valleys. Back in Omaha and in other eastern cities, another 7,000 men were employed, administering the project, arranging the finance, designing the bridges, ordering the rails and the spikes and the sleepers from the four corners of the earth and ensuring that they all reached 'End-of-track' at exactly the right time, so that the rhythm of the hammers never missed a beat. By the end of the year, the Union Pacific had laid 250 miles of track in less than nine months, an achievement never before accomplished anywhere in the world.

In his reminiscences, Evan briefly describes the excitement he felt when he glimpsed 'End-of-track' from the trail. 'From this hillside, afar down the river, could be seen the harbinger of another day. It was a large body of men laying the railroad track that was to cross the continent and make it unnecessary for ox-teams to ever cross the Plains again to bring the Saints to Zion.' He does not say where or when he saw 'End-of-track', but the company diaries tell us that his wagon train was about thirty miles west of Fort Kearny on August 16th and 'The New York Times reported on August 22nd that the railroad had reached Fort Kearney "less than a week ago".' Assuming the wagon train was making about 25 miles a day and the railway, a mile a day, Evan would have passed 'End-of-track' on either on August 14th or 15th, about a mile east of Fort Kearny.

Less than a month later, the train was running regular services between Omaha and Fort Kearney. There was a 1.00 p.m. service that got in to Fort Kearney at 5.10 the next morning, and a 7.00 p.m. service that arrived at 11.10 a.m. the next day – seventeen hours and ten minutes to make the journey that took Evan Stephens about fourteen days in 1866, Thomas Jeremy 24 days in 1855 and Brigham Young 25 days in 1847.

Evan's company had a relatively easy and uneventful crossing. A second Scandinavian company, which had left the Missouri ten days after them, suffered as badly as any company in the history of the trail. They were struck by the old enemy, cholera, and over a hundred of the four hundred in the company died. But nothing untoward disturbed Evan's company. Telegraph messages from Rawlins, the company Captain, arrived at the Emigration Office in Salt Lake City as regularly as the beat of the hammers at 'End-of-track'. 'August 21st, from Alkali Telegraph Office, ten miles up the North Platte. My train is all well. Traveling fine. J.S. Rawlins.' 'September 2nd, from Horseshoe Creek Office, 40 miles west of Fort Laramie. My company is all well. Traveling fine. J.S. Rawlins.' 'September 8th, from Fort Casper Office, another 100 miles up the North Platte. My train is all well. Traveling fine. No trouble with Indians. J.S. Rawlins.'

Day after day, Evan, with the rest of the children and the women and the old people, walked in advance of the wagons, in the clear air, on undisturbed ground. He remembered with delight the flowers in their path and the wildlife all around them. Before them, there were scouts keeping a watchful eye for dangers ahead. Far behind them, at the back of the column, walked the calves and the heifers, the milking cows and the spare oxen in the care of their dust-covered herdsmen and, in between, one long, twisting chain of 65 wagons.

Brigham had resumed the 'down-and-back' service this year and, once again, the 'boys' from the Valley had come to collect the emigrants. For a shy, twelve-year-old lad from a poor home in the barren Carmarthenshire uplands, 'the boys' represented all that was sophisticated and glamourous in American life. Evan remembered the dances they arranged in the evenings. 'When darkness set in, and the stars or moon turned on their lights, a clearing in a flat space was selected and the man with the "fiddle" or "concertina" was called for to furnish dance music. He struck up his tune while the boys laughingly urged the timid young ladies to join them as partners for a "cotillion", four couples to a "set". Several sets at times could be mustered and, with the experienced teamsters at hand to help guide the newcomers through the mazes of figures called out by the "caller" or prompter, all were soon in full swing, as the command of "Balance all", "Swing your partners", etc., was called out loudly and above the music... They looked so jaunty, hardy and good-natured, as well as manly in their valley tan boots, jean trousers, broad, shapely shirt waists, with loose coloured handkerchiefs around their necks, and broad-brimmed hats crowning their tousled heads.' Evan felt safe within the circle of their wagons. 'Soon all terror of traveling over the "dreary plain", almost uninhabited by white men for a thousand miles, was wiped out by the apparent peace and security of the camp.' Two months later, they came to the end of their journey. 'Afar in the distance, like a magnificent looking glass, the waters of the Great Salt Lake lie peacefully at the base of their mountain-islands. And nearer, the city of Salt Lake, its pretty houses dotted among the green foliage of its miles of fruit trees... The climax of the most wonderful experience of my life.'

When he arrived in Utah, Evan was a quiet, reserved boy, seemingly unremarkable and untalented. Apart from his shyness and his stutter, there was nothing to distinguish him from any other child in the wagon train. The family went to live in Willard with his brother and sister, and Evan went back to herding the family cattle. But there was a good choir in Willard, conducted by Daniel Tovey from Ebbw Vale, Shadrach Jones' partner in the stone house building business. Evan was invited to join the choir, and suddenly, his remarkable musical talent burst forth, filling and fulfilling the rest of his life. 'It was like finding oneself deeply in love,' he wrote. 'The world became a new creation, and rhythm began to manifest itself in everything. I walked in rhythmic motion through the fields and behind the cows and music was felt everywhere.' He threw himself into his new life. He took singing lessons, he learnt to play the organ on a small instrument bought for him by his brother Thomas. When he was seventeen, he was given the responsibility of conducting the Willard choir.

At that time, the most prestigious choir in the north of Utah was the Logan Choir, led by a man called Alexander Lewis, formerly of Merthyr. Lewis had heard of the success of the 'little shepherd boy' in Willard and had decided to employ him as the organist of his own choir. For three years, Evan lived with Alexander Lewis, composing new music for the choir and conducting when Alexander was away. He began giving singing lessons and lessons on the organ and saved enough to pay for a year in a college of music in Boston. On returning to Salt Lake City, he taught music, he produced operas and he formed his own choir. In 1890 came the call to lead the Mormon Tabernacle Choir, the greatest musical honour in the gift of the Church, and for the next 26 years he was the musical power in the land. He was made Professor of Music at the University of Utah, Supervisor of Music within the school system and finally Supervisor of State Music. But if he is remembered at all today, it is as the conductor of the great Tabernacle Choir. He quadrupled its size from a little over a hundred members to four hundred and more. The Tabernacle had to be extended to make room for them all. The choir competed in the Chicago World Fair in 1893, coming second to a choir from the Welsh coalmining city of Scranton, Pennsylvania. They competed in eisteddfodau and performed in concerts throughout the land, in Denver, Seattle, San Francisco, New York, the White House, and, of course, Salt Lake City itself. In 1895, the largest eisteddfod ever to be held in the United States, apart from the World Fair Eisteddfod, took place in Salt Lake City and Evan Stephens' choir was at its centre. Another great eisteddfod was held in the city in 1898, to which Dr Joseph Parry, the most famous Welsh musician of the day, came all the way from Wales to adjudicate.

But time has not been kind to Evan Stephens' reputation. Few people remember him today. The Victorian sentiment that typifies his work is no longer fashionable. Only seventeen of his hymns have kept their place in the new Mormon hymnal and the state anthem he composed has been supplanted by a tune with more 'go' to it. But throughout the fifty years that spanned the turn of the twentieth century, Evan Stephens was the composer-in-chief of his people and their leader in all things musical.

His experiences on the Plains remained an inspiration to him all his life. He liked to write the lyrics for his songs and it gave him immense pleasure to have won the prize in the 1895 eisteddfod for the best libretto for a cantata. The set subject was 'The Utah Pioneers'. He could not have been given a subject more to his liking. He used to say that everything he wrote, be it verse or music, always 'had a pinch of sagebrush in it'.

There is one other reason why Evan Stephens should be remembered. In all probability, he was the last of the Welsh Mormons to travel the whole length of the Mormon Trail, from the Missouri to Salt Lake City, in a wagon train. Only three large companies left the organizing camp on the Missouri after Evan's company. All three were mainly composed of Scandinavians and there are no Welsh surnames in their registers. The following year, no one walked the whole length of the trail. The emigrants travelled by train for the first three hundred miles. Evan was immensely proud to have been one of the last to come in this way to Zion. 'When the railroad brought the Pullman train across,' he wrote, 'then it ceased to be an event to cross the Plains. Those who came from the Old Country and arrived here in three weeks, missed the great joy and great experience of crossing that glorious and wild country.'

Of the 3,335 Saints that left Europe this year, 301 were Welsh. Amongst them was a 49 year old named John Evan Price, travelling with his wife, Ruth, and their three children. He had joined the Saints twenty years earlier, whilst working in a pit in the Amman Valley, and had given his whole life thereafter to the Church, preaching, selling tracts, surviving on handouts from church members and being constantly bullied and harried by the enemies of Mormonism. He writes in his diary, 'I preached in Cwm Twrch, Ystradgynlais, Cwmgors, Cross Hands, Llandybie, Gorslas, and many times in Gwaun-Cae-Gurwen. All manner of lies were told about us by the religious men of Llandeilo Fawr. I had to run many times with the mob after me.' Although he continued to live in the Amman Valley, he was called to start a branch of the church in Llangadog, and for six months he walked there and back every Sunday, in all weathers, thirty miles over the Black Mountain. When he eventually moved to live there, he failed to find work and he and his wife and children came very close to starvation. For months they lived on little more than bread and water, but John Evan Price continued to preach. 'My wife and I with our two children kept meeting twice a week with no one else present. The Lord was blessing us with the gift of the Holy Ghost, my wife speaking in tongues, interpreting and prophesying.'

A few days after the birth of another child, Ruth, his wife, fell very ill. 'She kept to her bed for many months. She felt the effects of this illness the rest of her life. I administered the ordinance day and night to her. I had to attend to the baby and everything else in the house including the baking and the washing. For months there was not a woman who would come near the place because we were Saints. I preached and kept Saints meeting every Sunday. I went to Llandovery for elder Benjamin Jones to administer to my wife [that is, to anoint her with the holy oil and bless her]... While we were blessing the oil, we heard the house making a noise as if it was going to fall and, while we were anointing her, one half of the house came down with a crash. Brother Jones took my wife out in his arms and I took the little children. Brother Jones said the devil was trying to kill us in our house.'

Poor John. Poverty surrounded him on all sides, sickness harried him constantly and bad luck seemed always to dog him. Time after time, he pleaded to be released from his call but each time his appeals were turned down. He was moved to Talgarth. He preached in Llangynidr and Bwlch and Talybont-on-Usk. Often, his landlady, Mrs Powell was pressing him hard for the rent. 'I had no money. I offered her anything I had but she wanted our pig. I offered her my coat which I had on and she took it, so I went home without one.' But John never grew sour, never gave up. Obedient to the Church authorities, he returned to his duties, ready for further trials.

Eventually, in 1856, he was allowed to take a job in a pit in Aberdare to raise the money to emigrate. Eight years later, he had saved eight pounds, enough to send two of his daughters to America. The following year, he and the rest of the family followed as far as Pittsburgh, where he had to work for a further year to earn the rest of their fare. But, at last, on July 16th, 1866, after twenty years of waiting and yearning, he started out on the final leg of his long journey and, three months later, walked into Salt Lake City, with the 350 others in his train, to be greeted by Brigham Young in person.

Eventually, John Evan Price was rewarded for his faithfulness and his endurance. As soon as he arrived in Utah, his luck changed. He heard that good land was to be had in the north, on the Idaho/Utah border, in the valley of the Malad River. Brigham Young had travelled through the valley in 1855, and had been impressed by the dependable flow of the river and the vigorous growth and ample yields of the wild crops in the valley. He is said to have encouraged the Welsh to settle there and, by the time John Evan Price arrived, the nucleus of a small community was already forming. John moved further out into the valley, laying claim to his 160 acres in an uninhabited section eight miles beyond the settlement. He arrived there with his sons at the beginning of February 1868, and by March, when the rest of the family came to join them, they had built a rough shelter of turf. There was a spring on the property which gave good water, whilst on the surrounding plain the grass grew 'as high as his horse's belly'. Two months on, four more families had settled nearby and one of the first things they did was form a branch of the Church. Then, in the spring of 1869, they cut a water channel to irrigate the community fields and, that autumn, they built a school and John was appointed one of the trustees. There were now nineteen families in the village. It was given the name 'Samaria' by the Church hierarchy, because the generosity of its inhabitants was a byword throughout the valley. Then came a saw mill and a branch of the Co-op and a blacksmith, a hotel and a jail and a milliner. And the highway from Utah to Montana ran through the middle of the village. Before the end of the century over eight hundred people were living in Samaria.

John Evan Price's son, John Evan Jnr, remembered his home becoming more comfortable and more affluent with every year that passed. He wrote of the orchard beginning to produce fruit, herds and flocks on the increase and the hum of bees in the orchard louder every year. Every autumn his larder was filled with apples and cherries and plums, and every winter the cellar was stocked with bottles of preserved fruit, pots of honey, pickled vegetables of all sorts. He built the first brick house in the village. Later, he brought the first piano to the village, the first bathroom with water pumped directly to the tap from the well, the first turbine to produce electricity, the first car and the first telephone. John Evan Snr didn't live to see all these blessings, but he lived long enough to know that he had brought his family through stormy seas to a fair haven.

In 1887, a large watercourse was built to bring more of the village fields into cultivation. The contract for the project was signed by 23 of the biggest landowners of the community. They were Richard Morse, Samuel Williams, David P. Davis, John Thomas, John Evan Price, David W. Davis, William W. Williams, Gomer Hughes, Charles Thomas, Owen Thomas, Joseph Morse, Thomas J. Davis, John Evan Price Jnr, James Griffiths, William Morse, Jeremiah Williams, William R. Thomas, Thomas S. Thomas, Samuel D. Davis, William E. Hawkins, Joseph Hawkins, Taliesin Hughes, and John Davis – Welshmen one and all, apart from the two Hawkinses. Undoubtedly, the village of Samaria had a good claim to be the spiritual home of the Welsh in Utah, even though, when the border between Utah and Idaho was drawn, it was adjudged to be in Idaho.

The people of Samaria were proud of their ancestry and proud of their language and, despite the Church's edict, they used it constantly. Samuel Daniel Williams never learnt to speak English, although he was appointed to a senior office in the Church in Samaria. Neither did Eleanore Morris of Pencader, one of the midwives of the Malad Valley, although she lived and worked in the valley for fifty years. And there are many similar examples. John Jones Davies, who emigrated in 1876, believed that the Welsh language would live forever amongst the Mormons. 'We, as a family, intend to speak Welsh so long as the breath of life is in us,' he wrote in an article published in *Tarian y Gweithiwr* [*The Workingman's Shield*], in Aberdare in 1885. 'My two sons, Ifor and Taliesin, speak the Old Tongue as fluently today as they ever did, although able to speak English as well as any Yankee. It is foolish to believe that Welsh is dying in America. I believe there's more chance of it dying in Wales first.'

But he was living in a fool's paradise. There were unmistakable signs that Welsh was fast losing ground in Samaria as it was throughout Utah. Ann Jenkins, for example, came to Samaria in 1876, from Llannon, near Llanelli. She and her husband, Evan Jenkins, farmed land on the edge of the village. Welsh was the language of the home and Welsh was their son's only language when he started school in Samaria.

354

But he had a hard time of it from the other pupils because he spoke no English. Ann and Evan decided to move into the village so that their child could learn English as quickly as possible.

Anna Evans Jenkins had many Welsh-speaking friends. Her granddaughter remembered she was very forthright in expressing herself and enjoyed talking and laughing with her friends in Welsh. 'The older people always used their native tongue. Even after they became fluent in English they always resorted to its use if they didn't want the young children to know what they were saying.' That's as good a sign as any of the increasing irrelevance of the language.

In fact, without the support of the Church, Welsh had very little chance of survival in Utah. Ever since John S. Davis, Thomas Jeremy and Dan Jones had written their letter to the *Udgorn* in 1856 urging the Welsh Saints to learn English and to forget their mother tongue, the death of the language in Utah was inevitable. Thomas Jeremy knew it was coming. 'I labour under a considerable disadvantage,' he wrote on the front page of his new diary in 1852, 'in trying to keep my diary in English, my being a Welshman. But I shall do my best, as I foresee my descendants will be reading and writing in English.' A poem, published in the *Millennium Star* in 1865, starts in Welsh and then changes to English halfway through. In the first five lines, the poet writes, 'In Babylon, longing to leave for beautiful Zion, I await joyful news in God's good time. The prophet Brigham Young says...' and then the rest of the poem is in English.

Hiraethu wyf ym Mabilon
Am fynd i Seion wiw,
Yn disgwyl am y newydd llon
Yn amser da fy Nuw.

Dywedai'r proffwyd Brigham Young
In English tongue so grand,
'A welcome you shall have among
The Saints in Zion's land.'

In the pages of his diary, we can follow the struggles of eighteen-year-old Henry Jones, a young man from Pencader, as he tries to learn English as he approaches Utah. He bought his diary in Llanelli before starting out for America and, for the first days, he attempts to keep it in English. But then, on the day his ship leaves Liverpool, he slips back into Welsh, describing the voyage over the Atlantic and the train journey to the Missouri in his mother tongue. Finally, as he crosses South Pass and starts the descent down the Rockies, he reverts to English, as if he knew that, from now on, English would be his language. The 1849 emigrants had recognised the same truth as they sang their farewell (in Welsh) on the dockside in Liverpool.

> Plant ydym a anwyd i deyrnas y nefoedd.
> Ni pherthyn gwlad Cymru ddim mwyach i ni.
> Ar dir yr Amerig y mae'n hetifeddiaeth,
> Cans yno mae'r Arglwydd yn galw ei lu.

[We are children born for the kingdom of heaven.
Wales no longer belongs to us.
On the land of America is our inheritance,
For it is there that the Lord is calling his hosts.]

The Welsh Mormons, unlike the German and the Scandinavian emigrants, never attempted to publish Welsh newspapers or magazines in Utah, and only on two of the hundreds if not thousands of Welsh graves recorded by Professor Dennis has he found Welsh inscriptions. But yet, as we shall see in the last chapters, one or two lingering ties still bind the Welsh Mormons in Utah to the old country.

356

1867

WHEN THE CIVIL War ended, American newspapers had to look elsewhere for copy to fill their columns. There was a growing interest in stories from the Wild West and there was spirited competition between rival newspapers for the latest and best tales from this new front. It was a front that was evolving at a prodigious pace. In the autumn of 1866, the town of North Platte at the confluence of the North and the South Platte rivers, did not yet exist. But when the *New York Times* correspondent arrived there in the spring of 1867, he found over 5,000 inhabitants and more than a hundred buildings, including a comfortable hotel. This was the temporary terminus of the Union Pacific. If passengers wished to travel beyond North Platte, to Denver or California, they had to take a stagecoach or walk.

There were now more than 10,000 men working for the Union Pacific. The work stopped over winter and many of them had spent the winter months in North Platte, idle and with pockets full of money. As a consequence, a rabble of ruffians were attracted to the town, outlaws and petty thieves, card sharpers and conmen, ladies of the night and their pimps and procurers, all with the same aim – to divert as much as possible of the railwaymen's money into their own pockets.

This motley crew and the railroad that had brought them here were not the only stories along the Mormon Trail in the spring of 1867. The Indian War was still continuing, and the army continued to rush from one bloody raid to another, seeking to teach the Indians a lesson they would never forget, but usually arriving long after the last of them had hightailed it to the hills. Gold, also, had been discovered, close to the trail near South Pass, and villages of tents and shacks, with romantic names like Miner's Delight and Atlantic City, had sprung up in those desolate wastes. As more and more stories about the colourful characters of this wild country were reported back east, the interest in the Wild West grew. Every reputable paper had to have a staff man out on this new front line.

Into this commotion of competing correspondents, early in the spring of 1867, the *Missouri Democrat* sent a promising young cub reporter, a Welshman, late of the St Asaph Workhouse in the Vale of Clwyd. His name was John Rowlands, but he now, in an effort to erase the memory of his impoverished upbringing, preferred to be called Henry Stanley. The middle name 'Morton' was to come later. Not yet 26 years old, this was his first assignment. In the colourful articles he filed, there is the clearest indication of the talent that took him, four years later, to darkest Africa, to the shores of Lake Tanganyika, to the meeting with Dr Livingston and to worldwide fame. 'Every gambler in the Union seems to have steered his course for North Platte,' he wrote, 'and every known game under the sun is played here. Every house is a saloon, and every saloon is a gambling den. Beardless youth imitate to the life the devil-may-care bull-whacker and blackleg, and here, for the first time, they try their hands at the "Mexican monte", "high-low-jack", "strap", "rouge-et-noir", "three card monte", and that satanic game, "chukka-luck", and lose their all. "Try again, my buck; nothing like 'spurious; you're cutting your eye-teeth now; by-and-by you will be a pioneer."'

The first North Platte was not a town but a camp, a bivouac that moved on two or three months later as 'End-of-track' continued to drive westwards. The hookers and thieves and gunmen followed the graders and the navvies and the track-laying gangs across the Plains. North Platte, Julesburg, Laramie and Benton, each in turn housed the same canvas hotels lining the same main streets, the same hastily built saloons operated by the same owners, the same girls dancing on the same tables and the same customers pouring in through the doorways. The name given to this fly-by-night, ephemeral community was 'Hell-on-Wheels'.

By the end of July, 'Hell-on-Wheels' was preparing to move on from North Platte, 85 miles down the line to Julesburg, the place that the Indians had burnt the previous summer. Henry Stanley visited Julesburg a few weeks before the circus arrived. 'Although it has only a population as yet of forty men and one woman, in six months it will have a population of 2,500 souls. North Platte intends a general exodus to Julesburg and next week the new town will have a newspaper, which is to be called the *Frontier Index*. In two weeks, the town will be a city; then the city will elect a mayor. In three weeks we predict it will have a theatre. In four weeks the citizens will have a branch railroad to Denver and St. Louis. In six weeks Julesburg may be the capital of Colorado.'

Two months later, Stanley visited Julesburg again. When he sat down to dinner in his hotel, he was astonished at the apparent wealth of the people sharing a table with him. 'Everybody had gold watches attached to expensive chains, and were dressed in well-made clothes, and several wore patent leather boots. I vow I thought these were great capitalists, but was astonished to find they were only clerks, ticket agents, conductors, engineers, and "sich like". Dinner over, I took a stroll through the streets and was really astonished at the extraordinary growth of the town and the energy of its people. I walked on till I came to a dance-house, bearing the euphonious title of "King of the Hills", gorgeously decorated and brilliantly lighted. Coming suddenly from the dimly lighted street to the kerosene-lighted restaurant, I was almost blinded by the glare and stunned by the clatter. The ground floor was as crowded as it could well be, and all were talking loud and fast, and mostly everyone seemed bent on debauchery. The women appeared to be the most reckless. They are expensive articles, and come in for a large share of the money wasted. In broad daylight they may be seen gliding through the sandy streets in Black Crook dresses, carrying fancy derringers slung to their waists.'

And these colourful little pistols were not just fashion

accessories. The women knew well how to handle them and God help the man who crossed them. Guns and revolvers were everywhere. Every man, from 'beardless youth' to 'be-whiskered old-timers' carried them. Murders were everyday occurrences. 'I verily believe that there are men here who would murder a fellow-creature for five dollars,' wrote Stanley. 'Nay, there are men who have already done it, and who walk abroad in daylight unwhipped of justice. Not a day passes but a dead body is found somewhere in the vicinity with pockets rifled of their contents.'

Stanley, even at this early stage of his career, possessed the one indispensable instinct of a good reporter, to be in the right place at the right time. And he knew what his customers wanted to read. Where did he learn to write English so well and to describe so vividly? Was it really in the workhouse in St Asaph? Earlier in 1867, he had managed to corner and interview Wild Bill Hickok. When Stanley met him, Hickok had yet to grow into the Wild West legend that he later became, but Stanley saw in him the makings of a story. 'The following dialogue took place between us: "I say, Mr. Hickok, how many white men have you killed to your certain knowledge?" After a little deliberation, he replied, "I suppose I have killed considerably over a hundred."' There was not much truth in Wild Bill's answer. His murderous career as a sharp shooting lawman had hardly begun. But as the newspaper man says at the end of 'The Man Who Shot Liberty Valance', 'This is the West, sir. When the legend becomes fact, print the legend.'

At this time, the end of the 1860s and beginning of the 1870s, many of the great Western folk heroes, later to be famous throughout the world, were in the process of being created, many of them cut from pretty shoddy cloth. In 1867, for example, in the gold rush village of Miner's Delight, there dwelt an orphan girl by the name of Martha Jane Carney. She was sucked into the heartless, frenzied whirl of 'Hell-on-Wheels' and later found work as a scout in a cavalry unit. She finished her life in Deadwood, South Dakota, a hopeless drunk and without a penny to her name. Out of this unpromising material was carved Calamity Jane, the evergreen heroine of the West. Another legend from the Plains glamorised for readers back east was the old scout, Kit Carson. After being deloused and scrubbed-up, he featured in over seventy novels. Some of them were based on fact, but not all by any means. He was once portrayed on the cover of one such novel, a beautiful girl on his arm and a pistol in his hand, fighting off half a dozen Indians. 'Do you remember this incident, Kit?' somebody asked. 'P'raps it 'appened,' answered the old man, 'But I ain't got no recollection of it.'

The most famous Western hero of them all was created on a summer's day in 1869 when a man called Ned Buntline stepped off the train in North Platte and wandered over to nearby Fort McPherson. Buntline was the author of over four hundred adventure books. He once wrote six in a week. He was in Fort McPherson to look for plotlines. Few of the soldiers had time to talk to him and he was eventually directed to a young man lying under a wagon outside the fort. The young man told Buntline tall tales of riding for the Pony Express, fighting off hordes of Indians, soldiering in the Civil War and killing 4,280 buffalo to feed the builders of the railway, all before he had reached his 24th birthday! There and then, Buffalo Bill was born.

These Western tales featuring Wild Bill Hickok, Kit Carson, Calamity Jane, Buffalo Bill, et al. were published in their thousands on both sides of the Atlantic from the 1870s onwards. In Britain, they were known as 'penny dreadfuls', in America as 'dime novels' or 'yellow-backs'. Their readers were the young men and women of the large cities and the factories, young people who longed for a little adventure and romance in their lives. For them, the railroad fired their imagination and opened up new horizons.

But it blighted and obscured other horizons. The buffalo retreated before it and the Indians followed them, abandoning their traditional hunting grounds. Later in the century, the homesteaders were driven from the Plains by the great cattle barons, who used the railway to take their herds to market.

The wagon trains disappeared, the stagecoaches followed and the old trails were no longer used – all displaced by the railway. In their place, to indulge the hunger of the city folk for romance, this world of myth and fantasy was created, a world ruled by the heroic figures of the old West whose hold on our imagination persists even to this day.

The Mormon staging camp in 1867 was convened at the temporary terminus of the Union Pacific in North Platte. Once again, Brigham Young did not encourage emigrants to come to Zion, nor did he send 'the boys' to meet them. It would all be so much cheaper and easier in a year or two when the line would be finally opened all the way to Utah. Nevertheless, 337 Saints left Liverpool that year, including fifty from Wales. Stanley noticed them amongst the bustle at the railhead. 'Encamped in the immediate vicinity of this town were 1,236 wagons,' he wrote. 'There were Mormon emigrants bound for Utah, settlers for far Idaho, and pilgrims to mountainous Montana, who were emigrating with their wives, children and worldly substance. The prairie around seemed to turn into a canvas city.'

They were joined there by Saints who had been working in the eastern states to earn their fare to the west. One of them was Thomas John Davis of Neath. Thomas was to become the great-great-grandfather of seven of the modern folk heroes of the West. After arriving in Utah, he and his wife, Elizabeth, and their four children, settled with their compatriots in Samaria where Thomas built a two-roomed wooden cabin. In it, three more sons were born, the eldest of them being the first white boy to be born in the village. Every winter Thomas went to Rock Springs in Wyoming to work in a coal mine so that they could pay for improvements on the farm. Elizabeth had worked in Wales as a maid and had learnt how to weave and sew, how to cook and bake and, above all, how to work tirelessly. They say that she always shared her bread with the Indians who lived and hunted in the Malad Valley. But despite their endless hard work, there was no great improvement in their estate. The small cabin was their home until the end of their lives.

When the two died, Thomas in 1891 and Elizabeth in 1903, Samaria was in its prime. The new school was built in 1898, a solid, two-floor brick building. Soon afterwards the village hall followed, a building of equal distinction. Their eldest son, John William Davis, had opened a general store in the village, in partnership with Elias Morris. Elias, no doubt, put up the capital and John William put in the labour. (It's remarkable how often Elias Morris' name crops up in any matter to do with the Welsh Mormons in business.)

Thomas and Elizabeth's second son, Samuel, with his wife, Mary Ann, went to live in the cabin when his parents died. Samuel lost his hand one summer whilst feeding corn sheaves into the threshing machine but, with his stump, he still managed most of the chores on the farm. Mary Ann made the best ice cream in the valley. She opened an ice cream parlour on the main street of Samaria and there, on summer evenings, the young folk gathered to enjoy sodas, sundaes and sarsaparilla. These were the good days, but the dark clouds were gathering. Ever since the railway entered the valley in 1906, the peace of village life had been disturbed. Samaria and the neighbouring village of Malad City had fought each other hard for the privilege of having the line run through their communities and, from the moment Malad City won, Samaria was in decline, her energies draining away.

In 1925, Samuel and Mary Ann's granddaughter, Vera, came home to the old cabin to give birth to her daughter, Olive. She was the third generation of Davises to be born in the cabin. But there was little life left in Samaria now. The village was dying. Thomas and Vera moved to Ogden, the leading city in the north of Utah and there Olive grew up and married a local man called George Osmond and had nine children. They all had glorious voices and seven of them got together to form a pop group, 'The Osmonds'. They may not have been the gun-slinging heroes of the 'penny dreadfuls' and the 'yellow-backs', but they just as surely created for their fans an escape from the humdrum tedium of their lives into a world of excitement and fantasy and fun.

When Samuel died in 1942, the old cabin was sold and it stood empty for a long while, slowly disintegrating, until a local high-school teacher, Luke Waldron, became interested in the history of the family who had lived there in the heyday of the village. He bought the cabin and carefully took down and marked every log and beam so that he could someday reassemble them again. Twenty years passed, and when Olive died, it seemed that the Davis family's links with Samaria had finally come to an end, but that was when Luke decided to rebuild the old cabin and to furnish it with as many of the family relics as he could find – the sewing machine, the stove and the old piano. In 2010, he opened it as a museum. People came from all over the world, even from Japan, to the opening. And the chief guests were Olive's children – Alan, Merrill, Jay, Donny and Jimmy Osmond – and the two deaf brothers, Virl and Tom. Only Wayne and Marie Osmond failed to make it. Their hope was that the old cabin should stand for many years to come as a tribute to Thomas John and Elizabeth Davis of Neath and as a memorial to the old Welsh community that had once thrived on these hills.

1868

'MY JOURNEY TO Utah was one I look upon and thank God that I had the privilege of making with an oxen team.' So wrote one of the emigrants of 1868. He very nearly didn't make it. Had he delayed his journey another year, he would have had to travel all the way by train. True grit was not needed after 1868, the emigrants were no longer pioneers. When the western 'End-of-track' met the eastern 'End-of-track' in Utah in May 1869, the 'Age of the Pioneers' was over.

But there was one last season, one last time for the pioneers to learn the ways of the trail. Aboard the *Colorado*, the last boat to leave Liverpool that year, Sarah Edwards of Rudbaxton in Pembrokeshire described in her diary how Franklin D. Richards, the President of the European Mission, had come aboard to address the passengers before they left. Out on the Plains, he said, their shortcomings would have nowhere to hide. They would be tested, their failings made apparent, and their faults revealed. But the trail was also their school and the lessons they learnt as they crossed to Utah would be the old lessons that the trail had taught from the beginning. He listed them as 'cleanliness, order, forbearance, and obedience to proper authority'. They would learn how to work together efficiently, how to respect each other, how to sacrifice for the common good. As one of the last companies, he told them, they had a duty to maintain those values that had sustained their predecessors on the trail in years past.

At the start of the emigrating season, the Union Pacific terminus was in Laramie, about four hundred miles from Salt

Lake City. This is not to be confused with the famous Fort Laramie that had played so colourful a role in the early history of the trail. The city of Laramie lay about a hundred miles to the south-west of the old fort. Today it is a respectable university town but, in 1868, it was the home of 'Hell-on-Wheels' and when the emigrants arrived there at the end of July, it was a dangerous place to be.

Big Steve Long and his two half-brothers, Ace and Con Moyer, ruled the town. They had been made deputy-marshals because of their dexterity with pistols and their readiness to use them. But the brothers had used their pistols to enrich themselves. They rarely arrested a lawbreaker. It was easier and less troublesome to shoot them down. The brothers' saloon was known as 'The Bucket of Blood'. When Long came across six drunken men fighting outside 'The Bucket of Blood' one evening, he killed five of them, in order, he said, to preserve the peace. It was believed the brothers had shot dead at least ten other men in 'Hell-on-Wheels' in that year alone, and they were probably responsible for seven more. When they were accused of shooting yet another denizen of the 'Bucket of Blood', an unruly mob rushed into the saloon, seized the three brothers, took them to a lonely cabin outside the town and hanged them. In a famous photograph taken after the lynching, the three bodies hang from the beams of the hut, one of them barefooted. Big Steve's last wish, so it was said, was to be allowed to take off his boots, because 'my mother always used to tell me that I was sure to die with my boots on and I wish to prove her wrong'.

This year, for the last time, Brigham Young sent out the 'Utah boys' to bring home the emigrants. In the week when the first wagons arrived to meet the trains, the *Frontier Index* reported that 82 of the citizens of 'Hell-on-Wheels' in Laramie had appeared in court on charges of drunkenness, unruly behaviour, firing guns and the heinous female crime of 'walking the streets in men's apparel'. It was noted that the Laramie town treasurer had run off with all the money and that the Mayor had resigned as a consequence. The Mormon emigrants were advised not to enter the town for fear of being corrupted or shot dead, but a few of the 'boys' ventured in and were obviously stunned by what they saw. 'I think it is the wickedest little town of its size in existence,' wrote Zebulon Jacobs. 'It is peopled with the scum of creation of both sexes.' Don Johnson's opinion was that 'everybody seemed to be safe in life and property so long as they minded their own business, kept out of the gambling games and didn't get in the path of flying bullets'. A separate camp was set up for the Mormons, three miles out of town. They hurried to get ready to leave. Within a few days everyone was sorted into four companies, places had been allotted to them on the wagons, all had been informed of their duties and the wagon train was ready to leave. Out in the Rockies, other temptations came their way from the smaller camps along the railway. Celestial Roberts, a girl from Pembroke Town, describes in her reminiscences how their Captain 'counselled them to drive out around the railroad camps and not to stop day or night till they got out of the way of the camps and thus they would avoid the rough element... as well as the Indians, which might be hanging around them.' Sometimes pretty women came from these camps to waylay the men with offers of good, well-paid work. But the Mormons were never tempted.

Despite the journey being six hundred miles shorter than in previous years, it still took them over a month to get to Salt Lake City, ample time for them to learn the basic lessons of the trail. The usual company rules set the pattern of their days. The trumpet sounded at four in the morning. They were to be at breakfast by five. At half past five, the companies were called to morning prayer. Before seven, they were expected to be on the trail. The usual trials befell them. 'One day, while camped for dinner, a scorpion stung me on the thumb. It was very painful, but one of the teamsters opened the wound with his pocket knife and sucked the blood from the wound, and covered it with tobacco which he had chewed. In a few days I was all right.' 'I fell into the river. A young Italian boy dove in after me and brought me to shore, but lost his watch and shoes rescuing me. I couldn't thank him in Italian, but when I revived I did my best to make him understand how much I appreciated his kindness to me.' 'We were covered with genuine "Emerald Isle" lice. Every seam in my pants shone with nits. I am sure there wasn't an immigrant who wasn't "lousy".' 'A young man about 20 years of age had been carrying a double barrelled shotgun. As he was getting in the wagon, he caught the trigger on the wagon tongue and killed himself.' 'A young brother by the name of James Powell, age 19, was drowned while crossing the Platt. He got into the deep water and was carried out of sight. His body could not be found. It cast a gloom over the camp. He was the eldest son of Sarah Powell, a widow. He was her main support, she being a cripple. It nearly breaks the old lady's heart.'

On the morning of the fourth day they passed another wagon train on its way to the terminus to pick up more emigrants. Its young teamsters had suffered a terrible accident whilst crossing the Green River some days earlier. One of the hawsers by which the ferry raft was being pulled over the river had broken and the raft had been swept away and six of the young 'down-and-back' boys had drowned. Now the company Captain was looking for volunteers to replace them. Amongst those who stepped forward was a young man from Llangyfelach, near Swansea, travelling to Utah with his brother and his two sisters. His name was Benjamin Perkins.

'I was one of the volunteers,' writes Ben in his memoirs. 'I was given charge of a team but of course it was necessary for me to have some assistance as they were the first oxen I had ever worked.' During the next weeks, Ben was to be thoroughly schooled in the skills of ox wagon driving. 'It was a practice of mine to be among the first to hitch up, but as a rule I was among the last to leave as I so often had the wrong ox, and frequently had the off ox on the near side very much to the disgust of the oxen and the teamsters. For some time I couldn't tell the oxen apart and often hitched up the wrong one. When a teamster would miss his oxen, he would come and examine my outfit and too often he would find there what he was looking for, and it became a byword among the crowd "Look out for that damned Welshman!"

'As I was a new hand they were all willing to let me show how much I could do around the camp. As soon as the oxen were unyoked, my orders came thick and fast from all sides. It was, "Ben get some water. Ben get some wood." When it had gone on for a week, I decided I had had enough of it. So after bringing in the wood, when the order came to get the water, I told them in my plainest English, for I was learning now to speak a little English, "Go to Hell!" The fellow jerked off his coat, and taking it as a warning, I jerked off mine. He asked if I meant what I said and in my broken Welsh and English I gave him to understand that I meant it all and more. After that I had considerable trouble with them and several times the boss threatened to show me my place.'

In Echo Canyon, sixty miles from Salt Lake City, Ben came across a gang of Mormons working on the line. Although the railway threatened the isolation of the Mormons, and was likely to bring 'Babylonians' in their thousands to Utah, Brigham Young had realized that its coming was inevitable and that nothing could be done to stop it. From the start, therefore, he had invested heavily in the project and had agreed to allow the Union Pacific to hire Mormon workers on condition that they did not have to mix with non-Mormons. Amongst the gang in Echo Canyon, Ben came across many old friends from Wales. 'After giving them an account of my trip, I had a hand full in keeping them from making a row over the way I had been treated, and the only way I could pacify them was by promising to stay with them in the camp. So I stayed, but I had difficulty getting the boss of the teams to let me off. When the boss found out that I wanted to earn money to send for my parents and the rest of my family in Wales, he gave me $40 with a "God bless you" and he promised I would soon have the necessary money.' Ben continued to work on the railroad for six months. His brother, Joseph, came to work with him, followed by his brother-in-law, John Evans.

Ben was a member of a much respected south Wales

Mormon family. His uncle was the Thomas Perkins who had shown such bravery on the Big Blue in 1855, helping Thomas Jeremy's company to cross. His grandmother was Elizabeth Perkins who, in her 71st year, had pulled a handcart in Bunker's company all the way to the Salt Lake. His father, William, had worked in a pit in Treboeth, near Swansea. When he joined the Mormons, he had lost his job and the whole family, Jane, his wife, and all his children, including Ben, were placed in the workhouse for a while. The 1851 census shows them back on their feet again, living in a house in Birchgrove, Swansea. In 1868, six of the children left together for America. Ruth went no further than St Louis. She had never accepted the Mormon faith and in St Louis she had decided there was no purpose in her going further. The other five went on without her. She was nineteen.

After a winter of hard work on the railroad, Ben, Joseph and John Evans had earned between them $900, enough to pay for their mother and father, their brothers, Hyrum and Daniel, their sister, Martha, and an orphaned cousin, another Daniel, to come over. And there was money left to pay for one more ticket. In Swansea, on his last day in Wales, whilst waiting for the train to Liverpool, Ben had noticed a young girl sitting near him. Mary Ann Williams was seventeen years old. He knew her well. They were members of the same church choir. Ben went to her and invited her to Utah and promised, if she should decide to come, that he would send her the money to pay her fare. In the spring of 1869, Mary Ann received her ticket and they were married in the autumn. A photograph of Mary Ann has survived, taken when she was still comparatively young. She appears in it as delicate as an autumn leaf, but, in reality, like her husband, she was as tough as bog oak.

Although he was only 25 years old, Ben had worked in a coal mine for nineteen years. On coming to Utah, he chose to work in the open air and was a shepherd on a co-operative farm near Cedar City for some years. But he had an adventurous spirit and was eager to put the skills he had learnt down the mine to some useful purpose. In 1879, the call came. The Church authorities wished to settle the valley of the San Juan River in the south-eastern corner of the state, close to Monument Valley, the spectacular location featured in so many Hollywood films from *Stagecoach* to *Easy Rider*. From the north, there was no easy access. A road would have to be carved through rugged country, 180 miles of the most difficult terrain in the state, which no wagon had crossed before. Cutting a deep gash across the route was the canyon of the Colorado River. Somehow a way would have to be found down that mile-deep ravine and back up the other side. Ben was called to help in this dangerous work.

He was happy to go. Mary Ann and his four children went with him, the eldest, six, the youngest, only four months old, and he invited his sister-in-law, Sarah, newly arrived from Wales, to accompany them, to help with the children. His brother Hyrum was also called to go, with his wife, Rachel, and their son, George. All told, there were about 250 people in the company, including ninety children. In addition to their private possessions, they took with them all that would be needed to settle in their new home – the building materials, the farm machinery, the tools and the seeds. They were also driving over a thousand head of cattle. They left Escalante, the last outpost in their path, on November 9th. By the middle of December they were corralled above the Colorado Canyon, looking down over the cliff edge, trying to fathom a route to the winding river a mile below. The weather worsened, there were snowstorms and freezing winds. Fodder for the animals was in short supply and running water was proving difficult to find, but not for a moment did they think of turning back. This was a calling from Brigham Young and they considered it an honour to have been chosen for the work. It was a duty they were bound to fulfil and a mission as sacred as any undertaken by the missionaries in foreign lands. And they had to be on the San Juan before spring, to prepare the ground for sowing and planting.

Santa Claus visited the camp on Christmas morning, leaving cakes and simple, home-made toys. And that night, as on other nights, there was dancing and singing around the camp fire. 'The contingents were favoured with a flock of good singers. Among them were the Perkins men and wives and Miss Sarah Williams,' wrote one diarist. And again, 'Among those who loved to dance was Benjamin Perkins. His snappy Welsh jigs furnished no end of entertainment and enjoyment for the company.'

The next day they were back at work. They found a narrow cleft in the wall of the gorge that gave access to the next level down, but it was hardly wide enough for a man to squeeze through, let alone a wagon. They widened the cleft with pick, shovel and black powder and as the two Perkins brothers were proficient in the use of explosives, they were given the responsibility of preparing and firing the charges. Throughout the camp they became known as 'The Blasters and Blowers from Wales' and the cleft they blasted was called 'Hole-in-the-Rock', a passage through a hundred feet of rock, wide enough for a wagon.

Below, there were further precipices to be negotiated, falling one foot in every two. One was a sheer drop of 45 feet. Ben had his men hanging on ropes, chiselling out a channel across the face of the rock, wide enough to take the wheel of a wagon. Then he marked a row of holes under the channel, one every eighteen inches, which the men, still hanging on ropes, drilled out to a depth of ten inches. Into the holes they pushed oak stakes and on these they laid planks of wood and slabs of stone to form a solid shelf, wide enough to take a wagon. The plan was for the inner wheels of the wagons to go down in the channel, whilst the outer wheels would be supported by the protruding shelf. This part of the road was called 'Uncle Ben's Dugway'. Whilst Ben was directing this work at the top of the gorge, further teams were building a raft at the bottom and a route out of the gorge on the other side.

By January 26th, all was ready. Ben brought his wagon to the edge of the ravine. The man who was to drive it down was Kumen Jones, son of Thomas Jones of Penderyn and Sage Treharne of Llangyndeyrn, both members of the company that sailed with Dan Jones on the *Buena Vista* in 1849. To pioneer this dangerous route there was no better man in all Utah than Kumen. All his life he had been out on the range, caring for his cattle, handling horses in the harshest conditions. More importantly, there were no better horses than his, brave, obedient and strong. They were harnessed up. Chains were bound to the wheels so that they could not turn, only slide. Long ropes were attached to the back of the wagon and each one grasped by ten or more men. Slowly, the wagon was eased over the side, into Hole-in-the-Rock and down Uncle Ben's Dugway. It all went smoothly and, before the day was out, 26 other wagons had followed. Two days later, all 83 had crossed the river, without a single accident.

It took them a week to climb out of the gorge and there were still another 120 miles to go, through a land that was just as difficult as any they had already crossed. The inclines were steep and slippery, polished by the wind and cut-through by the beds of dry rivers. At times, it took seven or eight yokes of horses to move the wagons, sliding as they sought for grip. 'The roughest country you have ever seen,' in the words of one traveller, 'it's nothing in the world but rocks and holes, hills and hollows.' And all this in the teeth of a hard winter, with layers of ice and drifts of snow in their paths. Six months after leaving Cedar City, the train finally reached journey's end. Six months to travel two hundred miles. That's how hard it had been!

Today, outside the village of Bluff, where the majority of the company settled, there stands a memorial carved with these words: 'This memorial is in honour of the men, women and children who came to the area in 1880 in answer to a call from their Church. These Mormon pioneers overcame challenges of unparalleled difficulty as they blazed a road through some of the most broken and rugged terrain in North America. No pioneer company ever built a wagon road through wilder, rougher, more inhospitable country. None ever demonstrated more courage, faith and devotion to cause.'

Having fought their way to the San Juan Valley, they

then had to fight again to snatch a living from the harsh surroundings – constant floods, poor soil, warlike Indians and extreme temperatures. But in the end, Bluff survived and many of the Hole-in-the-Rock company, including Hyrum Perkins, stayed there for the rest of their lives. But not Ben. He was preparing for another dangerous adventure. He had set his mind on taking his sister-in-law, Sarah, as his second wife, even though, when she started on her journey to Bluff, Sarah was a Welsh Calvinist Methodist.

Her father, Evan Williams, was an interesting man. He had joined the Mormon Church in his younger days, but had since become disenchanted and had left the faith, although the Saints were still welcome in his home. His wife however held fast to her allegiance. Evan had been in charge of setting and maintaining the pit props in a mine in Cwmbach, near Aberdare, an important and responsible job. He was one of the founders of the Cwmbach Co-op, the first successful co-op in Wales and he was also a literary man, one of the bards in Myfyr Morgannwg's oddball gorsedd which met on the common above Pontypridd. In 1871, he set out on the greatest adventure of his life, to work in the Ukraine with John Hughes, the founder of the iron industry in that country. Evan worked in Hughesovka, the city created by Hughes, which is today called Donetsk but, by 1879, he was a sick man, suffering from a lung complaint, and had been advised to seek a dryer and warmer climate. He had therefore taken his family to live near his eldest daughter, Mary Ann, in Cedar City. A few months after their arrival, Mary Ann had set out with Ben for the San Juan, taking Sarah with her.

The journey to Bluff was a turning point in Sarah's life. She felt at one with the company. 'The longer I lived among these people, the more I became convinced that Mormonism was the religion for me. There was always something lacking or wanting in my life until I joined the Mormon Church, and it came to me little by little – the things I had been wanting and didn't know I wanted. It was on the trip out to Bluff that my eyes began to be opened, that things began to come clearer a little at a time… The unity among the people, coming out with no conveniences, and yet they were just as happy as they could be; the testimony the people bore – I took so much interest in the testimonies; I was so impressed with the hymns and I read them over and over.' In June she was baptized in the waters of the San Juan.

But then Ben had begun to discuss polygamy with her, explaining to her what the Church expected of her and what her duty was. Years later, Sarah described her bewilderment to her son-in-law who recorded it in his memoir of her. 'Ben had been commanded to take another wife and after much prayer and fasting on the subject, he approached Mary Ann and informed her that he wanted to take, as his second wife, her younger sister, Sarah. Mary Ann was shocked and hurt. She had always feared that eventually she would be asked to give her consent to his having other wives but how could she bear to permit it. And yet she knew that to deny the family of this opportunity might affect their chances for eternal exaltation. Finally she gave her consent but not without presentiments of difficult times ahead and with some reservations. She would not attend the ceremony.'

Sarah returned to Cedar City in the summer of 1881 to discuss her predicament with the Church counsellors. 'Once she was thoroughly converted to the faith, the leaders told her polygamy was the thing she should be involved in, but she could foresee the hurt it would bring to her older sister and the sacrifices it would involve for all of them. It was an excruciating time for Sarah as well as for Mary Ann. And certainly Ben was not having an easy time. There was so much at stake and it wasn't the desire of any one of them to hurt or offend the others. Years later, Sarah said, 'I felt that Brother Perkins had the hardest deal of any of us.'

In the autumn, Ben and Mary Ann and the children returned to Cedar City. It was time for Sarah to make her decision. She never referred to him as Ben, but always as 'Brother Perkins'. The memoir says, 'Sarah had a lot of respect for him. She wouldn't go so far as to say she was in love with him.' 'But,' it continues, 'to her, a new and devout convert to the Church, that seemed less important than doing what she felt was right.' This, it said, was also the most painful decision of Mary Ann's life. 'Three people agonizing over what they all felt was their solemn duty, and yet knowing it would require more of them emotionally than they had ever faced before.'

Sarah looked to her parents for guidance. Her father was adamantly opposed to the marriage. 'You are old enough to know what you want to do,' he told her. 'I've always told my children they could choose what they wanted so long as they lived a good life but I would rather bury you than see you go into polygamy. I don't want to say goodbye to you if you are going to come back a plural wife. I won't be here when you go, because I'll leave home before you do.' This only added to her confusion, for she had always obeyed her parents. She went to Ben and told him she could not marry him. He took her back to the bishop and his advisors. 'They made me feel it was my clear duty,' said Sarah. 'They talked to me pretty straight and told me what it was like. And as I considered further what they were saying, it just seemed that my life was led to do it. They told me that the scriptures were plain enough; we should leave father and mother, all, for the gospel's sake. They told me to go home and think it over, that I wouldn't have the same feeling after that, and I didn't.'

'It was never in her nature to hurt anyone,' writes her son-in-law, 'and yet in her heart, she knew she must follow the counsel she had been given.' Before October had passed, she went with Ben to the temple to be married, and the only other member of her family who attended the ceremony was her sister, Naomi.

'Sarah couldn't bear the thought of not going back to her home to try to make peace with her parents. She arrived to find her younger sister holding Mary Ann's baby. Instinctively, she reached for the baby and was hugging him tenderly when he was snatched from her arms and Mary Ann's hand slapped her across her face with such force that her face held the mark of it for a week. It hurt her terribly, but it could not compare with the pain in her heart.' Her father, who had threatened to avoid her by leaving home if she married Ben, kept his word. She didn't see him again for some years. Her mother refused to speak to her. Sarah used to visit the family home every day, but was now turned away every time. A fortnight after the wedding, Ben went back to Bluff along the Hole-in-the-Rock road, taking his two wives with him. Her mother's last wish to Sarah was that she shouldn't darken her door again.

Life in the small cabin in Bluff could not have been easy. Two loving sisters who had hurt each other to the quick, two who had been so close but were now so distant. But slowly the anger cooled and they began to forgive. Their parents relented and letters came to Sarah from Cedar City inviting her to return. Ben built another cabin for Sarah where she might be mistress in her own home, and when her first child was born, Mary Ann could no longer spurn her.

By this time, another crisis was upon them. The tentacles of the law stretched even as far as Bluff, threatening every polygamous husband with imprisonment. Ben and Sarah separated, she to a farmhouse on Cedar Mountain, a desolate region, still little populated today, and Ben and Mary to the back hills of Boulder Mountain, seventy miles from her. When things quietened down, Ben built a cottage next door to Mary Ann's cottage and the two families lived as neighbours for some years. But then government detectives tracked them down again and came to arrest Ben. He spent six months in jail, and when he came out, instead of renouncing one of his marriages or fleeing to Mexico as did many of the Saints who could not live monogamously, Ben moved Sarah and her children out of the state, over the border to Colorado, where his brother John had settled, the only one of his brothers who was not a Mormon. Later, when the hounding of polygamous families became less persistent, he brought her back to Bluff, whilst he and Mary Ann moved to a village called Monticello, fifty miles further out into the hills. For a while, Ben drove the stagecoach between Monticello and Bluff, thus keeping in touch with both families, but farming remained his main livelihood. His two wives had ten children each, although four of Mary Ann's children died while they were still young. Mary Ann died in 1912 and Sarah moved to live with Ben in Monticello. He died in 1926 and she in 1943.

Back on the trail, halfway through this last pioneer season, the railway terminus moved on and a new 'Hell-on-Wheels' was erected in a place called Benton, 125 miles closer to Salt Lake City. This one proved to be the worst 'Hell-on-Wheels' of them all. It only existed for three months but in that time over a hundred murders were committed within its precincts. Out on the Plains, the Indians still seized every opportunity of attacking weak and underprotected wagon trains. On its way to Benton, McArthur's company, two weeks behind Ben's company, had passed the remains of a burnt-out telegraph station. 'The log house was still a mess of gleaming embers with the bones of the faithful, ill-fated operator in the cinders. It was reported that the agent fought the redskins and killed a number, but the besiegers finally succeeded in setting the log station on fire. Then for a terrible half-hour, with the flames roaring and crackling all around, with the deadly heat encompassing, he kept the key going and the wire hot, telling just how the battle was going, how hot it was getting, and at times actually joking about it. His hand kept the machine going to the last moment until there was a broken "goodbye boys, I wonder if hell is hotter!" The body was completely incinerated.' Outside Bear City, as they passed another of the railway camps on the trail, one the emigrants described a sight he would never forget. 'I saw six limp bodies hanging and dangling with ropes around their necks from telegraph poles. I wanted to stop and look into the matter but was told by my brother to keep going and keep my mouth shut. He said evidently vigilantes had been busy there last night.'

The very last company to cross was a company of Scandinavians. They had a horrendous voyage over the Atlantic. Their ship, the *Emerald Isle*, was one of the last sailing ships to be chartered by the Saints. They quarrelled with the captain, their water turned sour, measles broke out and 37 of them

378

died. In New York harbour, most of the 867 on board had been allowed to land but 61 were kept in an isolation hospital on Ward's Island until they were completely cured of the sickness. These 61 emigrants were part of the very last company to travel, at least part of the way, by ox wagon. They arrived in Salt Lake City, quietly and unheralded, on September 24th, only a few weeks before the rails of the Union Pacific arrived in Utah. And thus, with no ceremony and no fanfare, the Pioneer Age came to an end.

The following year, the first company to travel by train all the way from Omaha was enthusiastically welcomed by the *Deseret News*. 'Arrived Safely' was the headline on Saturday, June 26th. 'The first fruits of this year's emigration from Europe reached Utah last evening at 5 p.m. They left Liverpool on the 2nd of this month and a little more than three weeks has brought them the whole distance of the weary way that once took the best part of a year to travel. This being the first company that has come all the way across the continent from the Atlantic to Utah on the Great Highway, their journey will long be remembered as inaugurating an epoch in our history. The greater part of the company, 338 in all, came from the Welsh Principality, under the charge of Elder Elias Morris.'

Once again, as our story draws to its close, we catch a glimpse of Elias Morris, flickering momentarily into focus before slipping quietly back into the shadows. He was always there for the Welsh, advising, planning, contributing generously to their appeals, but always in the background. Was it the part he played in the catastrophe at Mountain Meadows that caused him thus to avoid the public eye? It had not always been so. On our journey along the Mormon Trail, my wife and I, one cold September morning, came to Independence Rock, high in the Rockies. A 150 years earlier, at exactly the same time of year, Elias and his wife had passed this way and had marvelled, as we did, at the thousands of names carved over its surface. We began to climb, searching out the Welsh names, a Hughes here, an Evans there. Eventually, we reached the summit and there, on the highest point, above every other carving, first in this remarkable register of all the travellers of the trail, Elias Morris had carved his own name: 'ELIAS & MARY MORRIS. N. WALES. SEPT 1852.'

Something of his turbulent life is reflected in the bizarre circumstances of his death. He had been chairing a meeting of the Cambrian Society committee which had been called to finalize the plans for the Great Salt Lake City Eisteddfod of 1898. The committee met in a room on an upper floor in a Co-op furniture store, built by one of Elias' many companies. At the end of the meeting, he left the room, crossed to the lift, waited for the door to open and stepped inside – into an empty shaft.

Postscript

TODAY THE TRAIL is fast disappearing. In South Pass, it is still possible, in the late evening light, to make out the wheel ruts winding like silver snakes towards the west. On Prospect Hill in Wyoming or the Hogsback in Utah, on the Murdock meadows or the Sandhills in Nevada, there are ridges and furrows that still mark the route of the wheels that once passed this way, in their tens of thousands, 150 years ago. But over most of its course, the winds have scoured the land clean and the desert storms have washed away the traces.

Yet the trail still lingers in the Mormon imagination, as clear today as ever. No people remember like the Mormons, and what they remember, above all else, are the sacrifices of their pioneer forefathers on the trail. Today, in the eyes of the Church, the forefathers are revered little short of saints. Although only a small minority pulled handcarts to Zion, some 3,000 perhaps out of the 70,000 who crossed the Plains, yet the Handcarters have today come to represent all Pioneers. In city parks, on the walls of public buildings, in the atria of luxury hotels, there are sculptures and paintings of the Handcarters, in the traces, under their heavy loads, straining painfully, but gloriously, towards Zion. Every summer, pageants are performed in festivals throughout the state, retelling the old stories of heroism and steadfastness. Every summer, they send the young folk out to isolated ranges where they pull carts across miles of trackless country, cooking their own food in the open and sleeping under the stars, so that they might always remember what the old people had to put up with to get to Salt Lake City. And on July 24th, they celebrate Pioneer

Day, commemorating the day upon which Brigham Young and his pioneers first entered the Valley. On this day, they haul handcarts in procession through the towns and cities of the state, marching down the main streets, surrounded by high school bands, majorettes twirling batons, cowboys spinning lariats and decorated lorries displaying slogans such as 'The spirit of our past is the hope of our future' and 'On, on with the Pioneers'. The trail continues to fire their imagination, as inspirational today as ever, no longer a route across the Plains to the Great Salt Lake, but a path through their history to the far horizons of their faith. And the diaries and the biographies of the Pioneers are their maps and compasses.

I would like to end this book in the Malad Valley, within sight of Samaria, the old Welsh stronghold. Today, although the population of the village has slipped to less than 150 and the language has long since ceased to be spoken, yet the spirit of the Welsh still persists. Many of the old community settled across the river in Malad City. As one community failed, so the other thrived. On their web page today, the people of Malad City proudly boast that there are more people of Welsh descent per capita in Malad City than anywhere else on earth, except in Wales itself, and every year, they come together to celebrate their Welshness.

Towards the end of June and the beginning of July, Welsh flags are raised throughout the town. This is the weekend of the Welsh Festival, a two-day celebration of all things Welsh. The visitors are led from the highway down a corridor of Welsh flags, past the Evans Co-op and the Davis Drugstore, Thomas Furnishers and Griffiths OK Tyres, towards the central green. From the walls of the museum the grim faces of the ancestors scowl down on them, Daniel Moroni Daniels, William Jenkins Williams, Gwen Lloyd Roberts Evans, Sarah Jane Evans, Catherine Elizabeth Owens Daniels, Phoebe Ann John Thomas and dozens more. On the green there are food stalls selling Welsh cakes and bara brith, copies of *The Malad Valley Welsh Heritage Cookbook* and a pancake breakfast for all. From the stage come the strains of an American-Celtic folk group and there are visits organised to the homes and the outlying villages of the Welsh, especially to Samaria. But the most important events of the festival are the lectures – Professor Ron Dennis on 'The Mormon Press in Nineteenth Century', Darris Williams, an expert on genealogy, on 'Searching Welsh Church Records on the Internet', other lecturers on the druids, on the history of the harp, on old Welsh legends and Evan Stephens' music. The first Welsh Festival was held in Malad City in 2004. Since then, it has been held annually. It now attracts over a thousand visitors to the town. The hope of the founders is that it will continue to flourish, to 'foster an awareness and pride in our Welsh heritage, creating a rich legacy for our children, before the ties that bind us to our past are completely lost'.

Sources

The two most important sources are the two websites – **https://history.lds.org/overlandtravels//** which contains the journals and the memoirs of pioneer Mormons from every corner of the world who travelled on the Mormon Trail between 1847 and 1869, and **http://welshmormon.byu.edu/** which records the histories of the Welsh families that travelled the same trail to Utah. Much of this book quotes directly from the pages of these websites. The third source which I found most useful was the magazine published in Welsh by the Mormon Church in Wales from 1846 to 1862. At first, it was called *Prophwyd y Jubilî* [*Prophet of the Jubilee*], but in 1849 it changed its name to *Udgorn Seion* [*Zion's Trumpet*]. All surviving issues have now been translated by Prof. Ron Dennis and are available on the 'welshmormon' website. Prof. Dennis has also compiled a bibliography of all the early Mormon works published in Welsh, *Welsh Mormon Writings from 1844 to 1862*, and has written numerous other books and articles on early Welsh Mormonism, which are all available on the 'welshmormon' site. A very readable account of the Mormon migration to the Salt Lake Valley is Wallace Stegner's book, *The Gathering of Zion*. Stegner was a successful novelist and his book brings alive the characters and incidents in the story. *Trail of Hope* by William Slaughter and Michael Landon also gives a comprehensive and well-told survey of the history of the trail. These are, of course, books about the migration in general. There are no books I know of written specifically about the Welsh on the trail. For the history of first twenty years of the Mormon settlement in the Valley, I found the following books very useful: *Establishing*

Zion: The Mormon Church in the American West (1847–1869) by Eugene E. Campbell, *Great Basin Kingdom* by Leonard J. Arrington and *The Mormon Experience: A History of Latter-day Saints* by Leonard J. Arrington and Davis Britton.

1847

For the story of the Bennions, see *Bennion Family History* by Harden Bennion which is available at **http://bennion.org/wp-content/uploads/2010/07/Bennion%20Family%20History%20Volume%20III.pdf** For the Joseph Smith story, I found *No Man Knows My History: The Life of Joseph Smith* by Fawn M. Brodie to be the most useful source. For Brigham Young I would recommend *Brigham Young: American Moses* by Leonard J. Arrington and for John Frémont, *Pathfinder: John Charles and the Course of American Empire* by Tom Chaffin. The stories of the Welsh individuals on the Trail are taken from the two websites. Gwenllian Williams' reminiscences, for example, can be accessed at **http://welshmormon.byu.edu/Resource_Info.aspx?id=2981** and Martha Williams' story is told in Joseph Gates' journal, see **https://history.lds.org/overlandtravels/sources/6349/gates-jacob-journals-1836-1861-vol-2**

1848

The Year of Decision: 1846 by Bernard De Voto is a marvellous description of the West as it was at the beginning of the Mormon migration. Life on the trail is well illustrated in *The Plains Across: The Overland Emigrants and Trans-Mississippi West, 1840–60* by John D. Unruh, and *The Great Platte River Road* by Merrill J. Mattes. There are also interesting chapters in *Wagons West* by Frank McLynn and *The Oregon Trail* by David Dary. Again, I found the accounts of the emigrants on the two websites. Some of Sarah's story is told in memoirs of her brother, Edward Jeremiah Price, at **http://welshmormon.byu.edu/Resource_Info.aspx?id=2577** Charles Smith's journal is held by the Harold B. Lee Library at Brigham Young University, Provo (MSS SC 554).

1849

Books about the early days of the Mormon mission in Wales are *Y Mormoniaid yng Nghymru* by T.H. Lewis, *Ar Drywydd y Mormoniaid* by Geraint Bowen and *Mormon Spirituality:Latter-day Saints in Wales and Zion* by Douglas James Davies. There's an excellent chapter by Prof. Dennis in *Truth Will Prevail: The Rise of The Church of Jesus Christ of Latter-day Saints in the British Isles, 1837–1987* (edited by V. Ben Bloxham, James R. Moss and Larry C. Porter), and a short chapter by E.M. Smith in *Merthyr Tydfil: 1500 Years* (edited by Huw Williams). I also found useful Aled Betts' 2010 M.A. thesis (University of Wales) 'The Price of Faith: The Mormons and South West Wales Society, 1844–1863'. Then, there are various articles, such as 'The Welsh Mormons' by Prof. David Williams (*The Welsh Review*, no. 7, 1948), 'Three Carmarthenshire Mormons' by T.H. Lewis (*Carmarthenshire Antiquary*, IV, 49–51), 'Mormon Baptists at the Brechfa Branch, 1846–56' by Lewis Evans (*Carmarthenshire Antiquary*, III, pp. 38–41), and 'William Lewis, Mormon' by D.G. Thomas (*Gelligaer*, XI, 1976–7, pp. 10–13). Two useful and readable volumes on the history of Mormonism in the early days in Britain are *Expectations Westward* by P.A.M. Taylor, and *Mormons in Early Victorian Britain*, co-edited by Richard L. Jensen and Malcolm R. Thorp. Prof. Ron Dennis has written a biography of Dan Jones, *A Steamboat for an Eldership*, which is to be found on the 'welshmormon' site at **http://welshmormon. byu.edu/Resources/pdf/21191.pdf** Many other articles on the life and times of Dan Jones (most of them again written by Prof. Dennis) can also be found on the 'welshmormon' website. Prof. Dennis has also published the tragic story of the *Buena Vista* and the *Hartley* pioneers in his book *The Call of Zion: The Story of the First Welsh Mormon Emigration*. This can be read at **http://archive.org/stream/TheCallOfZionTheStory OfTheFirstWelsh_MormonEmigration#page/n3/mode/2up** I read the story of the '49ers' in *The World Rushed In: The California Gold Rush Experience* by J.S. Holliday. I learnt about Brigham Young's involvement with the Madogwys in *Over the Rim: The Parley P. Pratt Exploring Expedition to Southern Utah, 1849–1850* by William B. and Donna T. Smart, and in Prof. Dennis' article on 'Dan Jones and the Welsh Indians' at **http://welshmormon.byu.edu/Resource Info. aspx?id=167** For Llewellyn Harris see the chapter on 'Myth and Legend' in *Mormon Country* by Wallace Stegner, and also his biography at **http://welshmormon.byu.edu/Immigrant View.aspx?id=1873** Daniel Edward Williams, George Adams and Edward Ashton's stories are on the 'welshmormon' website, as are the diaries and biographies of David D. Bowen, Isaac Nash, Elizabeth Lewis, John Parry, John Ormond et al. As in previous chapters, the stories of the non-Welsh are to be found at **https://history.lds.org/overlandtravels/**

1850
Prof. Dennis has a chapter on the 1850 emigration in his biography of Abel Evans, *Indefatigable Veteran,* to be found at **http://welshmormon.byu.edu/Resources/pdf/21184.pdf** The story of Winter Quarters is told in *Mormons on the Missouri: Winter Quarters, 1846–1852* by Richard E. Bennett, and that of the Perpetual Emigration Fund in the aforementioned *Great Basin Kingdom* and *Expectations Westwards*. I read Thomas Bullock's account of the flock of quail in *The Gathering: Mormon Pioneers on the Road to Zion* by Maurine and Scot Proctor. As usual, individual reminiscences of the pioneers are to be read on the two websites. Ann Roberts Griffiths', for example, at **http://welshmormon.byu.edu/Resource_Info.aspx?id=71** and Wilford Woodruff's description of the stampede at **https://history.lds.org/overlandtravels/trailExcerptMulti?lang=eng&companyId=325&sourceId=31967**

1851
A good description of the Saints' dealings with the '49ers' is to be found in *Gold Rush Sojourners in Great Salt Lake City* by Brigham D. Masden. I found the facts about unmarried Welsh girls aboard the *Joseph Bradlee* in *Indefatigable Veteran* and the story of Jones, the photographer, in *The Gathering of*

Zion (p. 294). John Ormond Jnr's story is recorded at **http://welshmormon.byu.edu/Resource_Info.aspx?id=514** and Lewis Bowen's letter to his son is at **http://welshmormon.byu.edu/Resource_Info.aspx?id=7536**

1852

William Morgan's letters can be read in *Zion's Trumpet* (7 August 1852; 8 January 1853; 27 August 1853), and also in Prof. Dennis' *The Call of Zion*. Prof. Dennis has also written William Howell's story in *Supporting Saints: Life Stories of Nineteenth-Century Mormons*, edited by Donald Cannon and David Whittaker. This essay is also available at **http://welshmormon.byu.edu/Resource_Info.aspx?id=12068** The *Saluda*'s story is to be found in *Explosion of the Steamboat 'Saluda'* by William G. Hartley and Fred E. Woods. R. Fred Roberts has written on the Parry family in 'Emigrant Stonemasons; Trelawnydd, Abergele and St. George' in *Denbighshire Historical Society Transactions* (Vol. 47, 1998) and on 'The Latter-day Saints in Nineteenth century Abergele', in Volume 38 (1989) of the same publication. Once more, the stories of the Welsh on the trail are on the 'welshmormon' site. Ann Rogers, for example, is at **http://welshmormon.byu.edu/Resource_Info.aspx?id=1254** and Elias Morris is at **http://welshmormon.byu.edu/Resource_Info.aspx?id=95** and at **http://welshmormon.byu.edu/Resource_Info.aspx?id=7507** and also at **http://welshmormon.byu.edu/Resource_Info.aspx?id=199**

1853

Two good books about the Mormons on the Atlantic are *Saints on the Seas: A Maritime History of Mormon Migration, 1830–1890* by Conway B. Sonne, and the relevant chapters in *Expectations Westwards*. The paragraphs describing the good life in Utah were taken from *Zion's Trumpet* (9 July 1853; 23 August 1851; October 1850). For more information on the cut-price emigration project, check out 'Bound for Zion: The Ten and Thirteen Pound Emigrating Companies, 1853–54', by Polly Aird in *Utah Historical Quarterly* (Autumn 2002). There is an abundance of books about Mormon polygamy, most of them prejudiced and judgemental. I found *Mormon Polygamy: A History* by Richard S. Van Wagoner to be balanced and fair. The full title of John E. Davis' book was *Mormonism Unveiled or a Peep into the Principles and Practices of the Latter Day Saints*. A copy can be found at **https://archive.org/details/ mormonismunveile00davi**

1854

On the website **http://mormonmigration.lib.byu.edu/** there is an excellent collection of the manifests of ships used by the Mormons, giving the name, ages, trades and nationalities of the passengers. For a history of the Grattan Massacre see *The First Sioux War: The Grattan Fight and Blue Water Creek, 1854– 1856* by Paul Norman Beck. I enjoyed reading about Crazy Horse and his long battle against the American army in *Crazy Horse and Custer* by Stephan E. Ambrose. The history of the Cedar City iron works is described in *A Trial Furnace: Southern Utah's Iron Mission* by Morris A. and Kathryn C. Shirts. As in previous chapters, the stories about the Welsh are from **http:// welshmormon.byu.edu**

1855

A description of the failed harvests of 1855 and 1856 and their consequences can be found in *Great Basin Kingdom* (pp. 148– 156). For the Battle of Ash Hollow see the aforementioned *The First Sioux War: The Grattan Fight and Blue Water Creek, 1854–1856*. William W. Davies' extraordinary history is to be read in *And There Were Men* by Russell Blankenship, and in *All Things New: American Communes and Utopian Movement, 1860–1914* by Robert S. Fogarty. Joseph Morris features in *Joseph Morris and the Saga of the Morrisites (Revisited)* by C. LeRoy Anderson.

1856

There are many attempts to chronicle the terrible events of 1856. As usual, *The Gathering of Zion* is very good, as is *Devil's*

Gate: Brigham Young and the Great Mormon Tragedy by David Roberts. A great deal of interest may be gleaned from *Handcarts to Zion* by Leroy ac Ann Hafen and also from *Emigrating Journals of the Willie and Martin Handcart Companies and the Hunt and Hodgetts Wagon Trains* by Lynne Slater Turner. The connection between the Welsh and the village of Wales can be read in *Chronicles of Courage*, Vol 6., 'Welsh Emigrants' by Jean S. Greenwood. This is on the web at **http://welshmormon.byu. edu/Resource_Info.aspx?id=3535** and **http://welshmormon. byu.edu/Resource_Info.aspx?id=3536** The suffering of the Griffiths family of Bangor is related by Mathew A. Misbach in his book entitled *The Griffiths Story*.

1857

There is a chapter on the Utah War and another on the Revival in *Establishing Zion: The Mormon Church in the American West, 1847–1869.* The book I found most useful in trying to understand the Mountain Meadows Massacre was *Massacre at Mountain Meadows* by Ronald W. Walker, Richard E. Turley Jr. and Glen M. Leonard. All three authors are Mormons, but I felt their account was thorough and fair. I felt *Blood of the Prophets: Brigham Young and the Massacre at Mountain Meadows* by Will Bagley, although fascinating and absorbing, to be less impartial. The diaries of Mary Lois Walker Morris, Elias Morris' second wife, were recently published (*Before the Manifesto: The Life Writings of Mary Lois Walker Morris*, edited by Melissa Lambert Milewski).

1858

Most of the information in this chapter was gleaned from journals and memoirs at **https://history.lds.org/overlandtravels/ companies/67/john-w-berry-company-1858#description**

1859

James Crane's diary is at **http://welshmormon.byu.edu/ Resource_Info.aspx?id=172** and that of his wife, Alice Davies, at **http://welshmormon.byu.edu/Resource_Info.**

aspx?id=2841 Shadrach Jones' biography is at **http:// welshmormon.byu.edu/Resource_Info.aspx?id=2521** and a little about the houses he built in Willard is recorded in 'A Heritage of Stone in Willard' by Teddy Griffith, *Utah Historical Quarterly*, 43 (Summer 1975). Taliesin Hughes' story is at **http:// welshmormon.byu.edu/Immigrant_View.aspx?id=641**

1860

I read about the Pony Express in *Orphans Preferred* by Christopher Corbett. I took Mark Twain's description of his encounter with the Pony Express from his book, *Roughing It*. Dale Boman has written the history of his great-great-great-grandmother, Catherine Jones Bennett. This can be read at **https://archive.org/stream/CatherineJonesBennett#page/ n5/mode/2up** Randy Brown wrote an article on the death of Annie John in the magazine of the Wyoming Branch of the OCTA (Oregon-California Trails Association) in February 2010. This is to be read at **http://welshmormon.byu.edu/ Resource_Info.aspx?id=4189** He published another on the discovery of Leah Edwards' grave. This can be read at **http://welshmormon.byu.edu/Resources/pdf/7510.pdf** See also the story of the discovery of Charlotte Dansie's grave at **http://wyoshpo.state.wy.us/trailsdemo/charlottedansie. htm** The diary of David John, Annie's father, one of the most detailed in the 'welshmormon' collection, can be read at **http:// welshmormon.byu.edu/Resource_Info.aspx?id=2427** and **http://welshmormon.byu.edu/Resource_Info. aspx?id=4080** and **http://welshmormon.byu.edu/Resource_ Info.aspx?id=4081**

1861

The story of the 'down-and-back' trains is told in 'Mormon Immigration in the 1860s: The Story of the Church Trains' by John K. Hulmston in *Utah Historical Quarterly* (Winter 1990, vol. 58, no. 1). It is also covered in *Great Basin Kingdom* (pp. 206–211) and in *Trail of Hope* (pp. 135–148). Martha Hughes Cannon's story is told in *Pioneer, Polygamist, Politician: The*

Life of Martha Hughes Cannon by Mari Graña. Her political career is described in *Utah Historical Quarterly* (vol. 38, no. 1) and her polygamous marriage in volume 48, no.1, of the same publication. Her letters to her husband are published in *Letters from Exile: The Correspondence of Martha Hughes Cannon and Angus M. Cannon, 1886–1888* by Constance L. Lieber and John Sillito.

1862

William Ajax's diary can be read, in his own handwriting, at **http://contentdm.lib.byu.edu/cdm/ref/collection/MMD/id/50834/rec/1** In *The Mormon Passage of George D. Watts: First British Convert, Scribe for Zion* by Ronald G. Watt, the story of the Salt Lake City shop is told. See also *Establishing Zion* (pp. 317–319). I found an article about William Ajax's second underground shop in the *Deseret Evening News* (July 14th, 1900). D.L. Davies' article on Dewi Elfed is in *Mormons in Early Victorian Britain*, ed. Richard L. Jensen and Malcolm R. Thorp. The stories of the other Welsh immigrants, people such as Thomas John and John Evans, are to be found, of course, at **http://welshmormon.byu.edu** John Evans' letter, for example, is at **http://welshmormon.byu.edu/Resource_Info.aspx?id=4208**

1863

The details of Titus Lazarus Davis' life are in an article written about him by his great-grandchild at **http://welshmormon.byu.edu/Resource_Info.aspx?id=56** and Thomas A. Davis, one of his sons, has an interesting autobiography at **http://welshmormon.byu.edu/Resource_Info.aspx?id=3275** A little of the history of Timothy, another of his sons, is to be found at **http://welshmormon.byu.edu/Resource_Info.aspx?id=4266** Benjamin Jones' story is at **http://welshmormon.byu.edu/Resource_Info.aspx?id=3054** There is more on the history of Mary Jones and her husband, George Harding, in the *Dwight Harding Family Book* (pp. 119–133). A copy of the text is available at **https://dcms.lds.**

org/delivery/DeliveryManagerServlet?dps_pid=IE98668
For John Lodwick Edwards, see **http://welshmormon.byu. edu/Resource_Info.aspx?id=3209** The relevant chapter in Dickens' *The Uncommercial Traveller* is 'Bound for the Great Salt Lake'. A little of the band's history is included in Thomas A. Davis' autobiography (see above), and I found more in an article bearing the title 'The Brass Band' in the *Ogden Standard Examiner*, March 13th, 1886 and in the bandmaster's obituary in the same paper on March 30th, 1925.

1864

I read Hervey Johnson's letters and his description of military life on the Plains in *Tending the Talking Wire*, ed. William E. Unrau. The story of the attack on the Kelly/Larimer Train is told in *Narrative of my Captivity among the Sioux Indians* by Fanny Kelly, and the Plum Creek Massacre and Nancy Morton's tale is told in *Captive of the Cheyenne: The Story of Nancy Jane Morton and the Plum Creek Massacre* by Russ Czaplewski. The recollections of other members of the William Warren wagon train are to be found at **https://history.lds. org/overlandtravels/companies/314/william-s-warren- company** Elizabeth Edwards' reminiscences are at **http:// welshmormon.byu.edu/Resource_Info.aspx?id=1146** and Margaret Reese's memoir is at **http://welshmormon.byu.edu/ Resource_Info.aspx?id=3972**

1865

I enjoyed reading about the construction of the railway in *Nothing Like It in the World: The Men Who Built the Railway that United America* by Stephen E. Ambrose. I found George Francis Train's story in *Around the World with Citizen Train* by Foster Allen. The relevant part of Albert Wesley Davis' autobiography is at **https://history.lds.org/overlandtravels/ sources/4782/davis-albert-wesley-autobiography-utah- genealogical-and-historical-magazine-oct-1926-246- and-ibid-jan-1927-6-7** Herber McBride's diary is at **https://**

history.lds.org/overlandtravels/sources/69089/mc-bride-heber-robert-autobiography-ca-1868-28-46 The messages sent to Brigham Young can be read on each wagon train's website on **https://history.lds.org/overlandtravels//**

1866

Much of the material in this chapter comes from *The Children Sang: The Life and Music of Evan Stephens* by Ray L. Bergman. There is a copy on 'welshmormon' at **http://welshmormon.byu.edu/Resource Info.aspx?id=4467** An article about him by Steve Dubé was published in *Carmarthenshire Antiquary* (volume 38, 2002). More can be found on the 'welshmormon' site under Evan Stephens' name and under that of his brother, David Evan Stephens. Also on the 'welshmormon' site there is much information about the other featured emigrants on the trail this year – Amos and Ann Clark, David Prossor Jones, Edward Giles Roberts and John Evan Price. I found some of Malad Valley's history in *Idaho's Malad Valley: A History* by Thomas J. McDevitt and Samaria's history in *We, the People of Samaria*, ed. Clarence Ralph Hughes.

1867

I read *The Frontier Index*, the newspaper of 'Hell on Wheels', in the Nebraska Historical Society Library in Lincoln, Nebraska. It was more exciting than any Wild West 'penny dreadful'. Stanley's articles are to be found in *My Early Travels and Adventures in America and Asia*. The story of Thomas John Davis is chronicled in *The Children and Ancestors of Thomas Martin Davis and Vera Ann Nicholas* by the Davis Family Society, and much of their story after they arrived in Samaria is in *We, the People of Samaria*. I found the story of the opening of the renovated cabin in the *Deseret News* (May 3rd, 2010).

1868

Most of the information in this chapter comes from *The Personal Histories of Benjamin Perkins and his Two Wives Mary Ann Williams & Sarah Williams* by Lyman De Platt which can be read at **http://welshmormon.byu.edu/Resource Info. aspx?id=4472** Sarah's story is recorded by her granddaughter, Alberta Lyman O'Brien, at **https://archive.org/stream/The StoryOfSarahWilliamsPerkins#page/n101/mode/2up** The struggle to build the road to the San Juan Valley has been chronicled in *Hole-in-the-Rock: An Epic in the Colonization of the Great American West* by David E. Miller. The memoirs of the Welsh emigrants, such as Sarah Edwards of Rudbaxton and Celestial Roberts, are to be read, of course, at **http:// welshmormon.byu.edu**

Acknowledgements

My heaviest debt is to Emeritus Professor Ronald D. Dennis, formerly of Brigham Young University, Utah. Ron was a member of the Portuguese department at the university, but his leisure time was devoted to researching the history of the Mormons in nineteenth-century Wales. He learnt to speak Welsh fluently in order to better understand their history, and he spent months in the National Library of Wales and in other libraries, in Wales and in the United States, reading their publications. Many of these he has translated and published. All are available on his remarkable website **http://welshmormon.byu.edu/** now administered by Brigham Young University. He has also invited the descendants of the Welsh immigrants to contribute their family reminiscences to this website, be they journals or letters or memoirs or biographies, and many hundreds have done so. I'm grateful to them all for the permission I have received from Prof. Dennis to quote from their material. I'm also grateful for the kind advice he has always readily offered me whilst writing this book, and for his friendship and his generosity.

I have also quoted extensively from the diaries and memoirs which are to be found on the website of the archives of the Church of Jesus Christ of Latter-day Saints at **https://history. lds.org/overlandtravels//** I'm grateful to the administrators for permission to use them.

I had much help and good advice from Dr Huw Walters, formerly of the National Library of Wales, from Christine Cox of the Church History Library in Salt Lake City and from my brother, John, who, amongst other things, found the grave of Shadrach Jones in Ravenshill, Swansea.

I'm also grateful for the kindness and attention I have received from the descendants of the Welsh in Utah, especially from the late Mrs Anna Lou Giles Jeffs.

Thanks are also due to Eirian Jones, my editor at Y Lolfa, to the map-maker, Elgan Griffiths, and, above all, to Lefi Gruffudd, the Commissioning Editor at Y Lolfa, who has so skilfully guided my book through both its Welsh and English impressions.

Index of Principal Participants